ちょびっツ

Chobits

CLAMP

Satsuki Igarashi
Nanase Ohkawa
Mick Nekoi
Mokona Apapa

ALSO AVAILABLE FROM TOKYOPOP®

MANGA

CINE-MANGA™

NOVELS

TOKYOPOP KIDS

ART BOOKS

ANIME GUIDES

5-12-03

Volume 7 of 8

Story and Art By
CLAMP

Los Angeles • Tokyo • London

Translator - Shirley Kubo
English Adaptation - Jake Forbes
Associate Editor - Paul Morrissey
Retouch and Lettering - Christine Holmes
Cover Layout - Anna Kernbaum

Senior Editor - Jake Forbes
Managing Editor - Jill Freshney
Production Coordinator - Antonio DePietro
Production Manager - Jennifer Miller
Art Director - Matthew Alford
Director of Editorial - Jeremy Ross
VP of Production - Ron Klamert
President & C.O.O. - John Parker
Publisher & C.E.O. - Stuart Levy

Email: editor@TOKYOPOP.com
Come visit us online at www.TOKYOPOP.com

A  Manga

TOKYOPOP® is an imprint of Mixx Entertainment, Inc.
5900 Wilshire Blvd. Suite 2000, Los Angeles, CA 90036

ISBN: 1-59182-258-0

First TOKYOPOP® printing: August 2003

10 9 8 7 6 5 4 3 2 1
Printed in the USA

www.Contents.com

Chapter 73 - 7
Chapter 74 - 25
Chapter 75 - 43
Chapter 76 - 63
Chapter 77 - 81
Chapter 78 - 99
Chapter 79 - 119
Chapter 80 - 139
Chapter 81 - 159

MUST SEE Persocoms

address:

HOT Chobits

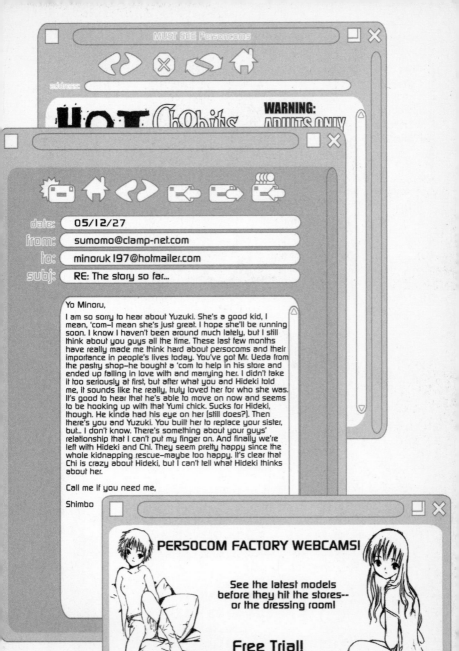

WARNING:
ADULTS ONLY

date: 05/12/27

from: sumomo@clamp-net.com

to: minoruk197@hotmailer.com

subj: RE: The story so far...

Yo Minoru,

I am so sorry to hear about Yuzuki. She's a good kid, I mean, 'com–I mean she's just great. I hope she'll be running soon. I know I haven't been around much lately, but I still think about you guys all the time. These last few months have really made me think hard about persocoms and their importance in people's lives today. You've got Mr. Ueda from the pastry shop–he bought a 'com to help in his store and ended up falling in love with and marrying her. I didn't take it too seriously at first, but after what you and Hideki told me, it sounds like he really, truly loved her for who she was. It's good to hear that he's able to move on now and seems to be hooking up with that Yumi chick. Sucks for Hideki, though. He kinda had his eye on her (still does?). Then there's you and Yuzuki. You built her to replace your sister, but... I don't know. There's something about your guys' relationship that I can't put my finger on. And finally we're left with Hideki and Chi. They seem pretty happy since the whole kidnapping rescue–maybe too happy. It's clear that Chi is crazy about Hideki, but I can't tell what Hideki thinks about her.

Call me if you need me,

Shimbo

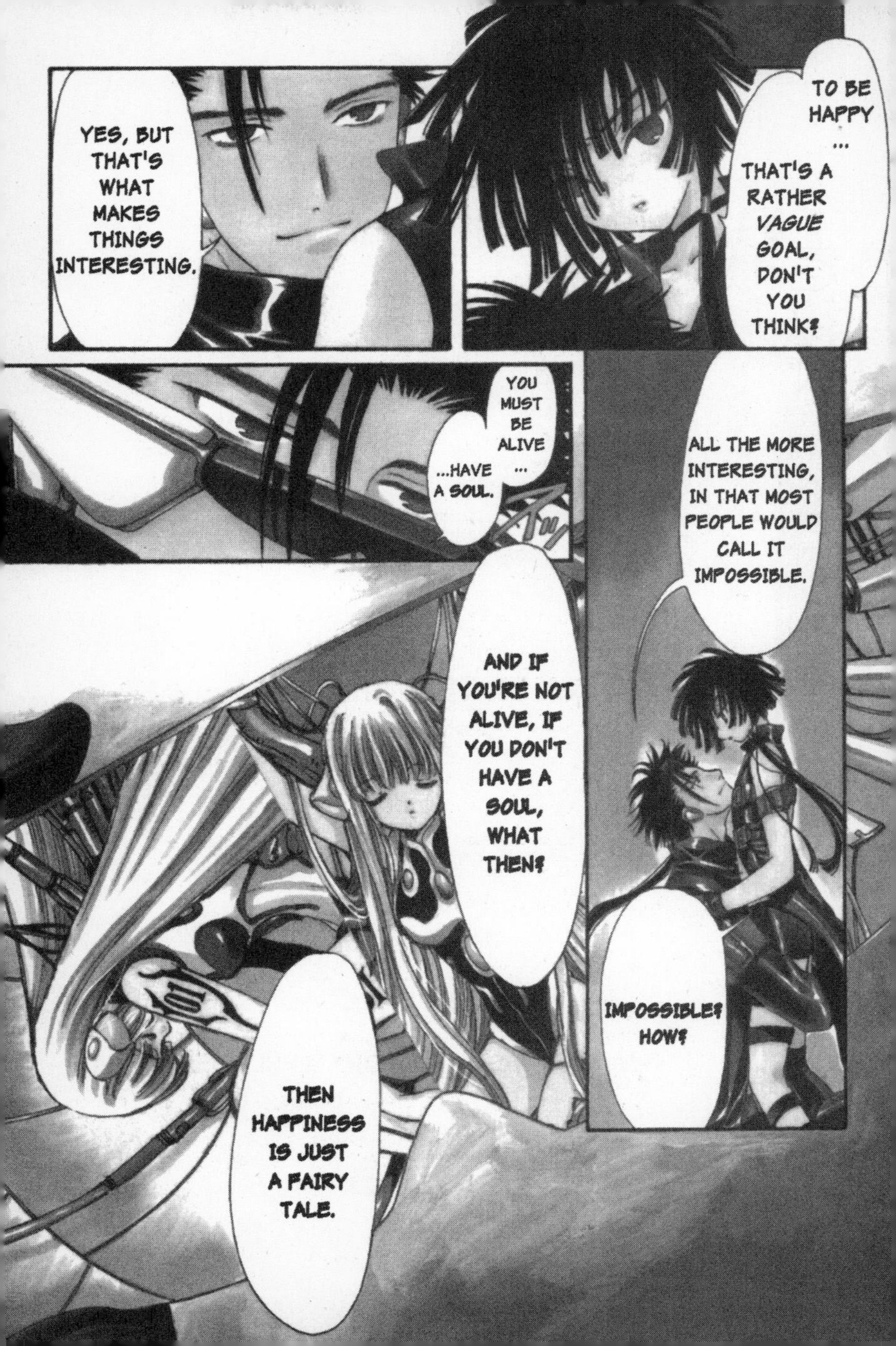
TO BE HAPPY ...
THAT'S A RATHER *VAGUE* GOAL, DON'T YOU THINK?
YES, BUT THAT'S WHAT MAKES THINGS INTERESTING.
ALL THE MORE INTERESTING, IN THAT MOST PEOPLE WOULD CALL IT IMPOSSIBLE.
IMPOSSIBLE? HOW?
YOU MUST BE ALIVE ...
...HAVE A SOUL.
AND IF YOU'RE NOT ALIVE, IF YOU DON'T HAVE A SOUL, WHAT THEN?
THEN HAPPINESS IS JUST A FAIRY TALE.

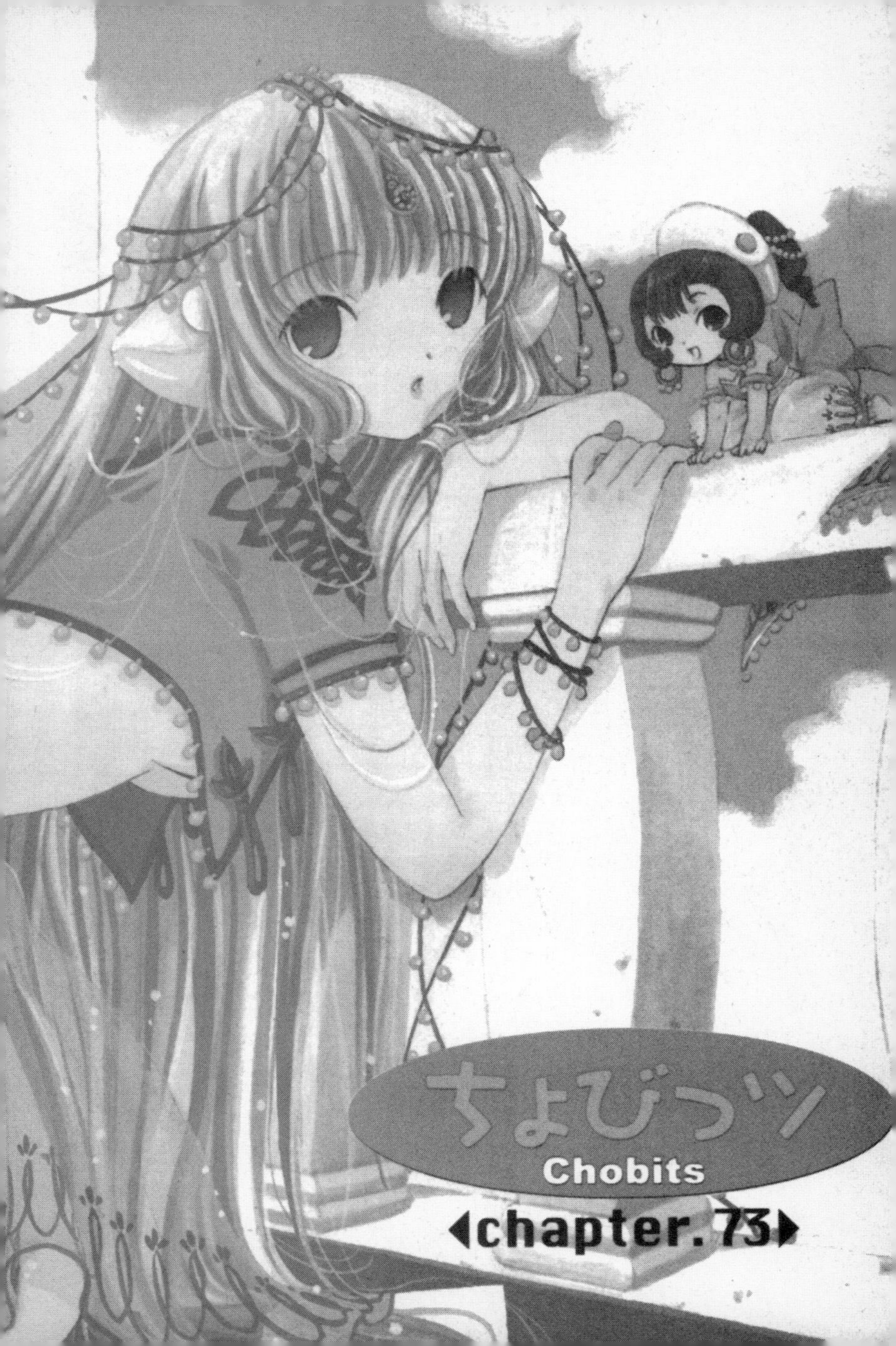
ちょびっツ
Chobits
chapter. 73

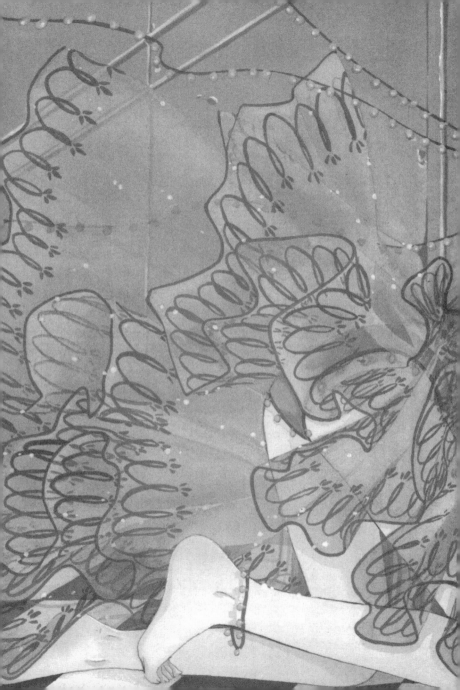

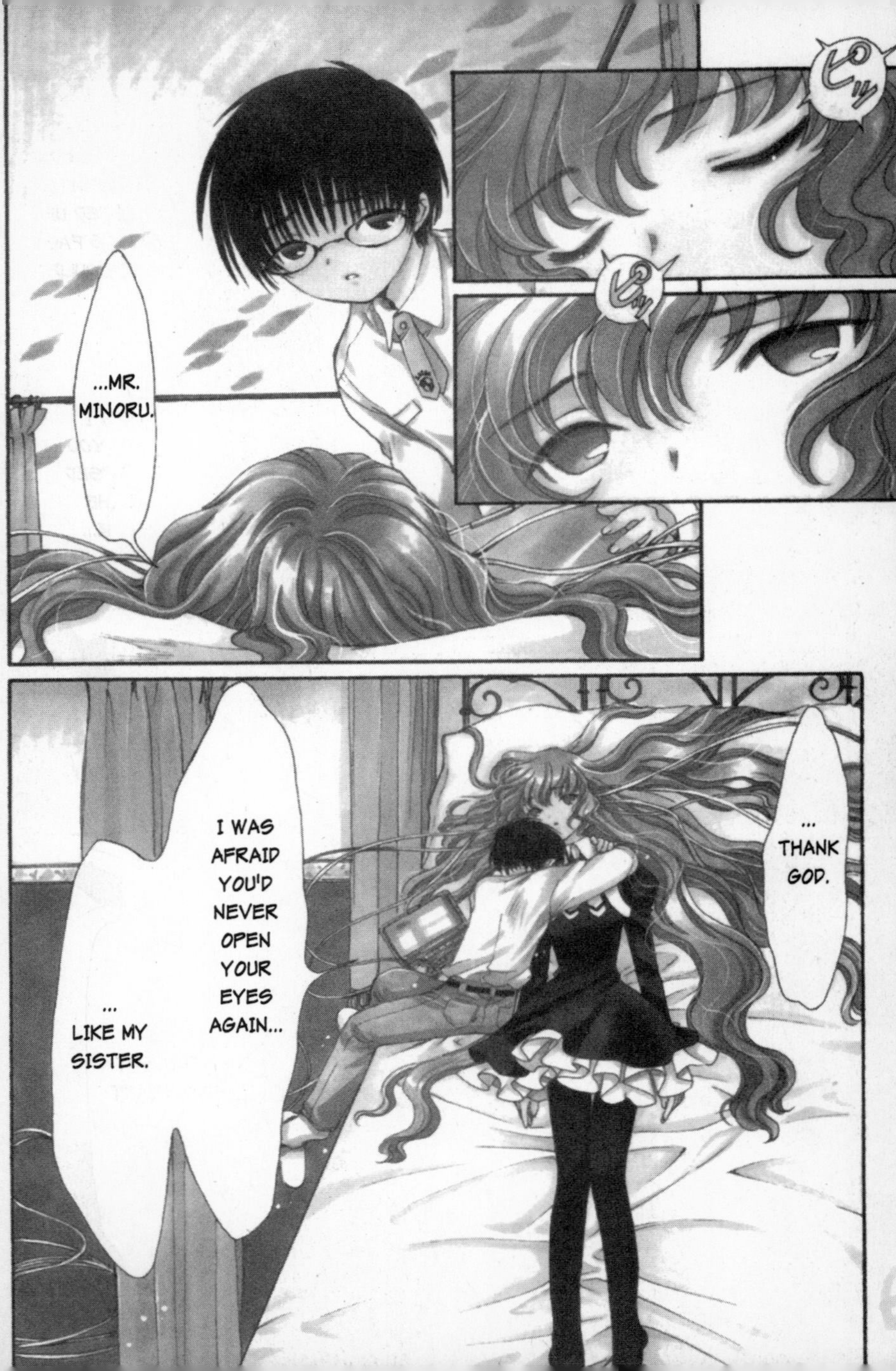
ピッ
ピッ
...MR. MINORU.
... THANK GOD.
I WAS AFRAID YOU'D NEVER OPEN YOUR EYES AGAIN...
... LIKE MY SISTER.

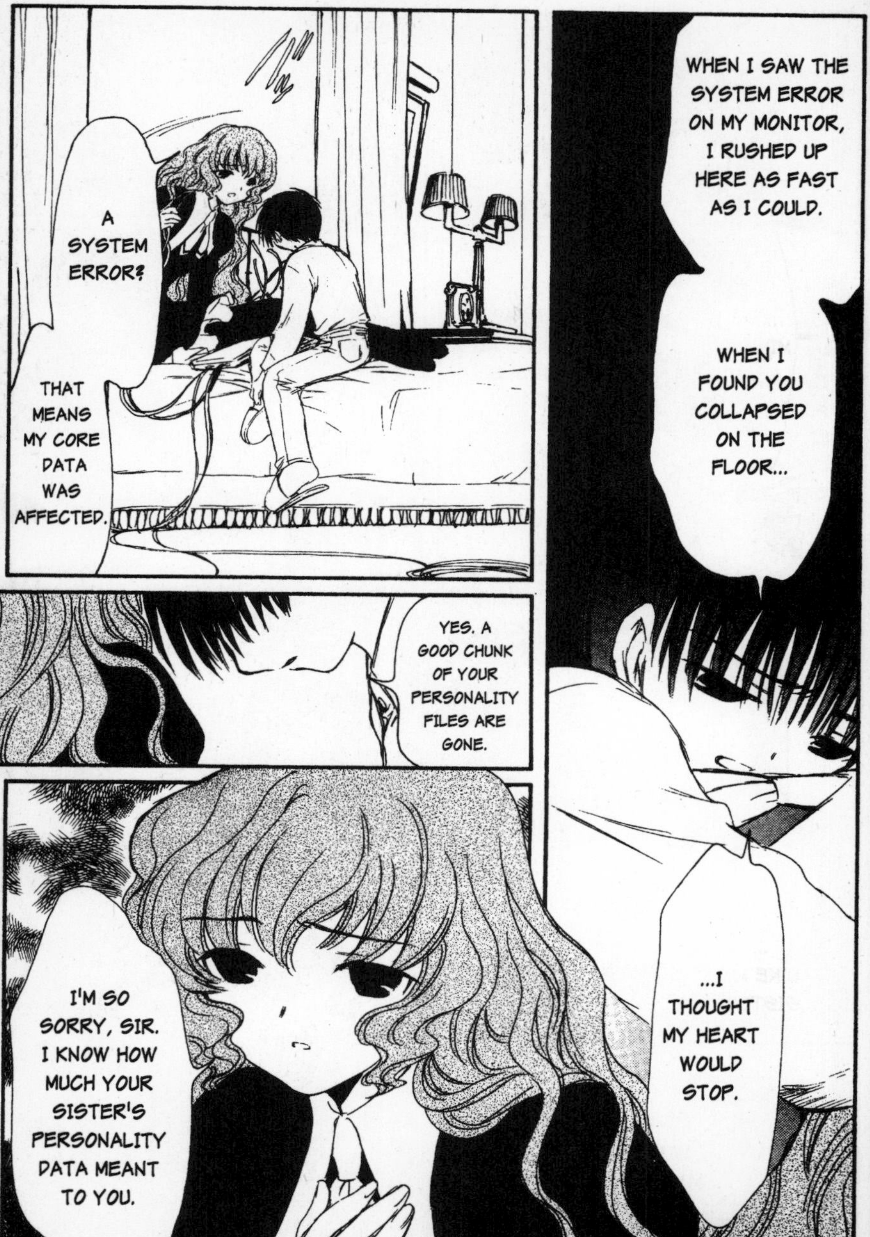
WHEN I SAW THE SYSTEM ERROR ON MY MONITOR, I RUSHED UP HERE AS FAST AS I COULD.
WHEN I FOUND YOU COLLAPSED ON THE FLOOR...
...I THOUGHT MY HEART WOULD STOP.
A SYSTEM ERROR?
THAT MEANS MY CORE DATA WAS AFFECTED.
YES. A GOOD CHUNK OF YOUR PERSONALITY FILES ARE GONE.
I'M SO SORRY, SIR. I KNOW HOW MUCH YOUR SISTER'S PERSONALITY DATA MEANT TO YOU.

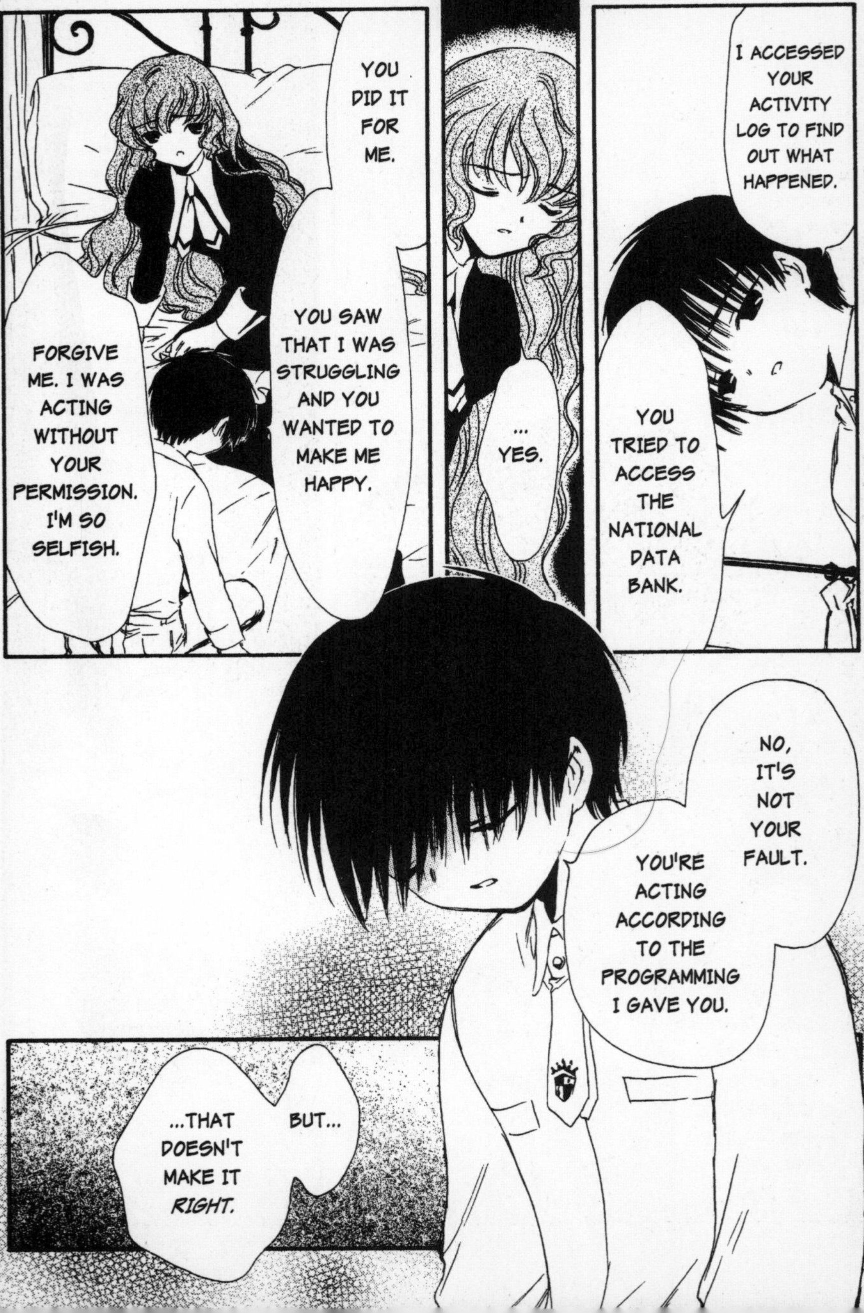
I ACCESSED YOUR ACTIVITY LOG TO FIND OUT WHAT HAPPENED.
YOU TRIED TO ACCESS THE NATIONAL DATA BANK.
... YES.
YOU DID IT FOR ME.
YOU SAW THAT I WAS STRUGGLING AND YOU WANTED TO MAKE ME HAPPY.
FORGIVE ME. I WAS ACTING WITHOUT YOUR PERMISSION. I'M SO SELFISH.
NO, IT'S NOT YOUR FAULT.
YOU'RE ACTING ACCORDING TO THE PROGRAMMING I GAVE YOU.
BUT...
...THAT DOESN'T MAKE IT *RIGHT*.

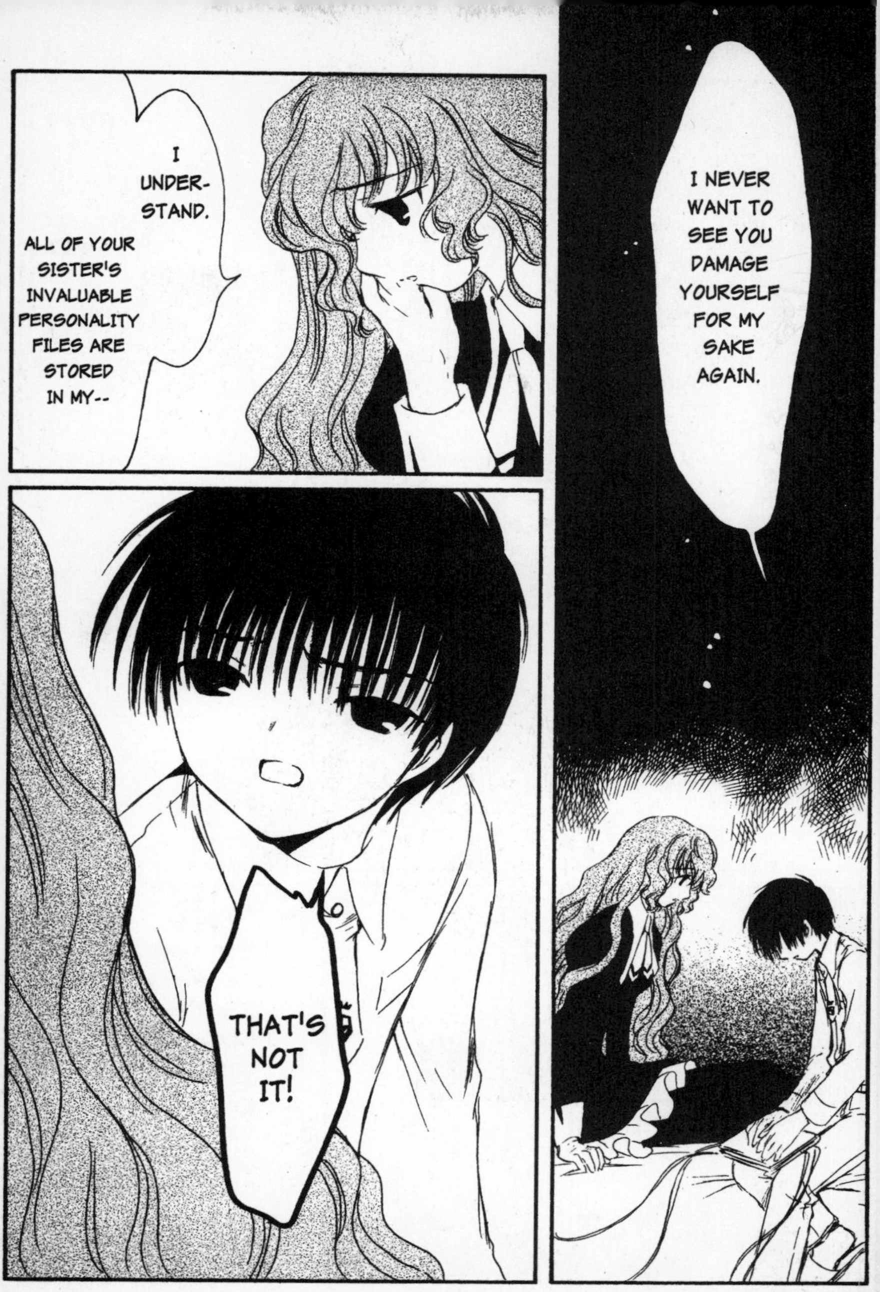
I NEVER WANT TO SEE YOU DAMAGE YOURSELF FOR MY SAKE AGAIN.
I UNDER-STAND.
ALL OF YOUR SISTER'S INVALUABLE PERSONALITY FILES ARE STORED IN MY--
THAT'S NOT IT!

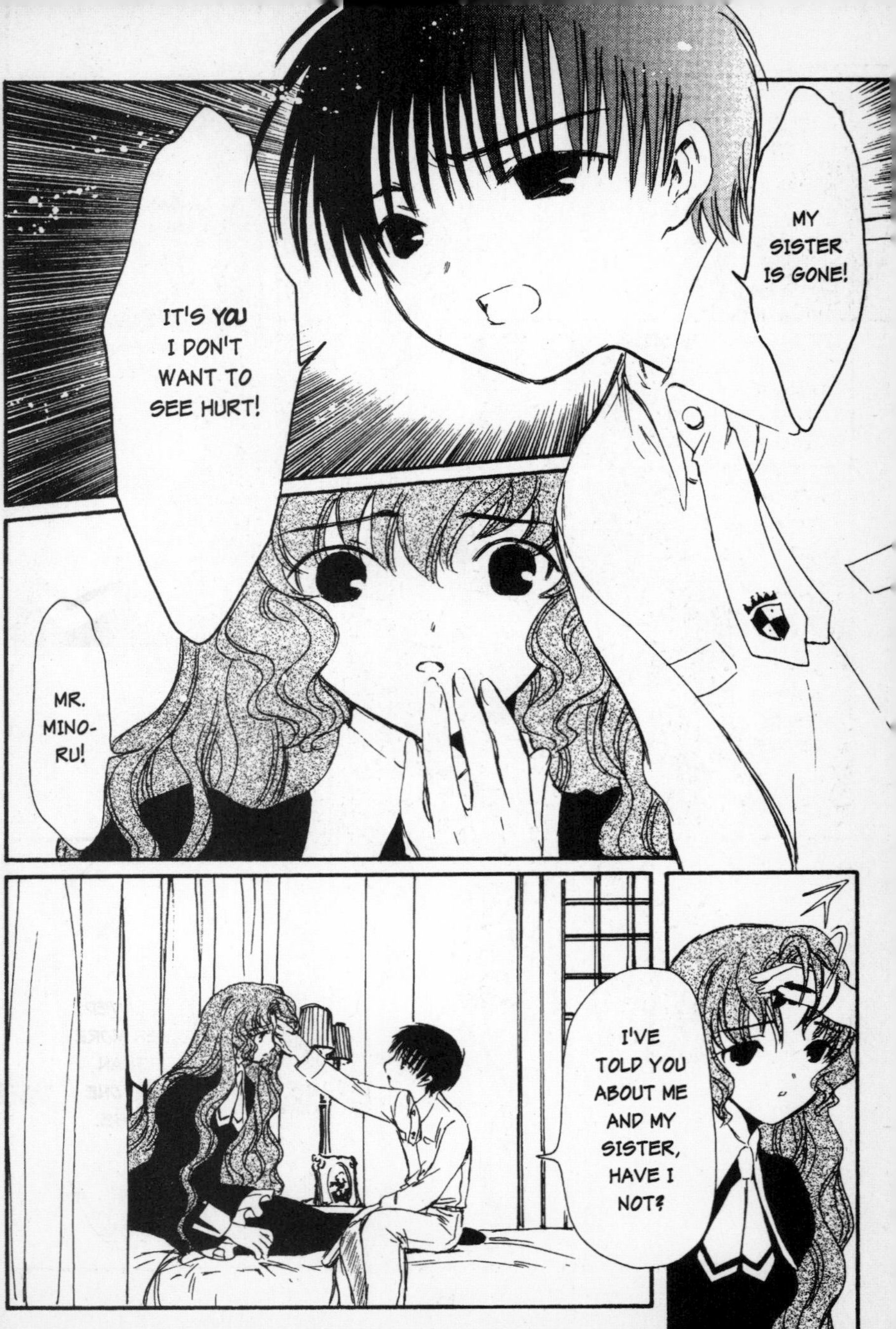
MY SISTER IS GONE!
IT'S YOU I DON'T WANT TO SEE HURT!
MR. MINO-RU!
I'VE TOLD YOU ABOUT ME AND MY SISTER, HAVE I NOT?

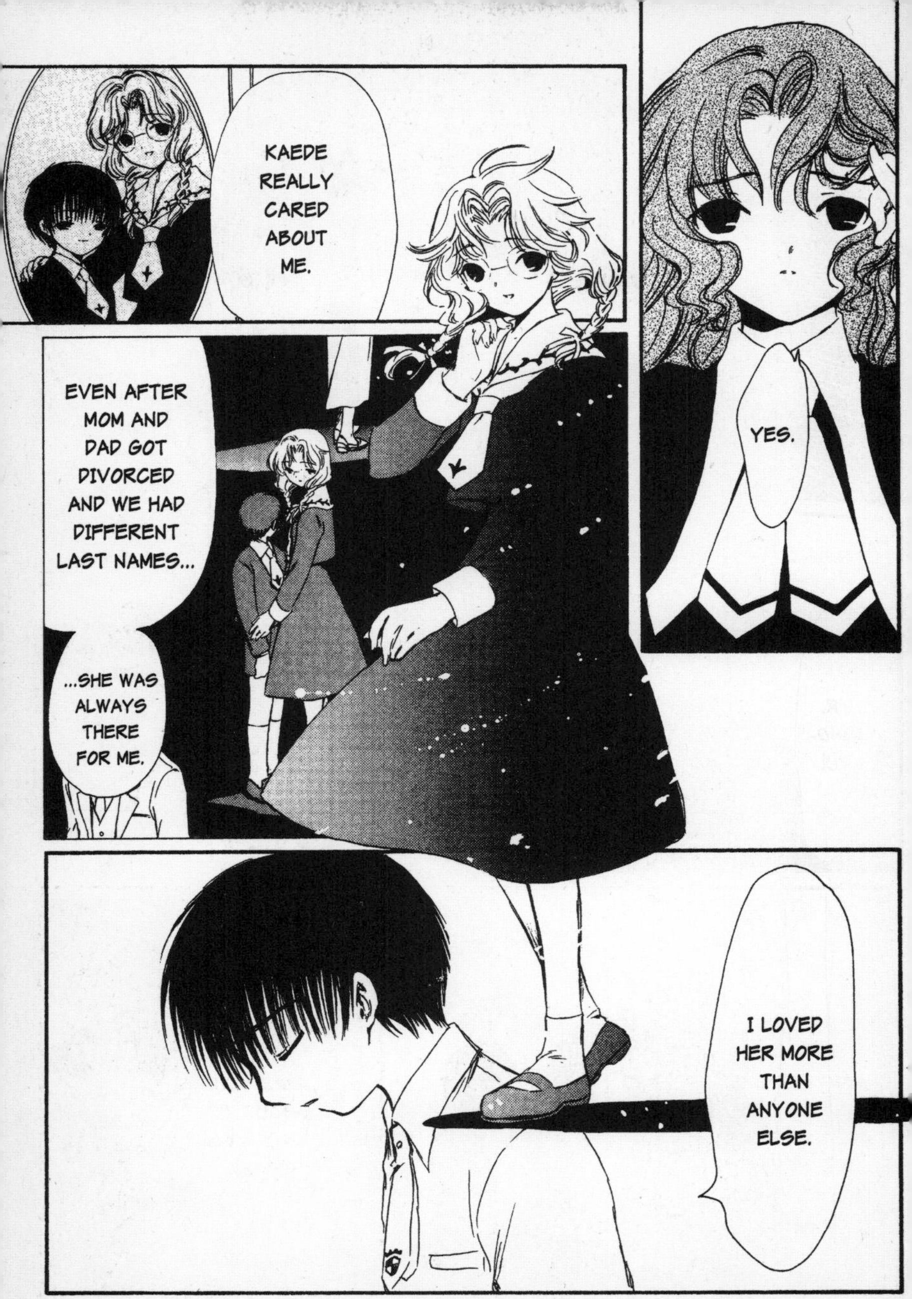
YES.
KAEDE REALLY CARED ABOUT ME.
EVEN AFTER MOM AND DAD GOT DIVORCED AND WE HAD DIFFERENT LAST NAMES...
...SHE WAS ALWAYS THERE FOR ME.
I LOVED HER MORE THAN ANYONE ELSE.

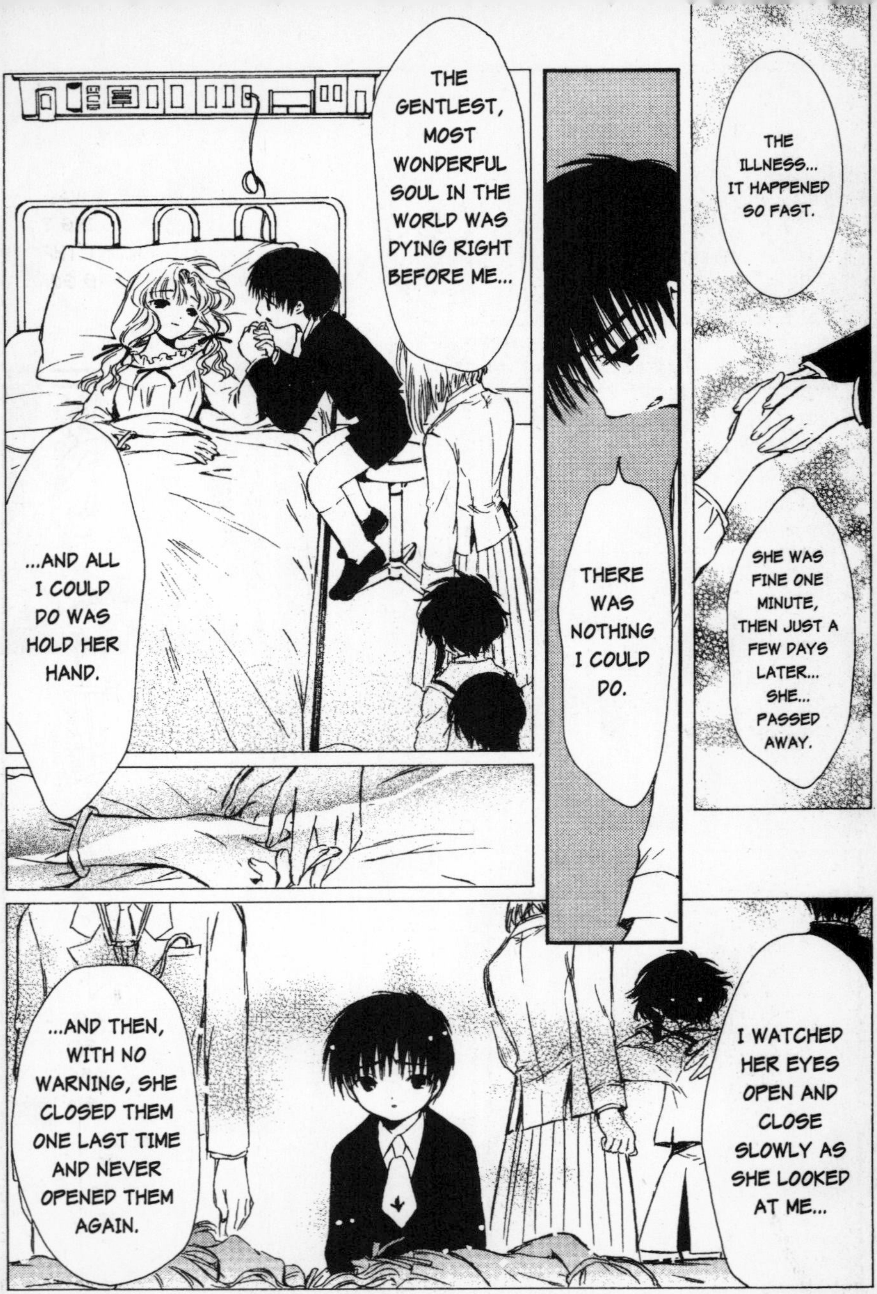
THE ILLNESS... IT HAPPENED SO FAST.
SHE WAS FINE ONE MINUTE, THEN JUST A FEW DAYS LATER... SHE... PASSED AWAY.
THERE WAS NOTHING I COULD DO.
THE GENTLEST, MOST WONDERFUL SOUL IN THE WORLD WAS DYING RIGHT BEFORE ME...
...AND ALL I COULD DO WAS HOLD HER HAND.
I WATCHED HER EYES OPEN AND CLOSE SLOWLY AS SHE LOOKED AT ME...
...AND THEN, WITH NO WARNING, SHE CLOSED THEM ONE LAST TIME AND NEVER OPENED THEM AGAIN.

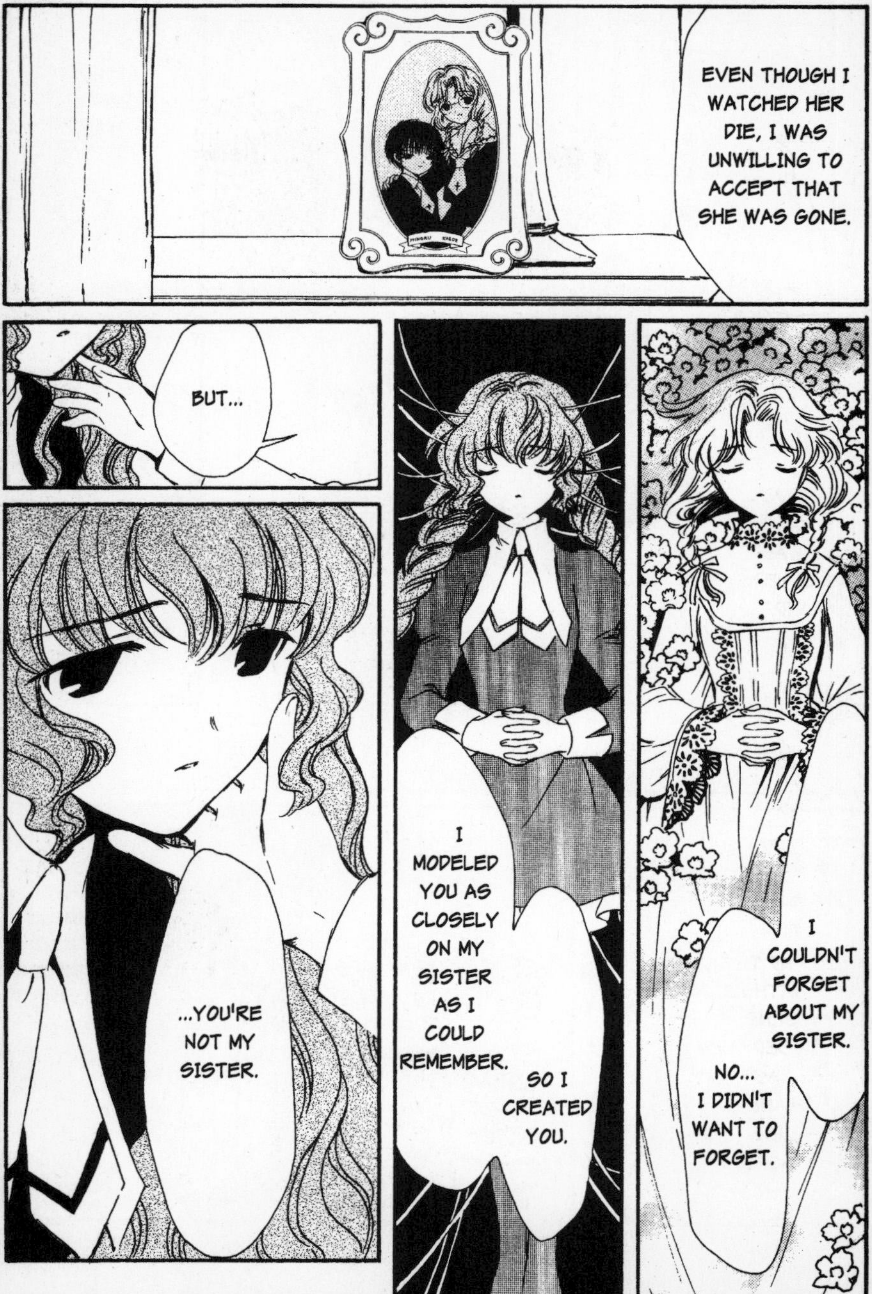
EVEN THOUGH I WATCHED HER DIE, I WAS UNWILLING TO ACCEPT THAT SHE WAS GONE.
I COULDN'T FORGET ABOUT MY SISTER.
NO... I DIDN'T WANT TO FORGET.
I MODELED YOU AS CLOSELY ON MY SISTER AS I COULD REMEMBER.
SO I CREATED YOU.
BUT...
...YOU'RE NOT MY SISTER.

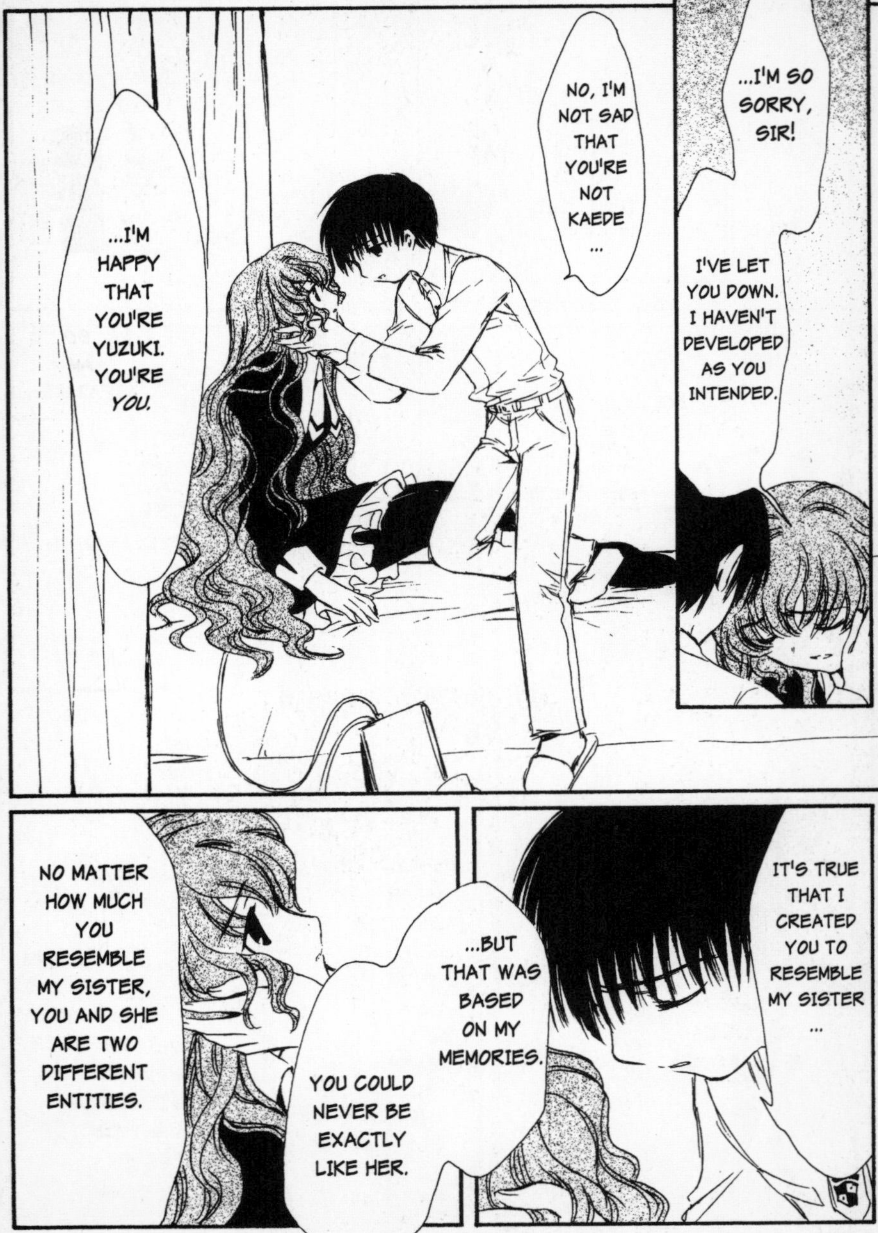
...I'M SO SORRY, SIR!
I'VE LET YOU DOWN. I HAVEN'T DEVELOPED AS YOU INTENDED.
NO, I'M NOT SAD THAT YOU'RE NOT KAEDE ...
...I'M HAPPY THAT YOU'RE YUZUKI. YOU'RE *YOU.*
IT'S TRUE THAT I CREATED YOU TO RESEMBLE MY SISTER ...
...BUT THAT WAS BASED ON MY MEMORIES.
YOU COULD NEVER BE EXACTLY LIKE HER.
NO MATTER HOW MUCH YOU RESEMBLE MY SISTER, YOU AND SHE ARE TWO DIFFERENT ENTITIES.

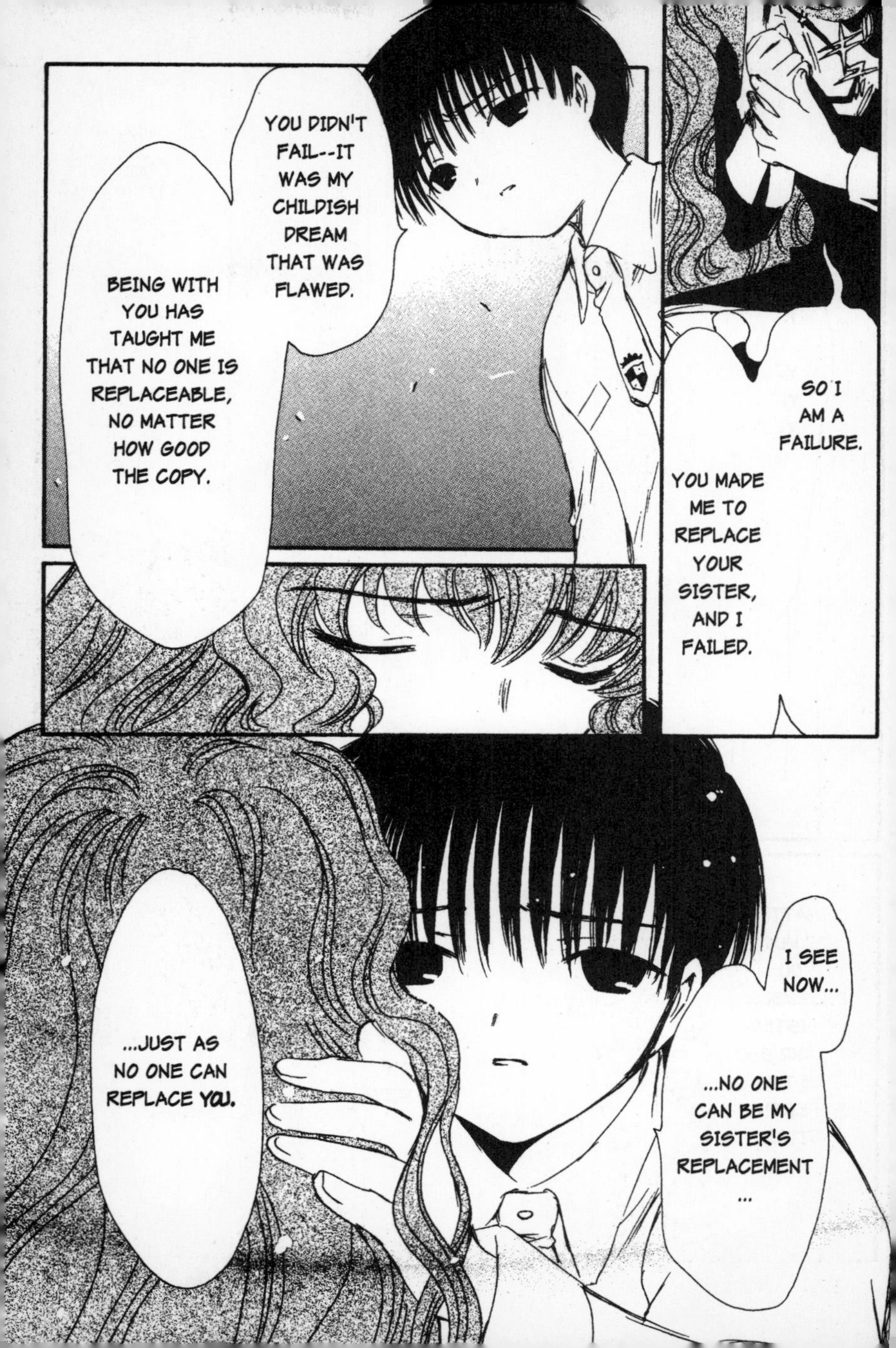
SO I AM A FAILURE.
YOU MADE ME TO REPLACE YOUR SISTER, AND I FAILED.
YOU DIDN'T FAIL--IT WAS MY CHILDISH DREAM THAT WAS FLAWED.
BEING WITH YOU HAS TAUGHT ME THAT NO ONE IS REPLACEABLE, NO MATTER HOW GOOD THE COPY.
I SEE NOW...
...NO ONE CAN BE MY SISTER'S REPLACEMENT ...
...JUST AS NO ONE CAN REPLACE YOU.

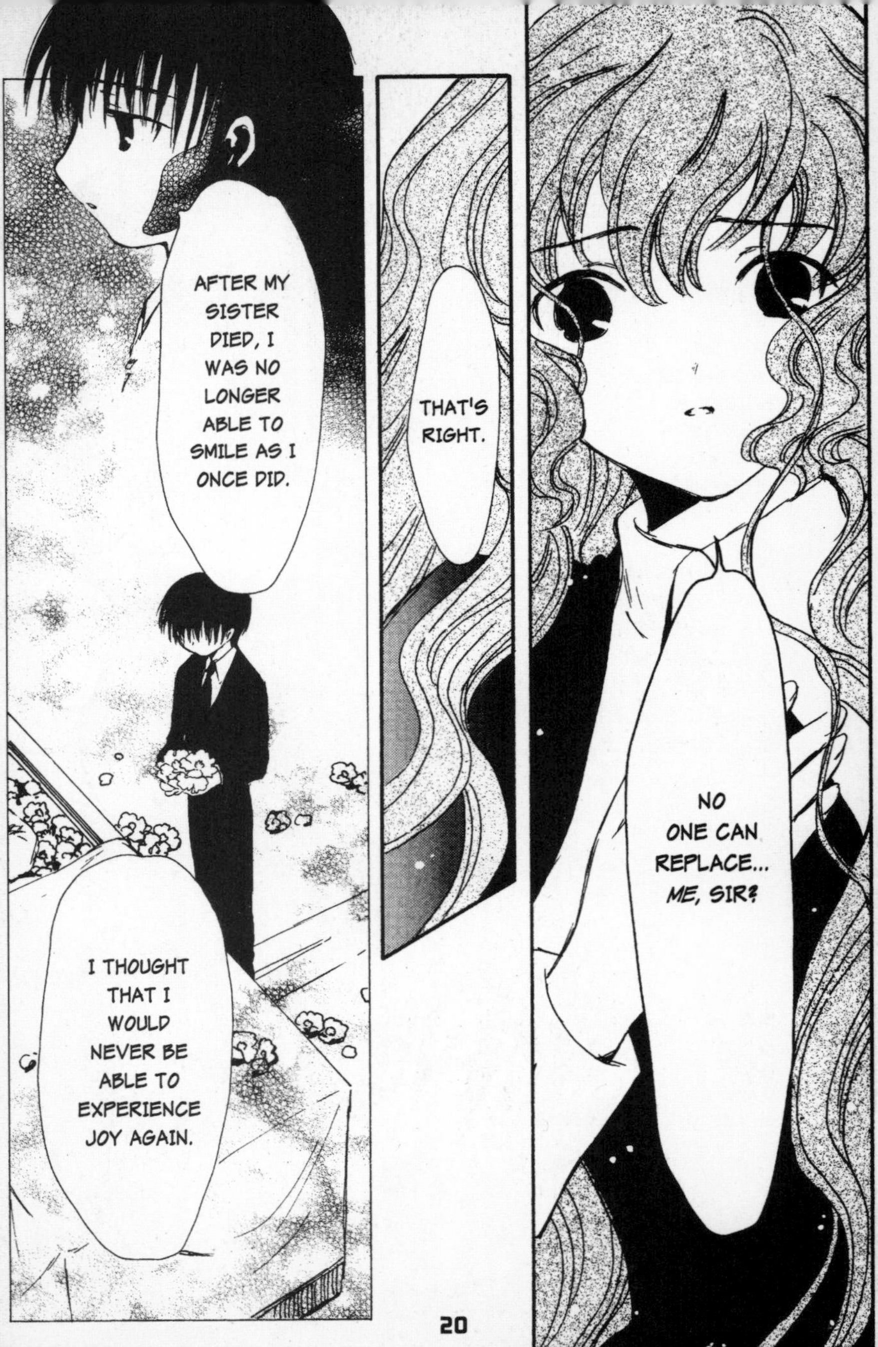
NO ONE CAN REPLACE... *ME*, SIR?
THAT'S RIGHT.
AFTER MY SISTER DIED, I WAS NO LONGER ABLE TO SMILE AS I ONCE DID.
I THOUGHT THAT I WOULD NEVER BE ABLE TO EXPERIENCE JOY AGAIN.

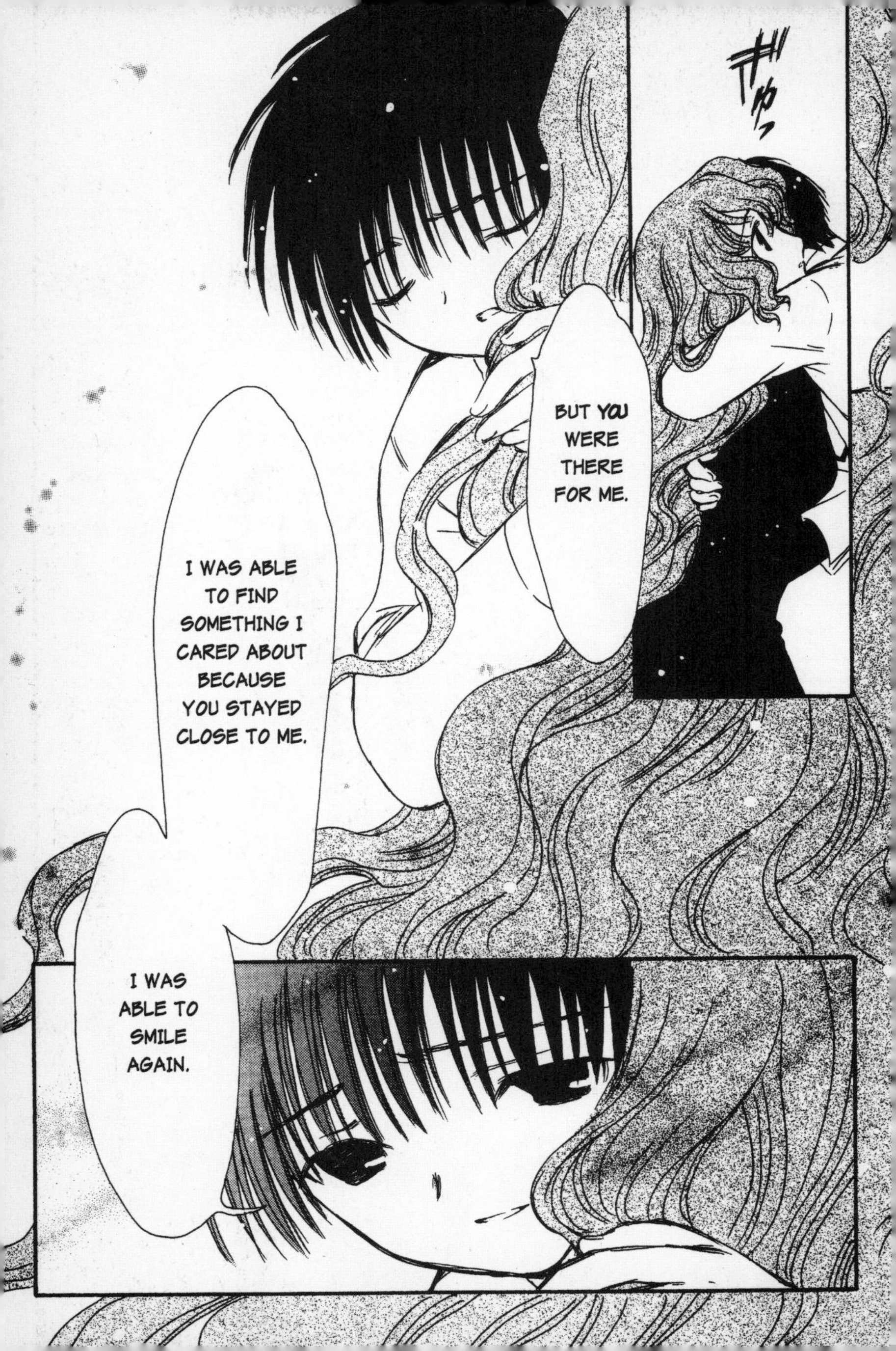
BUT YOU WERE THERE FOR ME.
I WAS ABLE TO FIND SOMETHING I CARED ABOUT BECAUSE YOU STAYED CLOSE TO ME.
I WAS ABLE TO SMILE AGAIN.

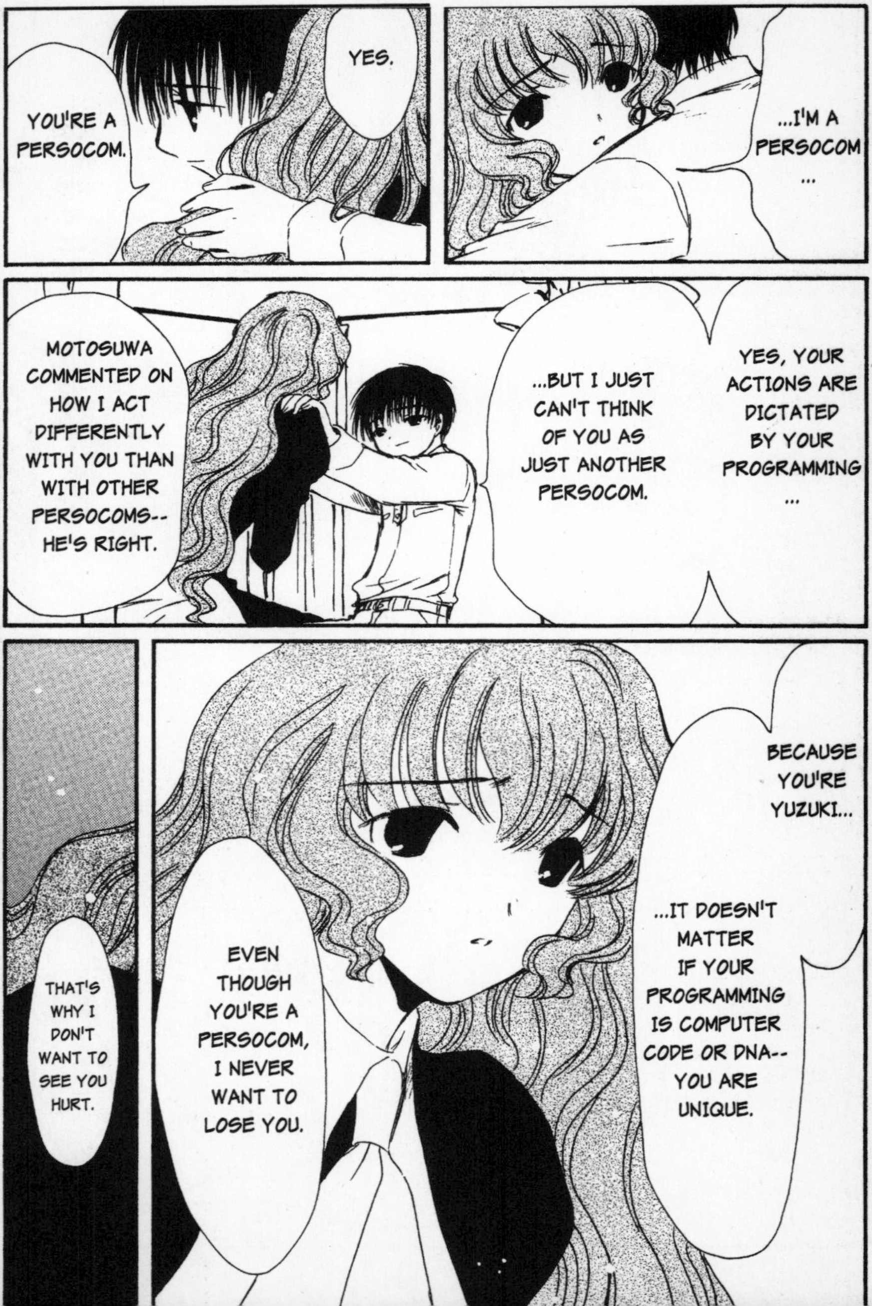
...I'M A PERSOCOM ...
YES.
YOU'RE A PERSOCOM.
YES, YOUR ACTIONS ARE DICTATED BY YOUR PROGRAMMING ...
...BUT I JUST CAN'T THINK OF YOU AS JUST ANOTHER PERSOCOM.
MOTOSUWA COMMENTED ON HOW I ACT DIFFERENTLY WITH YOU THAN WITH OTHER PERSOCOMS-- HE'S RIGHT.
BECAUSE YOU'RE YUZUKI...
...IT DOESN'T MATTER IF YOUR PROGRAMMING IS COMPUTER CODE OR DNA-- YOU ARE UNIQUE.
EVEN THOUGH YOU'RE A PERSOCOM, I NEVER WANT TO LOSE YOU.
THAT'S WHY I DON'T WANT TO SEE YOU HURT.

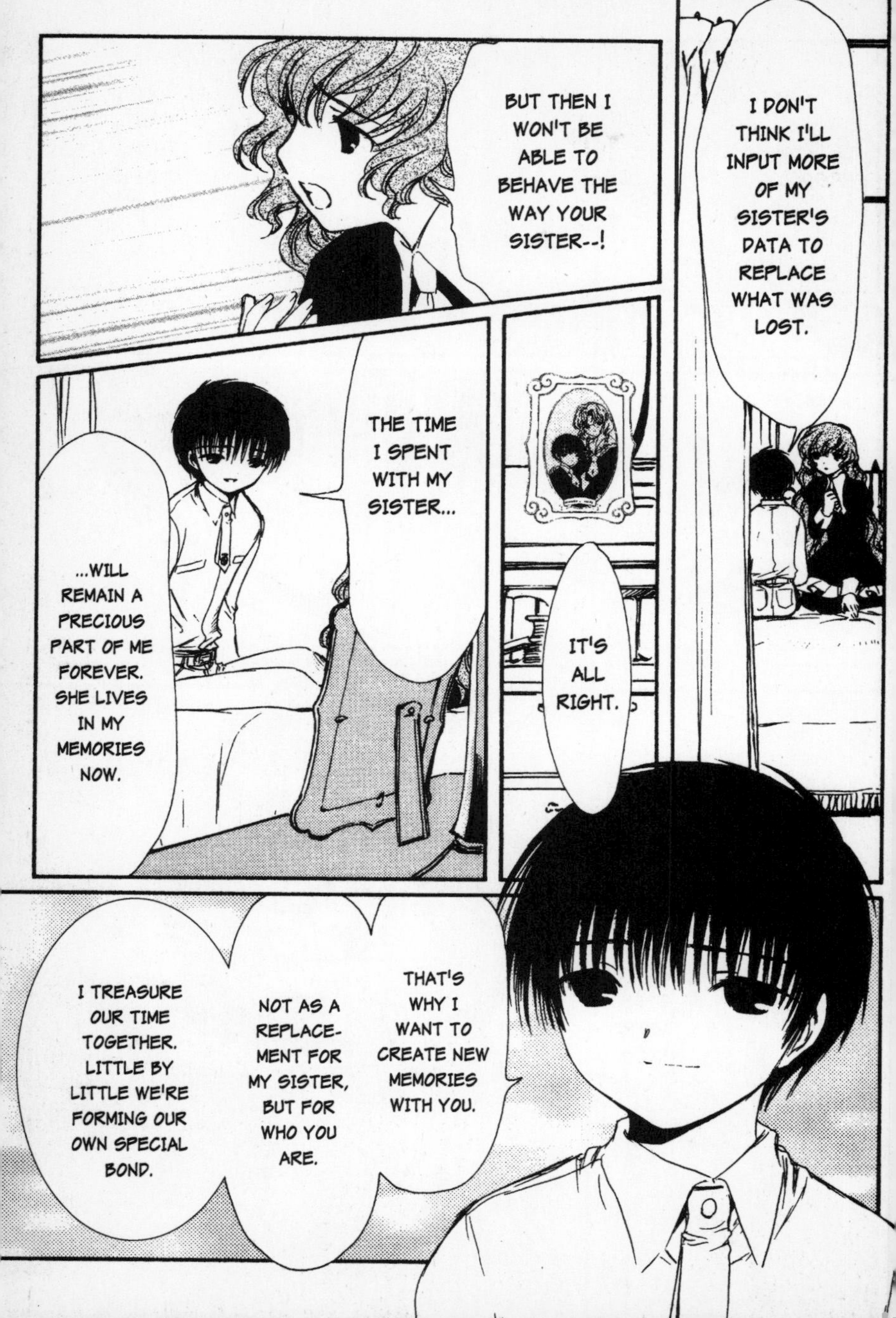
I DON'T THINK I'LL INPUT MORE OF MY SISTER'S DATA TO REPLACE WHAT WAS LOST.
BUT THEN I WON'T BE ABLE TO BEHAVE THE WAY YOUR SISTER--!
IT'S ALL RIGHT.
THE TIME I SPENT WITH MY SISTER...
...WILL REMAIN A PRECIOUS PART OF ME FOREVER. SHE LIVES IN MY MEMORIES NOW.
THAT'S WHY I WANT TO CREATE NEW MEMORIES WITH YOU.
NOT AS A REPLACE-MENT FOR MY SISTER, BUT FOR WHO YOU ARE.
I TREASURE OUR TIME TOGETHER. LITTLE BY LITTLE WE'RE FORMING OUR OWN SPECIAL BOND.

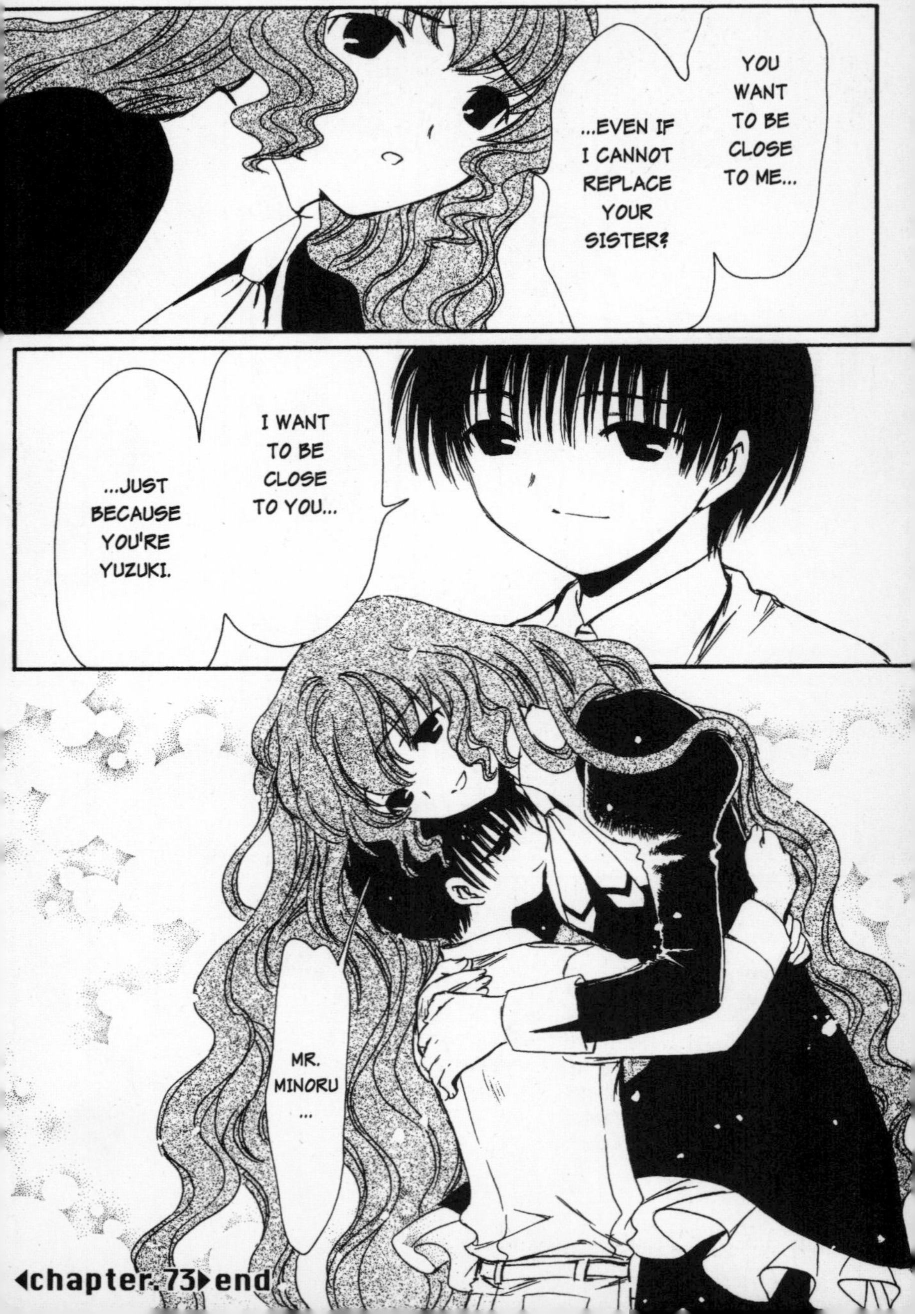
YOU WANT TO BE CLOSE TO ME...
...EVEN IF I CANNOT REPLACE YOUR SISTER?
I WANT TO BE CLOSE TO YOU...
...JUST BECAUSE YOU'RE YUZUKI.
MR. MINORU ...
chapter. 73 end

ちょびっツ
Chobits

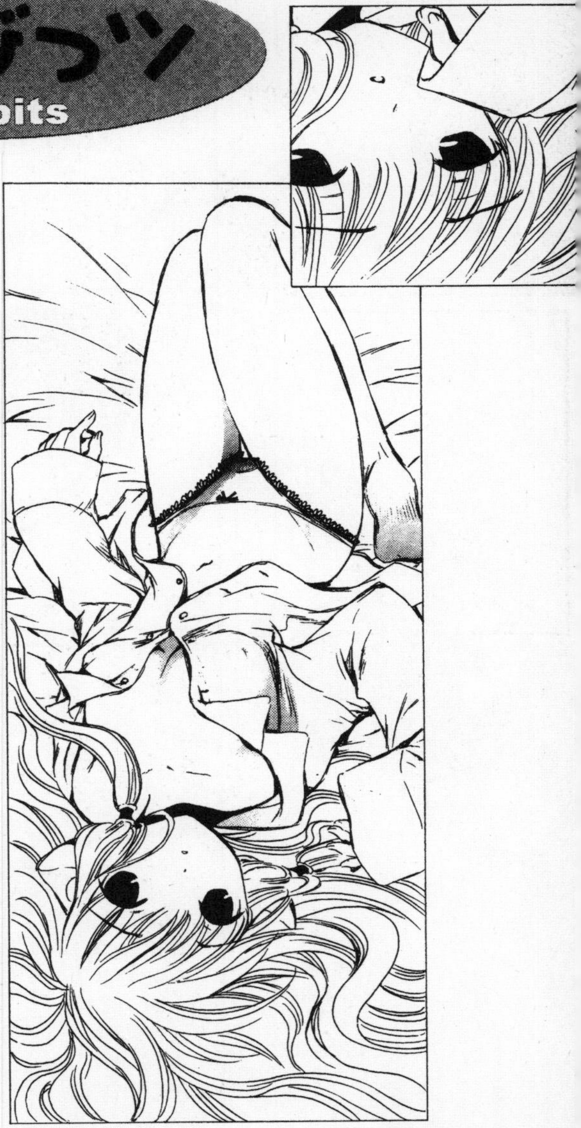

◀chapter. 74▶

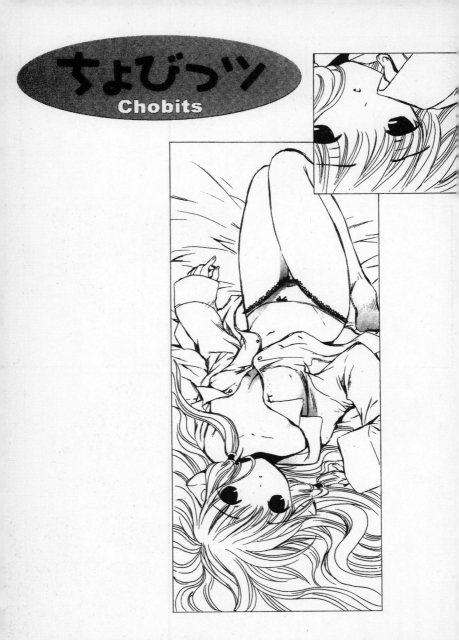

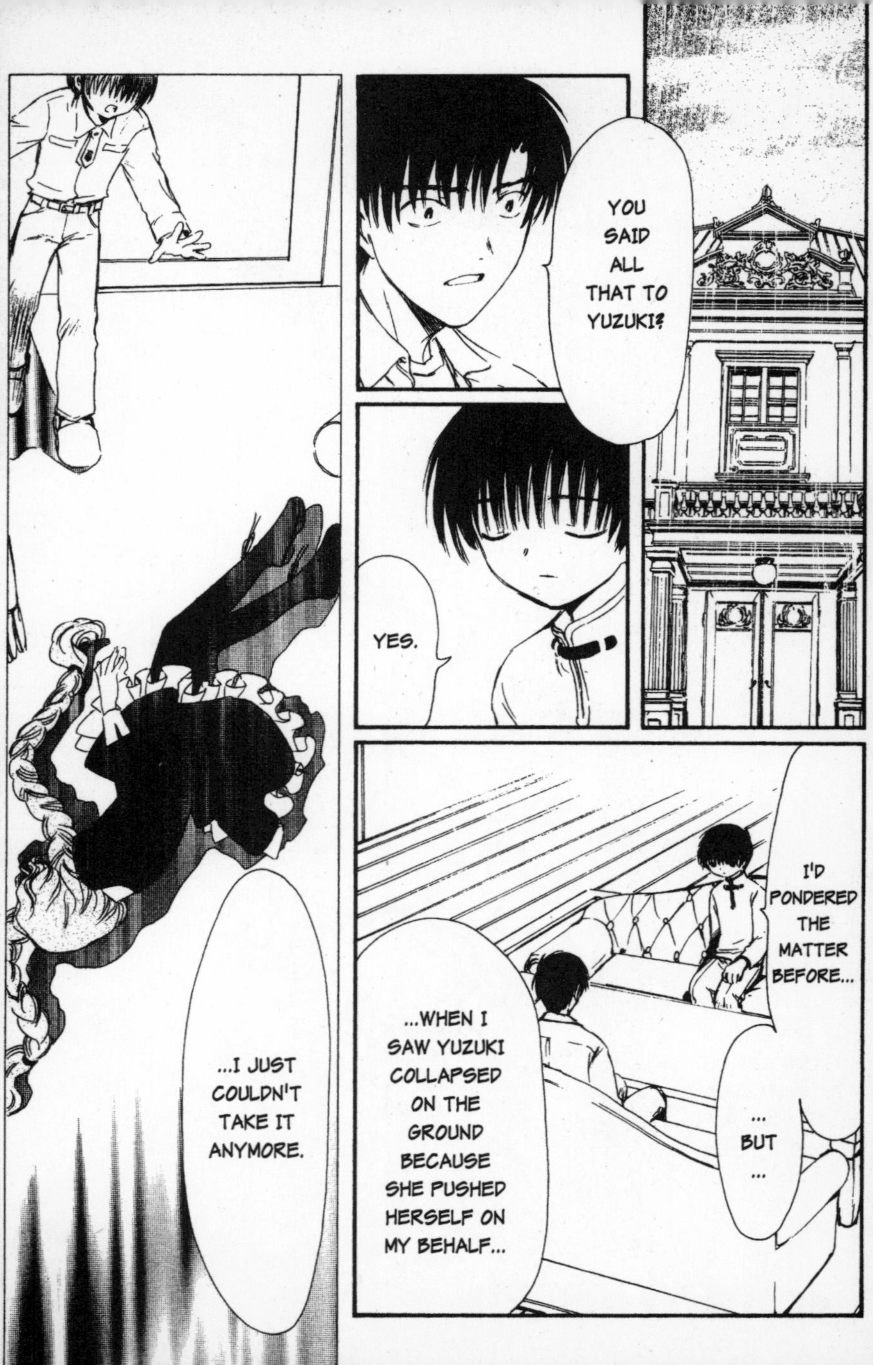
YOU SAID ALL THAT TO YUZUKI?
YES.
I'D PONDERED THE MATTER BEFORE...
... BUT ...
...WHEN I SAW YUZUKI COLLAPSED ON THE GROUND BECAUSE SHE PUSHED HERSELF ON MY BEHALF...
...I JUST COULDN'T TAKE IT ANYMORE.

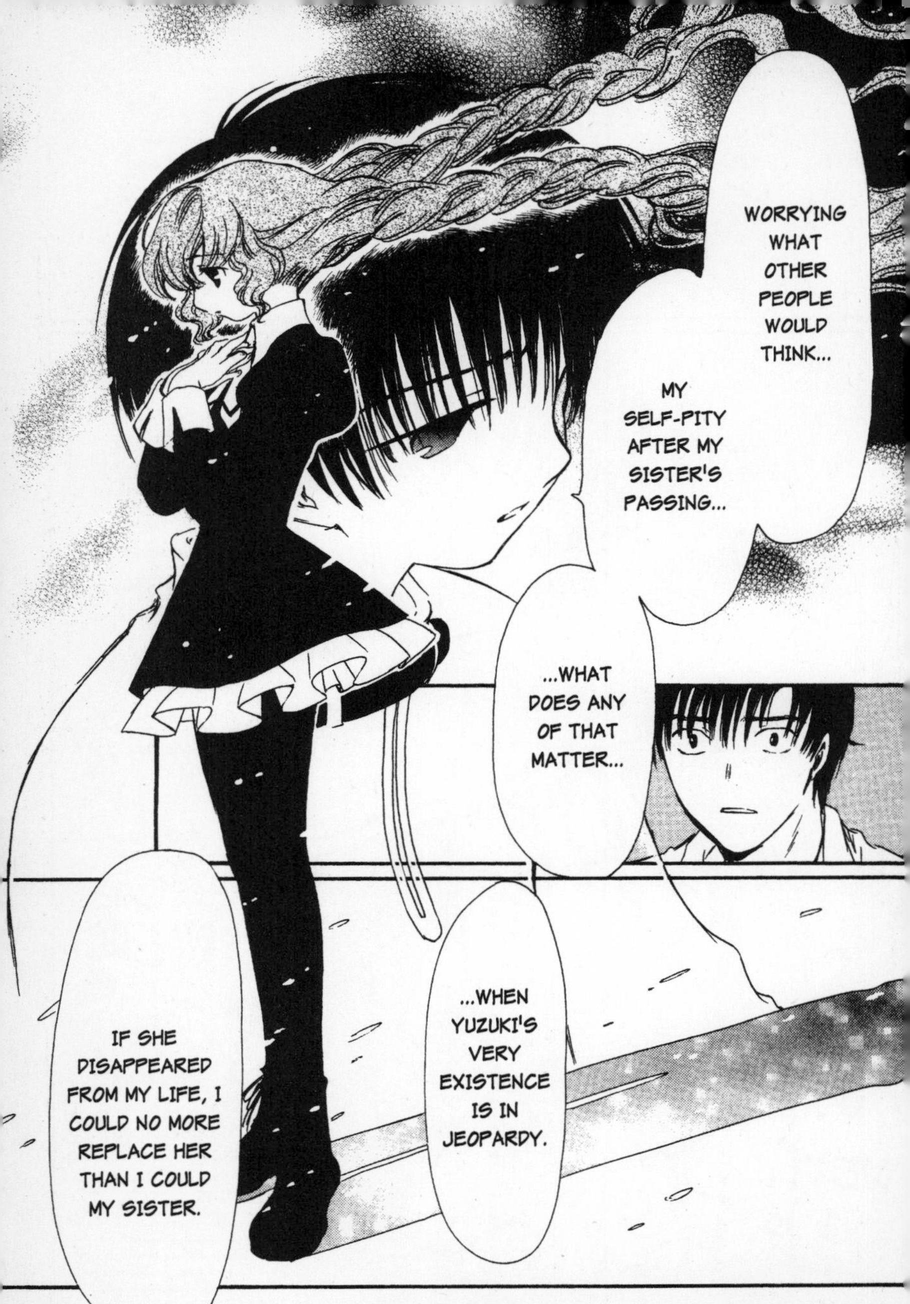
WORRYING WHAT OTHER PEOPLE WOULD THINK...
MY SELF-PITY AFTER MY SISTER'S PASSING...
...WHAT DOES ANY OF THAT MATTER...
...WHEN YUZUKI'S VERY EXISTENCE IS IN JEOPARDY.
IF SHE DISAPPEARED FROM MY LIFE, I COULD NO MORE REPLACE HER THAN I COULD MY SISTER.

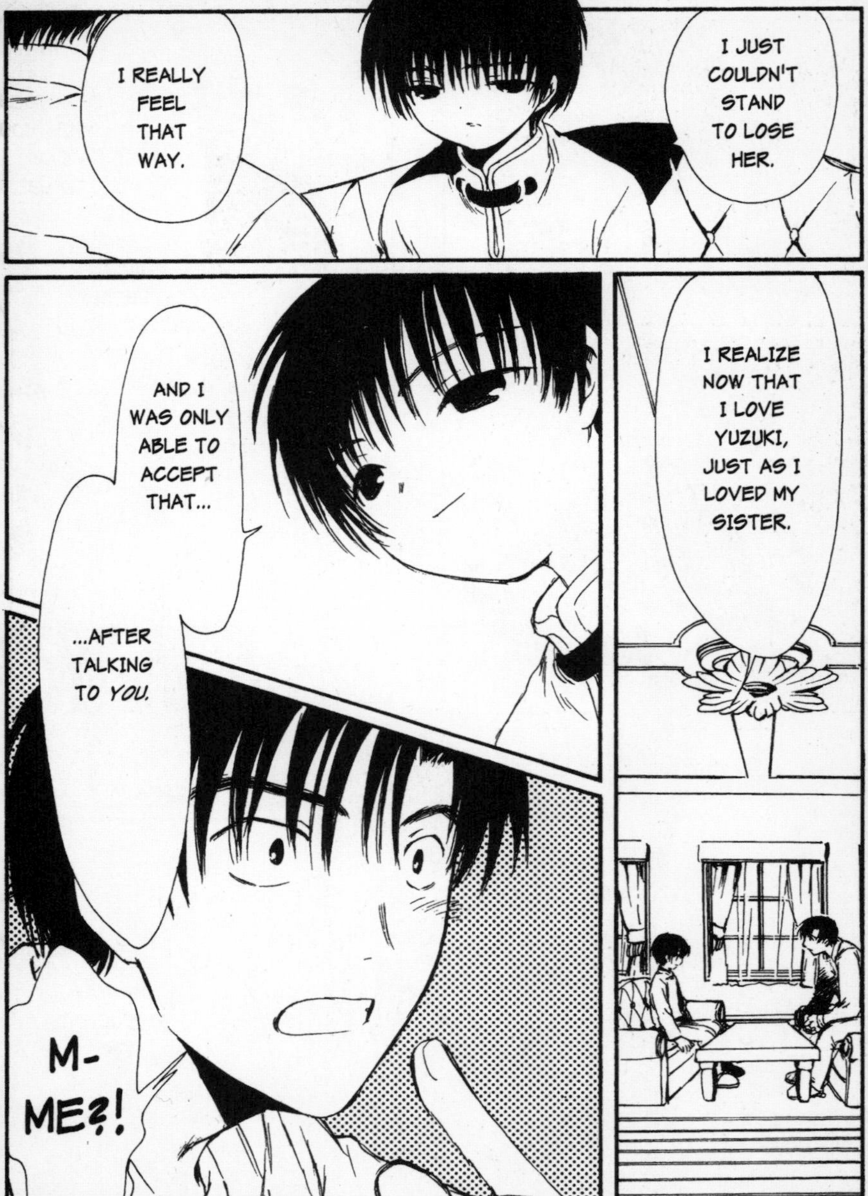
I JUST COULDN'T STAND TO LOSE HER.
I REALLY FEEL THAT WAY.
I REALIZE NOW THAT I LOVE YUZUKI, JUST AS I LOVED MY SISTER.
AND I WAS ONLY ABLE TO ACCEPT THAT...
...AFTER TALKING TO *YOU.*
M-ME?!

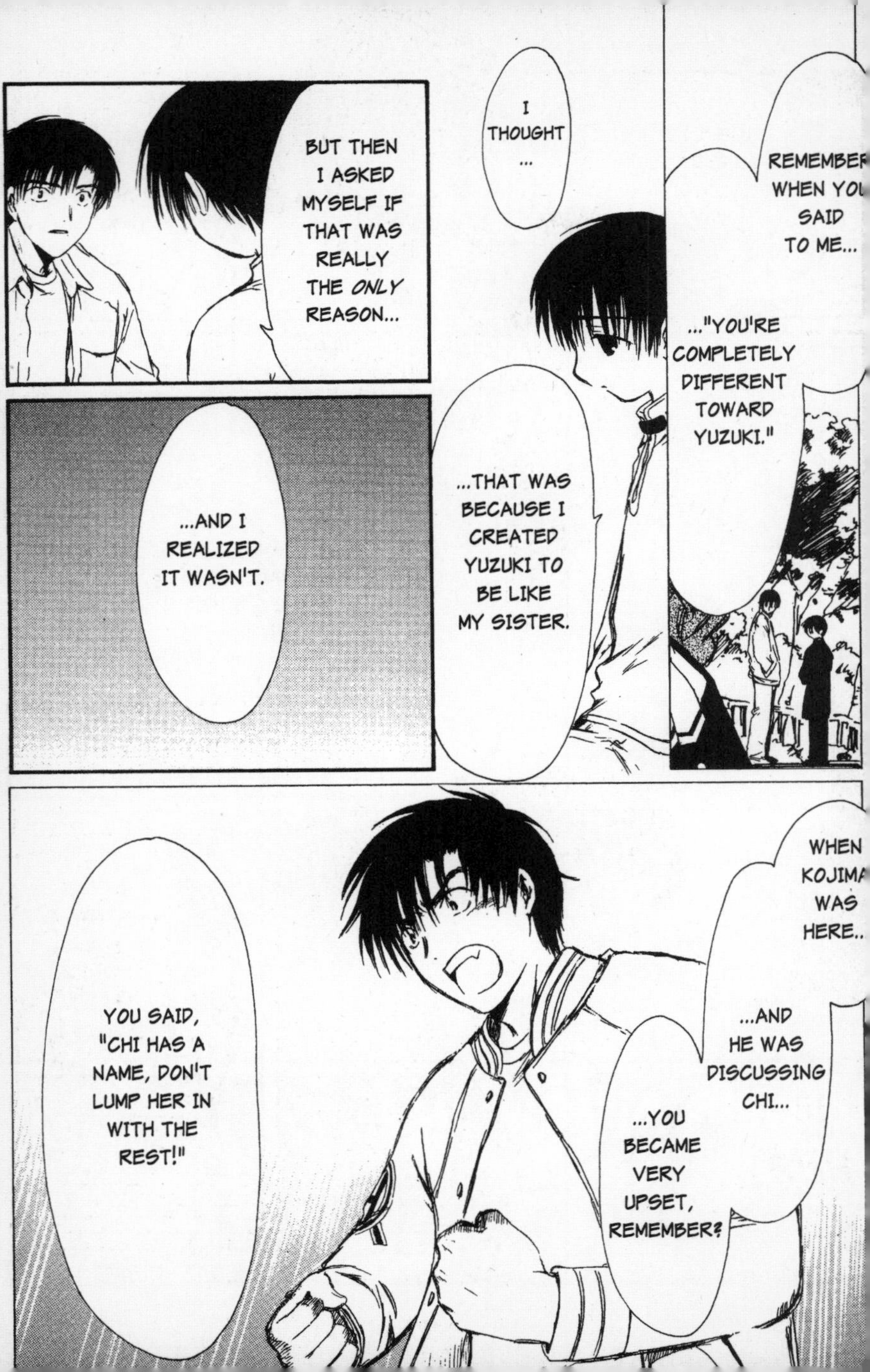
REMEMBER WHEN YOU SAID TO ME...
..."YOU'RE COMPLETELY DIFFERENT TOWARD YUZUKI."
I THOUGHT ...
...THAT WAS BECAUSE I CREATED YUZUKI TO BE LIKE MY SISTER.
BUT THEN I ASKED MYSELF IF THAT WAS REALLY THE *ONLY* REASON...
...AND I REALIZED IT WASN'T.
WHEN KOJIMA WAS HERE...
...AND HE WAS DISCUSSING CHI...
...YOU BECAME VERY UPSET, REMEMBER?
YOU SAID, "CHI HAS A NAME, DON'T LUMP HER IN WITH THE REST!"

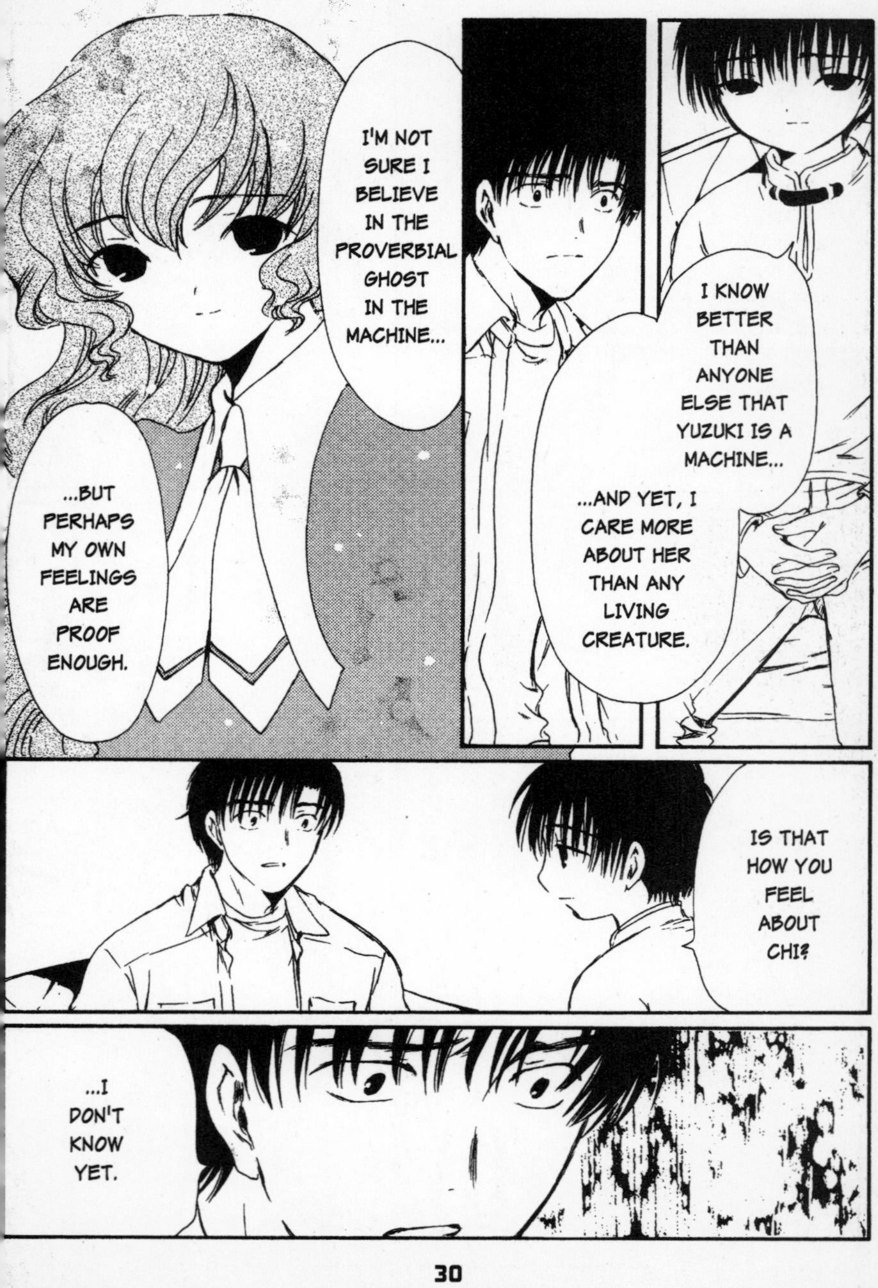
I KNOW BETTER THAN ANYONE ELSE THAT YUZUKI IS A MACHINE...
...AND YET, I CARE MORE ABOUT HER THAN ANY LIVING CREATURE.
I'M NOT SURE I BELIEVE IN THE PROVERBIAL GHOST IN THE MACHINE...
...BUT PERHAPS MY OWN FEELINGS ARE PROOF ENOUGH.
IS THAT HOW YOU FEEL ABOUT CHI?
...I DON'T KNOW YET.

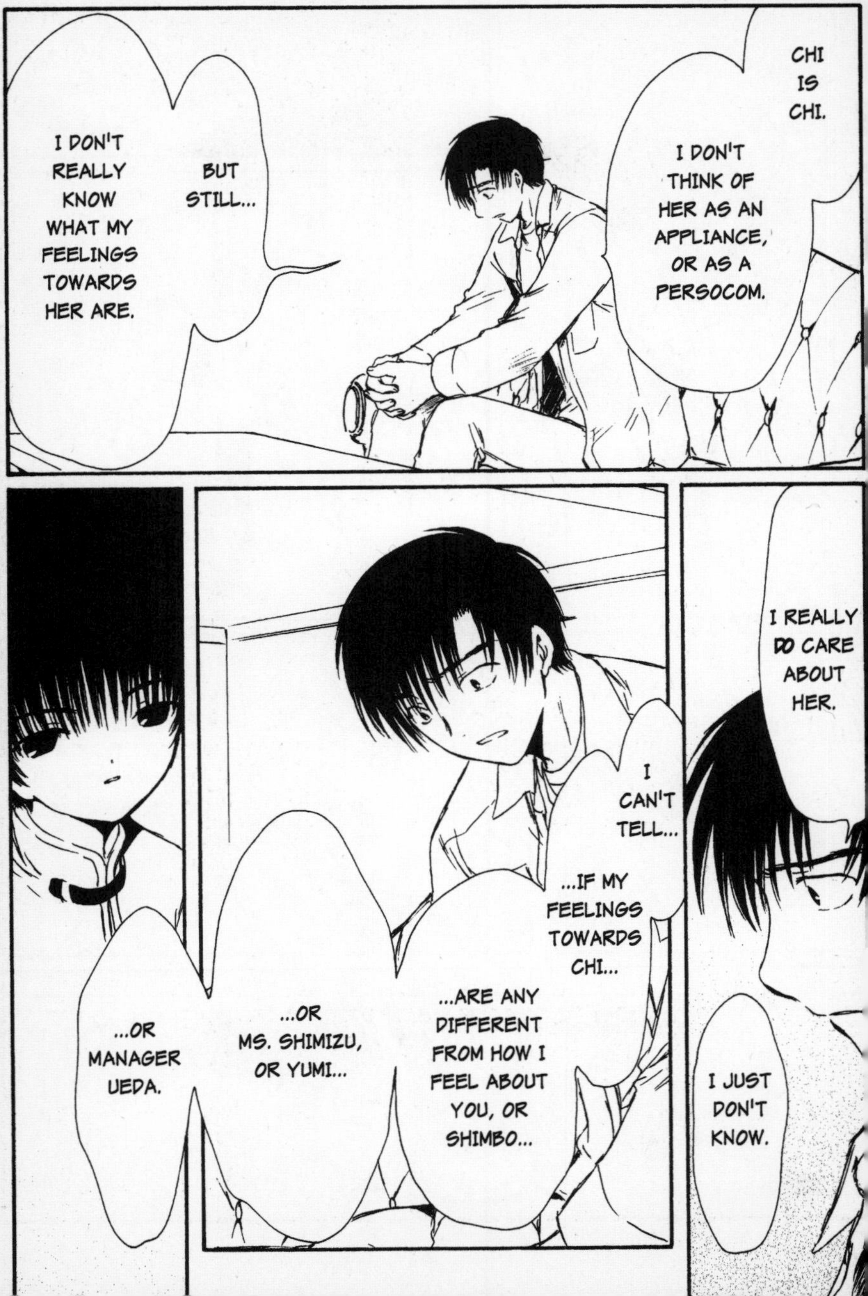
CHI IS CHI.
I DON'T THINK OF HER AS AN APPLIANCE, OR AS A PERSOCOM.
BUT STILL...
I DON'T REALLY KNOW WHAT MY FEELINGS TOWARDS HER ARE.
I REALLY DO CARE ABOUT HER.
I JUST DON'T KNOW.
I CAN'T TELL...
...IF MY FEELINGS TOWARDS CHI...
...ARE ANY DIFFERENT FROM HOW I FEEL ABOUT YOU, OR SHIMBO...
...OR MS. SHIMIZU, OR YUMI...
...OR MANAGER UEDA.

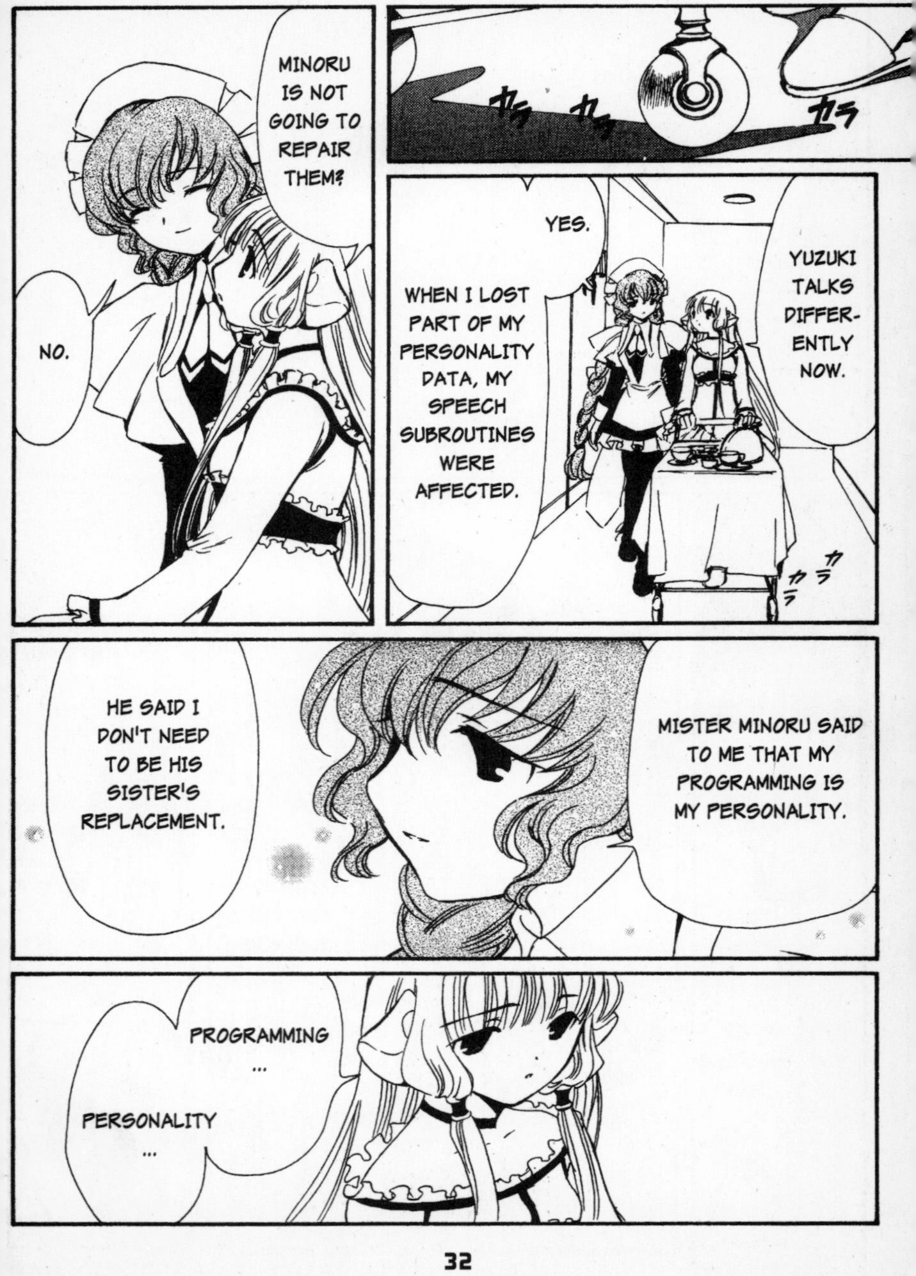

カラ
カラ
カラ
YUZUKI TALKS DIFFER-ENTLY NOW.
YES.
WHEN I LOST PART OF MY PERSONALITY DATA, MY SPEECH SUBROUTINES WERE AFFECTED.
カラ
カラ
MINORU IS NOT GOING TO REPAIR THEM?
NO.
MISTER MINORU SAID TO ME THAT MY PROGRAMMING IS MY PERSONALITY.
HE SAID I DON'T NEED TO BE HIS SISTER'S REPLACEMENT.
PROGRAMMING ...
PERSONALITY ...

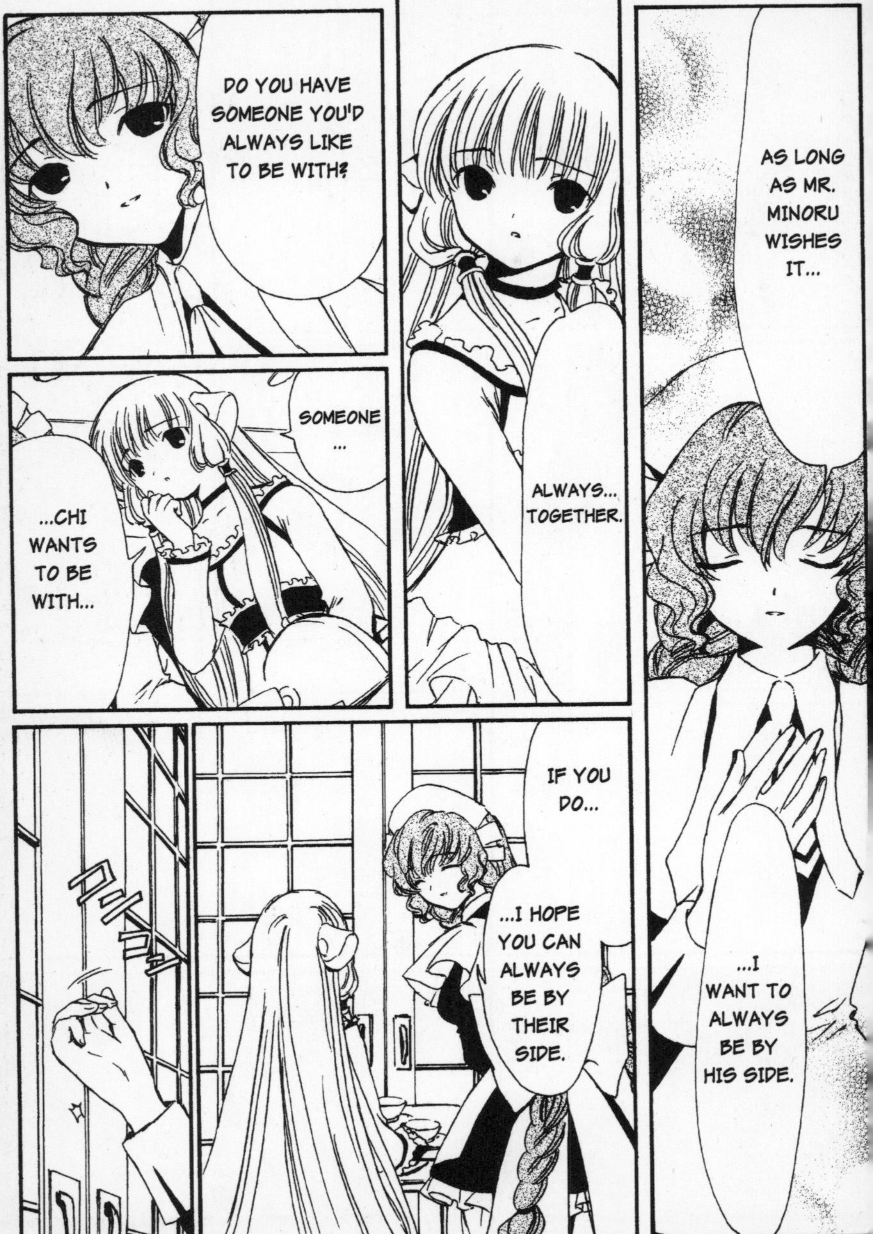
AS LONG AS MR. MINORU WISHES IT...
...I WANT TO ALWAYS BE BY HIS SIDE.
ALWAYS... TOGETHER.
DO YOU HAVE SOMEONE YOU'D ALWAYS LIKE TO BE WITH?
SOMEONE ...
...CHI WANTS TO BE WITH...
IF YOU DO...
...I HOPE YOU CAN ALWAYS BE BY THEIR SIDE.

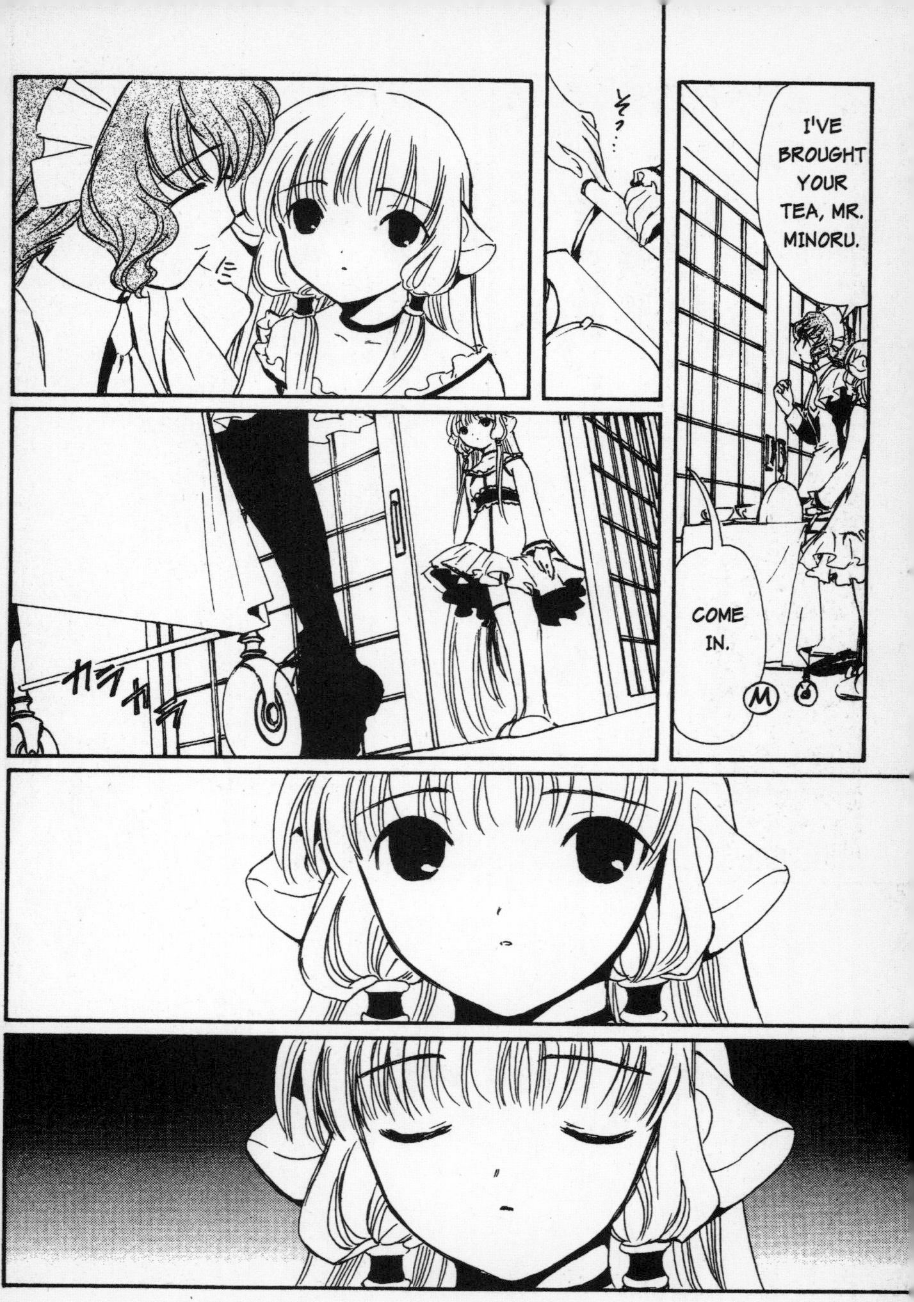
I'VE BROUGHT YOUR TEA, MR. MINORU.
COME IN.
カラカラ

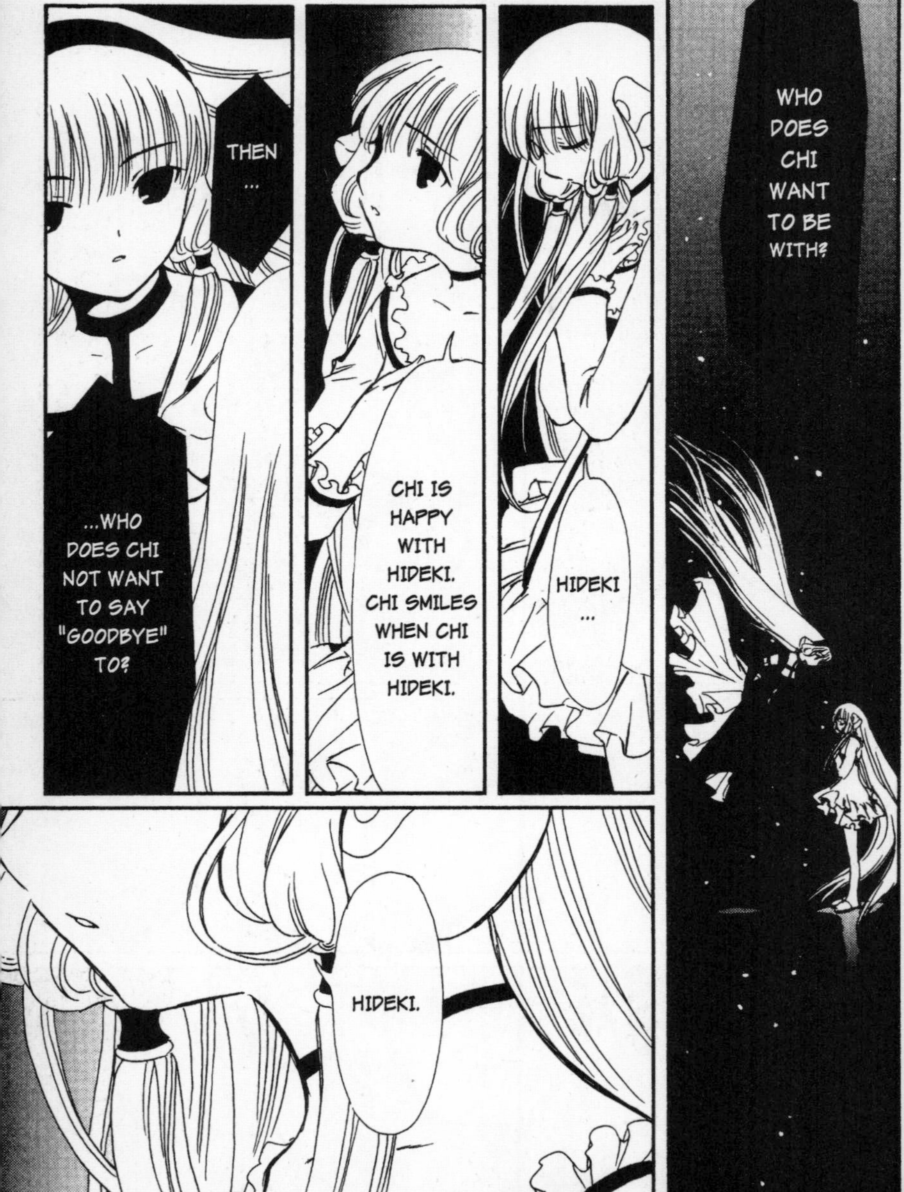
WHO DOES CHI WANT TO BE WITH?
HIDEKI ...
CHI IS HAPPY WITH HIDEKI. CHI SMILES WHEN CHI IS WITH HIDEKI.
THEN ...
...WHO DOES CHI NOT WANT TO SAY "GOODBYE" TO?
HIDEKI.

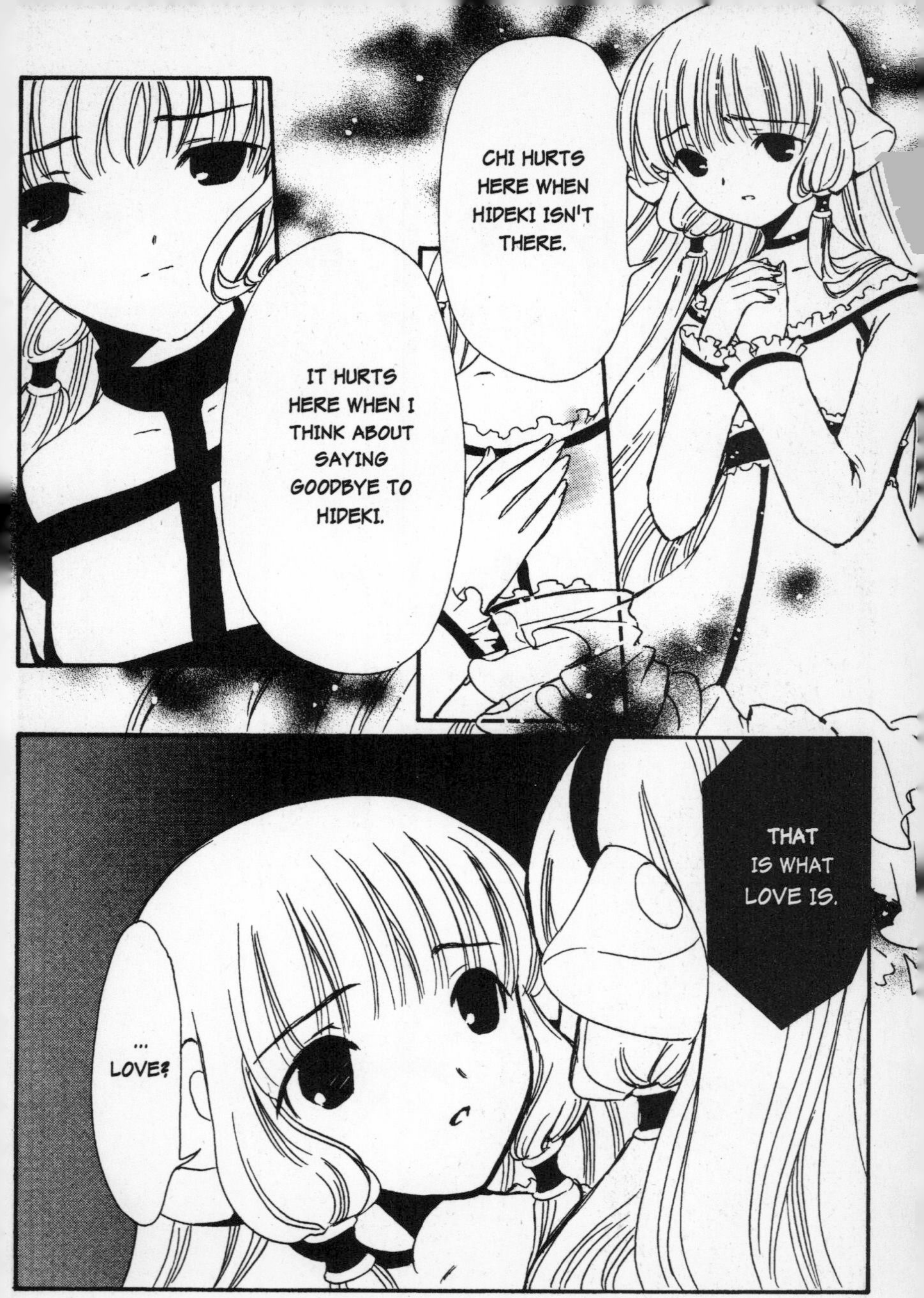
CHI HURTS HERE WHEN HIDEKI ISN'T THERE.
IT HURTS HERE WHEN I THINK ABOUT SAYING GOODBYE TO HIDEKI.
THAT IS WHAT LOVE IS.
... LOVE?

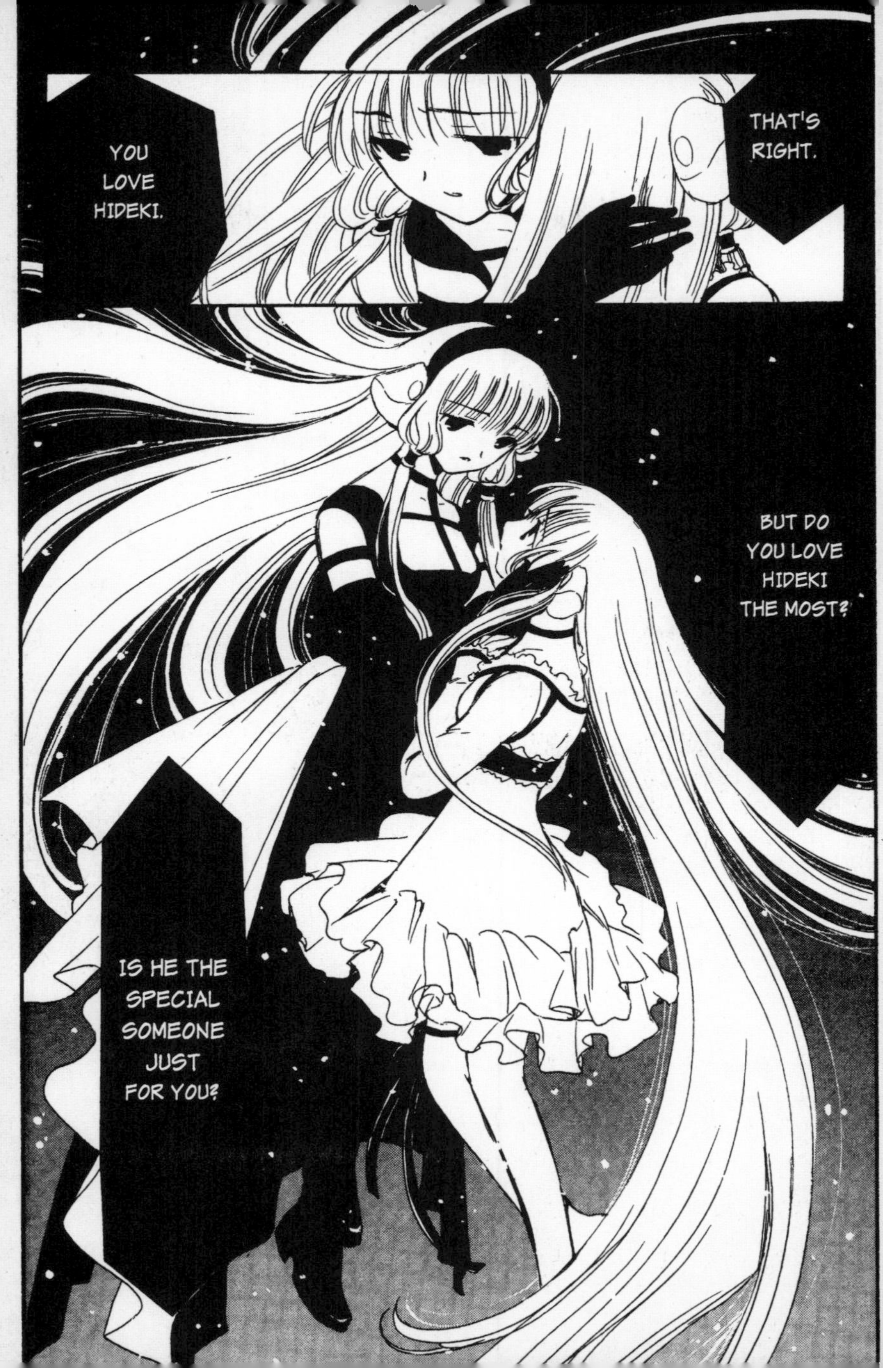
THAT'S RIGHT.
YOU LOVE HIDEKI.
BUT DO YOU LOVE HIDEKI THE MOST?
IS HE THE SPECIAL SOMEONE JUST FOR YOU?

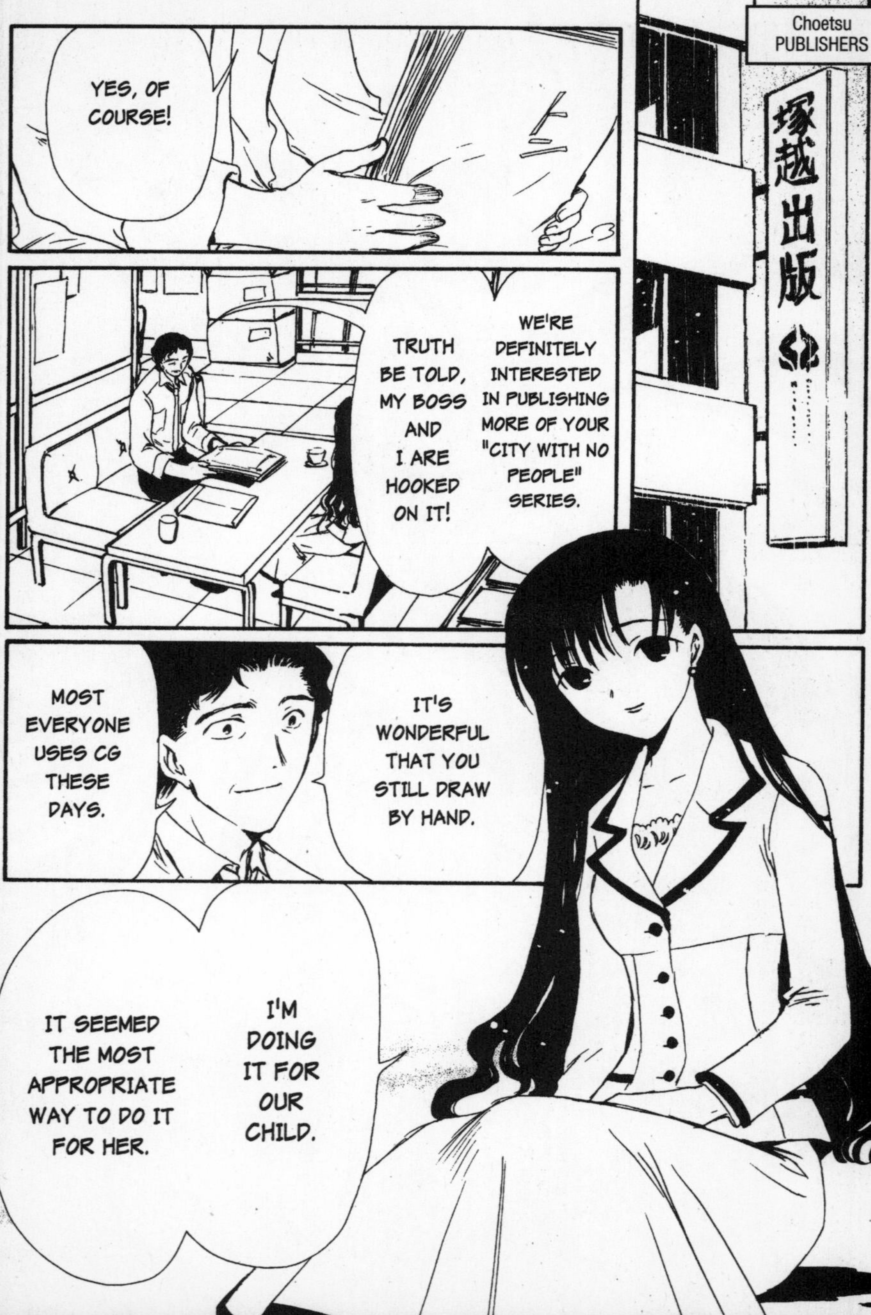
Choetsu PUBLISHERS
塚越出版
YES, OF COURSE!
WE'RE DEFINITELY INTERESTED IN PUBLISHING MORE OF YOUR "CITY WITH NO PEOPLE" SERIES.
TRUTH BE TOLD, MY BOSS AND I ARE HOOKED ON IT!
IT'S WONDERFUL THAT YOU STILL DRAW BY HAND.
MOST EVERYONE USES CG THESE DAYS.
I'M DOING IT FOR OUR CHILD.
IT SEEMED THE MOST APPROPRIATE WAY TO DO IT FOR HER.

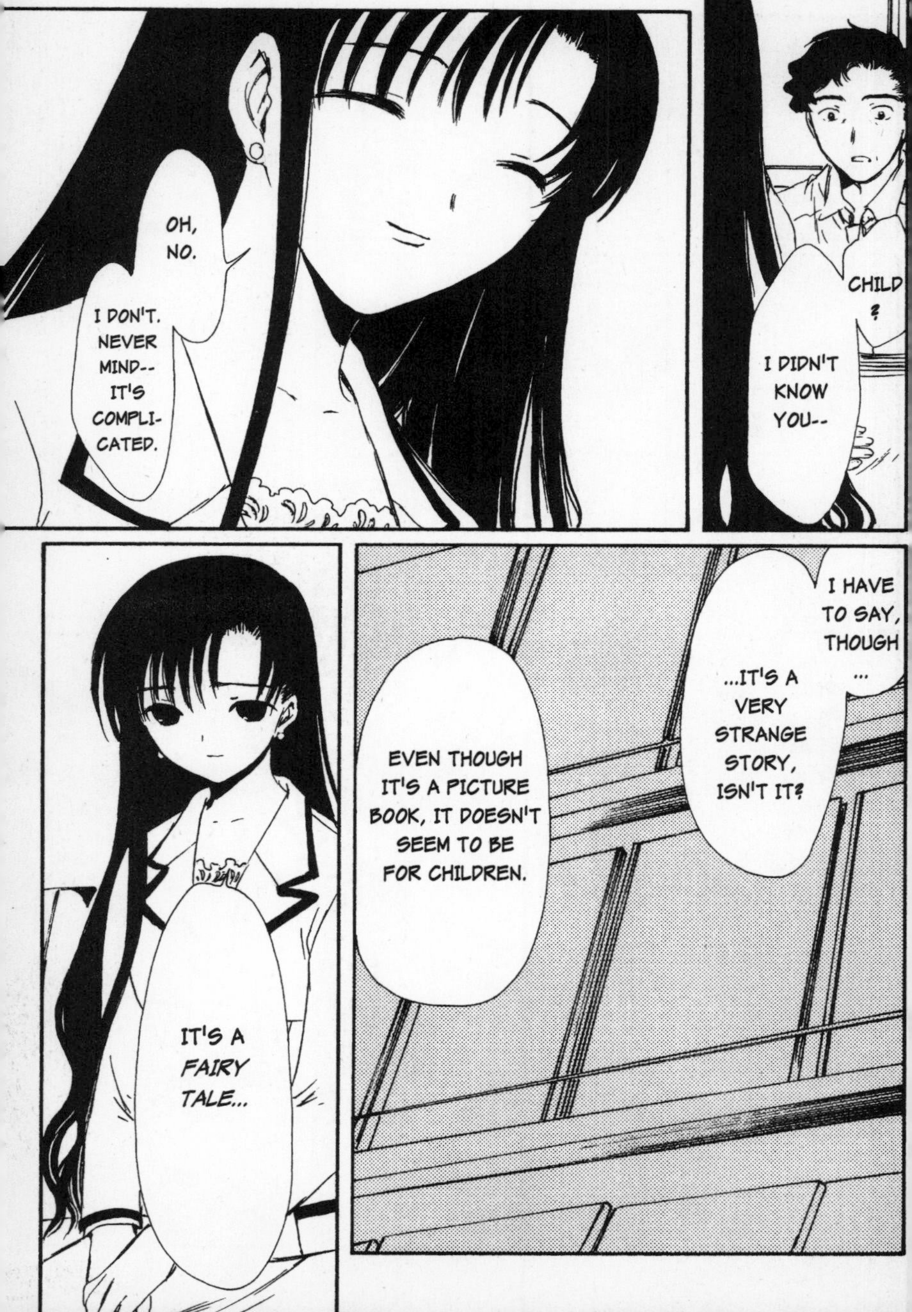
CHILD?
I DIDN'T KNOW YOU--
OH, NO.
I DON'T. NEVER MIND-- IT'S COMPLICATED.
I HAVE TO SAY, THOUGH...
...IT'S A VERY STRANGE STORY, ISN'T IT?
EVEN THOUGH IT'S A PICTURE BOOK, IT DOESN'T SEEM TO BE FOR CHILDREN.
IT'S A *FAIRY TALE*...

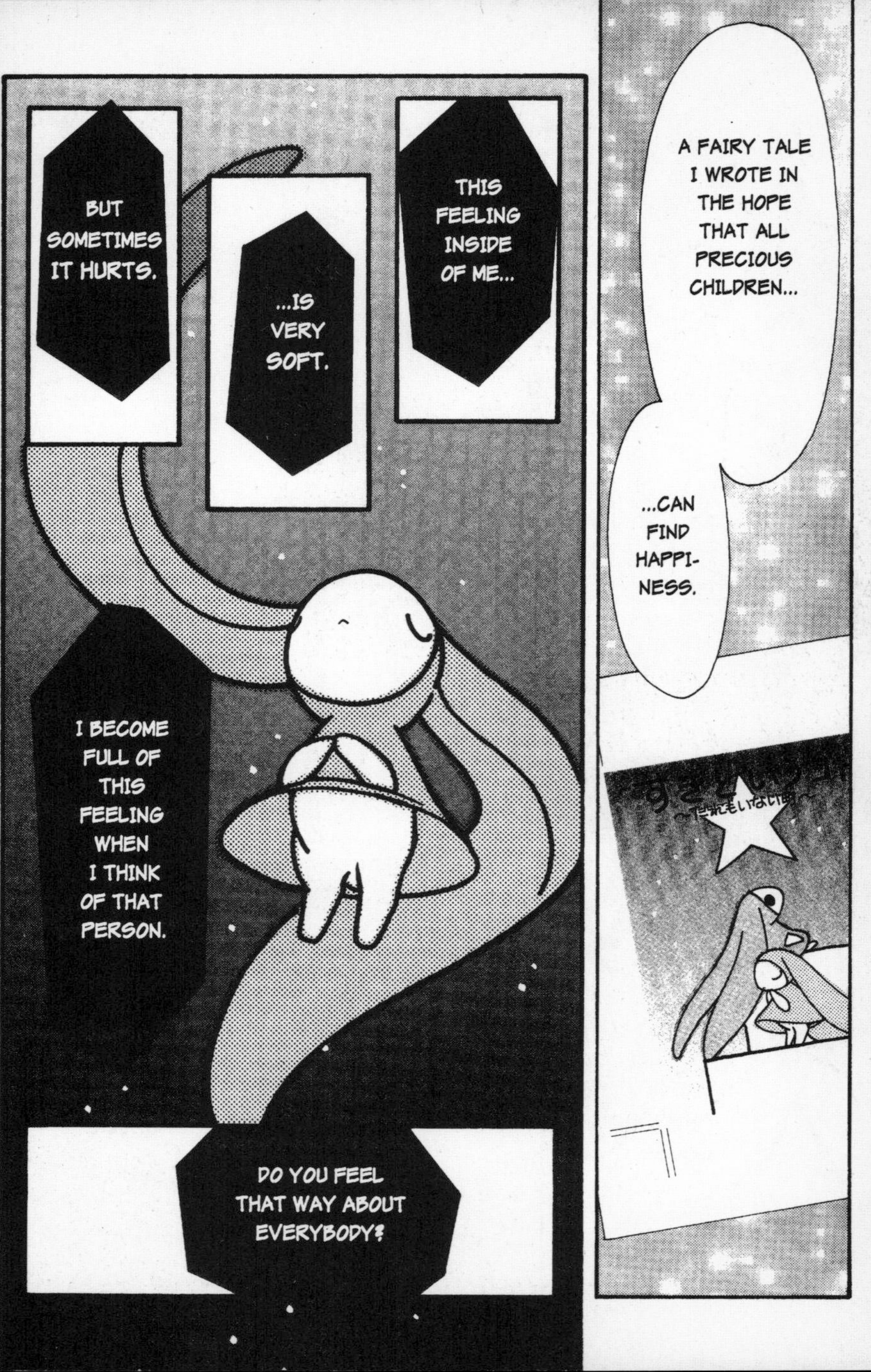
A FAIRY TALE I WROTE IN THE HOPE THAT ALL PRECIOUS CHILDREN...
...CAN FIND HAPPI-NESS.
THIS FEELING INSIDE OF ME...
...IS VERY SOFT.
BUT SOMETIMES IT HURTS.
I BECOME FULL OF THIS FEELING WHEN I THINK OF THAT PERSON.
DO YOU FEEL THAT WAY ABOUT EVERYBODY?

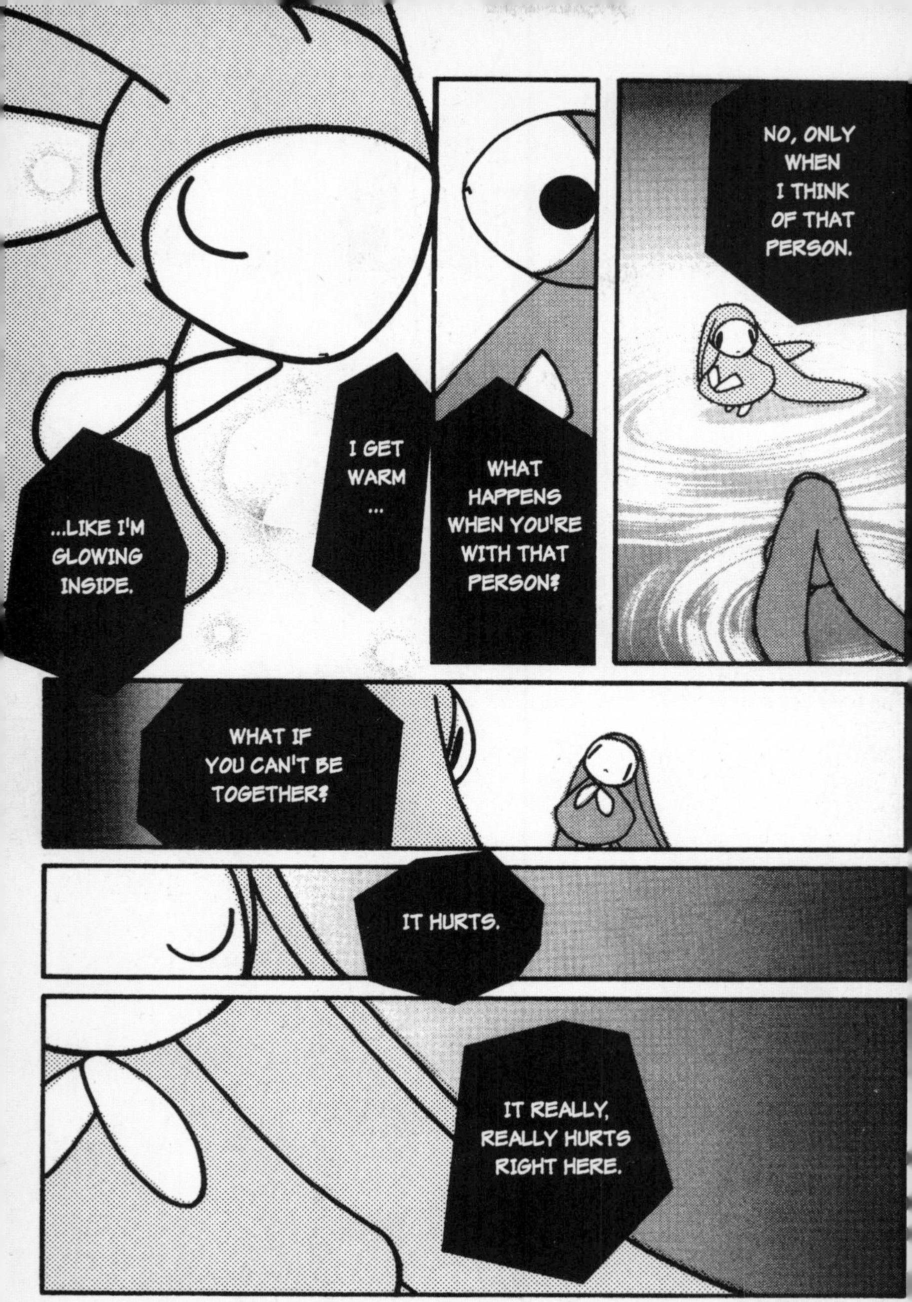
NO, ONLY WHEN I THINK OF THAT PERSON.
WHAT HAPPENS WHEN YOU'RE WITH THAT PERSON?
I GET WARM ...
...LIKE I'M GLOWING INSIDE.
WHAT IF YOU CAN'T BE TOGETHER?
IT HURTS.
IT REALLY, REALLY HURTS RIGHT HERE.

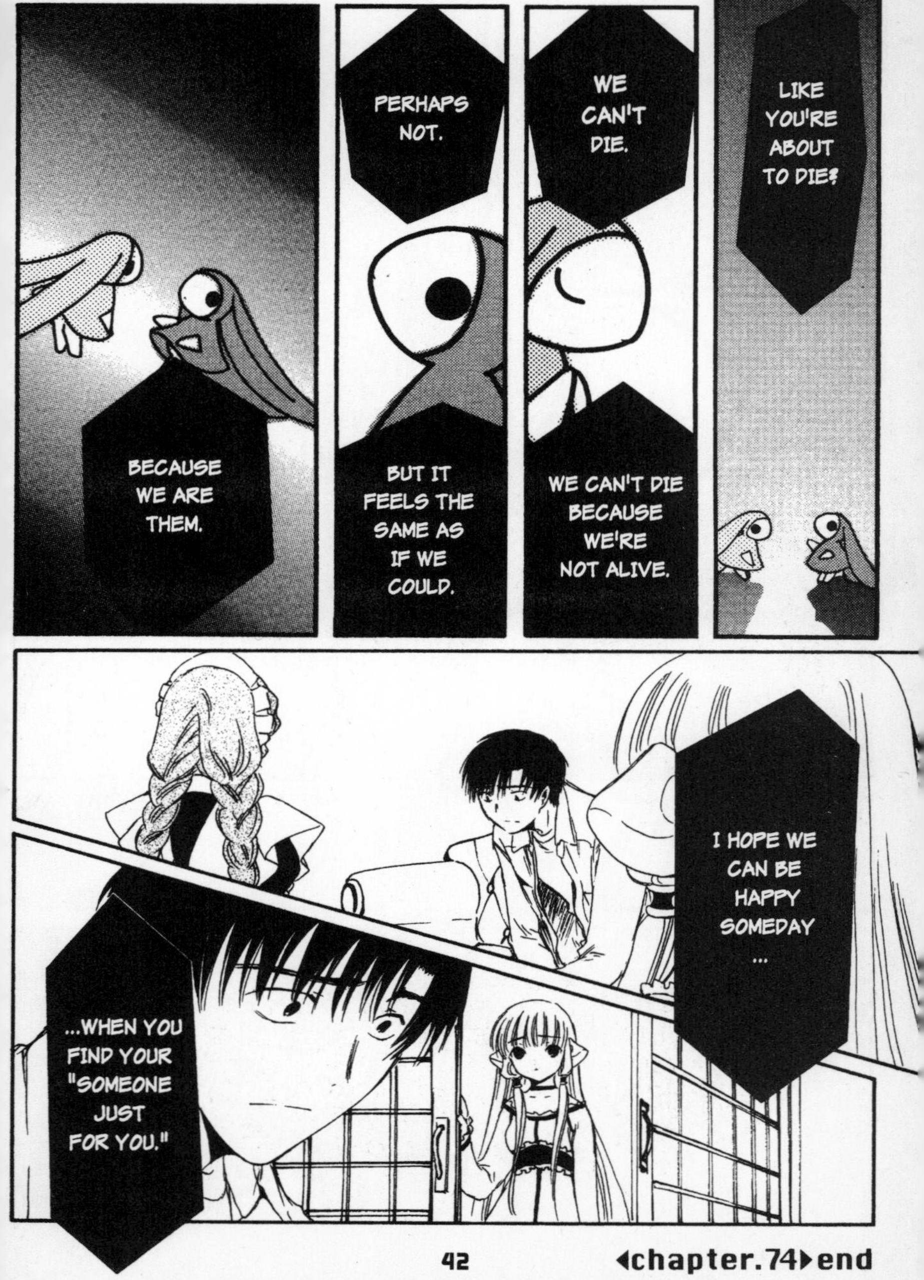
LIKE YOU'RE ABOUT TO DIE?
WE CAN'T DIE.
WE CAN'T DIE BECAUSE WE'RE NOT ALIVE.
PERHAPS NOT.
BUT IT FEELS THE SAME AS IF WE COULD.
BECAUSE WE ARE THEM.
I HOPE WE CAN BE HAPPY SOMEDAY ...
...WHEN YOU FIND YOUR "SOMEONE JUST FOR YOU."

chapter.74 end

◂chapter.75▸

ちょびっツ
Chobits

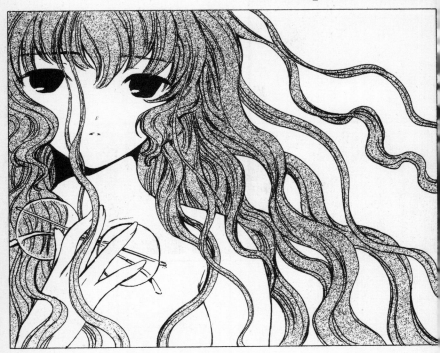

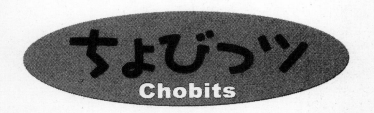

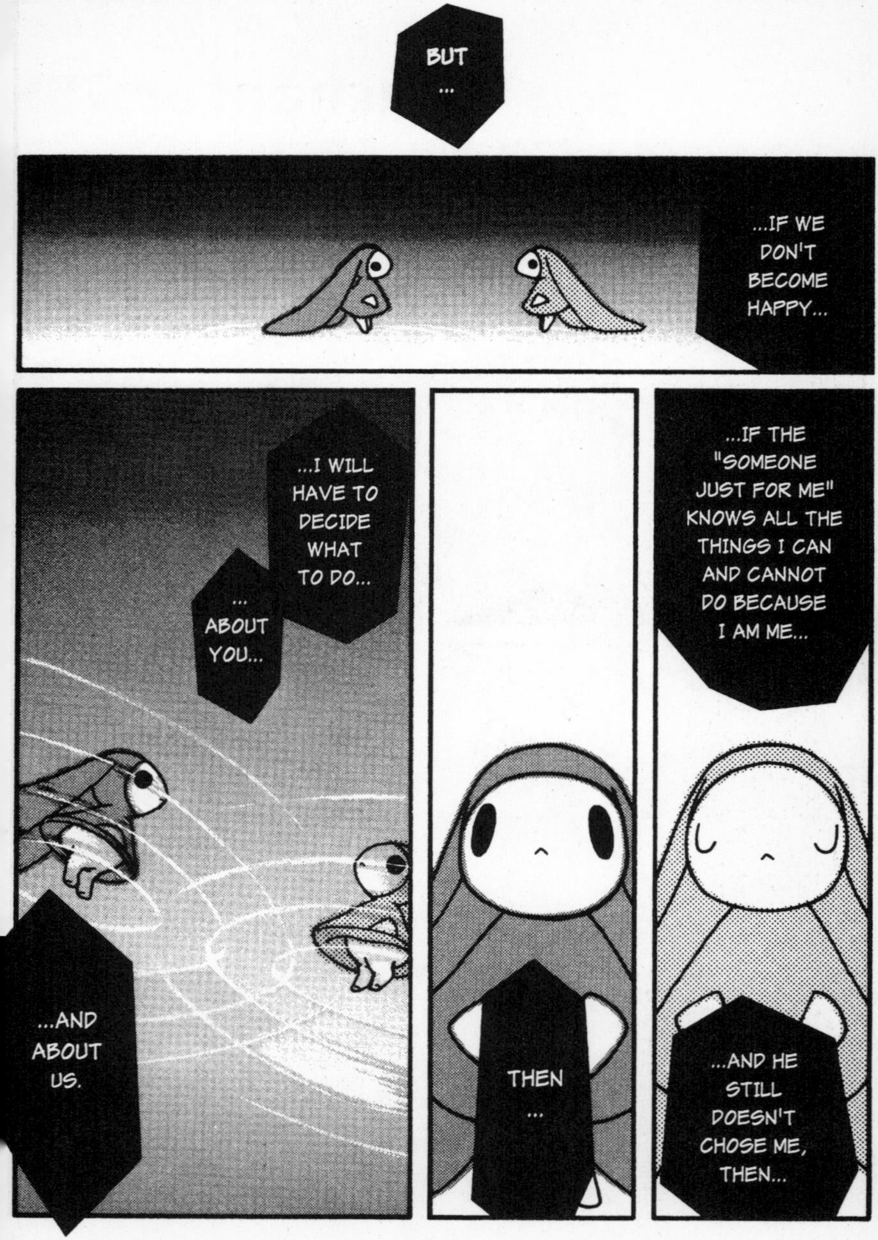
BUT ...
...IF WE DON'T BECOME HAPPY...
...IF THE "SOMEONE JUST FOR ME" KNOWS ALL THE THINGS I CAN AND CANNOT DO BECAUSE I AM ME...
...AND HE STILL DOESN'T CHOSE ME, THEN...
THEN ...
...I WILL HAVE TO DECIDE WHAT TO DO...
... ABOUT YOU...
...AND ABOUT US.

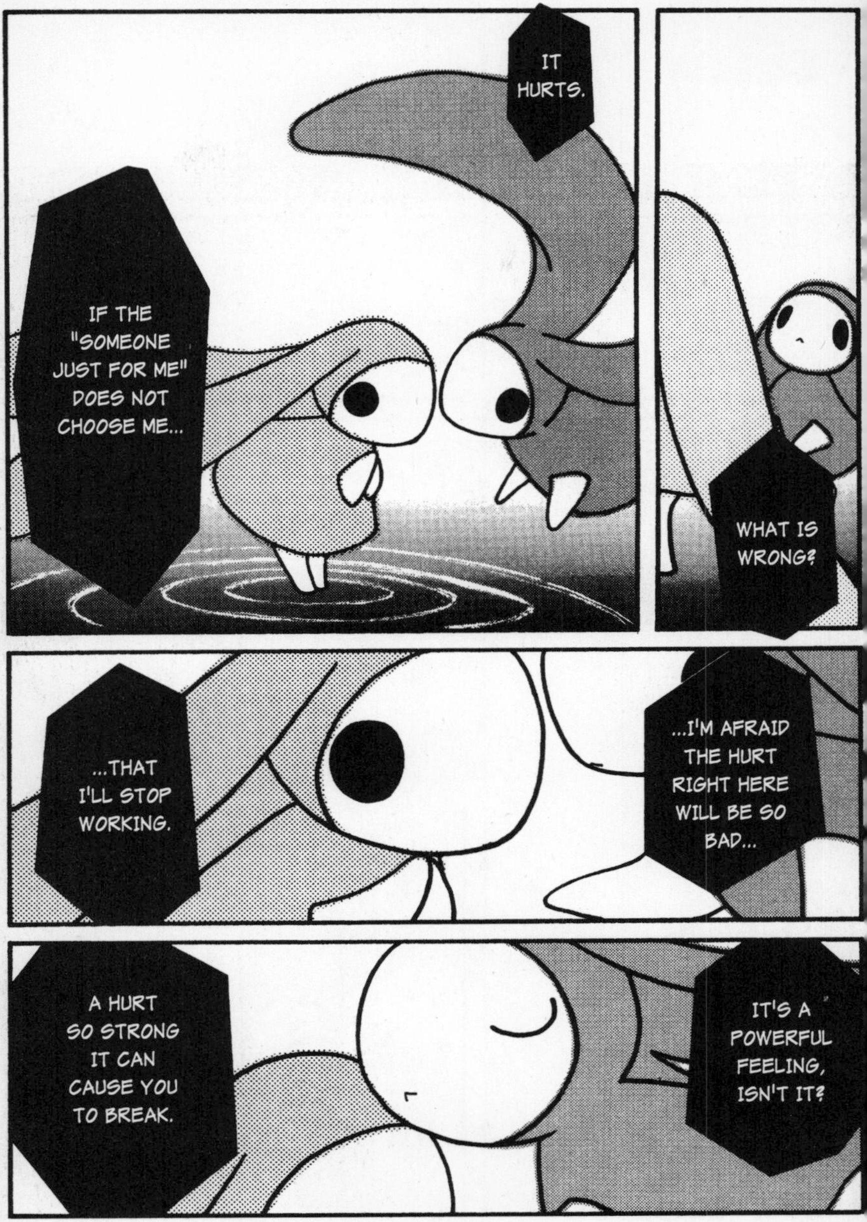
WHAT IS WRONG?
IT HURTS.
IF THE "SOMEONE JUST FOR ME" DOES NOT CHOOSE ME...
...I'M AFRAID THE HURT RIGHT HERE WILL BE SO BAD...
...THAT I'LL STOP WORKING.
IT'S A POWERFUL FEELING, ISN'T IT?
A HURT SO STRONG IT CAN CAUSE YOU TO BREAK.

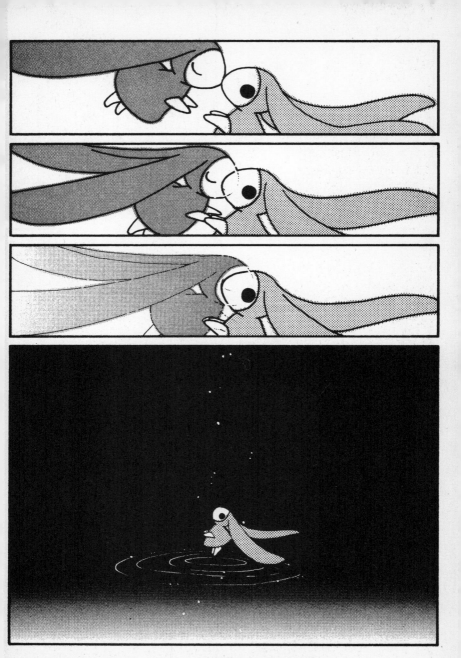

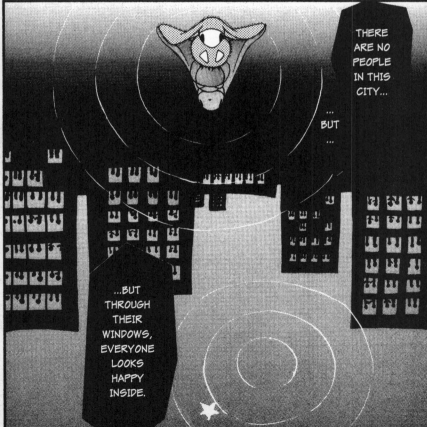

THERE ARE NO PEOPLE IN THIS CITY...

...BUT...

...BUT THROUGH THEIR WINDOWS, EVERYONE LOOKS HAPPY INSIDE.

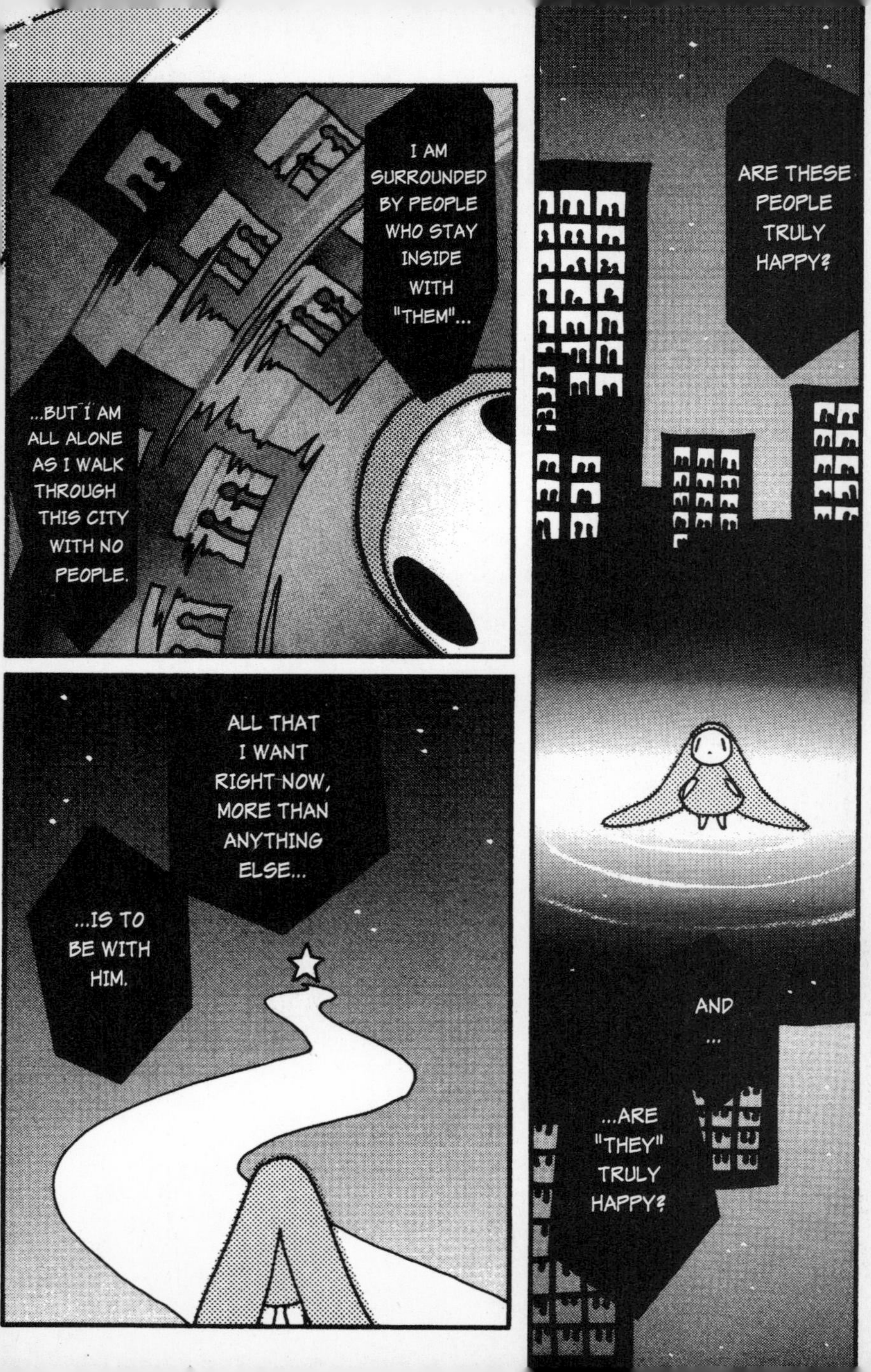
ARE THESE PEOPLE TRULY HAPPY?
AND ...
...ARE "THEY" TRULY HAPPY?
I AM SURROUNDED BY PEOPLE WHO STAY INSIDE WITH "THEM"...
...BUT I AM ALL ALONE AS I WALK THROUGH THIS CITY WITH NO PEOPLE.
ALL THAT I WANT RIGHT NOW, MORE THAN ANYTHING ELSE...
...IS TO BE WITH HIM.

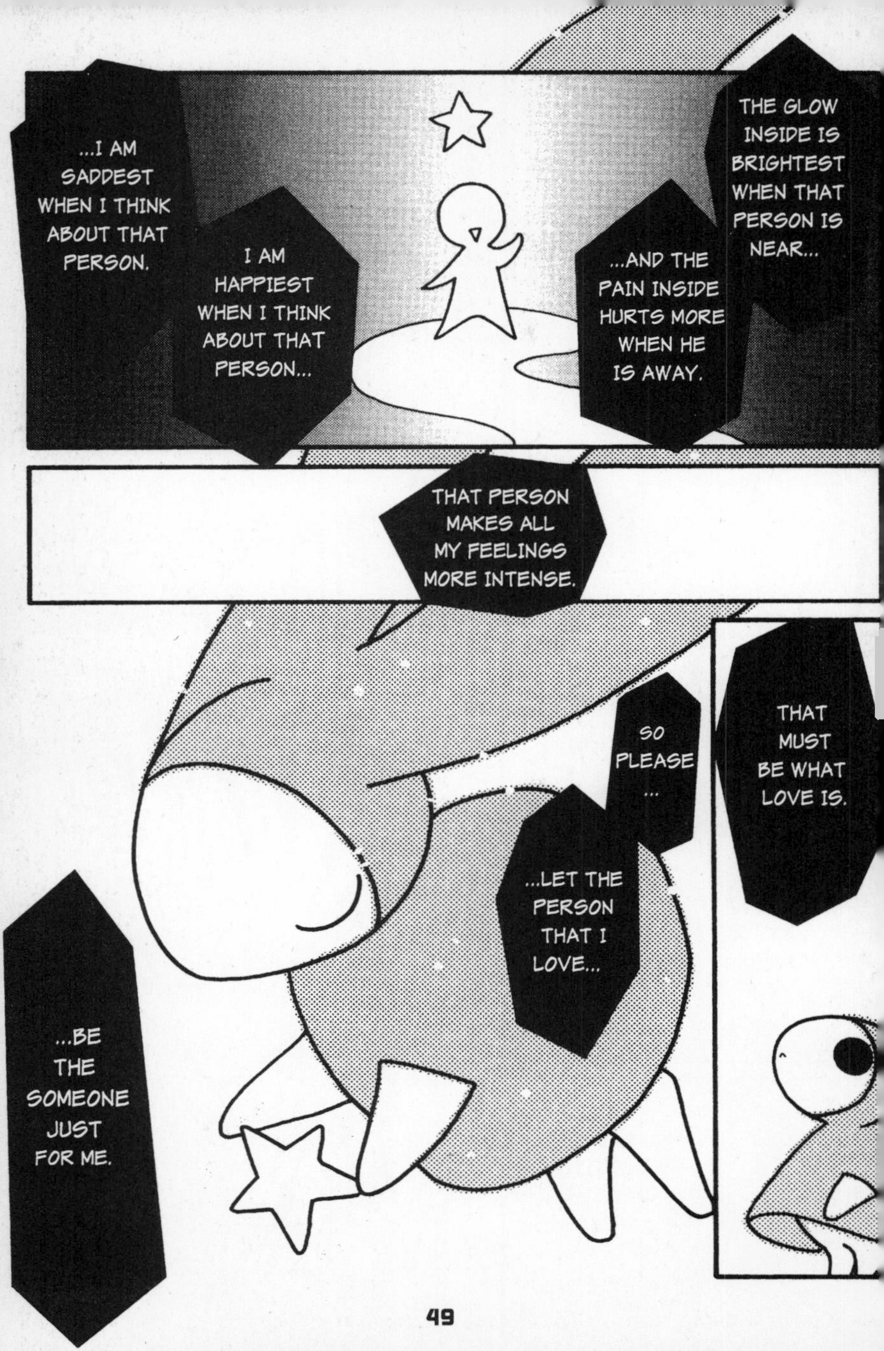
THE GLOW INSIDE IS BRIGHTEST WHEN THAT PERSON IS NEAR...
...AND THE PAIN INSIDE HURTS MORE WHEN HE IS AWAY.
I AM HAPPIEST WHEN I THINK ABOUT THAT PERSON...
...I AM SADDEST WHEN I THINK ABOUT THAT PERSON.
THAT PERSON MAKES ALL MY FEELINGS MORE INTENSE.
THAT MUST BE WHAT LOVE IS.
SO PLEASE ...
...LET THE PERSON THAT I LOVE...
...BE THE SOMEONE JUST FOR ME.

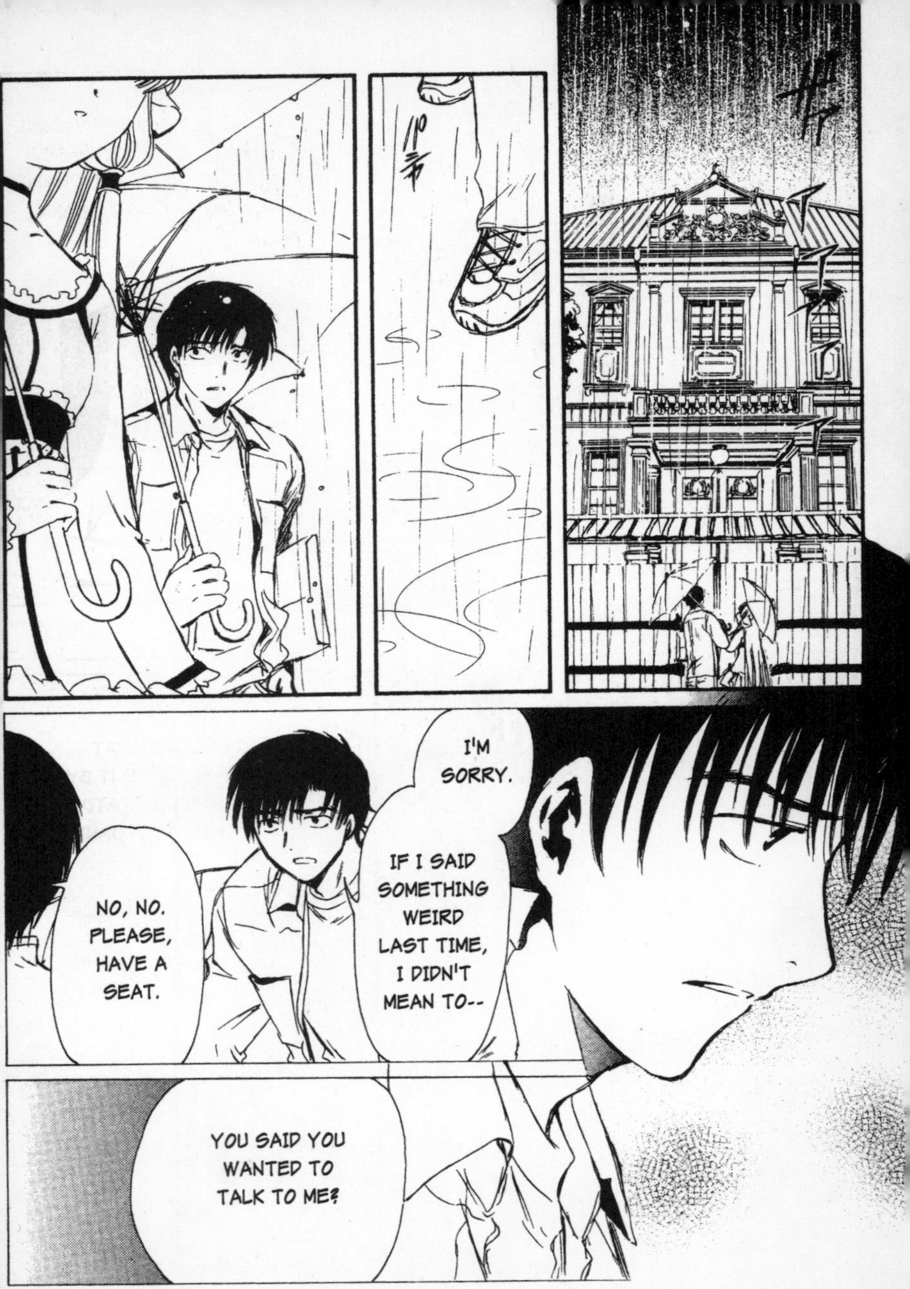
I'M SORRY.
IF I SAID SOMETHING WEIRD LAST TIME, I DIDN'T MEAN TO--
NO, NO. PLEASE, HAVE A SEAT.
YOU SAID YOU WANTED TO TALK TO ME?

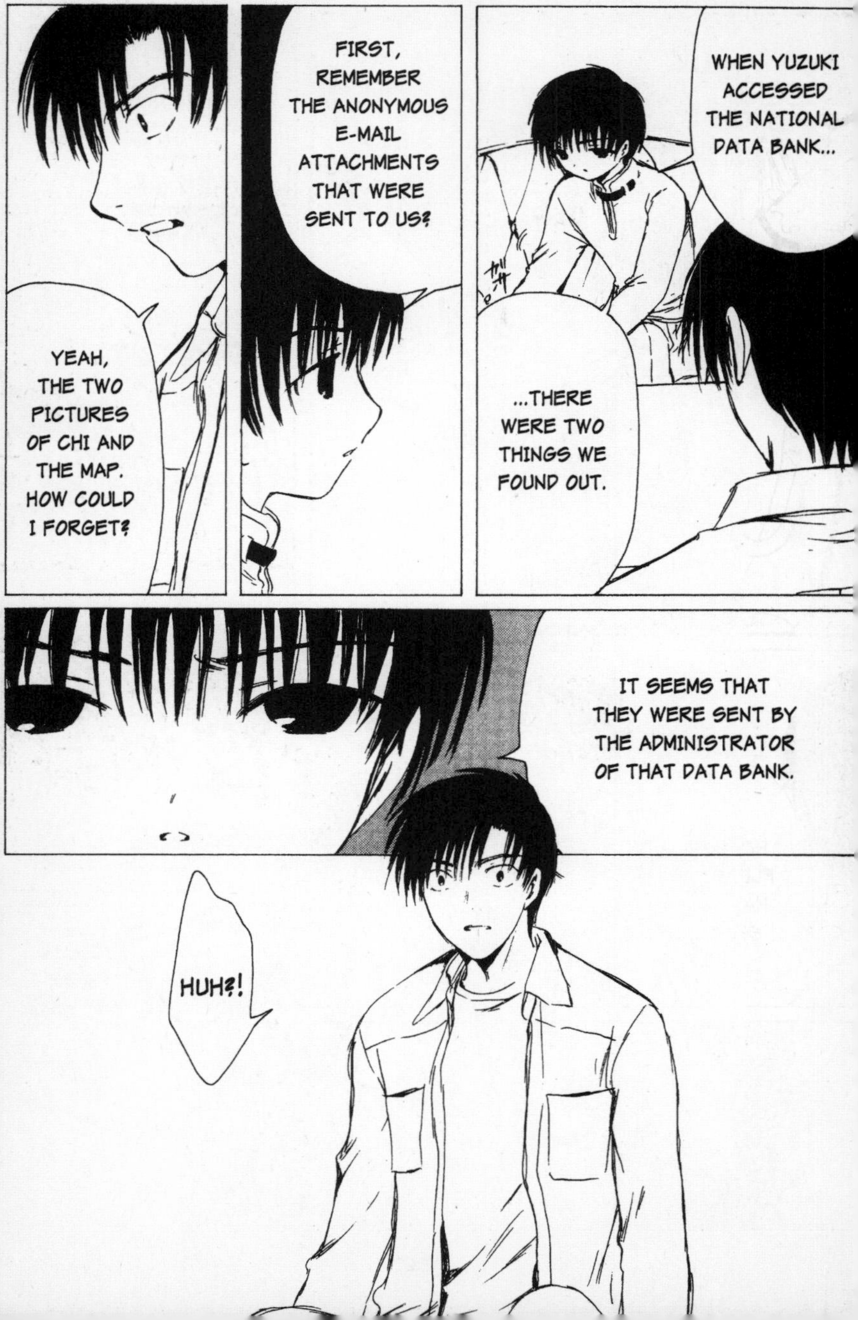
WHEN YUZUKI ACCESSED THE NATIONAL DATA BANK...
...THERE WERE TWO THINGS WE FOUND OUT.
FIRST, REMEMBER THE ANONYMOUS E-MAIL ATTACHMENTS THAT WERE SENT TO US?
YEAH, THE TWO PICTURES OF CHI AND THE MAP. HOW COULD I FORGET?
IT SEEMS THAT THEY WERE SENT BY THE ADMINISTRATOR OF THAT DATA BANK.
HUH?!

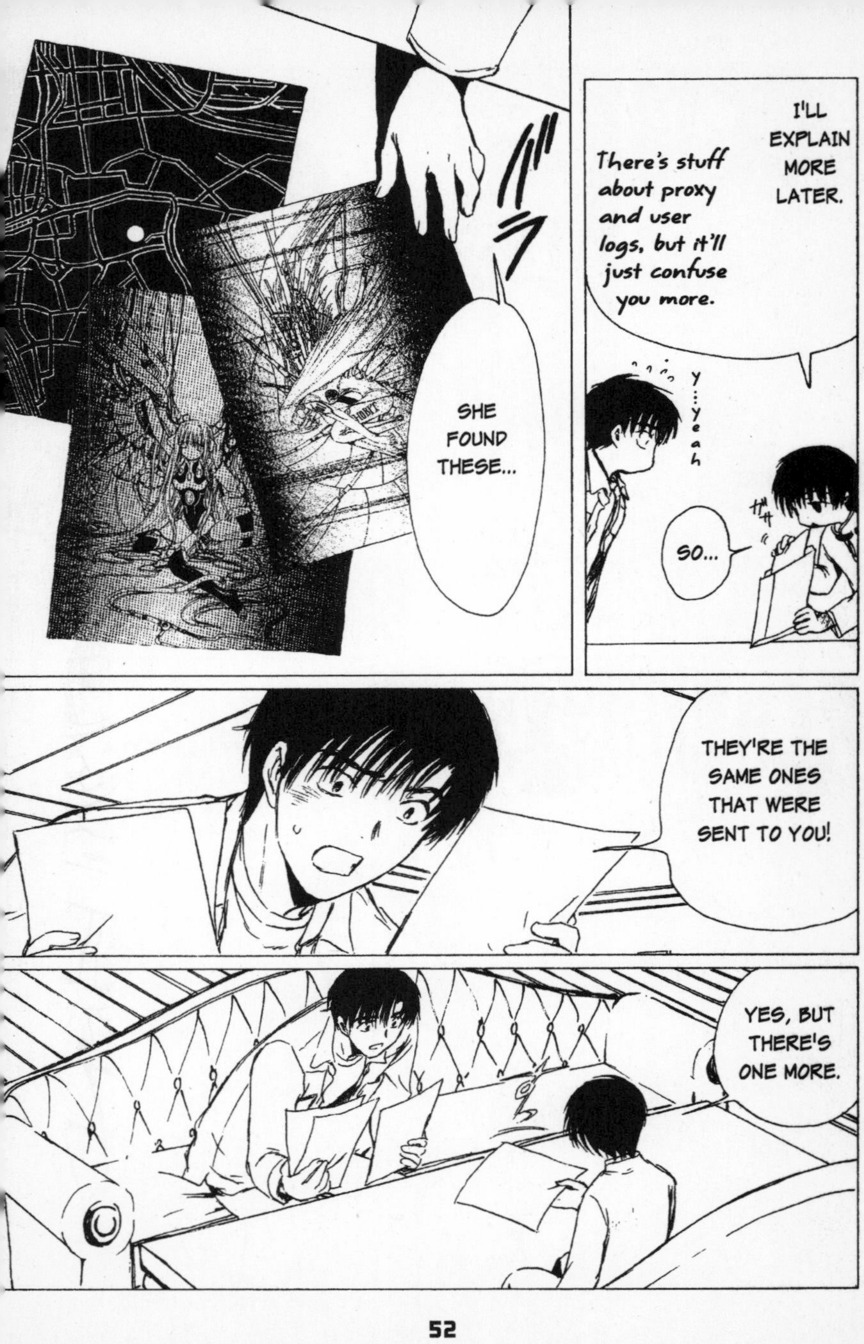
I'LL EXPLAIN MORE LATER.
There's stuff about proxy and user logs, but it'll just confuse you more.
Y...Yeah
SO...
SHE FOUND THESE...
THEY'RE THE SAME ONES THAT WERE SENT TO YOU!
YES, BUT THERE'S ONE MORE.

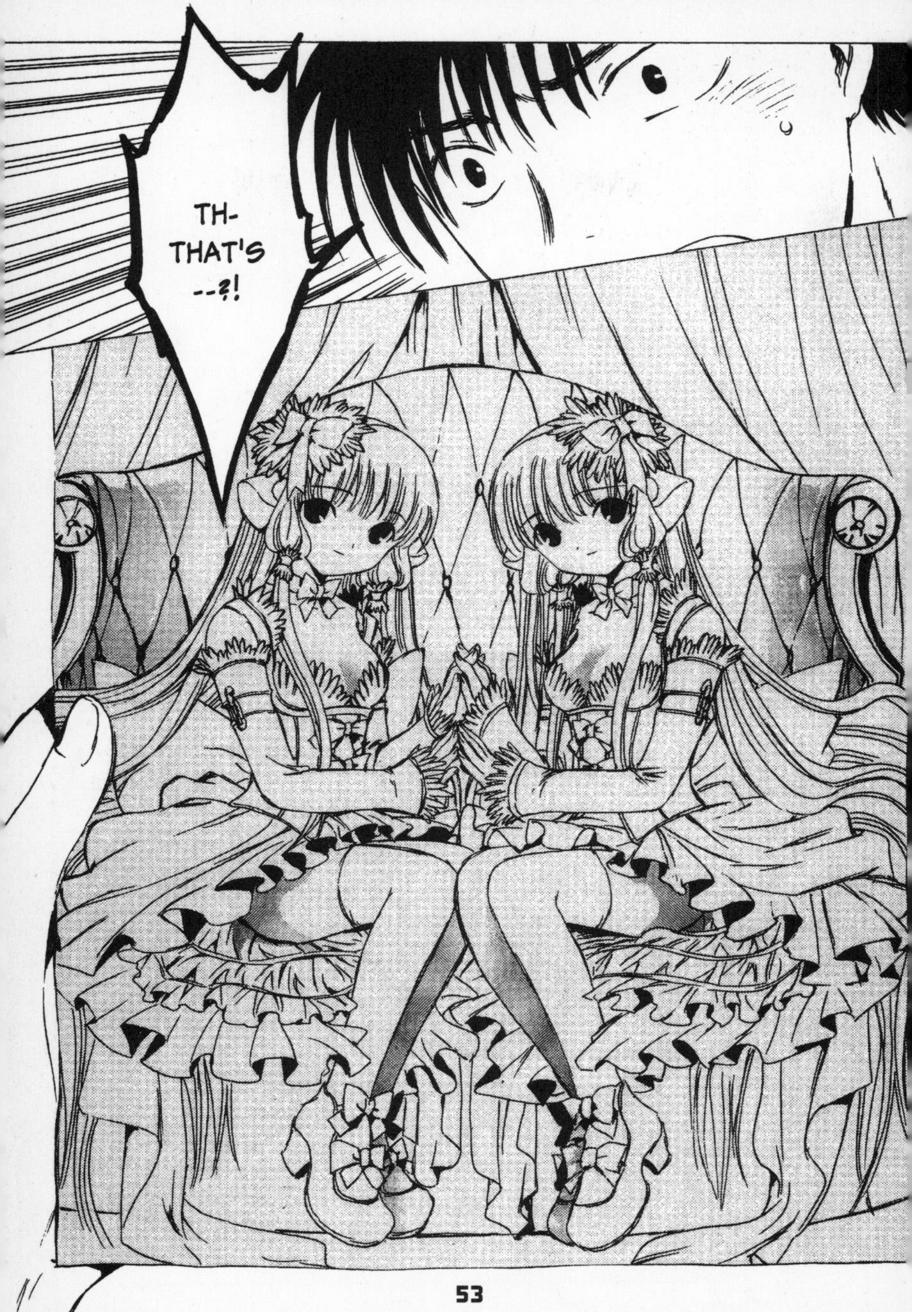
TH- THAT'S --?!

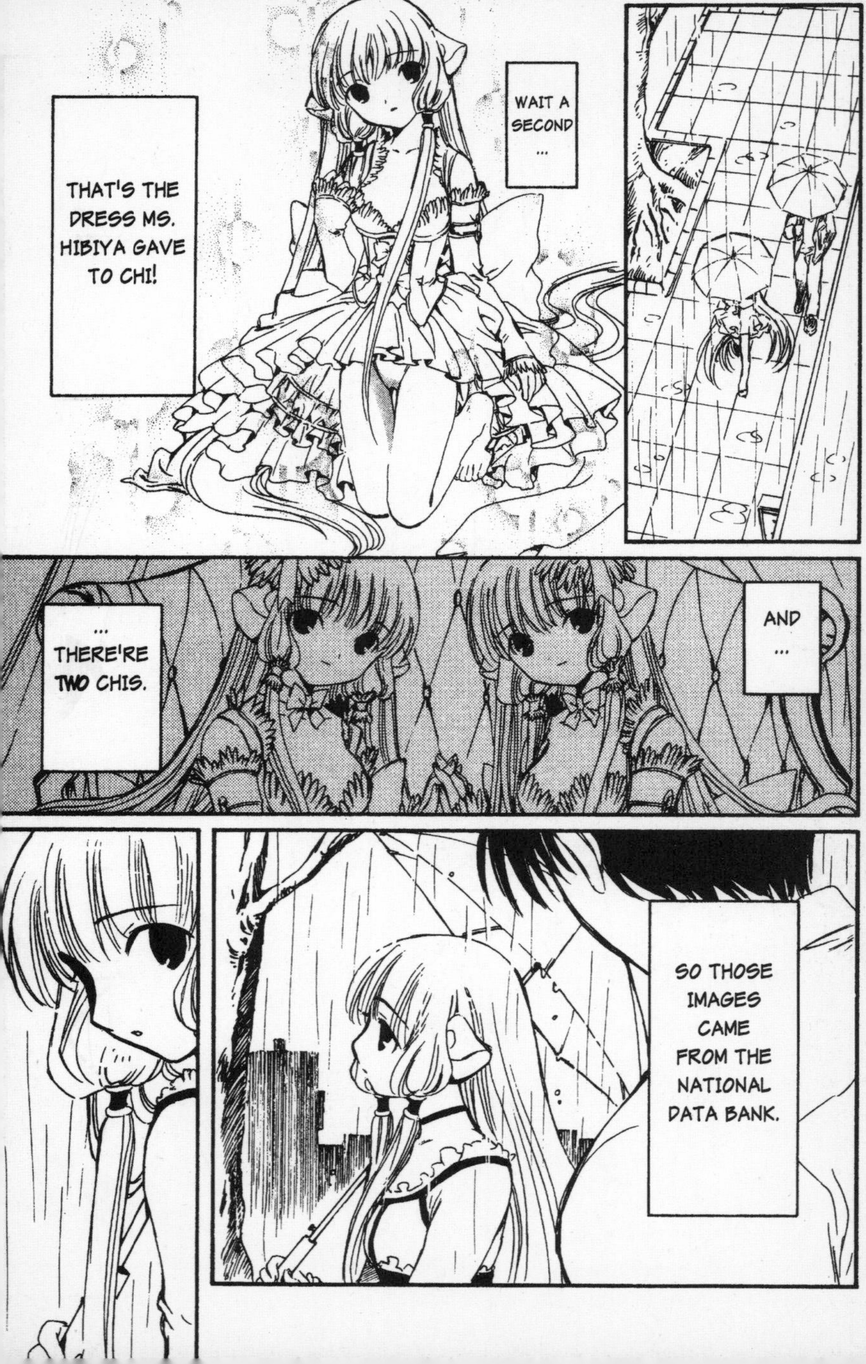
WAIT A SECOND ...
THAT'S THE DRESS MS. HIBIYA GAVE TO CHI!
AND ...
... THERE'RE TWO CHIS.
SO THOSE IMAGES CAME FROM THE NATIONAL DATA BANK.

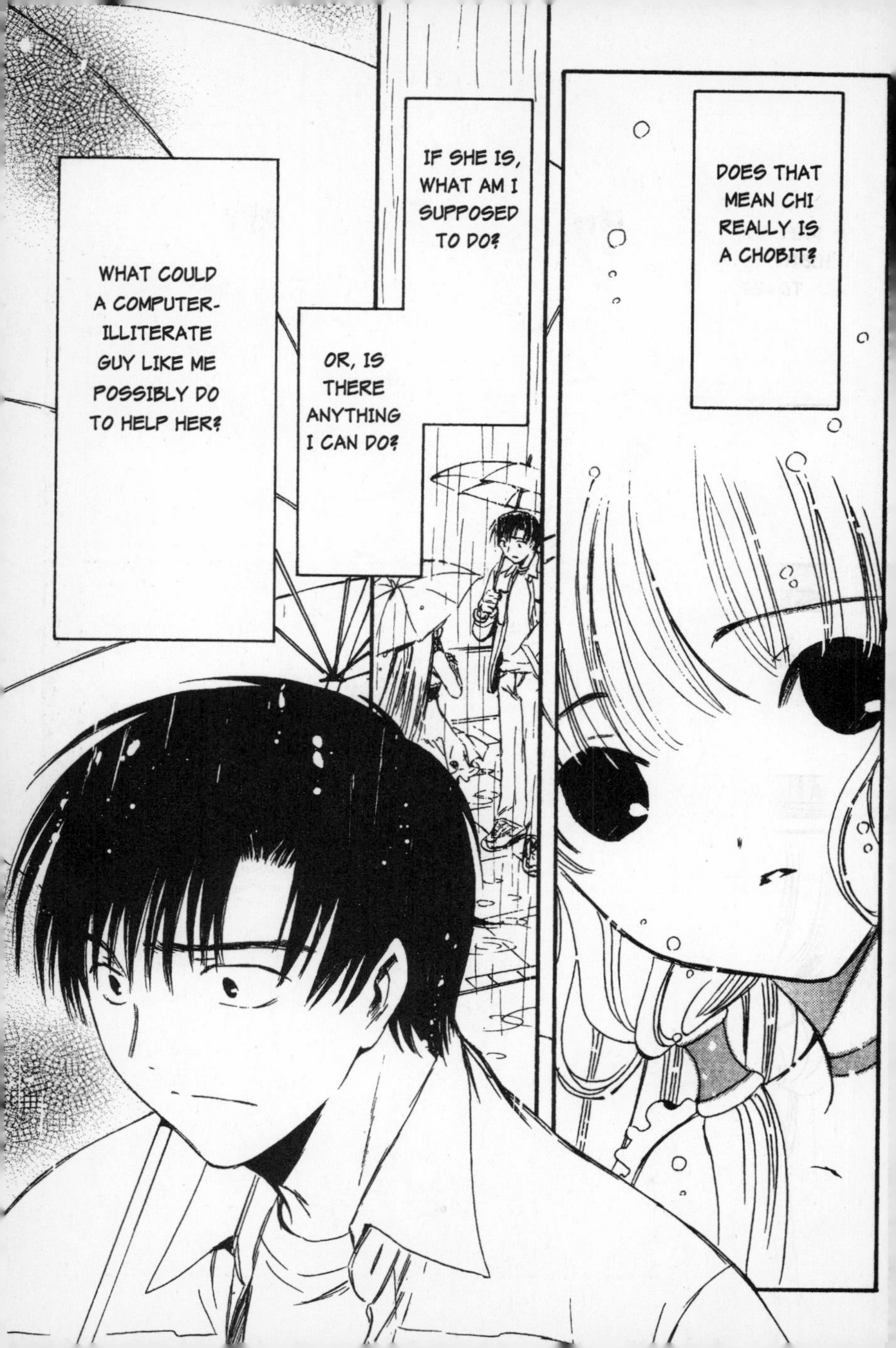
DOES THAT MEAN CHI REALLY IS A CHOBIT?
IF SHE IS, WHAT AM I SUPPOSED TO DO?
OR, IS THERE ANYTHING I CAN DO?
WHAT COULD A COMPUTER-ILLITERATE GUY LIKE ME POSSIBLY DO TO HELP HER?

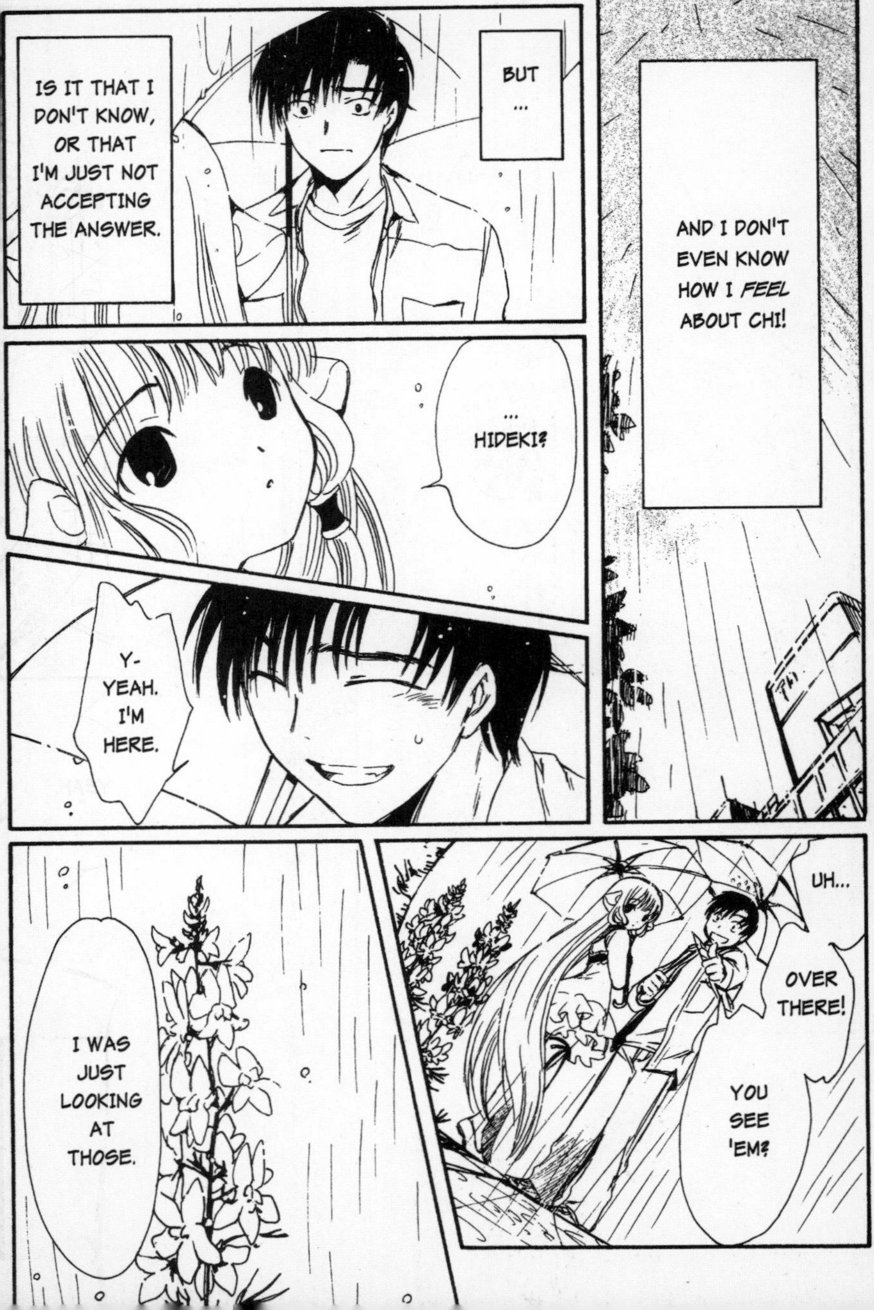
AND I DON'T EVEN KNOW HOW I FEEL ABOUT CHI!
BUT ...
IS IT THAT I DON'T KNOW, OR THAT I'M JUST NOT ACCEPTING THE ANSWER.
... HIDEKI?
Y-YEAH. I'M HERE.
UH...
OVER THERE!
YOU SEE 'EM?
I WAS JUST LOOKING AT THOSE.

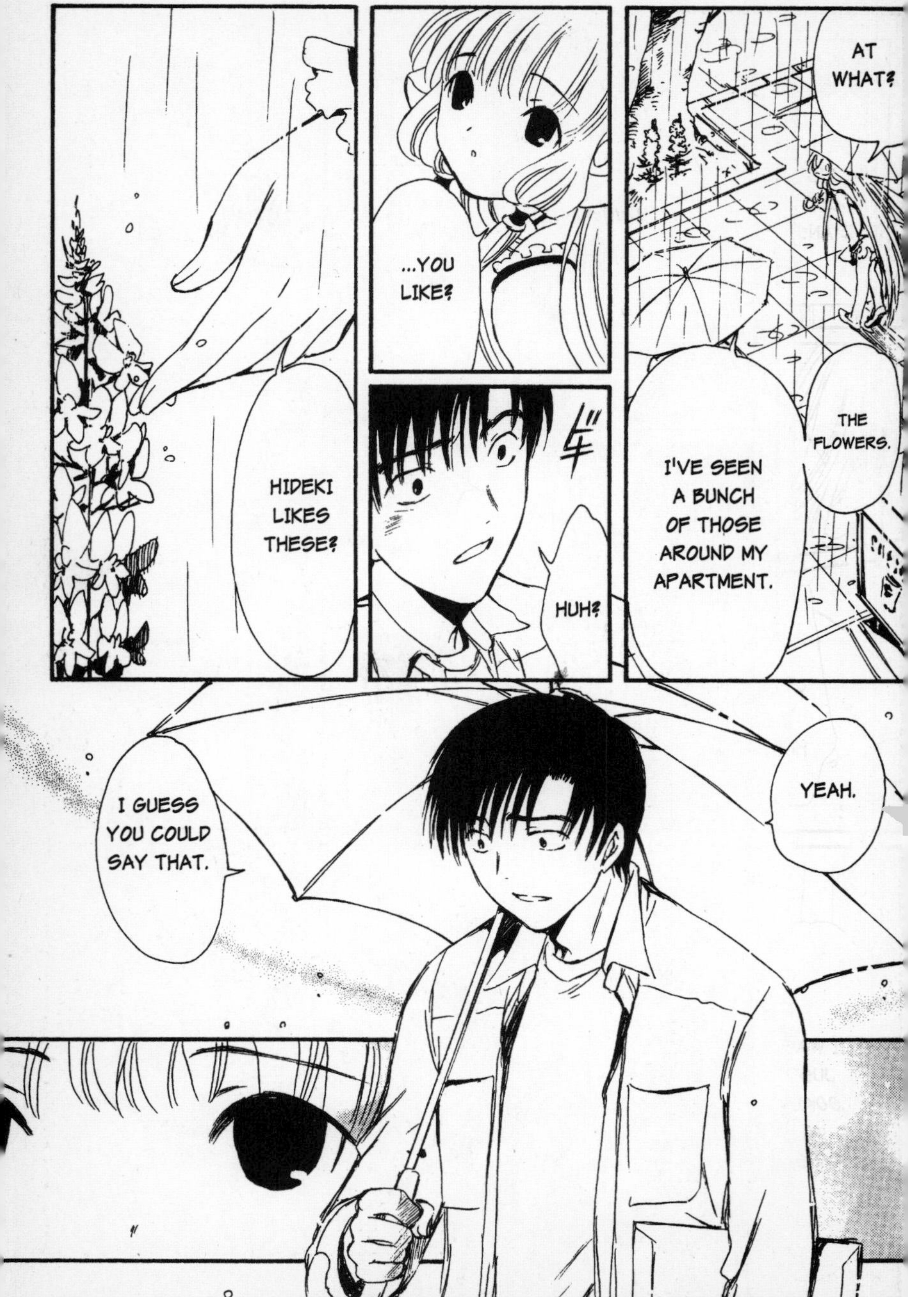
AT WHAT?
THE FLOWERS.
I'VE SEEN A BUNCH OF THOSE AROUND MY APARTMENT.
...YOU LIKE?
HUH?
HIDEKI LIKES THESE?
YEAH.
I GUESS YOU COULD SAY THAT.

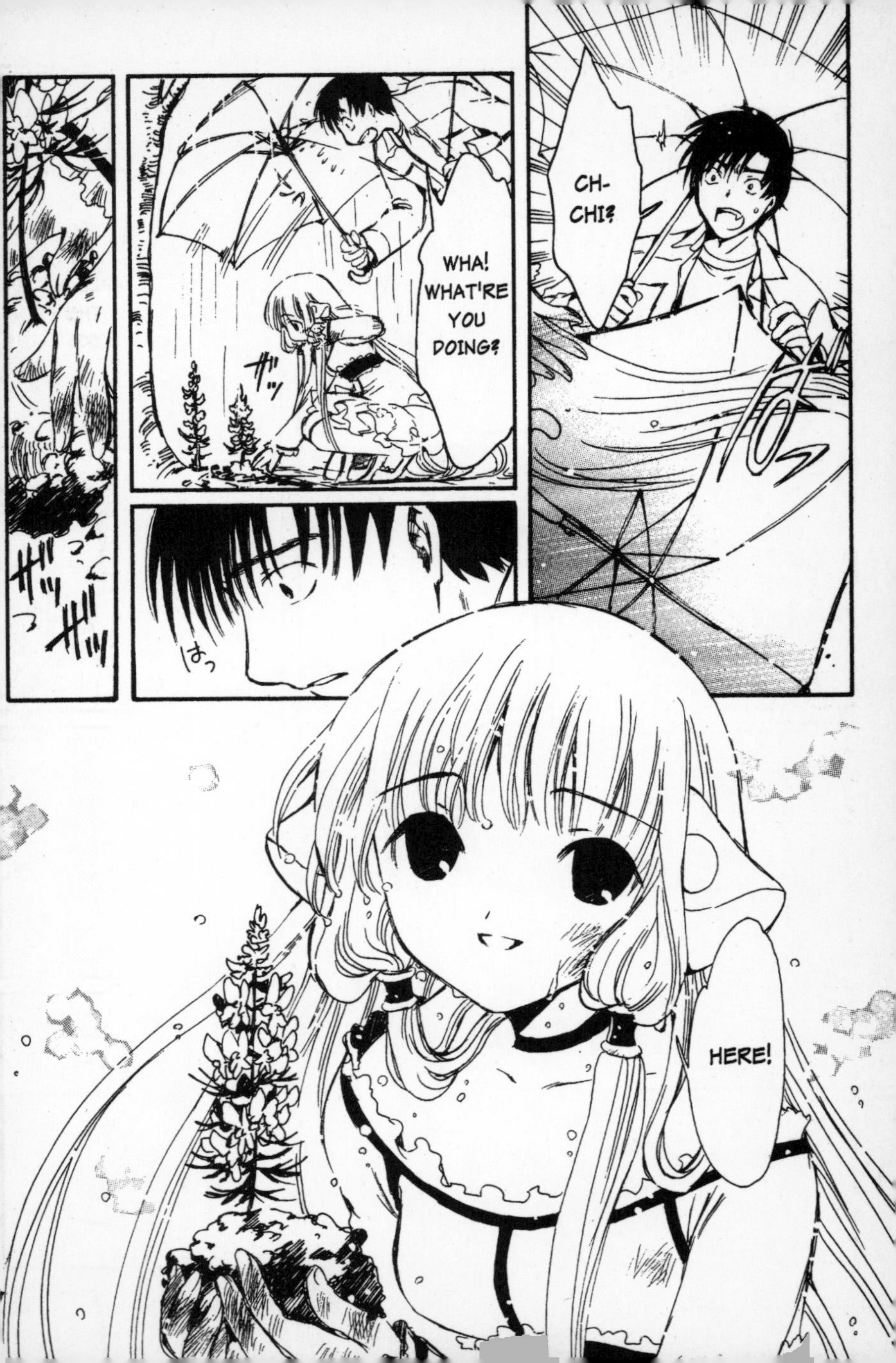
CH-
CHI?
WHA! WHAT'RE YOU DOING?
HERE!

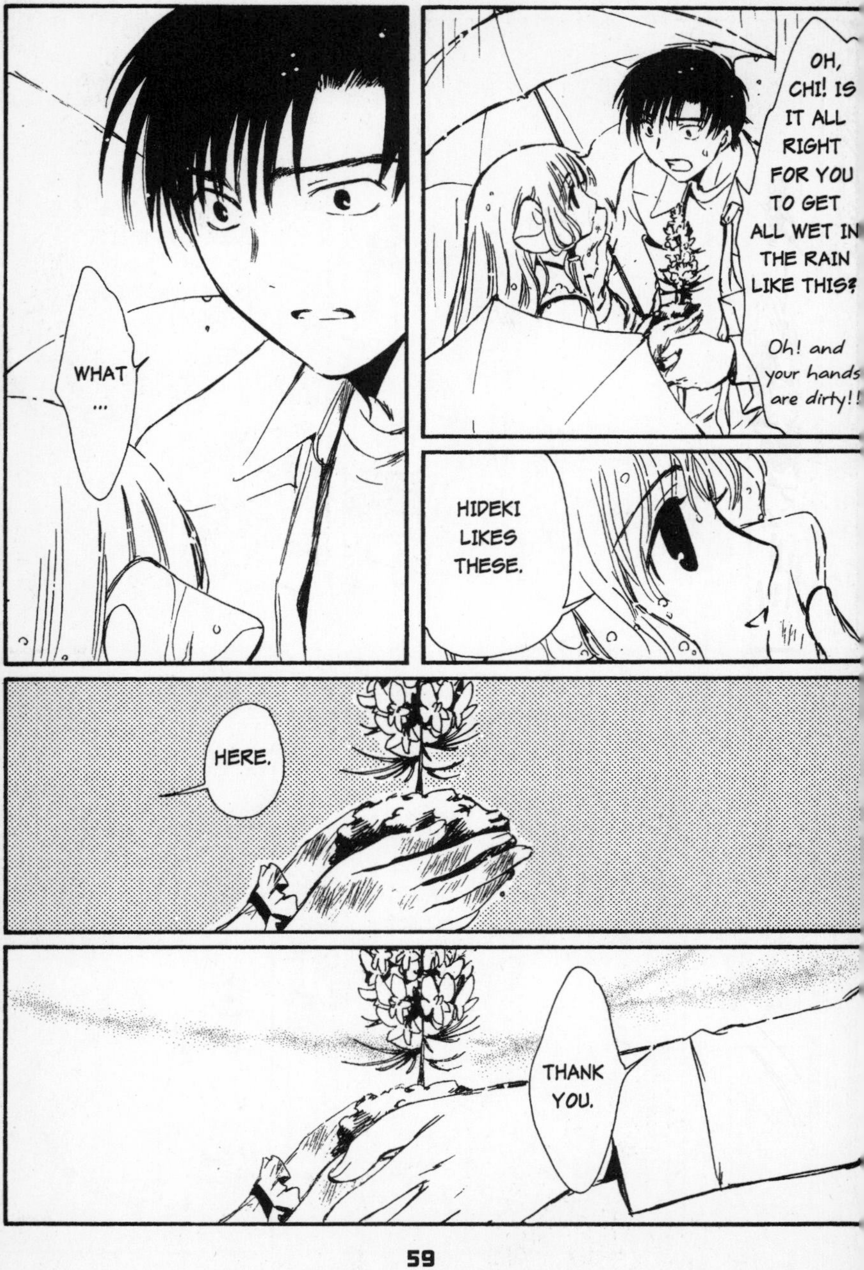
OH, CHI! IS IT ALL RIGHT FOR YOU TO GET ALL WET IN THE RAIN LIKE THIS?
Oh! and your hands are dirty!!
HIDEKI LIKES THESE.
WHAT ...
HERE.
THANK YOU.

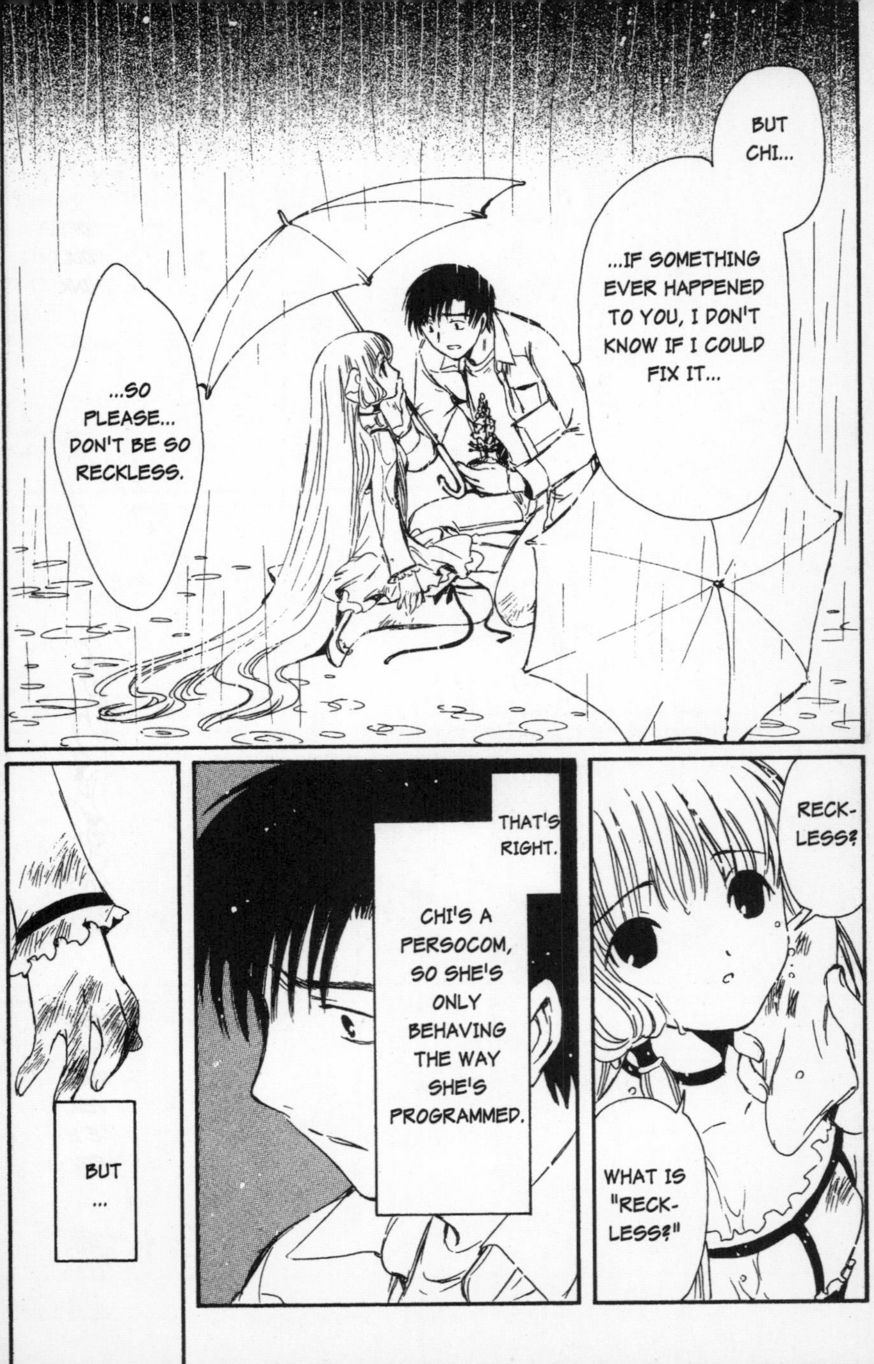
BUT CHI...
...IF SOMETHING EVER HAPPENED TO YOU, I DON'T KNOW IF I COULD FIX IT...
...SO PLEASE... DON'T BE SO RECKLESS.
RECK-LESS?
WHAT IS "RECK-LESS?"
THAT'S RIGHT.
CHI'S A PERSOCOM, SO SHE'S ONLY BEHAVING THE WAY SHE'S PROGRAMMED.
BUT ...

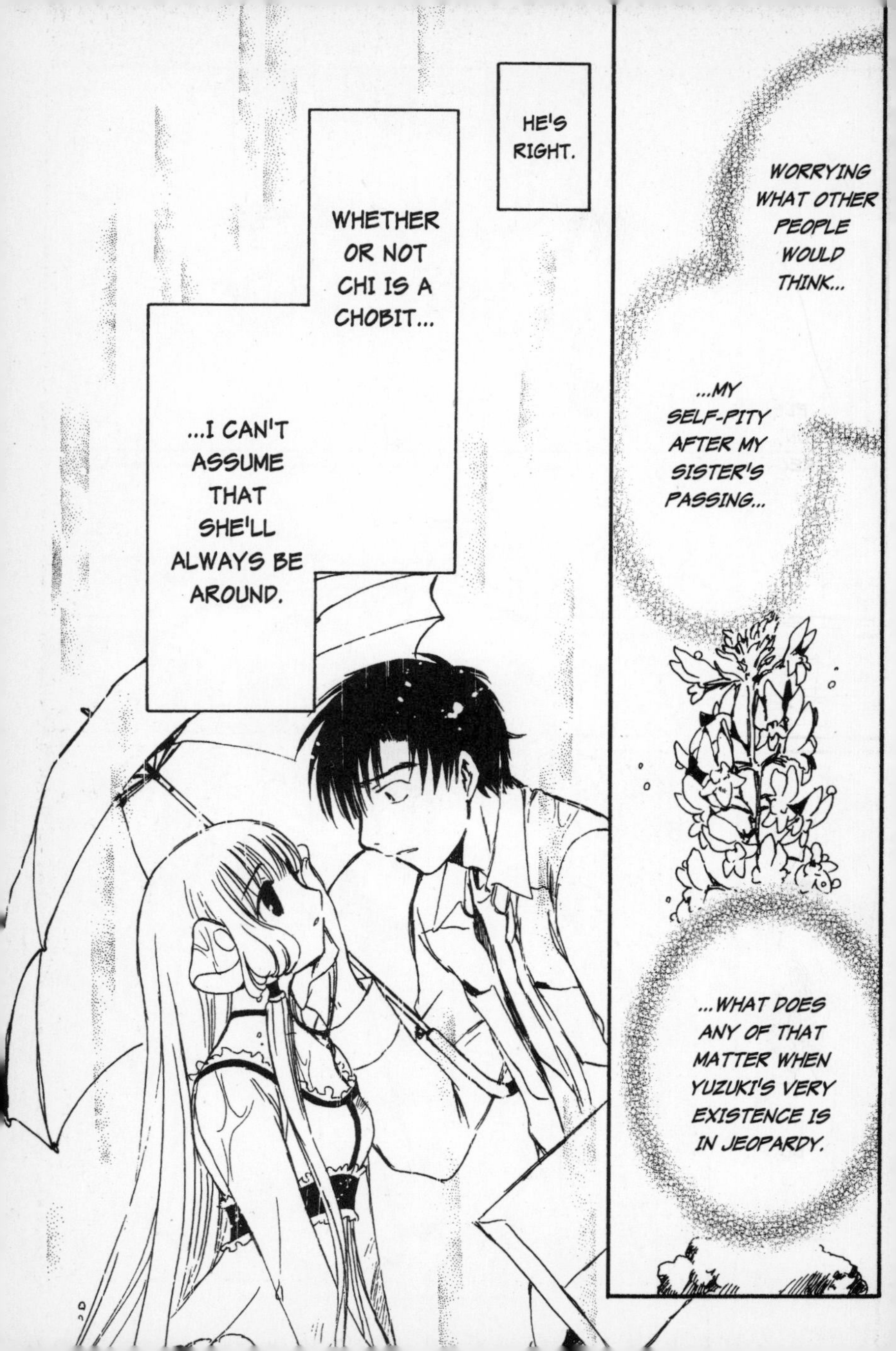
WORRYING WHAT OTHER PEOPLE WOULD THINK...
...MY SELF-PITY AFTER MY SISTER'S PASSING...
...WHAT DOES ANY OF THAT MATTER WHEN YUZUKI'S VERY EXISTENCE IS IN JEOPARDY.
HE'S RIGHT.
WHETHER OR NOT CHI IS A CHOBIT...
...I CAN'T ASSUME THAT SHE'LL ALWAYS BE AROUND.

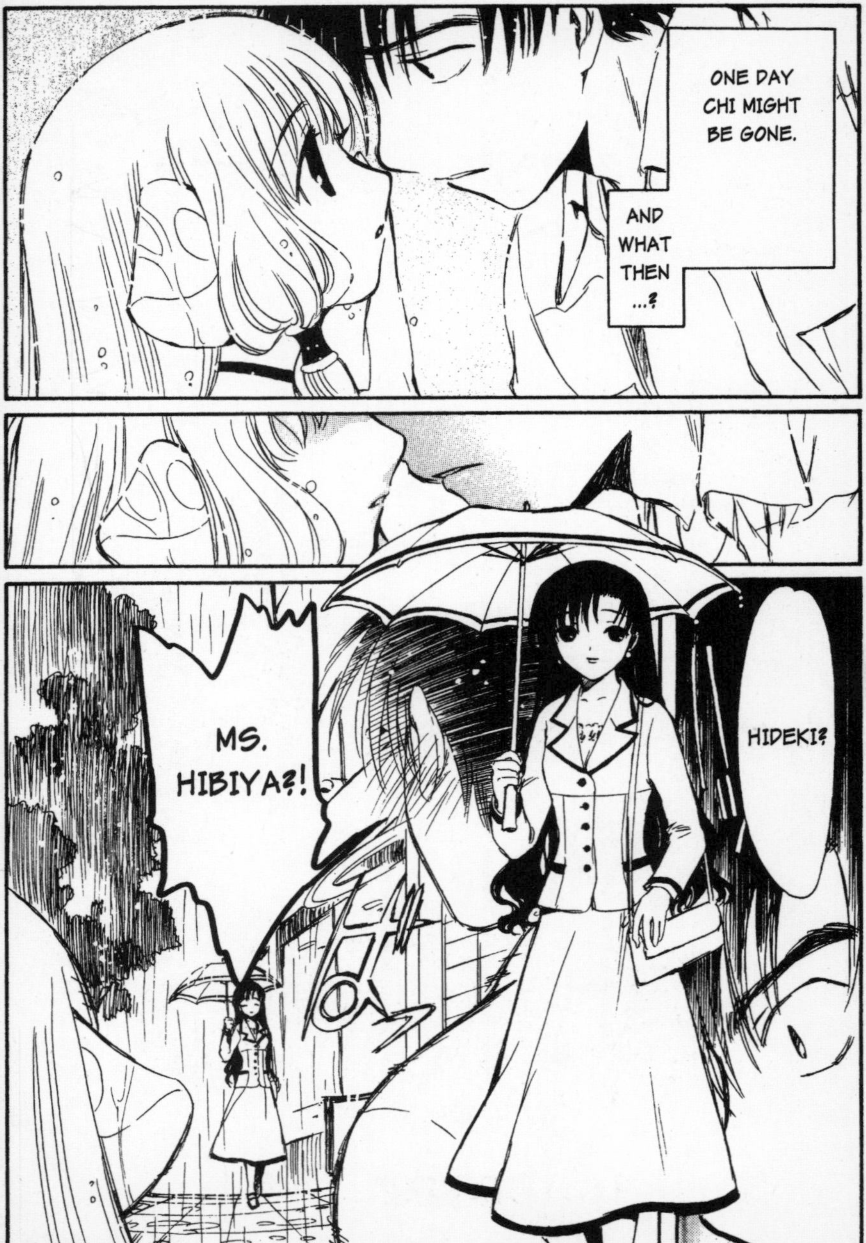
ONE DAY CHI MIGHT BE GONE.
AND WHAT THEN ...?
HIDEKI?
MS. HIBIYA?!

◀chapter.75▶ end

ちょびっツ
Chobits

◀ **chapter.76** ▶

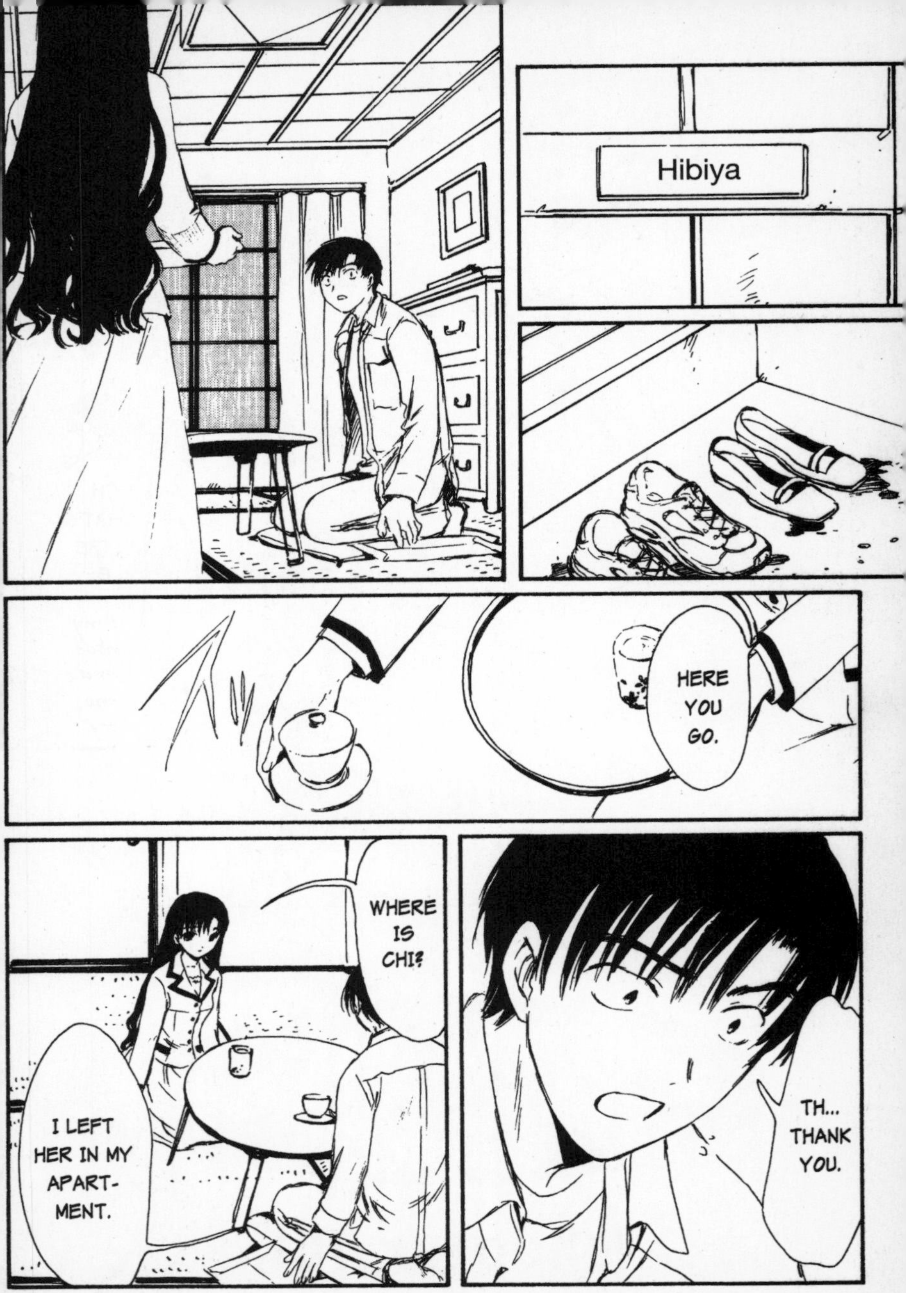
Hibiya
HERE YOU GO.
TH... THANK YOU.
WHERE IS CHI?
I LEFT HER IN MY APART-MENT.

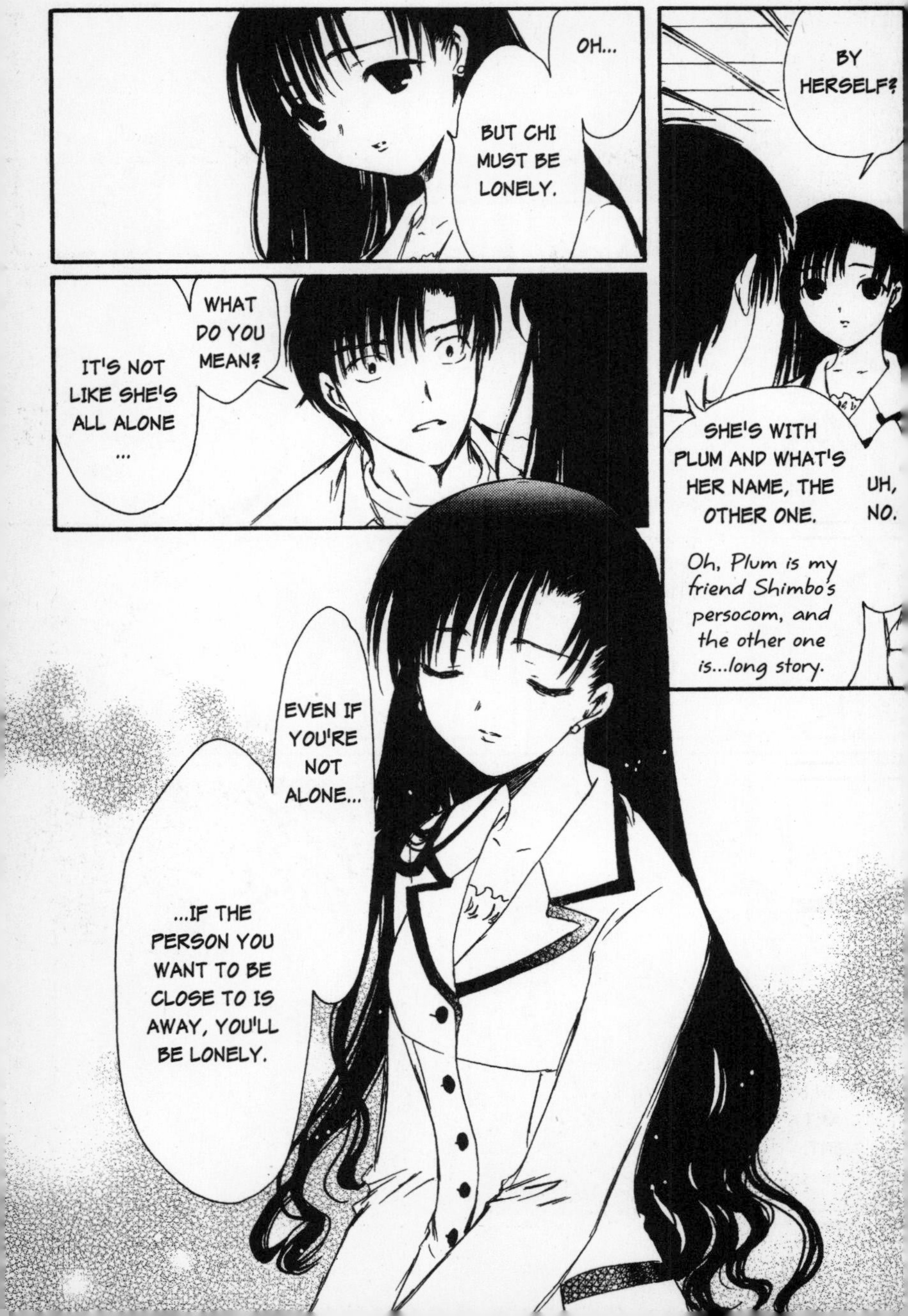
BY HERSELF?
UH, NO.
SHE'S WITH PLUM AND WHAT'S HER NAME, THE OTHER ONE.
Oh, Plum is my friend Shimbo's persocom, and the other one is...long story.
OH...
BUT CHI MUST BE LONELY.
WHAT DO YOU MEAN?
IT'S NOT LIKE SHE'S ALL ALONE ...
EVEN IF YOU'RE NOT ALONE...
...IF THE PERSON YOU WANT TO BE CLOSE TO IS AWAY, YOU'LL BE LONELY.

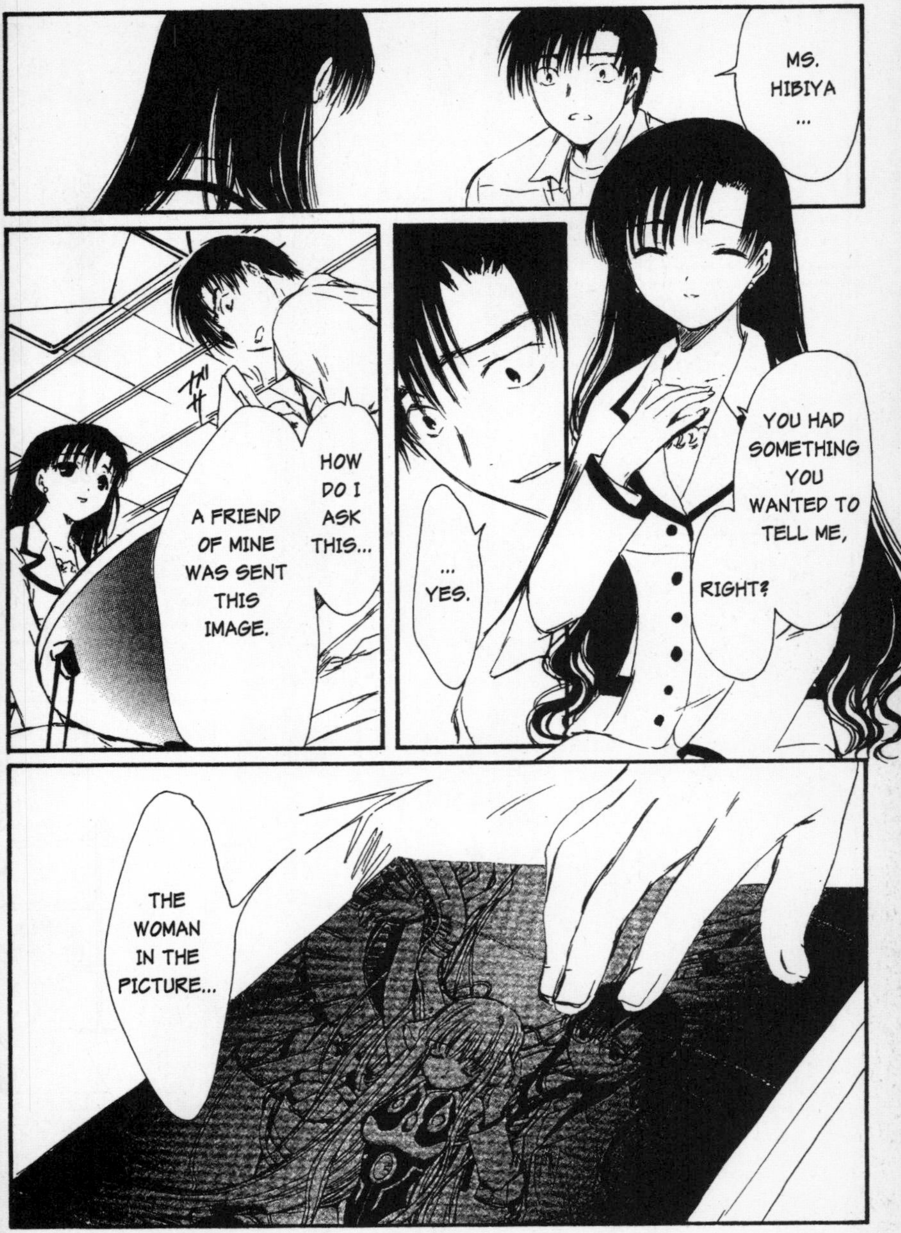
MS. HIBIYA ...
YOU HAD SOMETHING YOU WANTED TO TELL ME,
RIGHT?
... YES.
HOW DO I ASK THIS...
A FRIEND OF MINE WAS SENT THIS IMAGE.
THE WOMAN IN THE PICTURE...

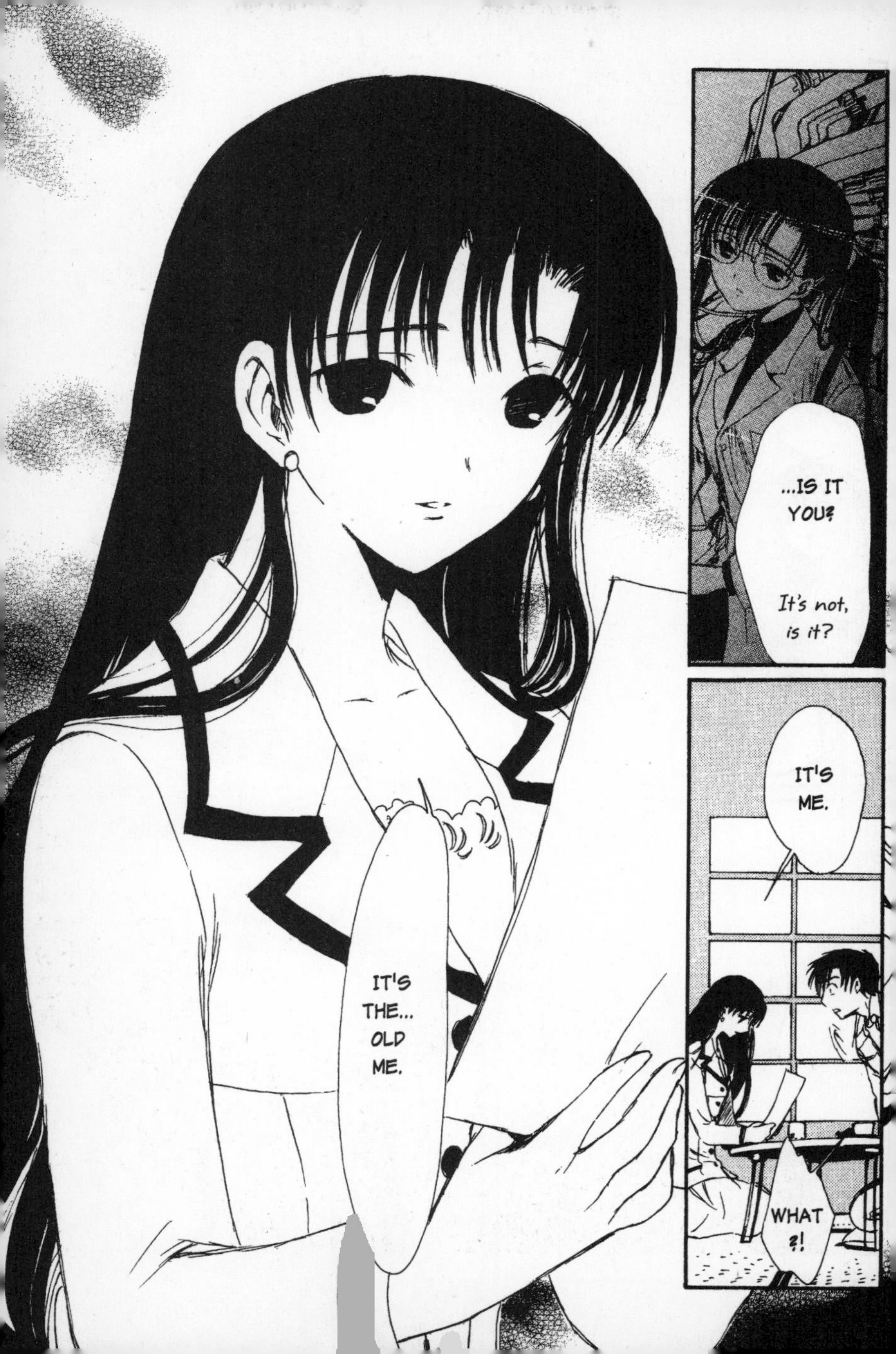
...IS IT YOU?
It's not, is it?
IT'S ME.
WHAT?!
IT'S THE... OLD ME.

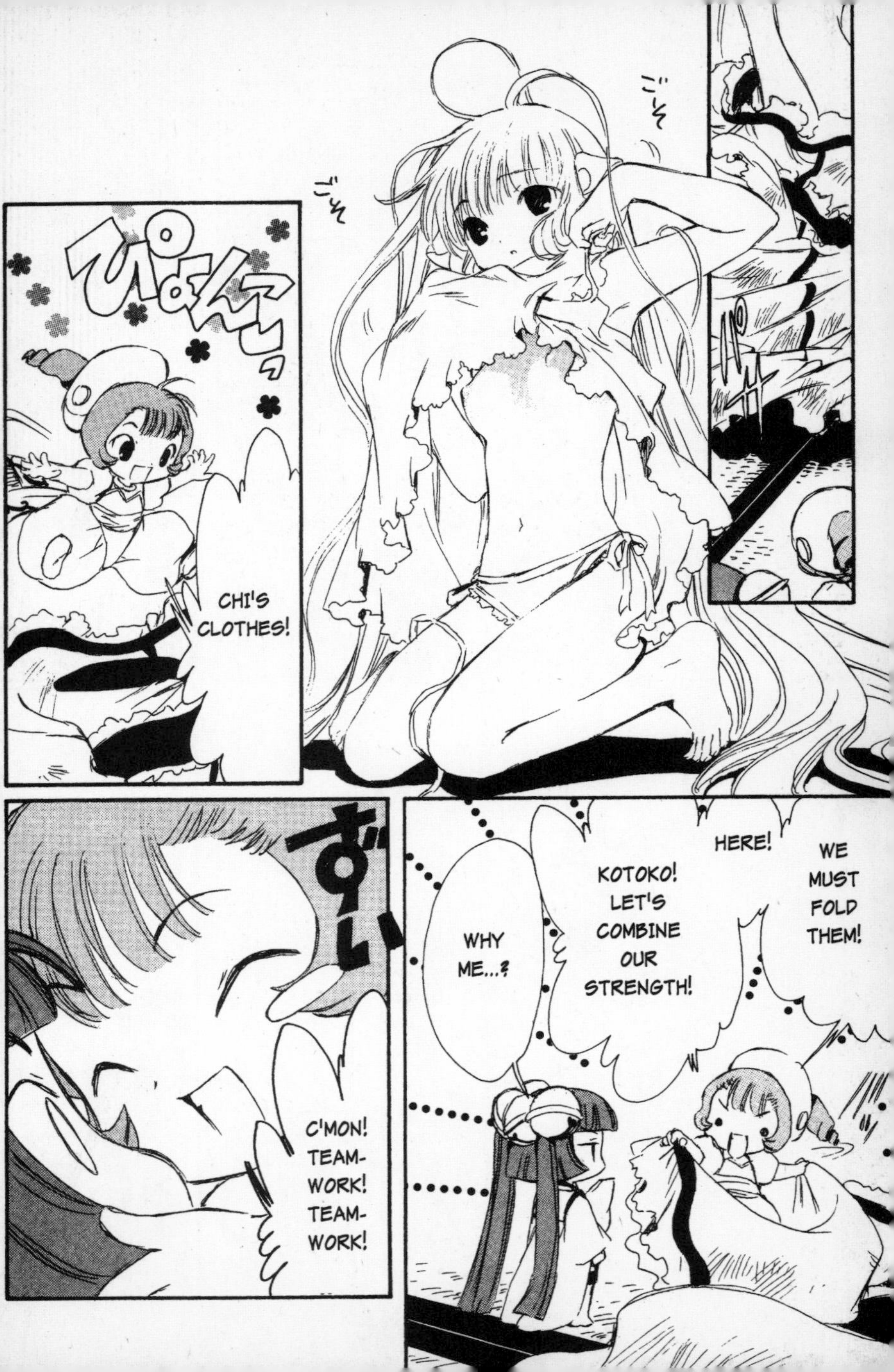
ごそ
ごそ
ぴょんっ
CHI'S CLOTHES!
WE MUST FOLD THEM!
HERE!
KOTOKO! LET'S COMBINE OUR STRENGTH!
WHY ME...?
ずい
C'MON! TEAM-WORK! TEAM-WORK!

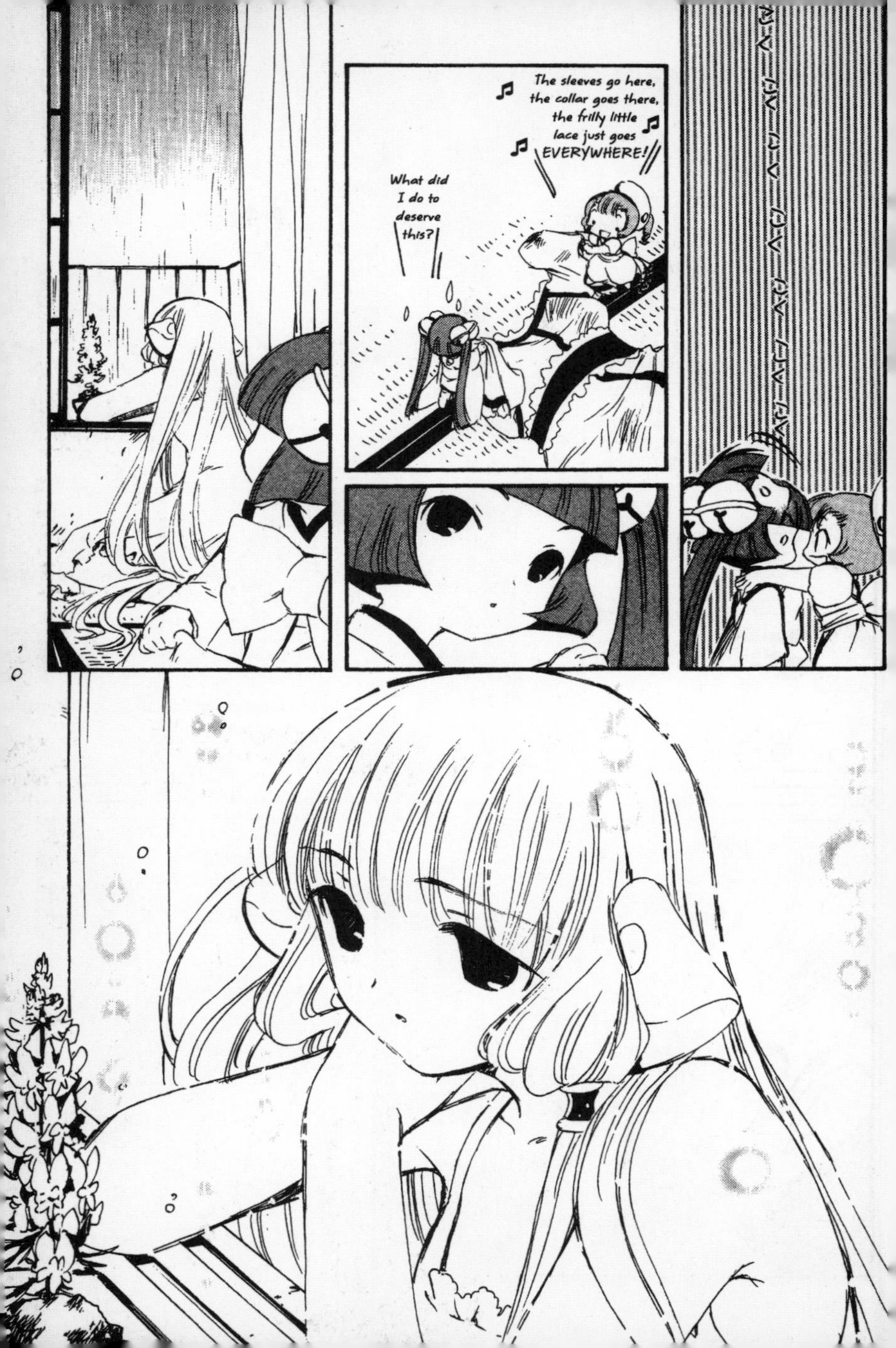
The sleeves go here, the collar goes there, the frilly little lace just goes EVERYWHERE!
What did I do to deserve this?

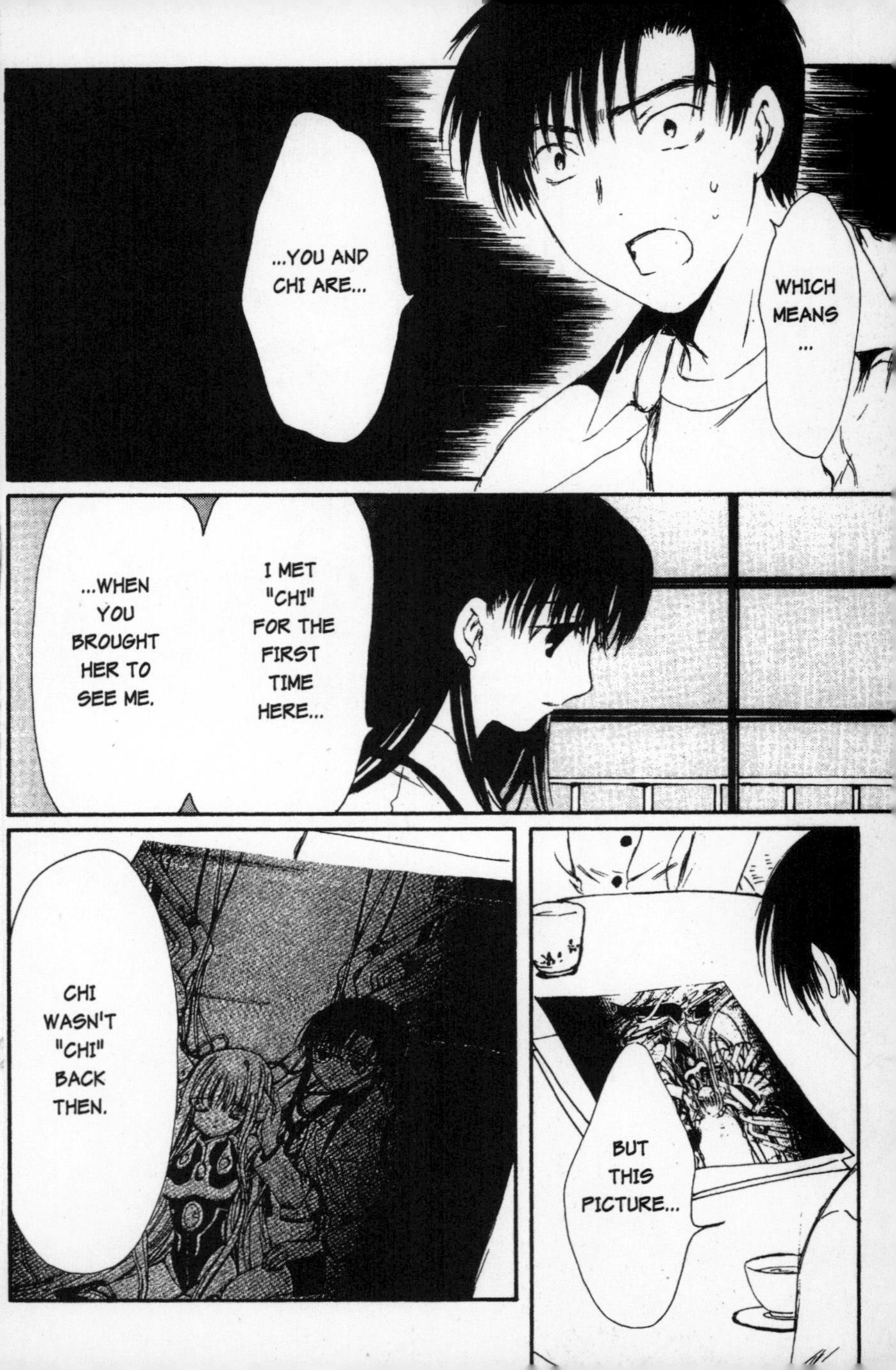
WHICH MEANS ...
...YOU AND CHI ARE...
I MET "CHI" FOR THE FIRST TIME HERE...
...WHEN YOU BROUGHT HER TO SEE ME.
BUT THIS PICTURE...
CHI WASN'T "CHI" BACK THEN.

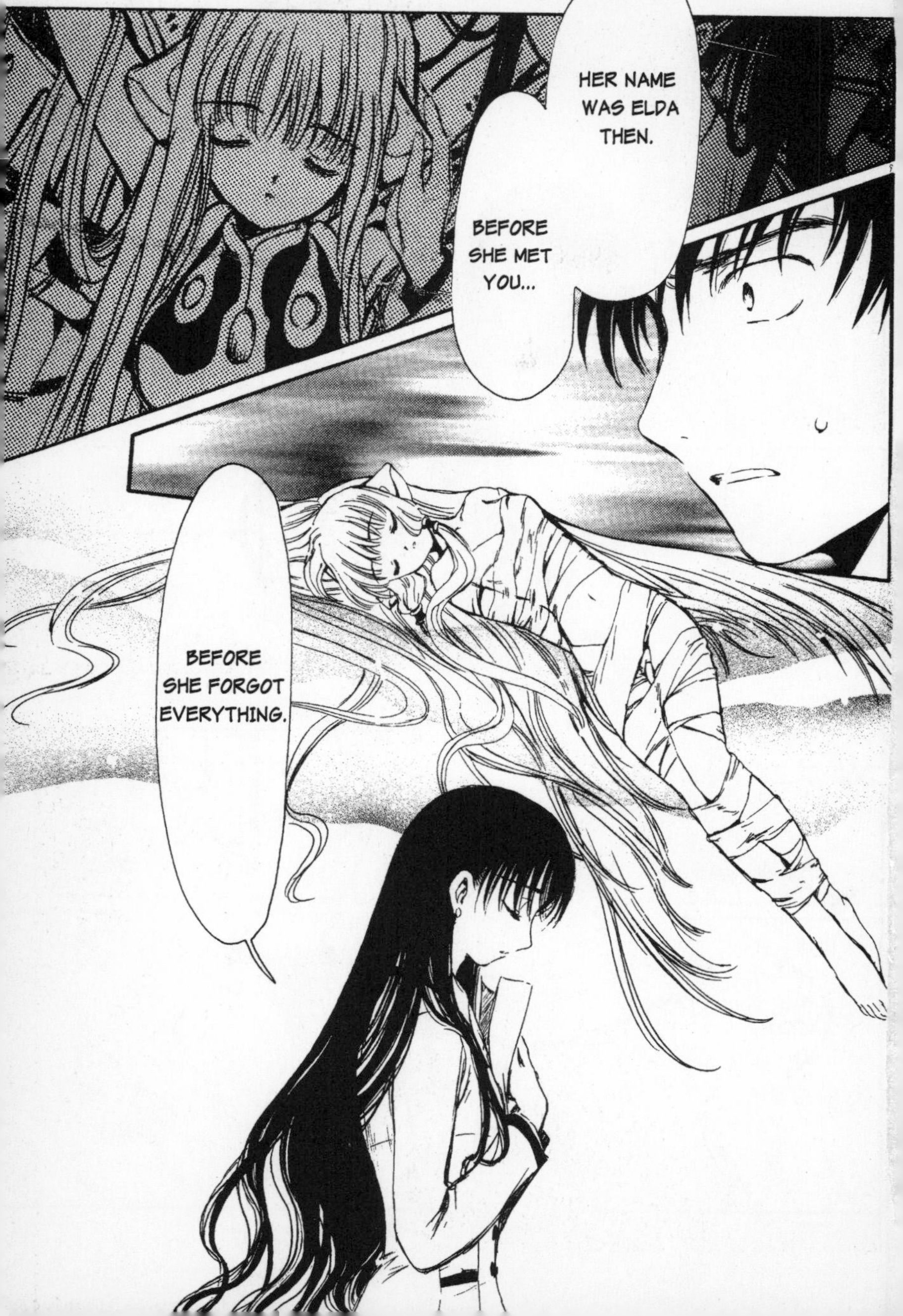
HER NAME WAS ELDA THEN.
BEFORE SHE MET YOU...
BEFORE SHE FORGOT EVERYTHING.

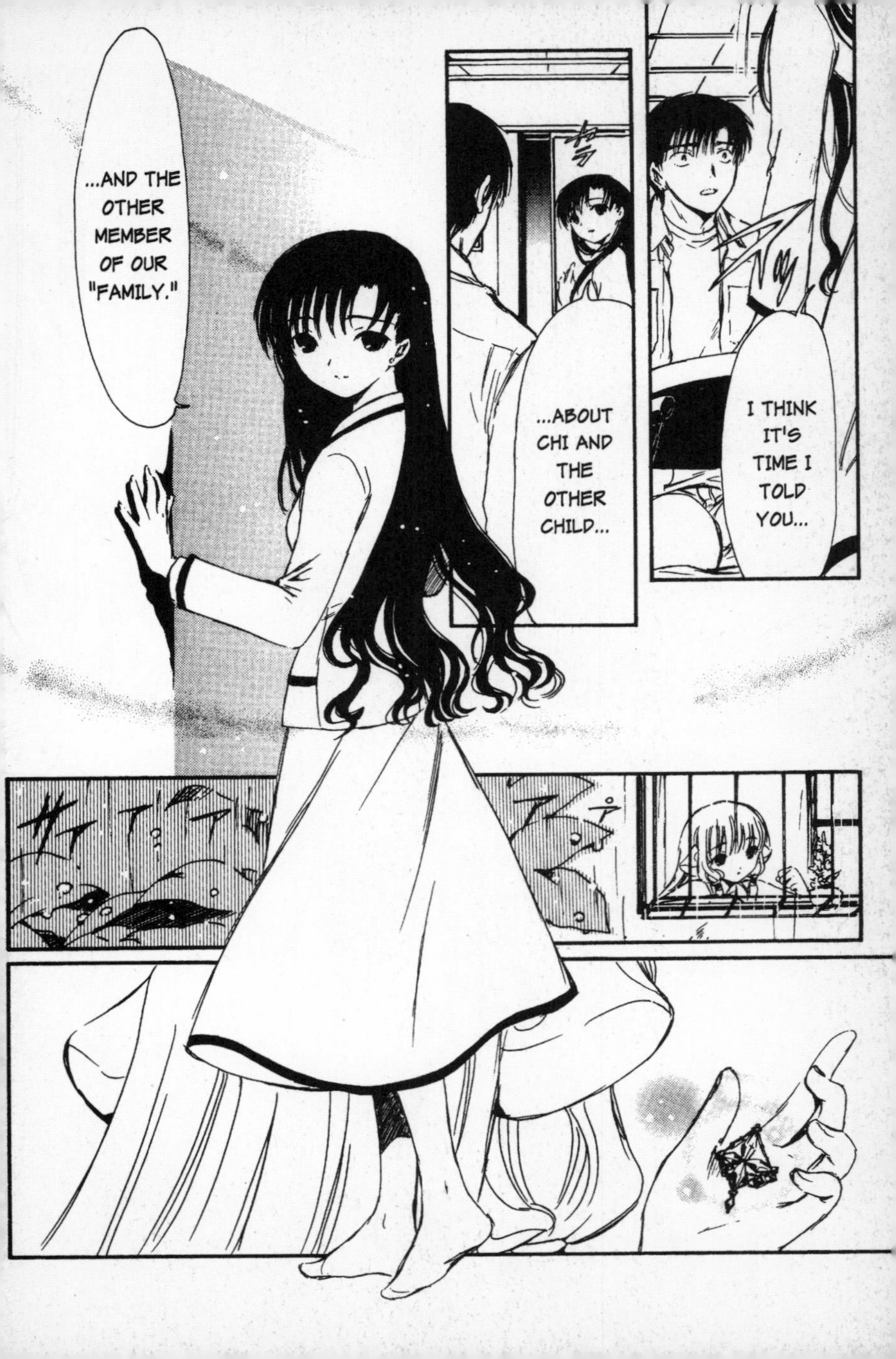
I THINK IT'S TIME I TOLD YOU...
...ABOUT CHI AND THE OTHER CHILD...
...AND THE OTHER MEMBER OF OUR "FAMILY."

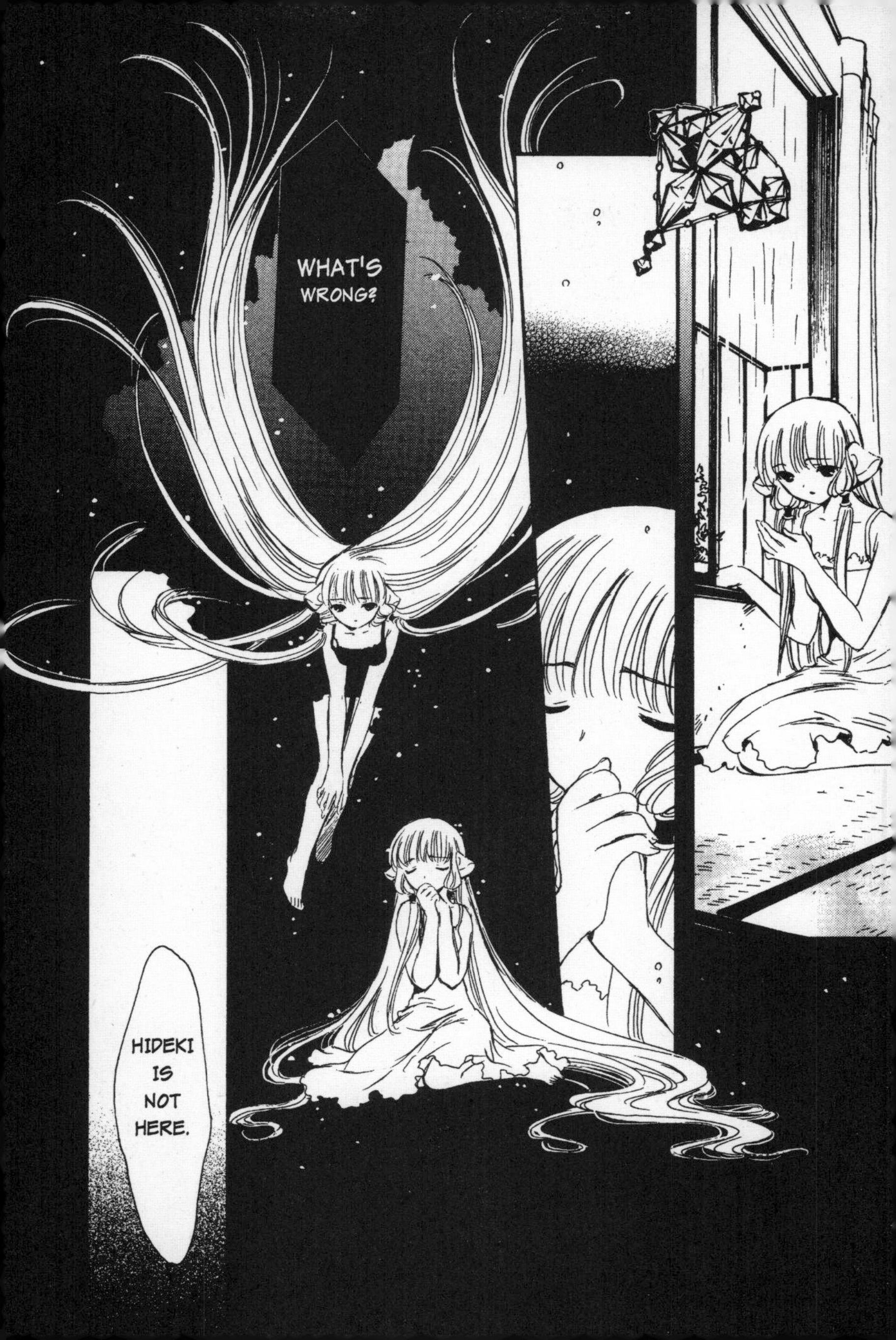
WHAT'S WRONG?
HIDEKI IS NOT HERE.

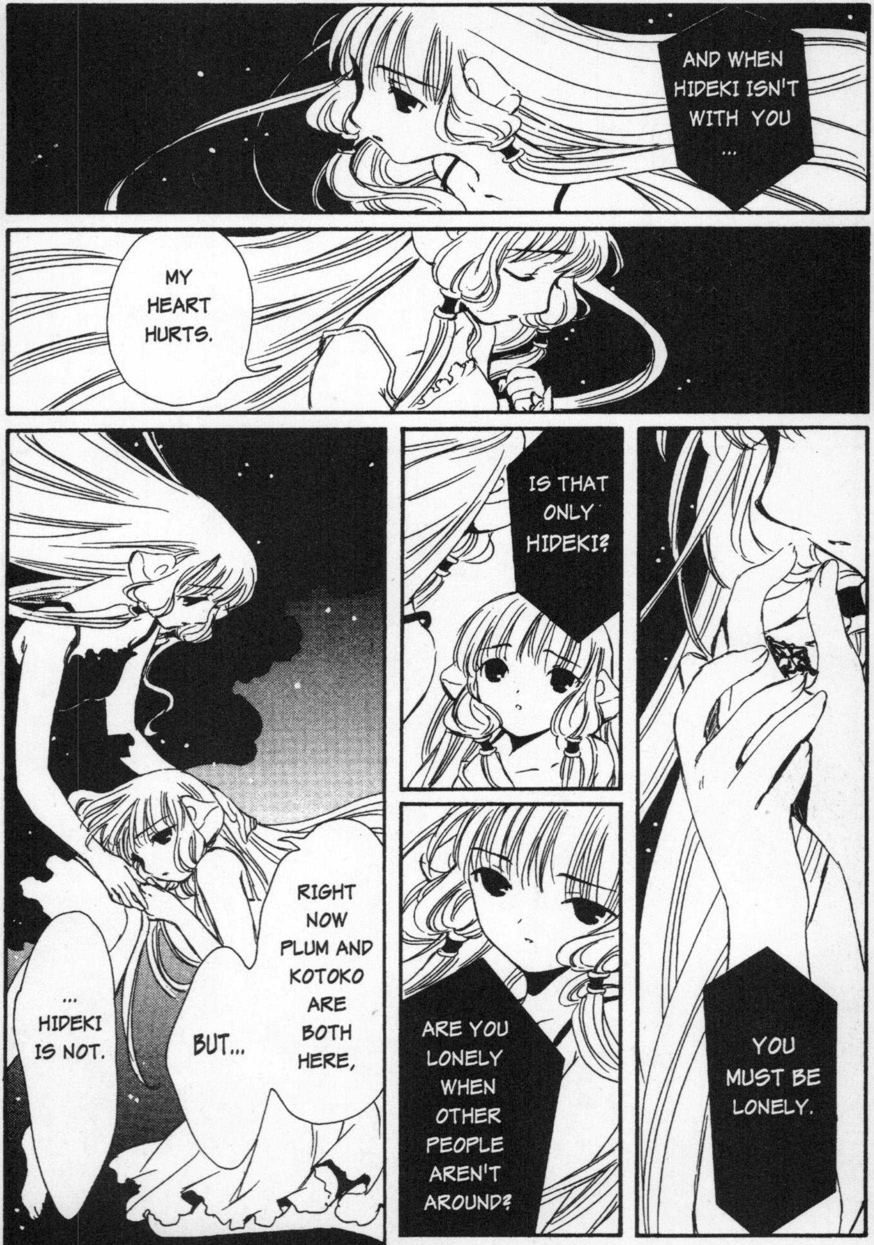
AND WHEN HIDEKI ISN'T WITH YOU ...
MY HEART HURTS.
YOU MUST BE LONELY.
IS THAT ONLY HIDEKI?
ARE YOU LONELY WHEN OTHER PEOPLE AREN'T AROUND?
RIGHT NOW PLUM AND KOTOKO ARE BOTH HERE,
BUT...
... HIDEKI IS NOT.

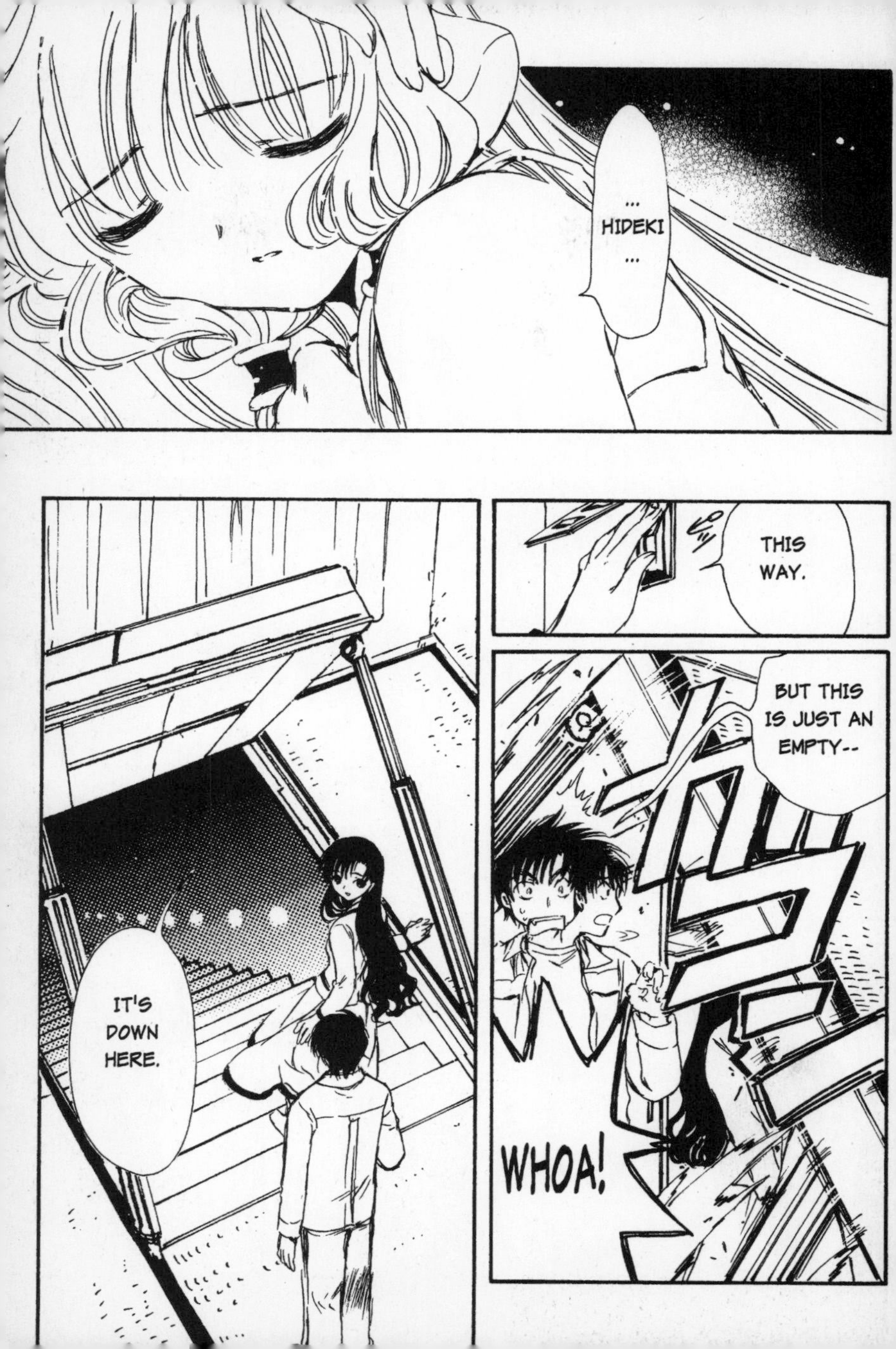
... HIDEKI ...
THIS WAY.
BUT THIS IS JUST AN EMPTY--
WHOA!
IT'S DOWN HERE.

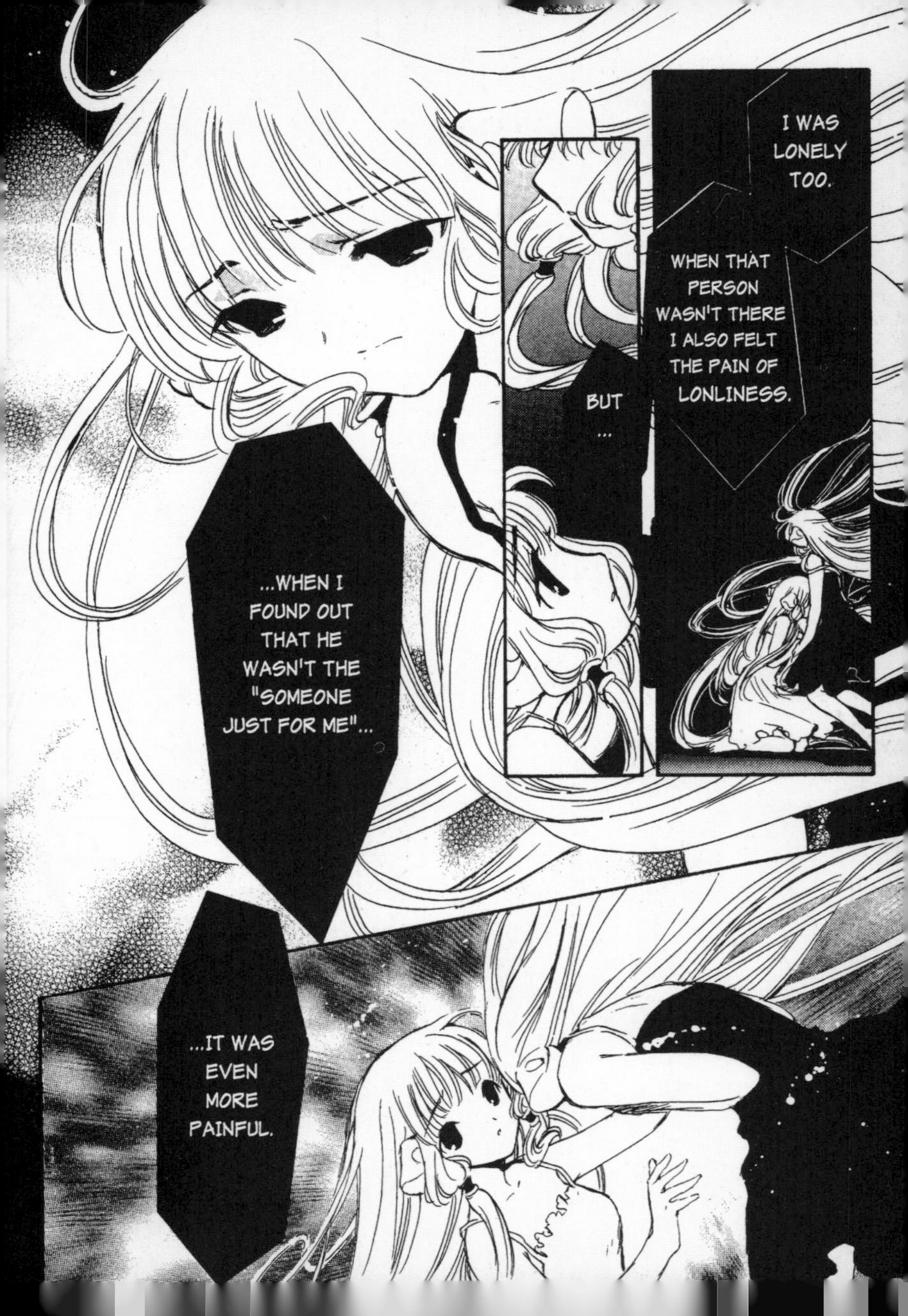
I WAS LONELY TOO.
WHEN THAT PERSON WASN'T THERE I ALSO FELT THE PAIN OF LONLINESS.
BUT ...
...WHEN I FOUND OUT THAT HE WASN'T THE "SOMEONE JUST FOR ME"...
...IT WAS EVEN MORE PAINFUL.

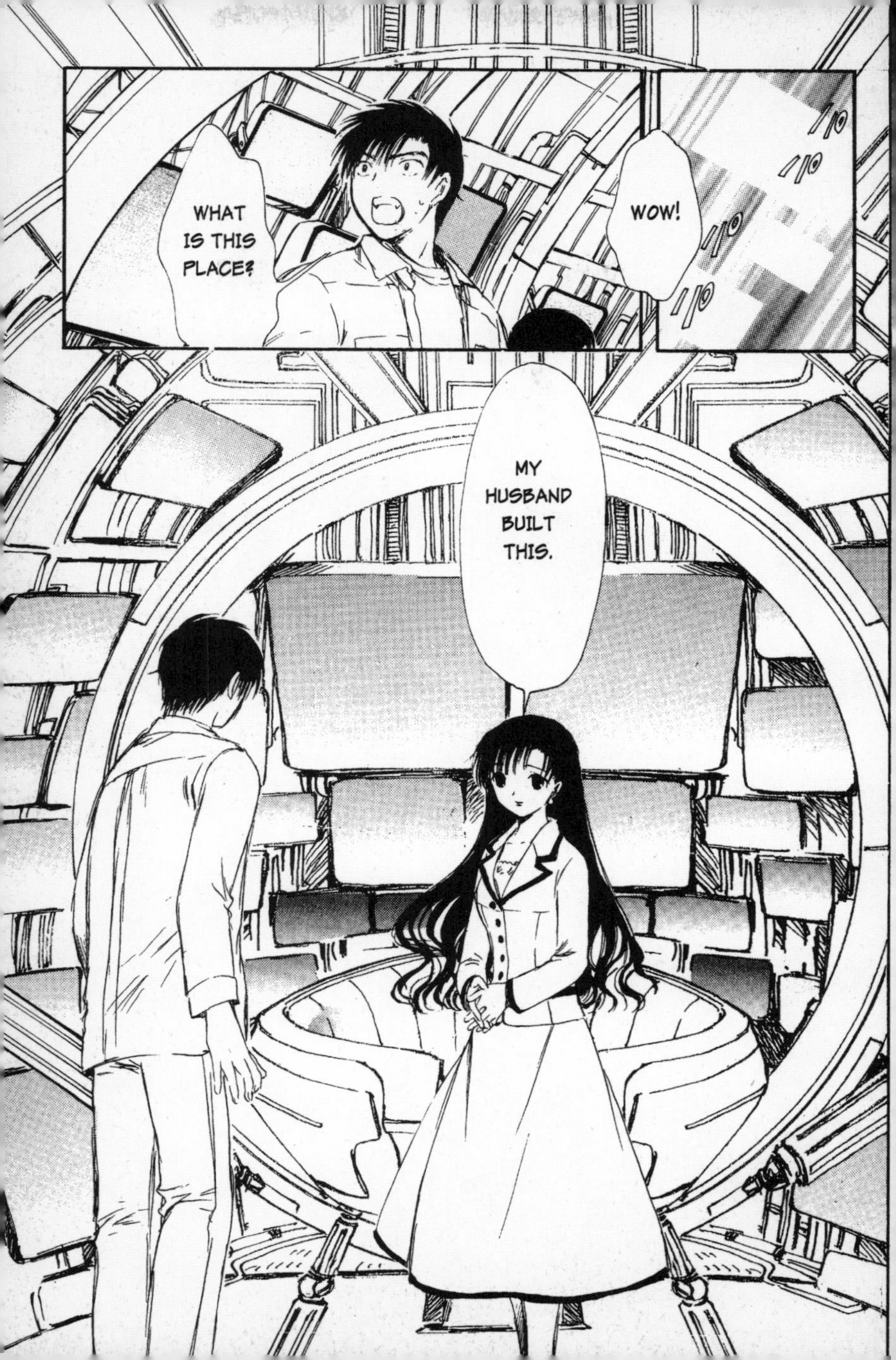
WOW!
WHAT IS THIS PLACE?
MY HUSBAND BUILT THIS.

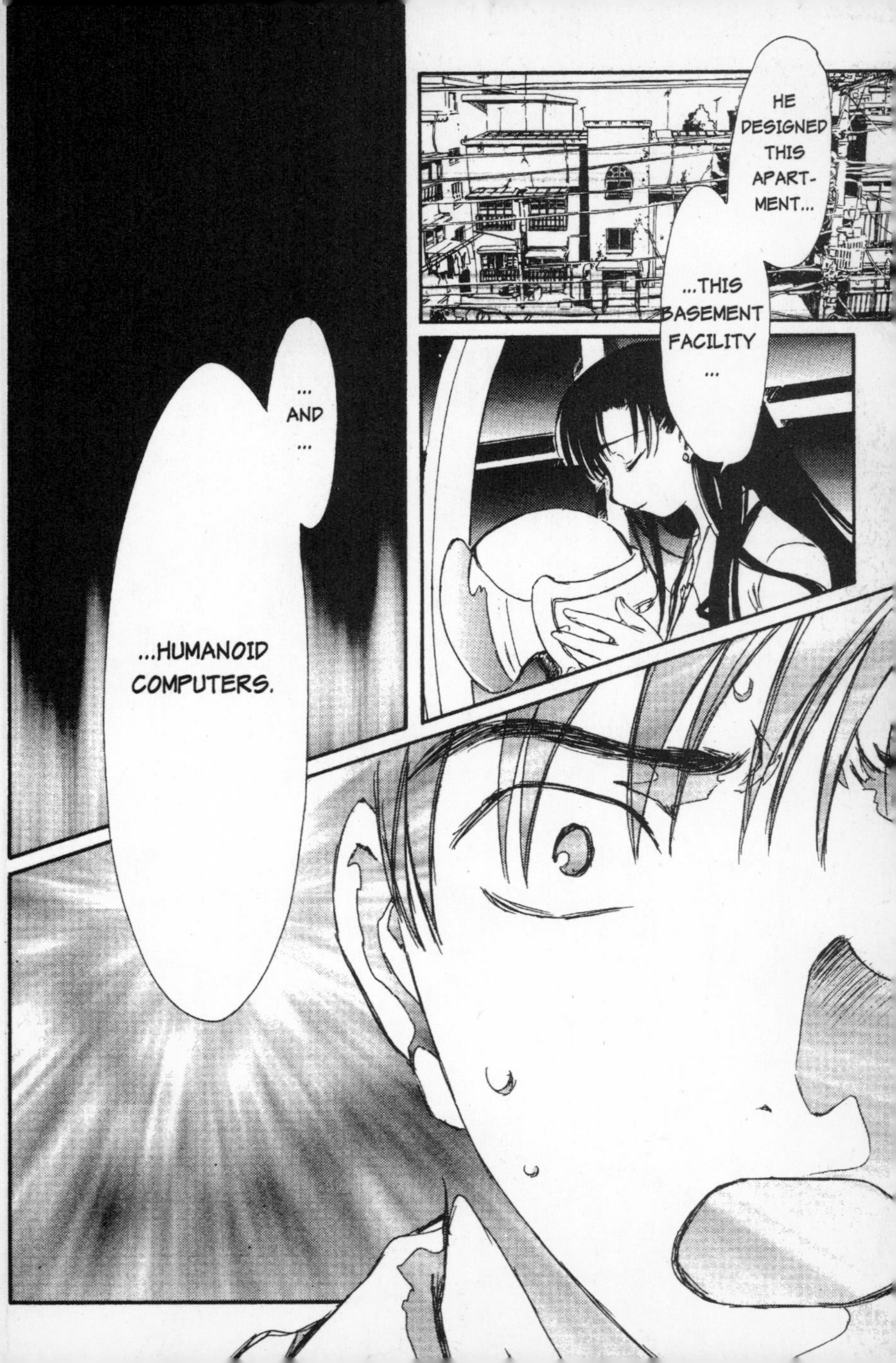
HE DESIGNED THIS APART-MENT...
...THIS BASEMENT FACILITY ...
... AND ...
...HUMANOID COMPUTERS.

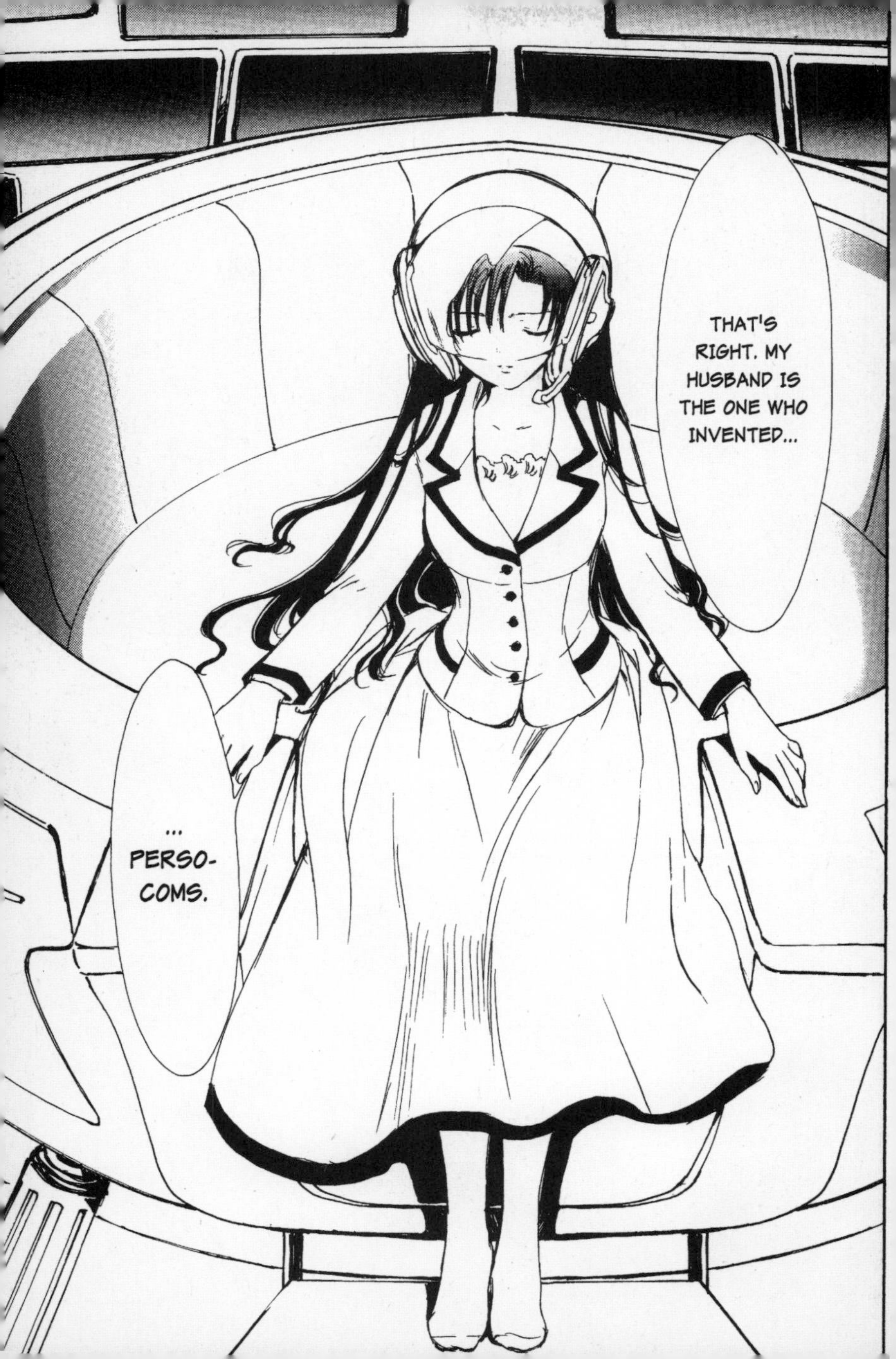
THAT'S RIGHT. MY HUSBAND IS THE ONE WHO INVENTED...
... PERSO-COMS.

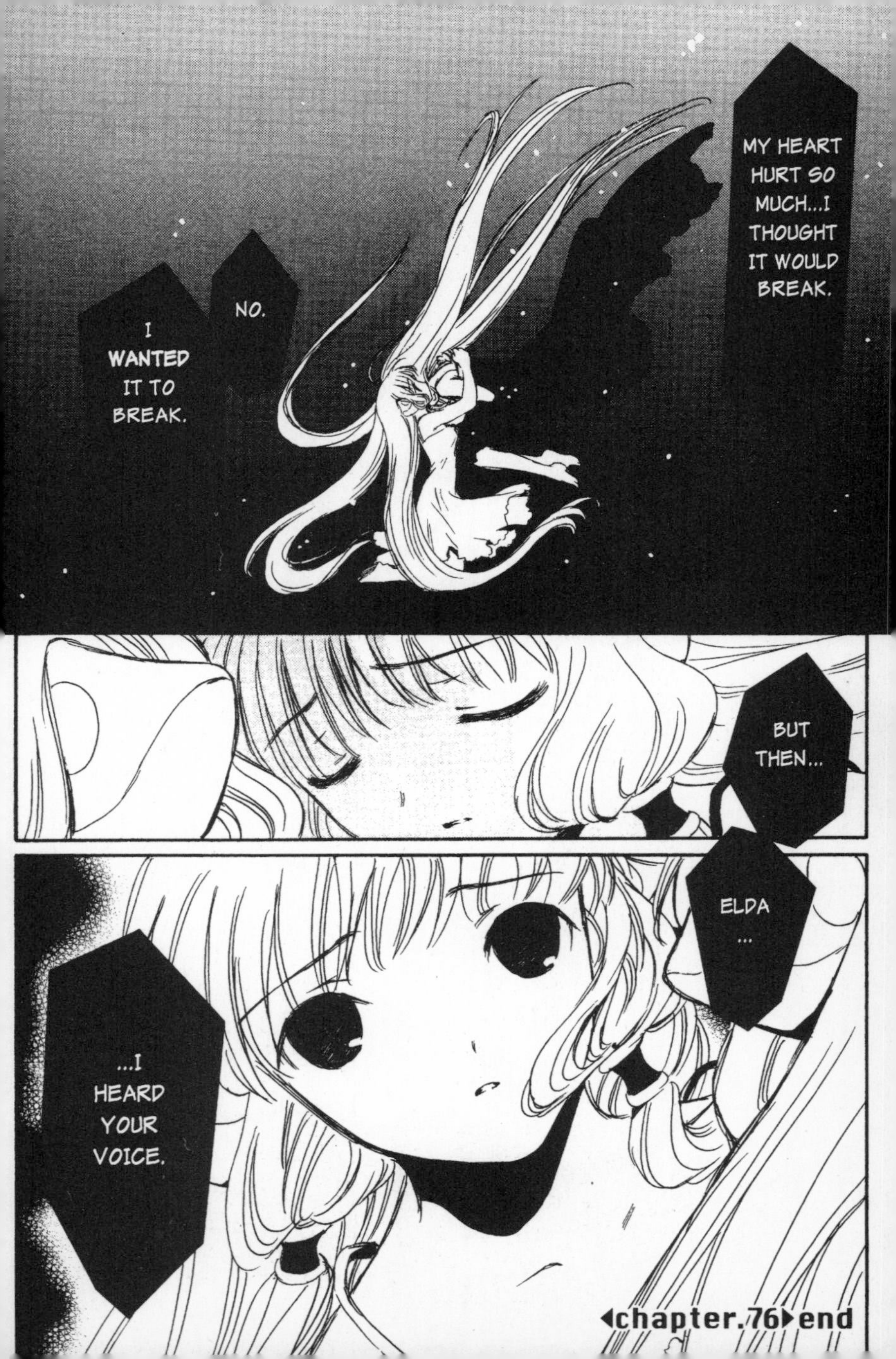
MY HEART HURT SO MUCH...I THOUGHT IT WOULD BREAK.
NO.
I WANTED IT TO BREAK.
BUT THEN...
ELDA ...
...I HEARD YOUR VOICE.
chapter.76 end

◀chapter.77▶

ちょびっツ
Chobits

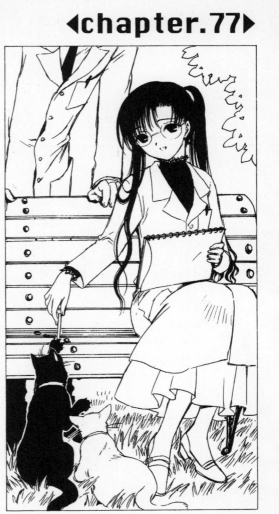

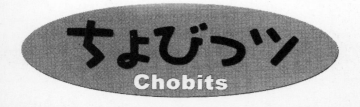

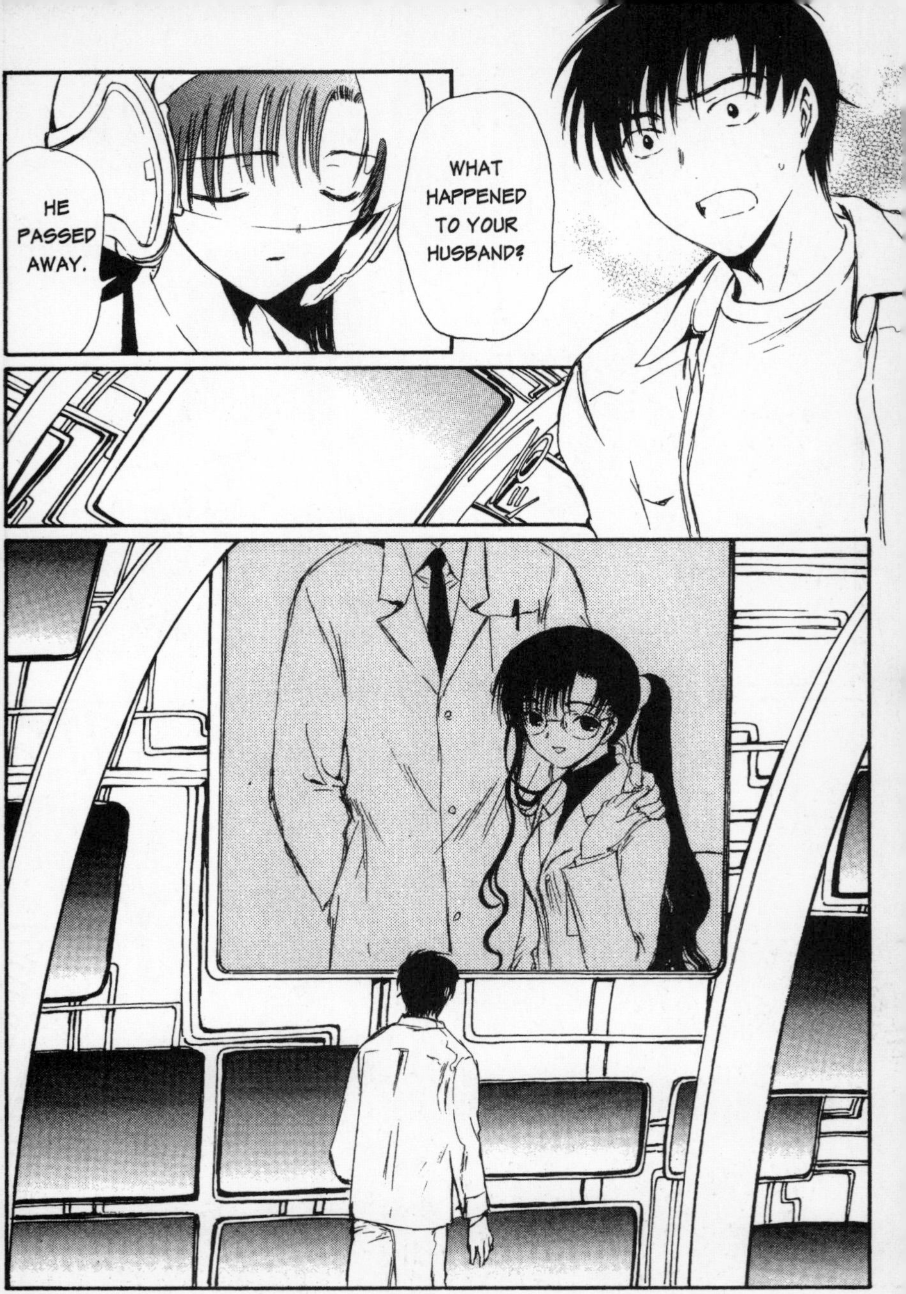
WHAT HAPPENED TO YOUR HUSBAND?
HE PASSED AWAY.

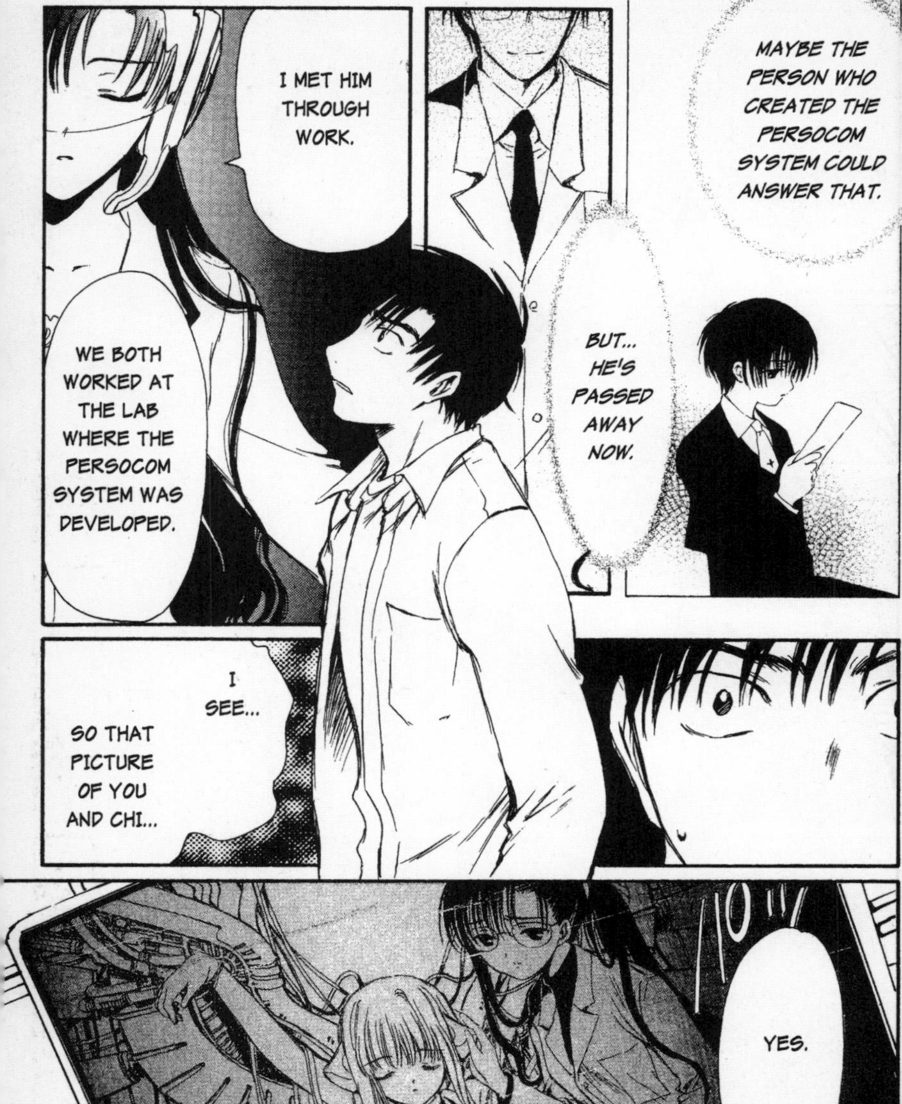
MAYBE THE PERSON WHO CREATED THE PERSOCOM SYSTEM COULD ANSWER THAT.
BUT... HE'S PASSED AWAY NOW.
I MET HIM THROUGH WORK.
WE BOTH WORKED AT THE LAB WHERE THE PERSOCOM SYSTEM WAS DEVELOPED.
I SEE...
SO THAT PICTURE OF YOU AND CHI...
YES.

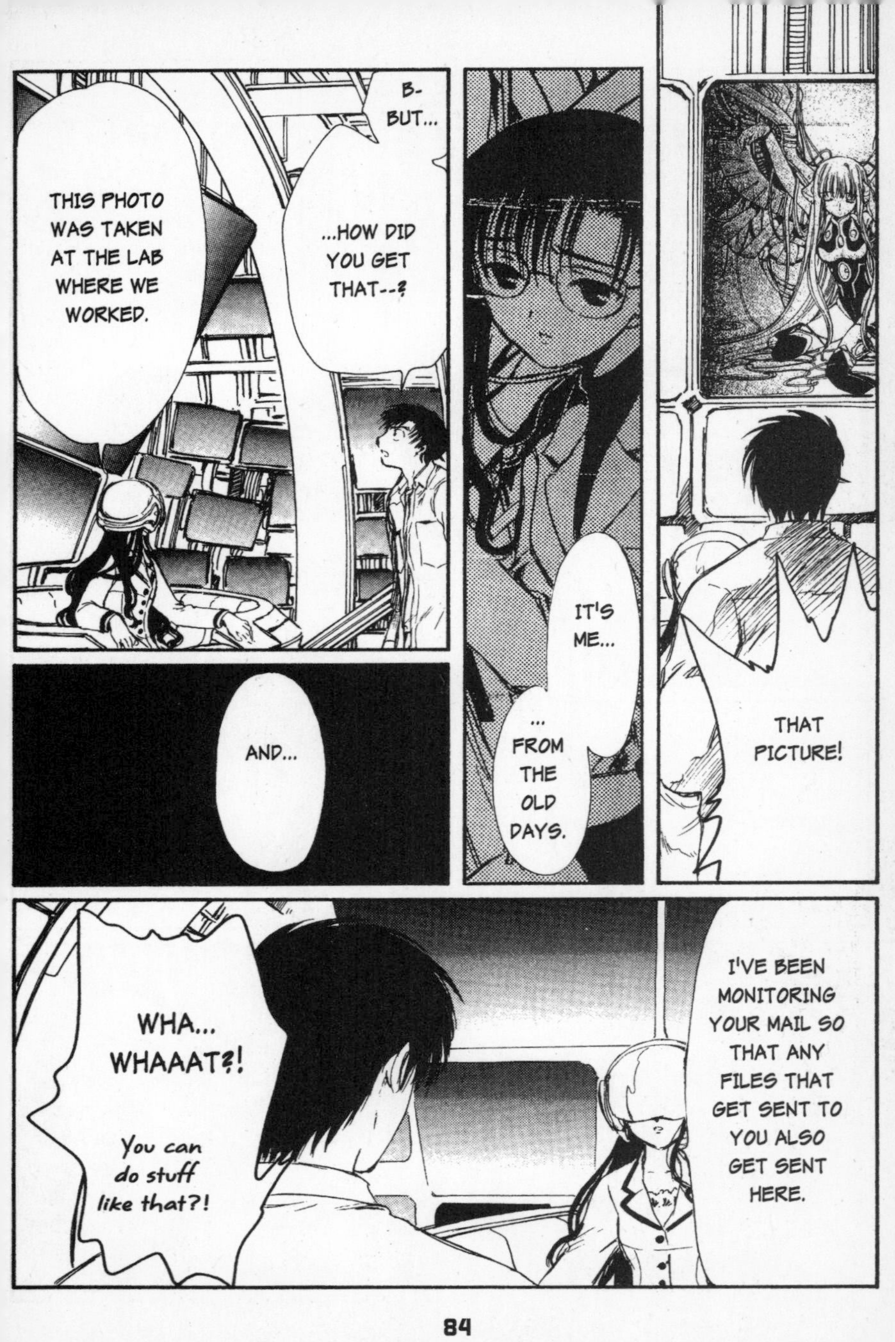
THAT PICTURE!
IT'S ME...
...FROM THE OLD DAYS.
B-BUT...
...HOW DID YOU GET THAT--?
THIS PHOTO WAS TAKEN AT THE LAB WHERE WE WORKED.
AND...
I'VE BEEN MONITORING YOUR MAIL SO THAT ANY FILES THAT GET SENT TO YOU ALSO GET SENT HERE.
WHA... WHAAAT?!
You can do stuff like that?!

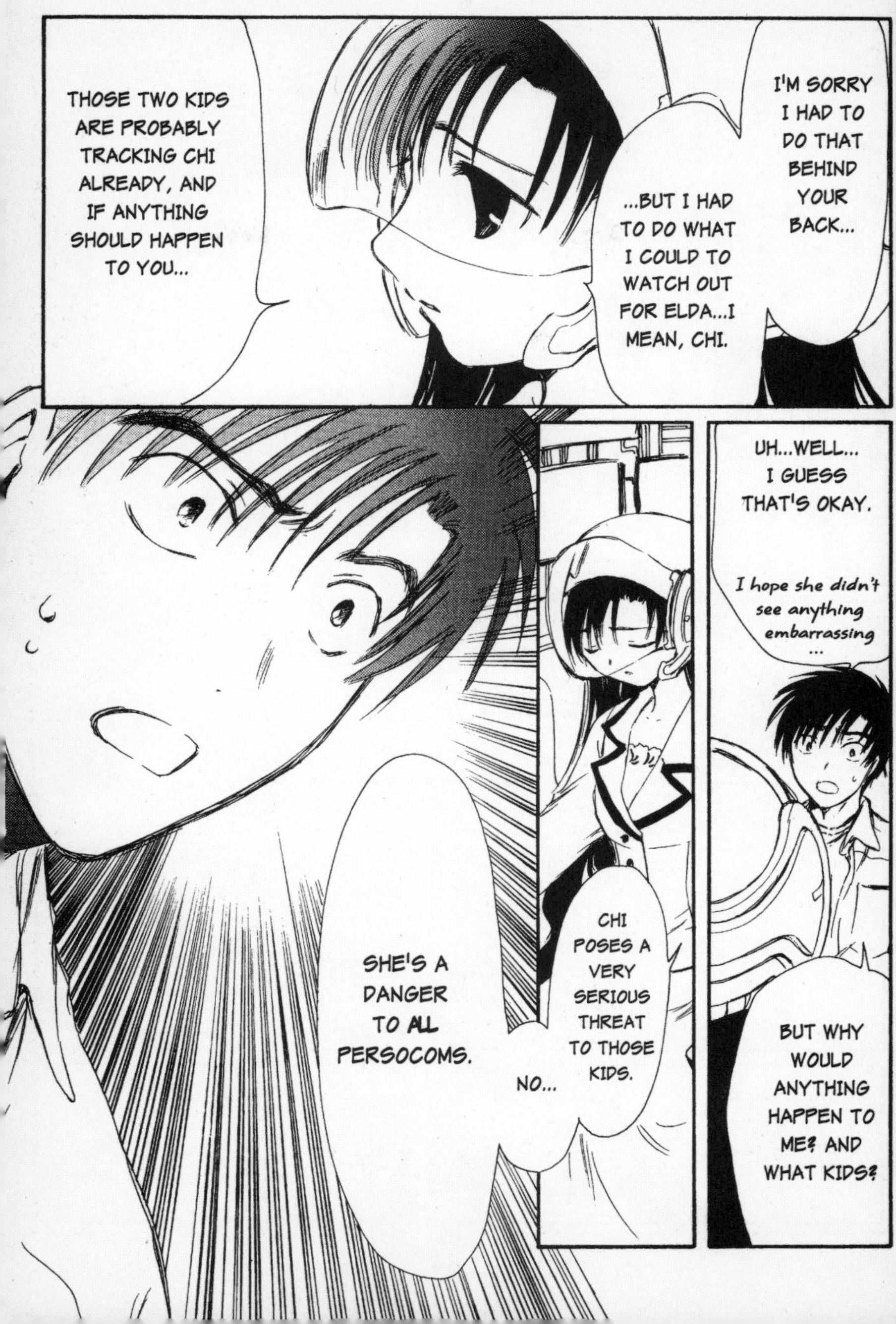

I'M SORRY I HAD TO DO THAT BEHIND YOUR BACK...
...BUT I HAD TO DO WHAT I COULD TO WATCH OUT FOR ELDA...I MEAN, CHI.
THOSE TWO KIDS ARE PROBABLY TRACKING CHI ALREADY, AND IF ANYTHING SHOULD HAPPEN TO YOU...
UH...WELL... I GUESS THAT'S OKAY.
I hope she didn't see anything embarrassing ...
BUT WHY WOULD ANYTHING HAPPEN TO ME? AND WHAT KIDS?
CHI POSES A VERY SERIOUS THREAT TO THOSE KIDS.
NO...
SHE'S A DANGER TO ALL PERSOCOMS.

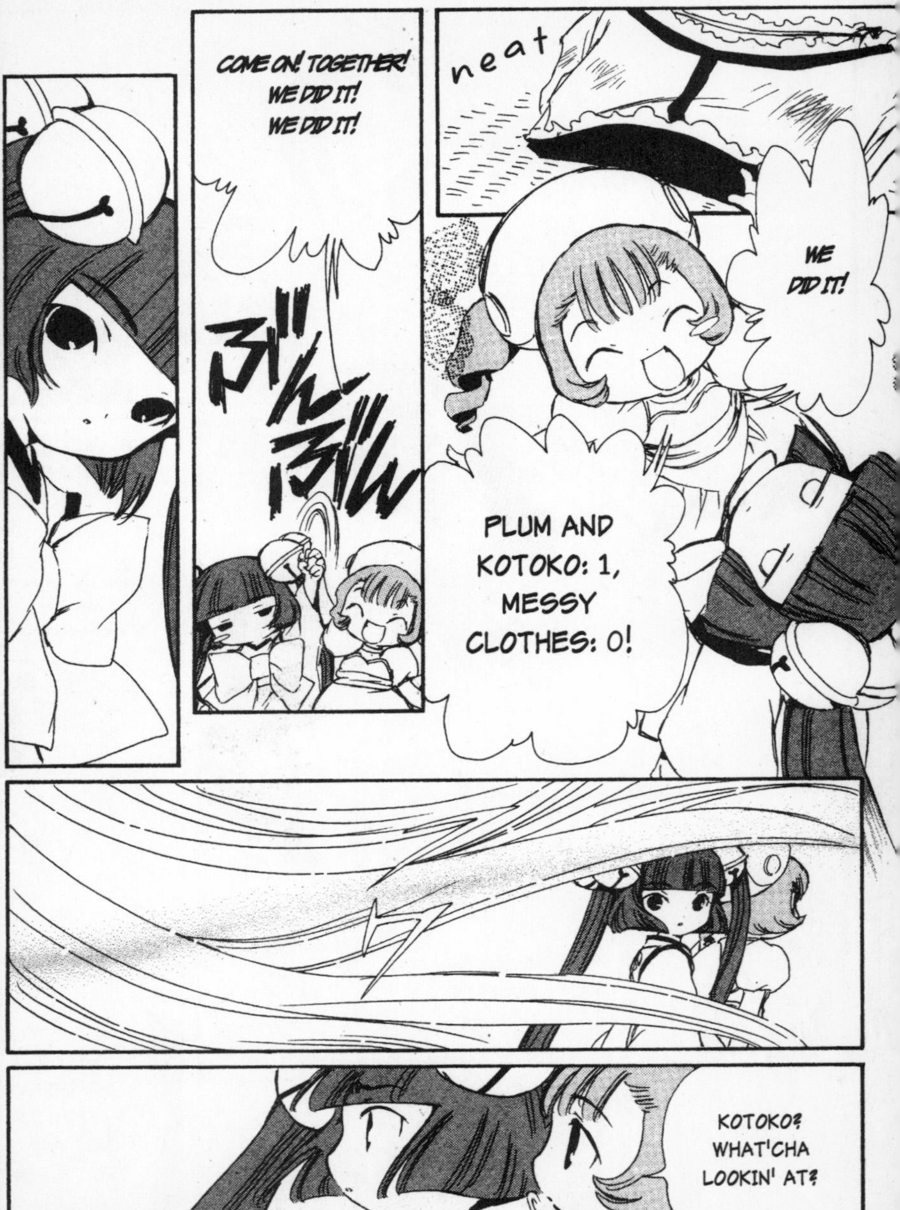
neat
WE DID IT!
PLUM AND KOTOKO: 1, MESSY CLOTHES: 0!
COME ON! TOGETHER! WE DID IT! WE DID IT!
ぶんぶん
KOTOKO? WHAT'CHA LOOKIN' AT?

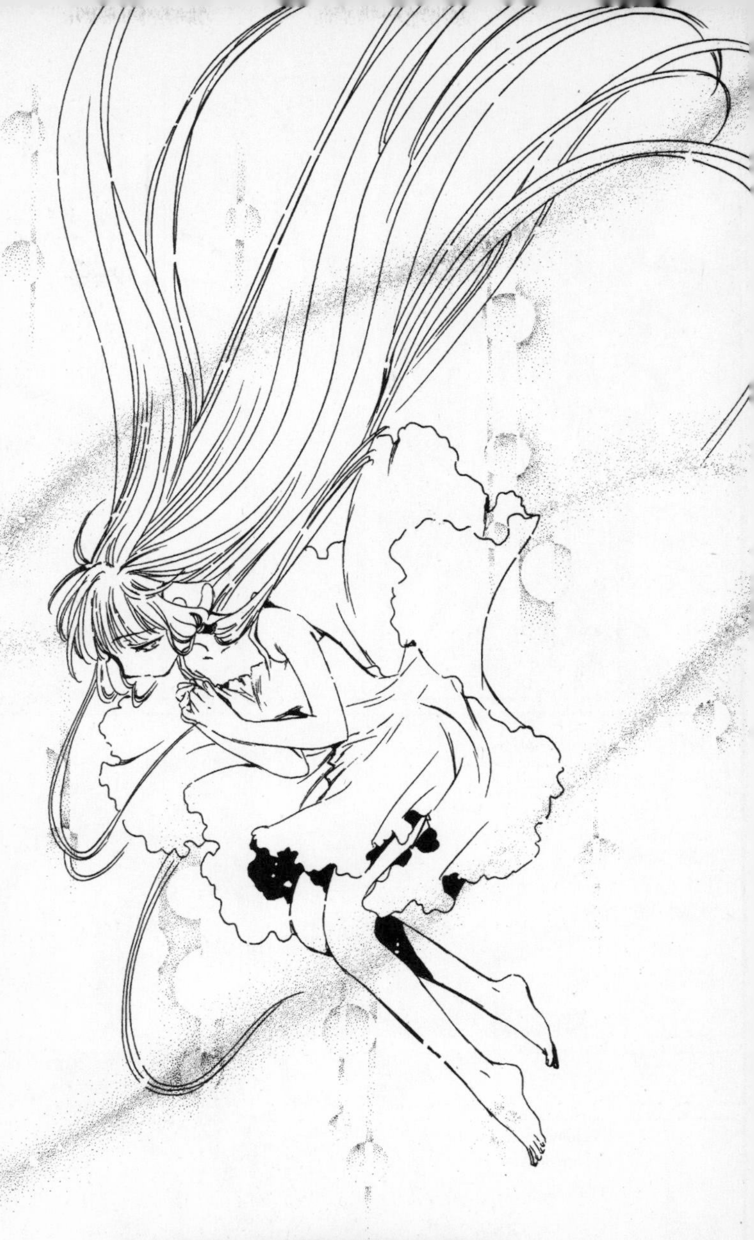

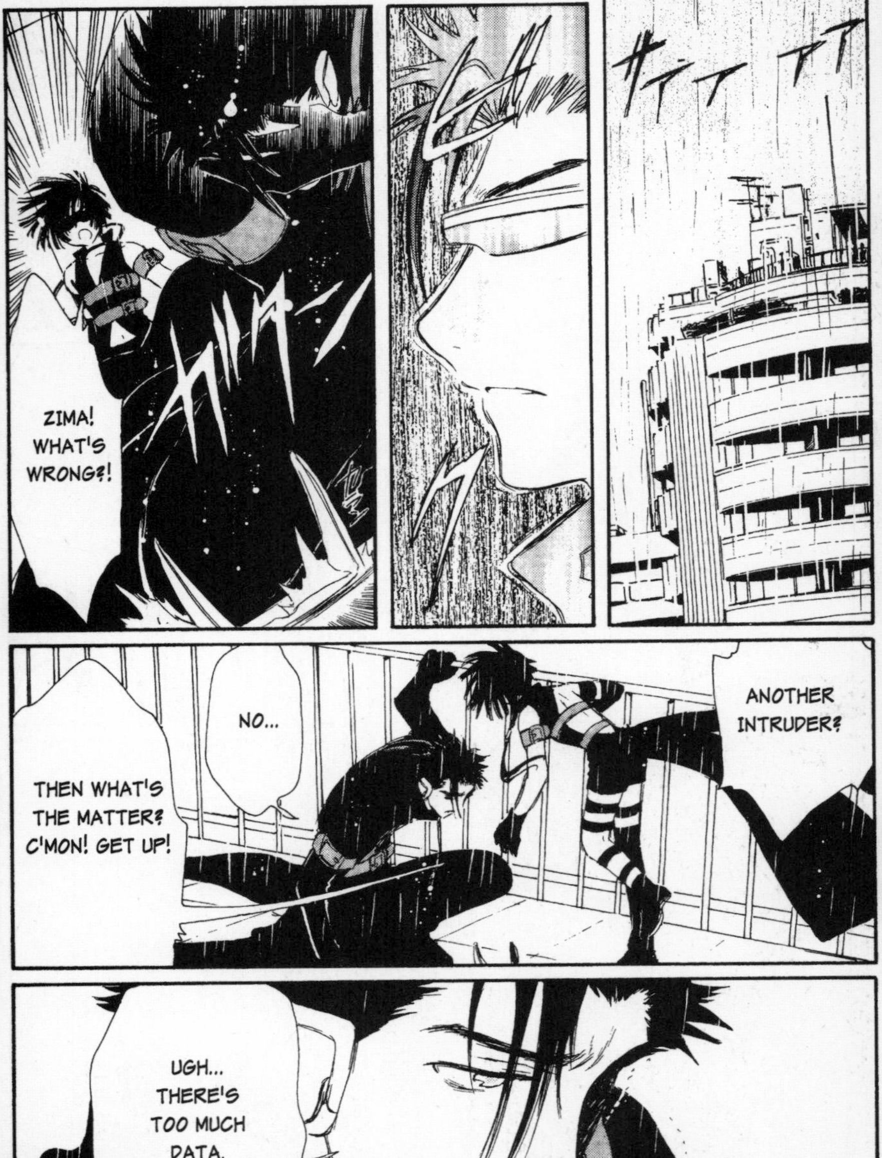
ZIMA! WHAT'S WRONG?!
ANOTHER INTRUDER?
NO...
THEN WHAT'S THE MATTER? C'MON! GET UP!
UGH... THERE'S TOO MUCH DATA.

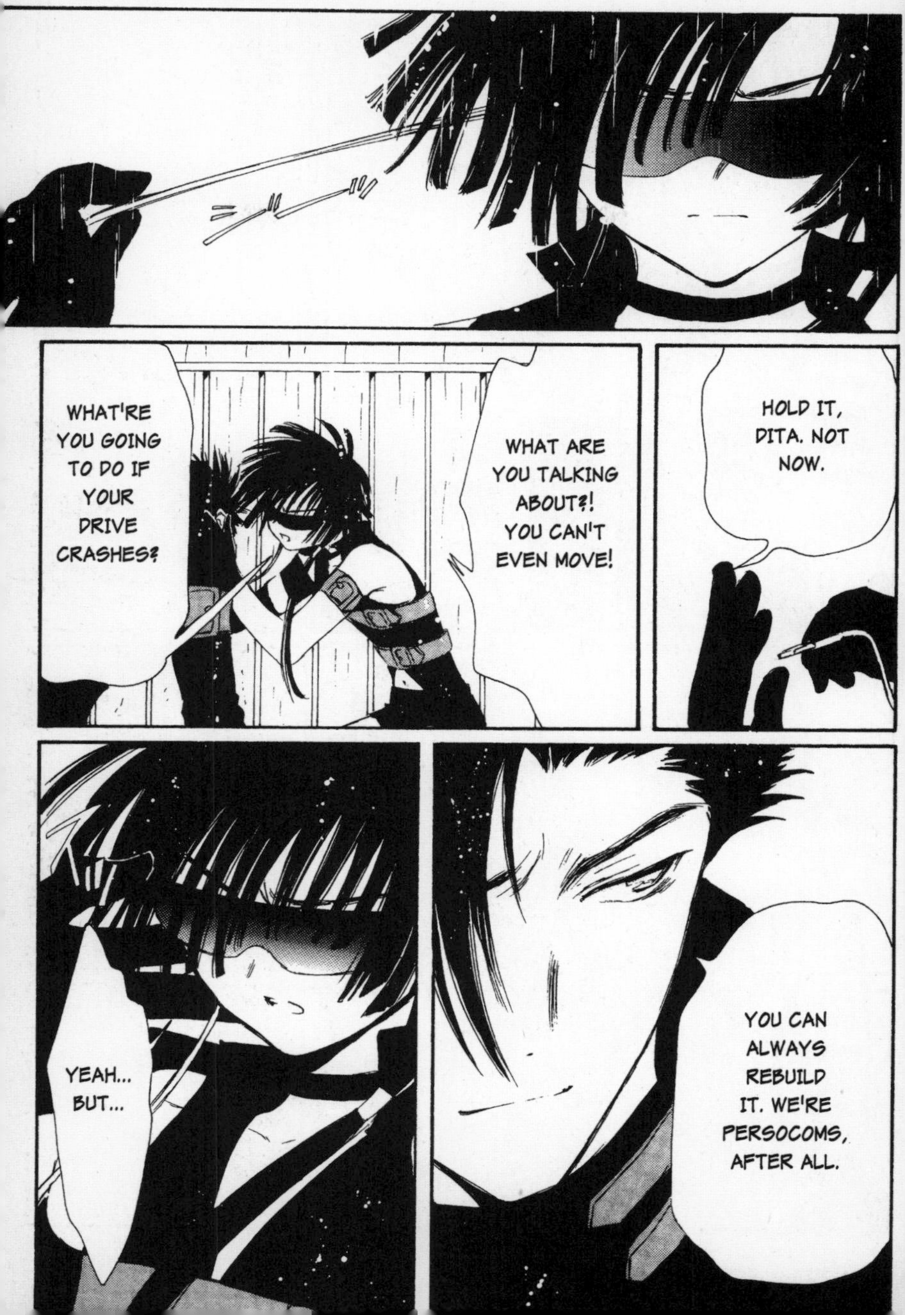
HOLD IT, DITA. NOT NOW.
WHAT ARE YOU TALKING ABOUT?! YOU CAN'T EVEN MOVE!
WHAT'RE YOU GOING TO DO IF YOUR DRIVE CRASHES?
YOU CAN ALWAYS REBUILD IT. WE'RE PERSOCOMS, AFTER ALL.
YEAH... BUT...

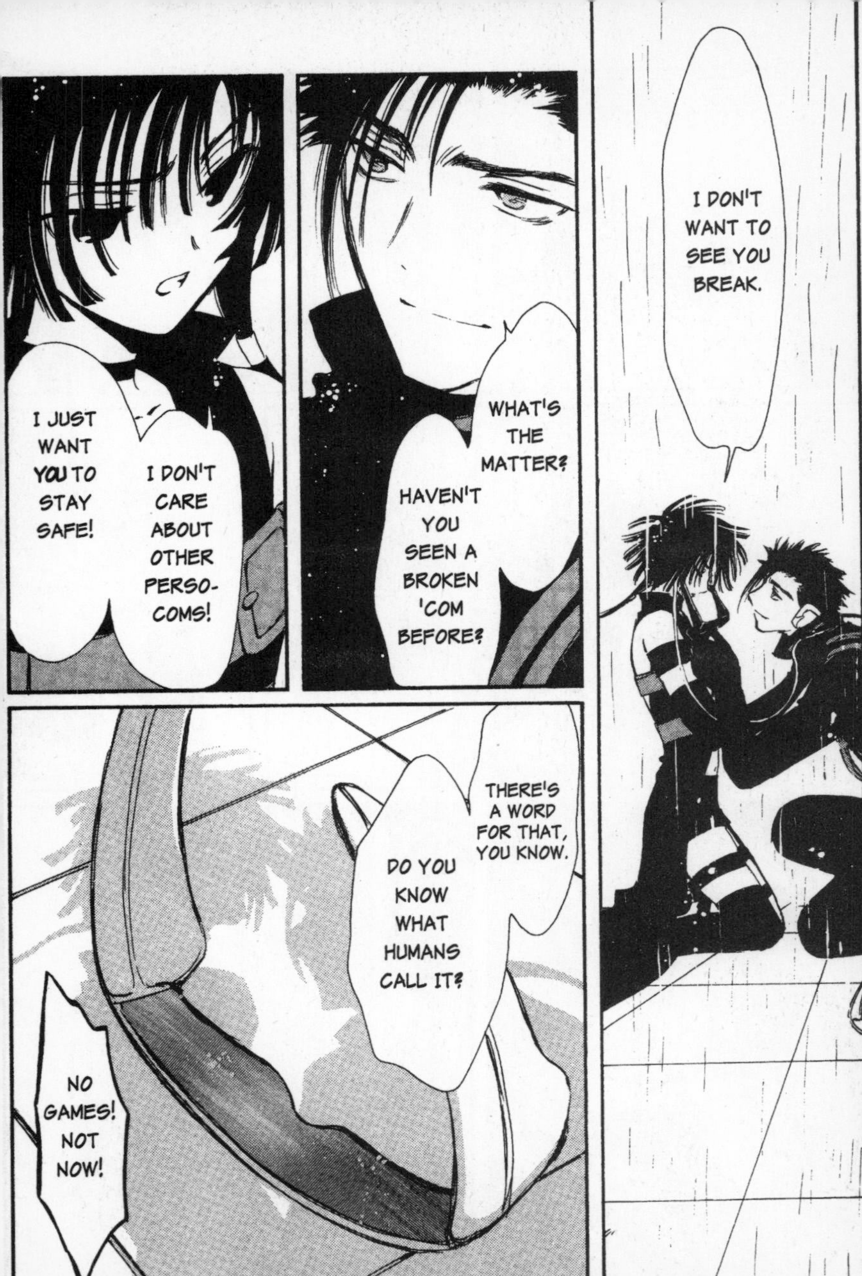
I DON'T WANT TO SEE YOU BREAK.
WHAT'S THE MATTER?
HAVEN'T YOU SEEN A BROKEN 'COM BEFORE?
I DON'T CARE ABOUT OTHER PERSO-COMS!
I JUST WANT YOU TO STAY SAFE!
THERE'S A WORD FOR THAT, YOU KNOW.
DO YOU KNOW WHAT HUMANS CALL IT?
NO GAMES! NOT NOW!

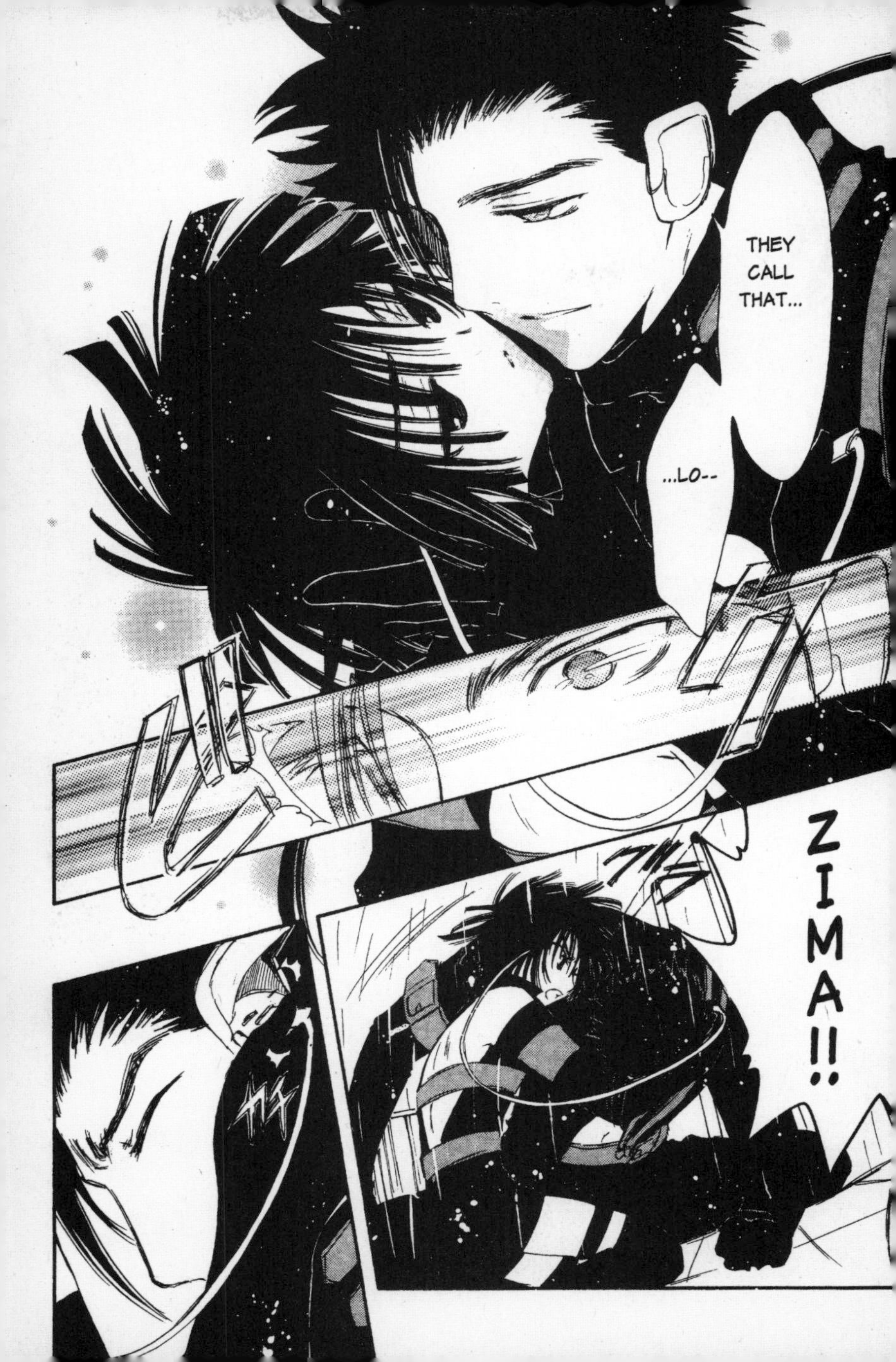
THEY CALL THAT...
...LO--
ZIMA!!

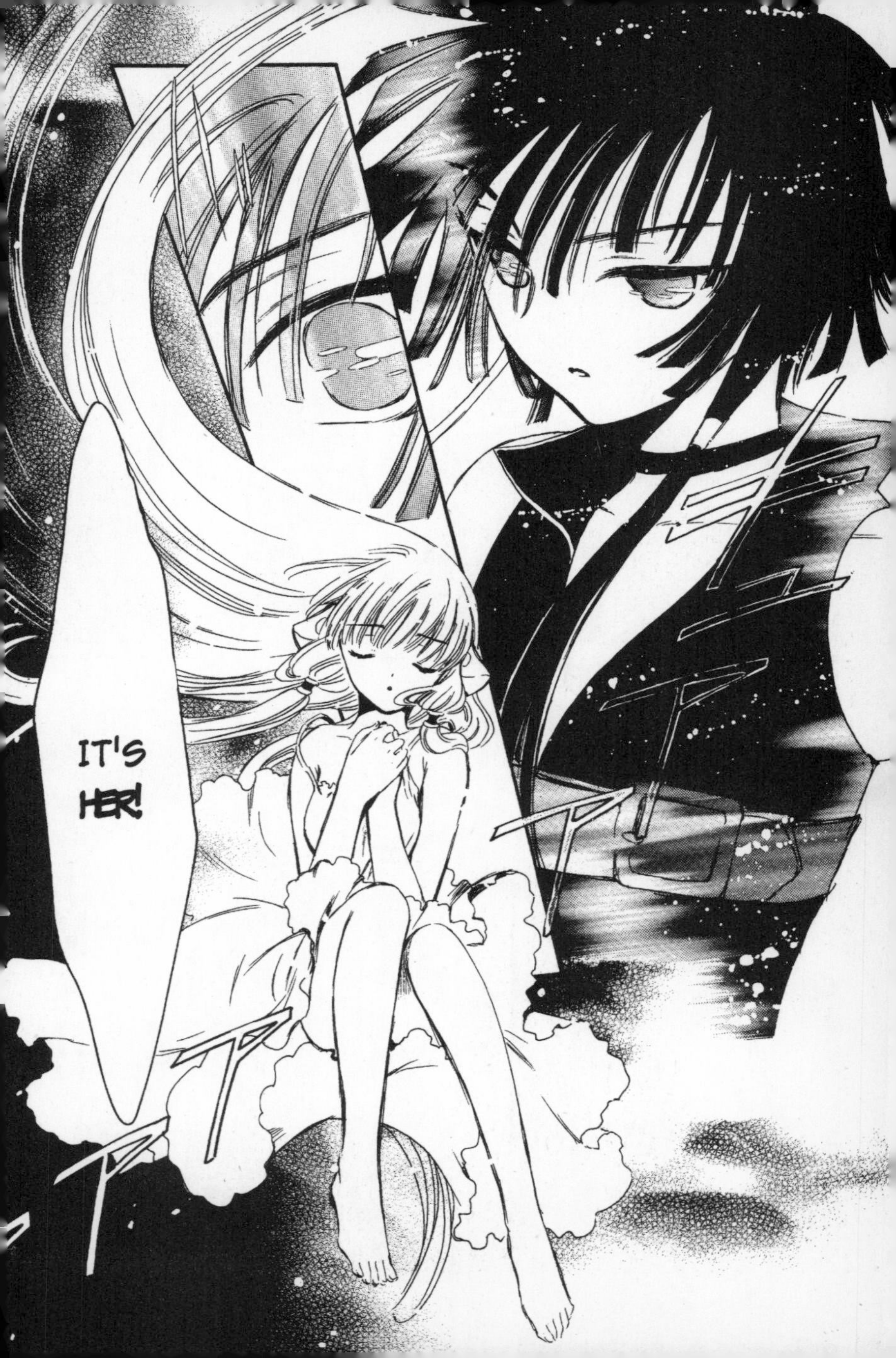
IT'S HER!

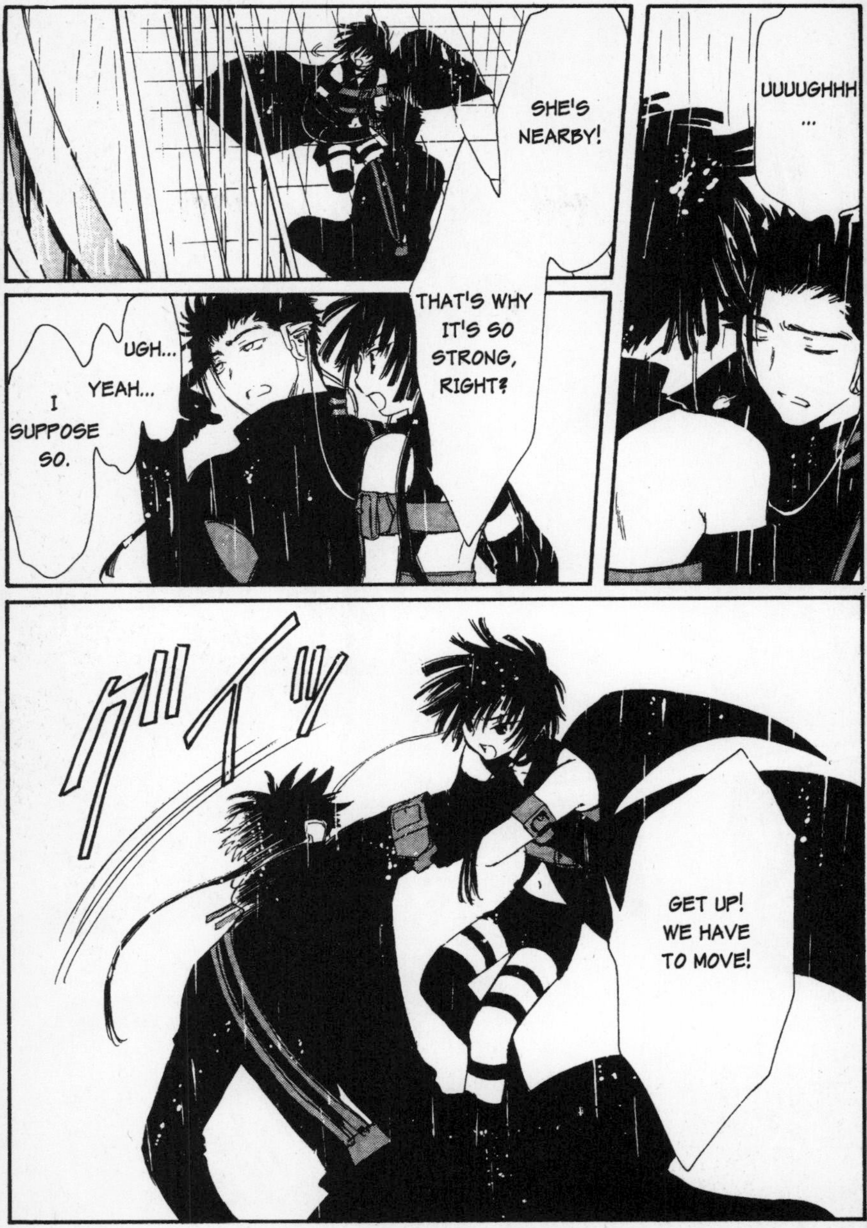
UUUUGHHH ...
SHE'S NEARBY!
THAT'S WHY IT'S SO STRONG, RIGHT?
UGH... YEAH... I SUPPOSE SO.
グイッ
GET UP! WE HAVE TO MOVE!

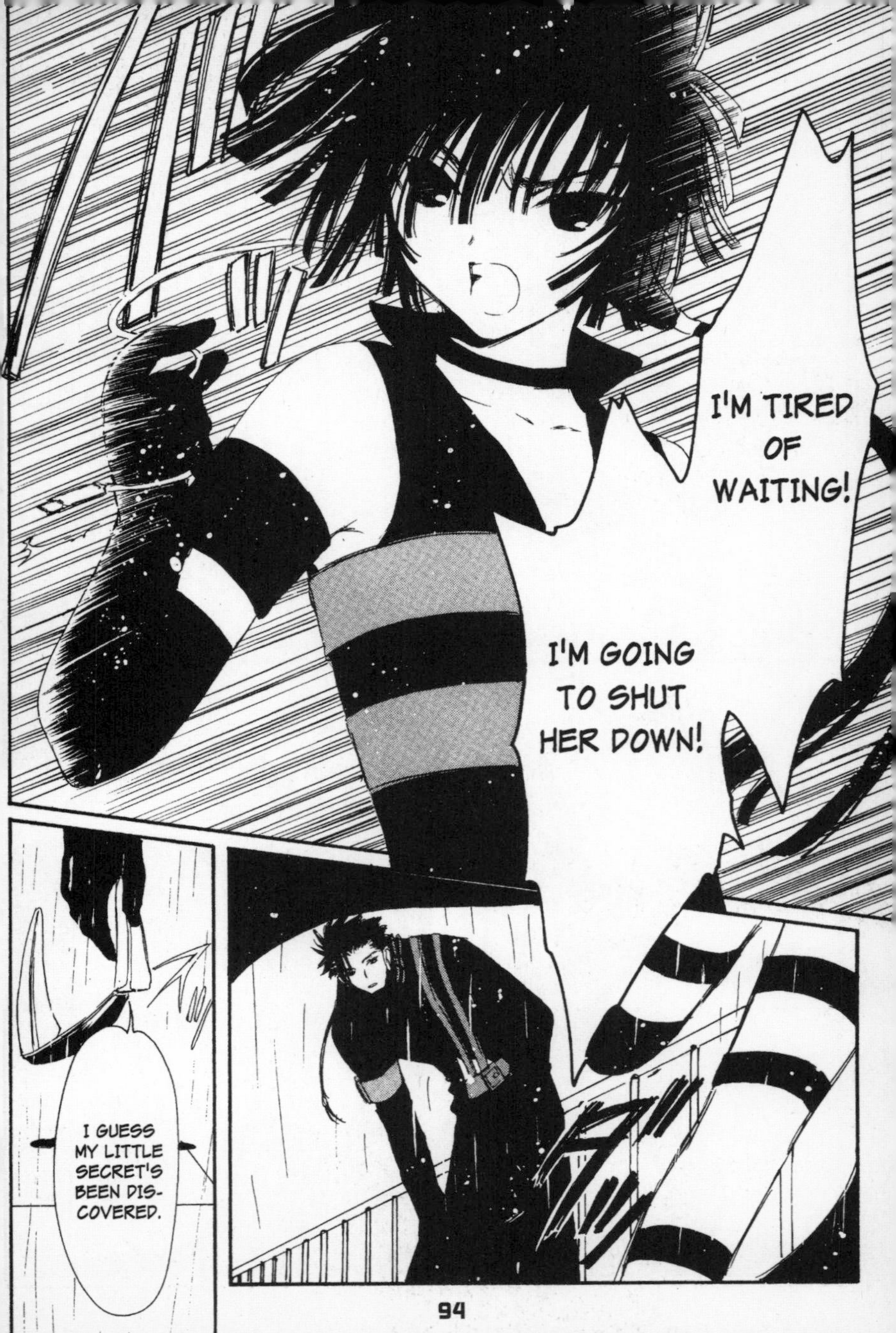
I'M TIRED OF WAITING!
I'M GOING TO SHUT HER DOWN!
I GUESS MY LITTLE SECRET'S BEEN DIS-COVERED.

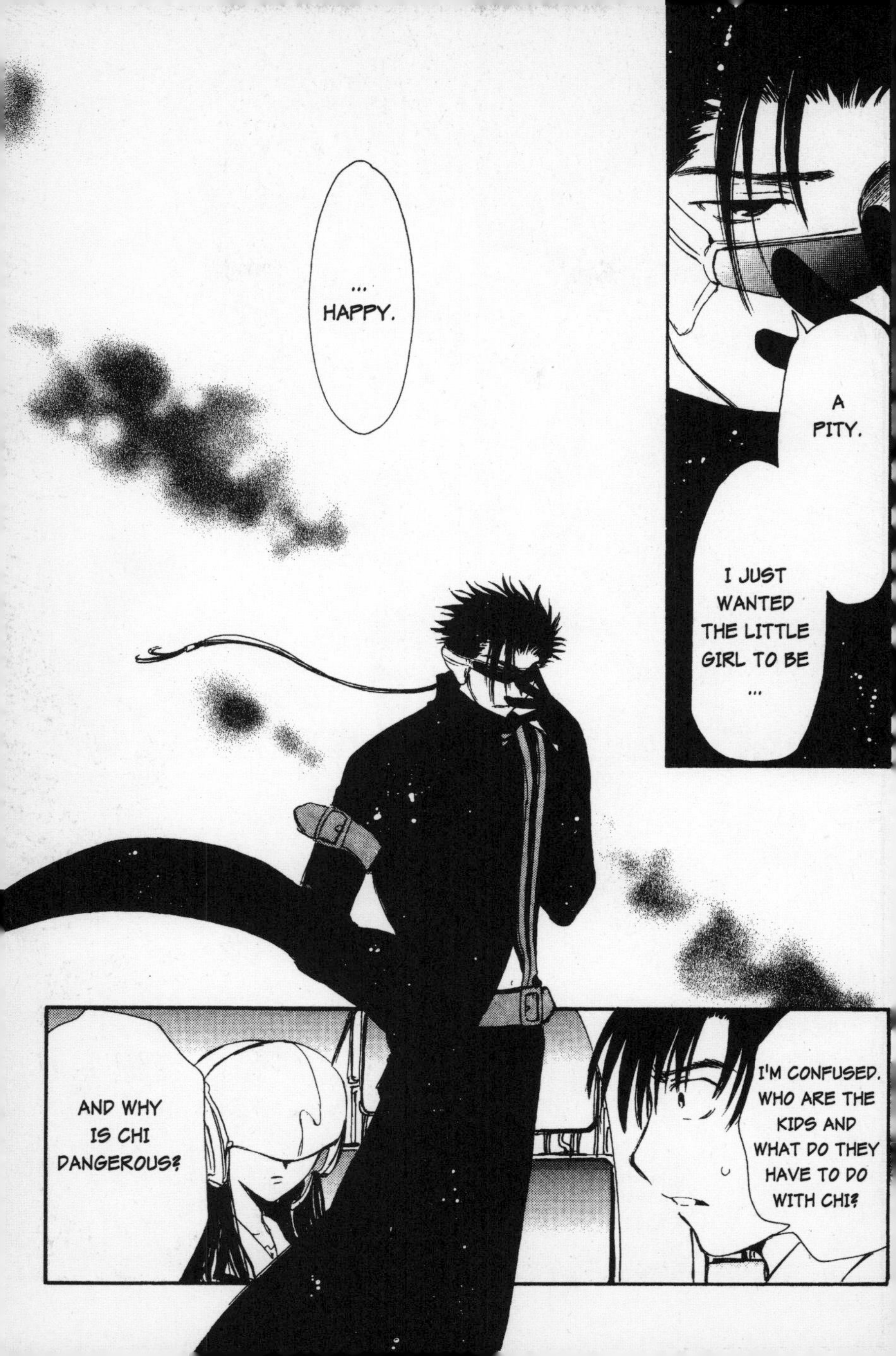
A PITY.
I JUST WANTED THE LITTLE GIRL TO BE ...
... HAPPY.
I'M CONFUSED. WHO ARE THE KIDS AND WHAT DO THEY HAVE TO DO WITH CHI?
AND WHY IS CHI DANGEROUS?

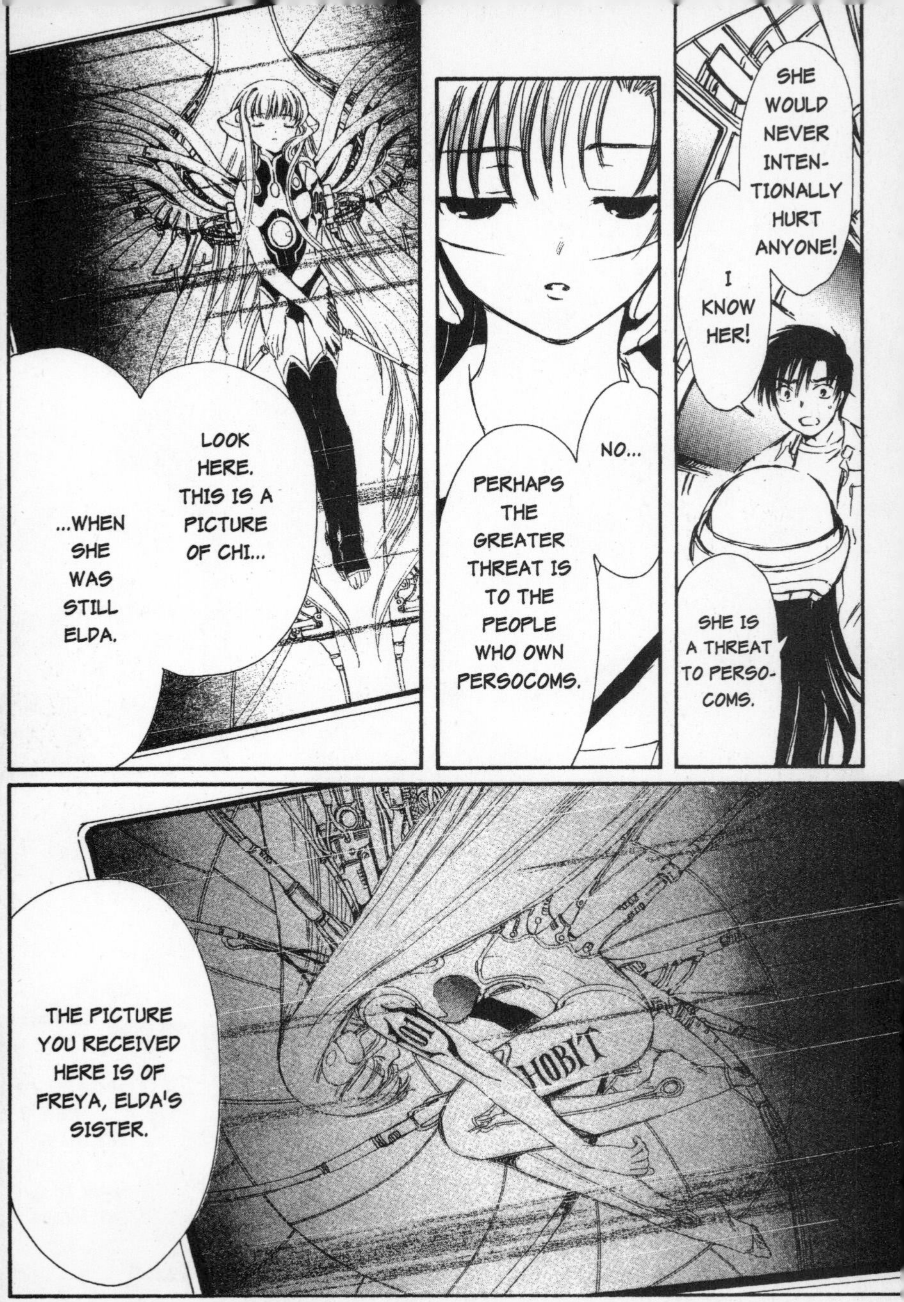
SHE WOULD NEVER INTENTIONALLY HURT ANYONE!
I KNOW HER!
SHE IS A THREAT TO PERSOCOMS.
NO...
PERHAPS THE GREATER THREAT IS TO THE PEOPLE WHO OWN PERSOCOMS.
LOOK HERE. THIS IS A PICTURE OF CHI...
...WHEN SHE WAS STILL ELDA.
HOBIT
THE PICTURE YOU RECEIVED HERE IS OF FREYA, ELDA'S SISTER.

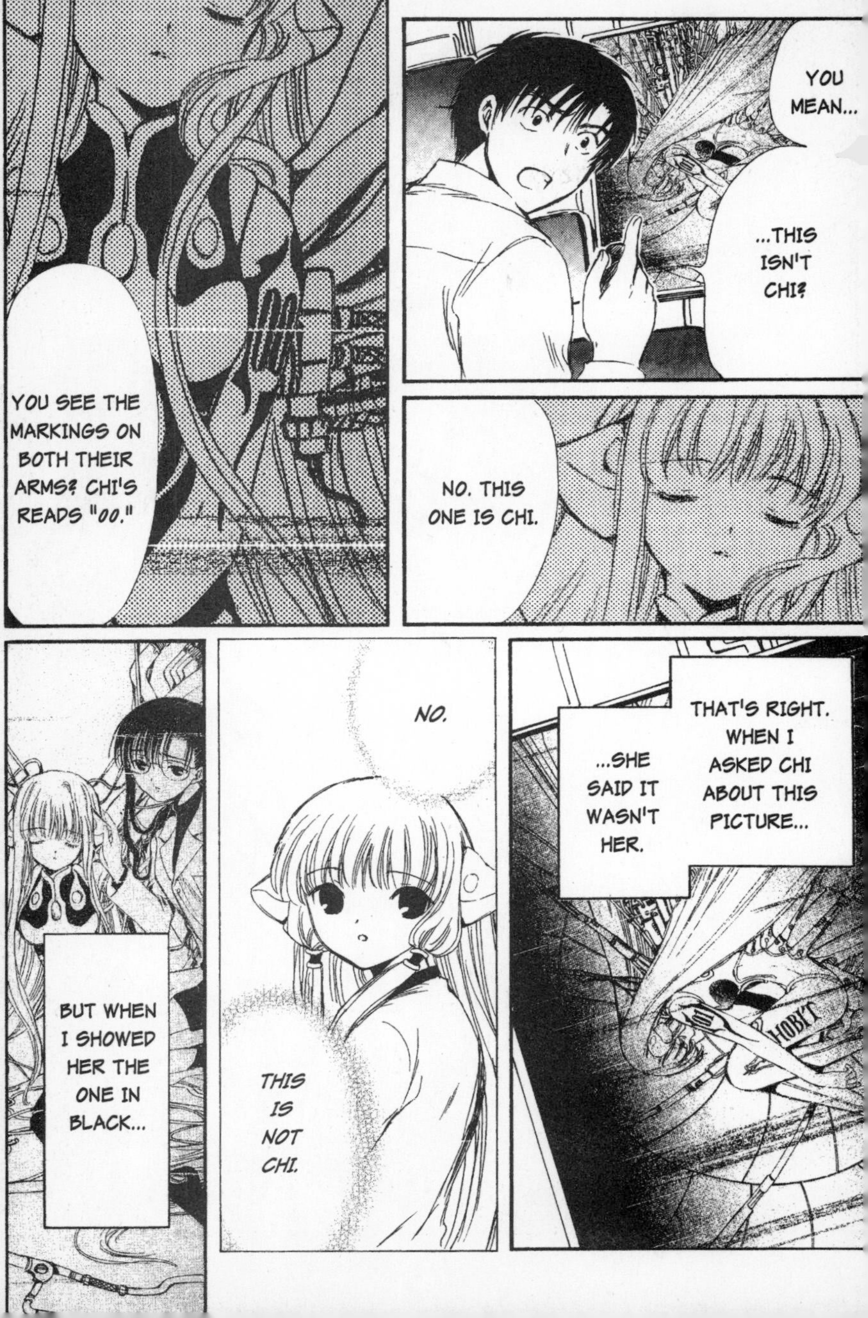
YOU MEAN...
...THIS ISN'T CHI?
NO. THIS ONE IS CHI.
YOU SEE THE MARKINGS ON BOTH THEIR ARMS? CHI'S READS "00."
THAT'S RIGHT. WHEN I ASKED CHI ABOUT THIS PICTURE...
...SHE SAID IT WASN'T HER.
NO.
THIS IS NOT CHI.
BUT WHEN I SHOWED HER THE ONE IN BLACK...

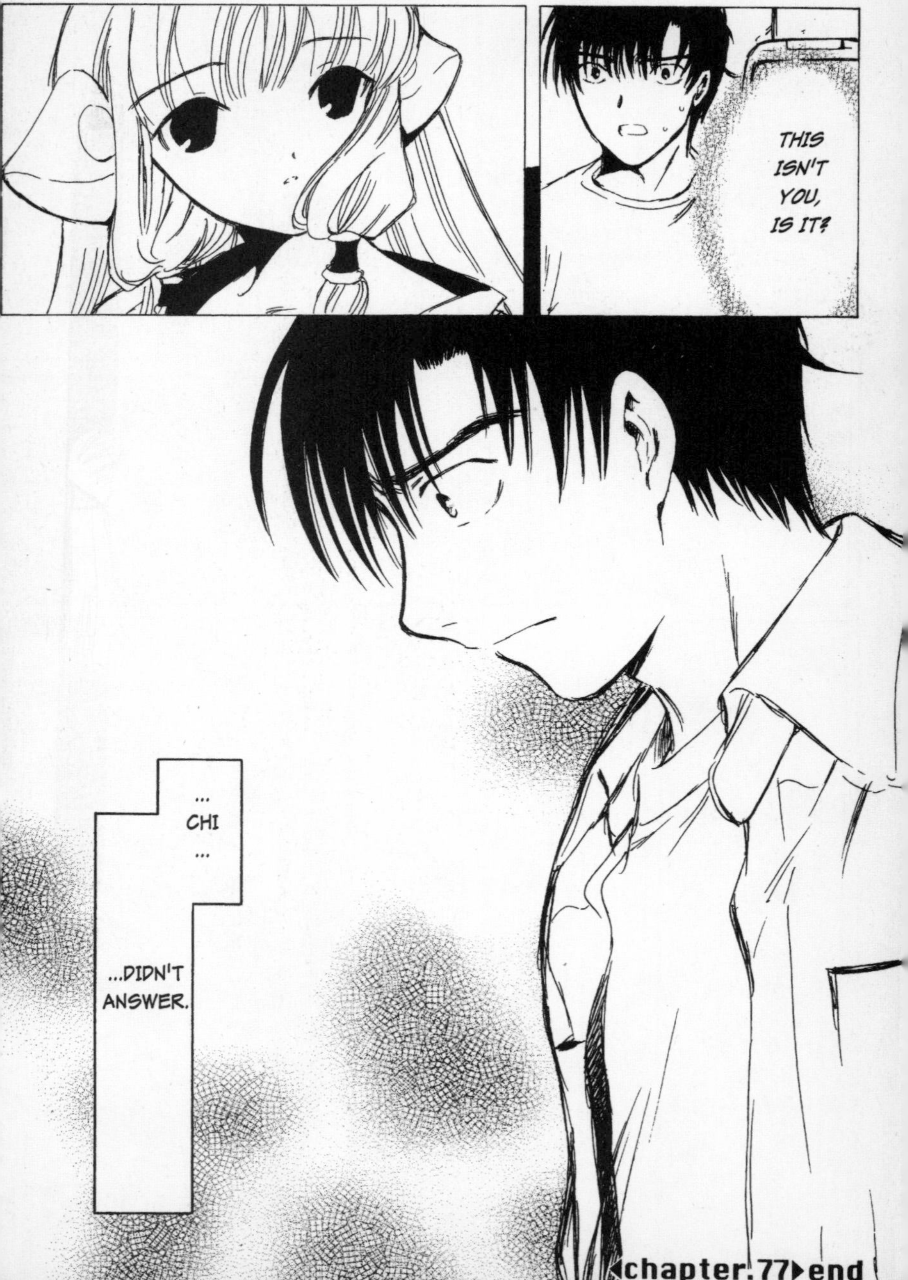
THIS ISN'T YOU, IS IT?
... CHI ...
...DIDN'T ANSWER.

chapter. 77 end

ちょびっツ
Chobits

◀**chapter.78**▶

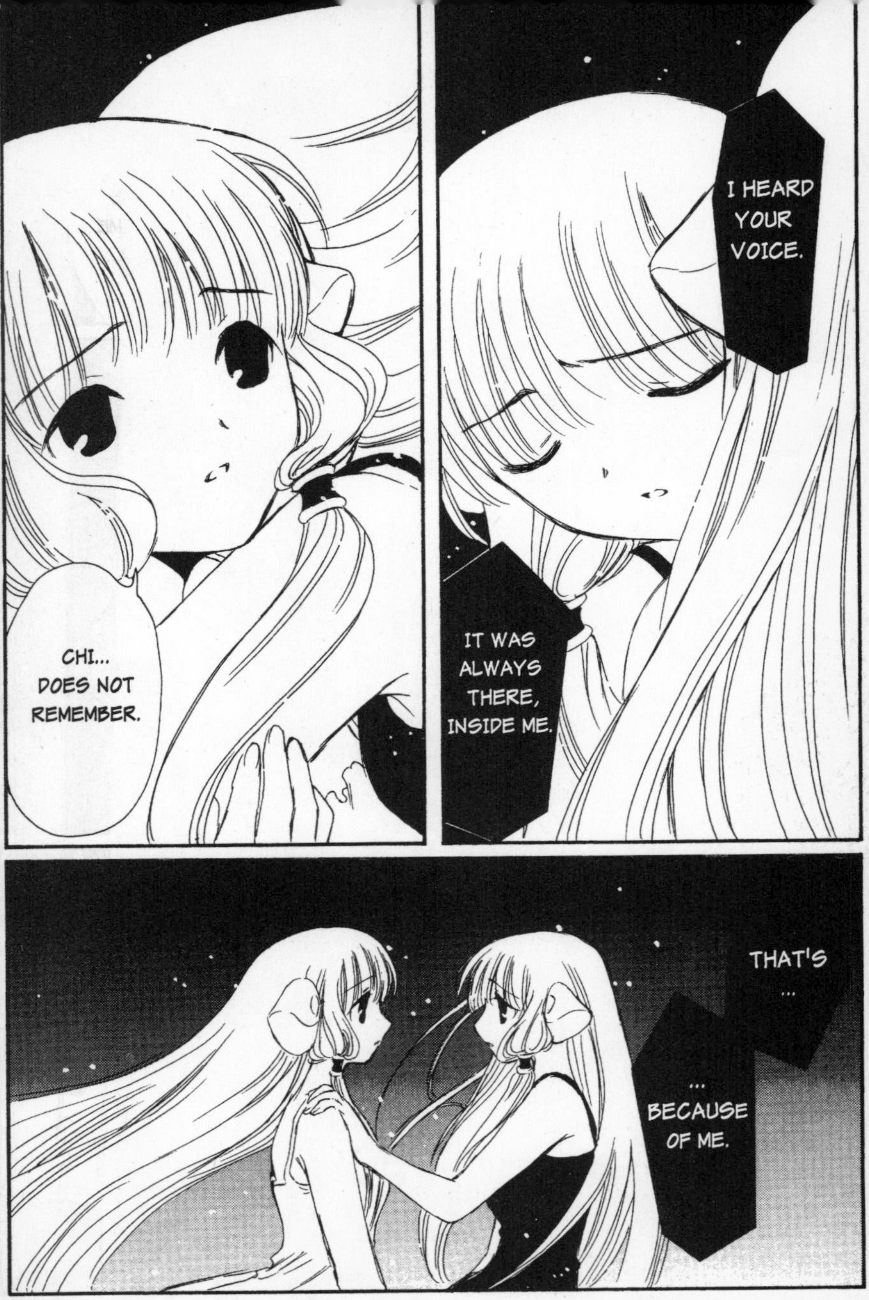
I HEARD YOUR VOICE.
IT WAS ALWAYS THERE, INSIDE ME.
CHI... DOES NOT REMEMBER.
THAT'S ...
... BECAUSE OF ME.

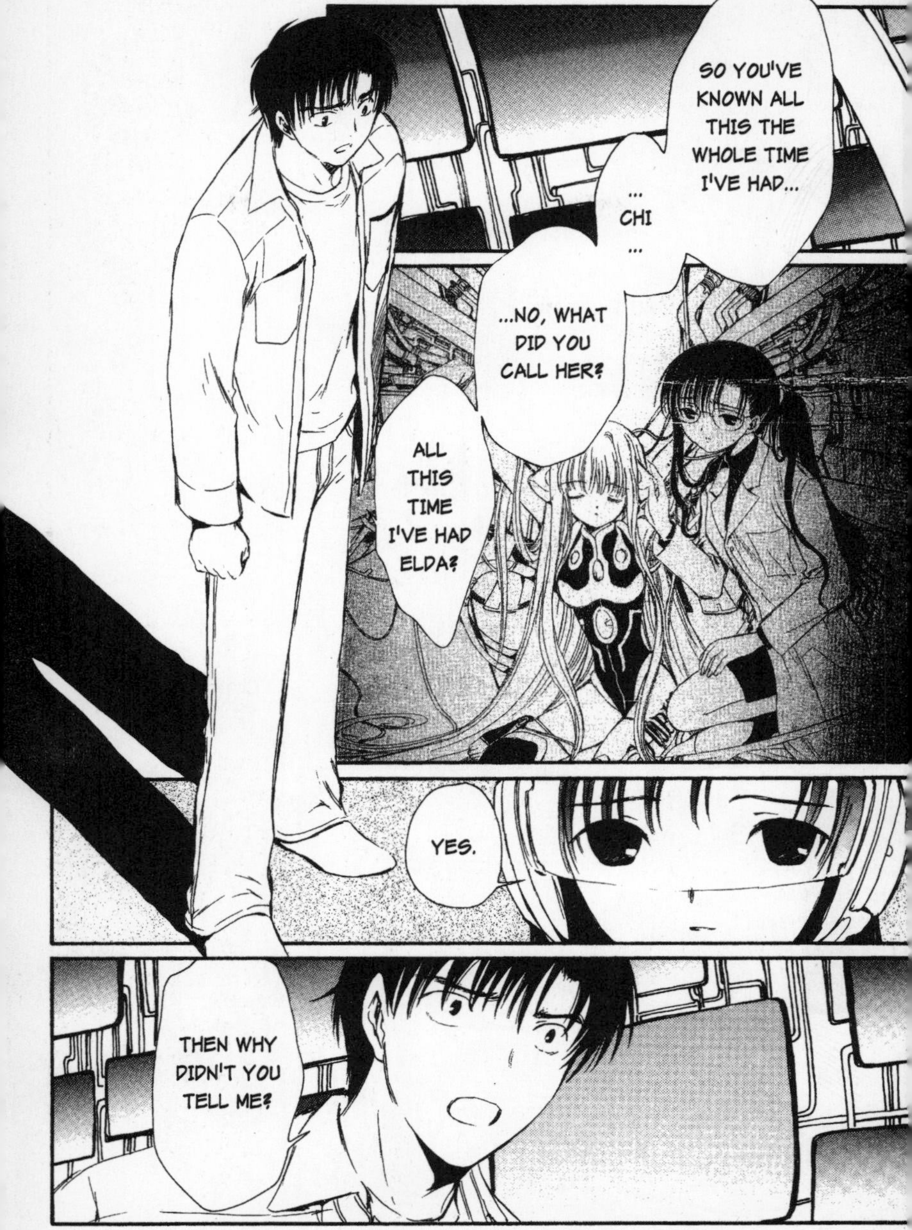
SO YOU'VE KNOWN ALL THIS THE WHOLE TIME I'VE HAD...
... CHI ...
...NO, WHAT DID YOU CALL HER?
ALL THIS TIME I'VE HAD ELDA?
YES.
THEN WHY DIDN'T YOU TELL ME?

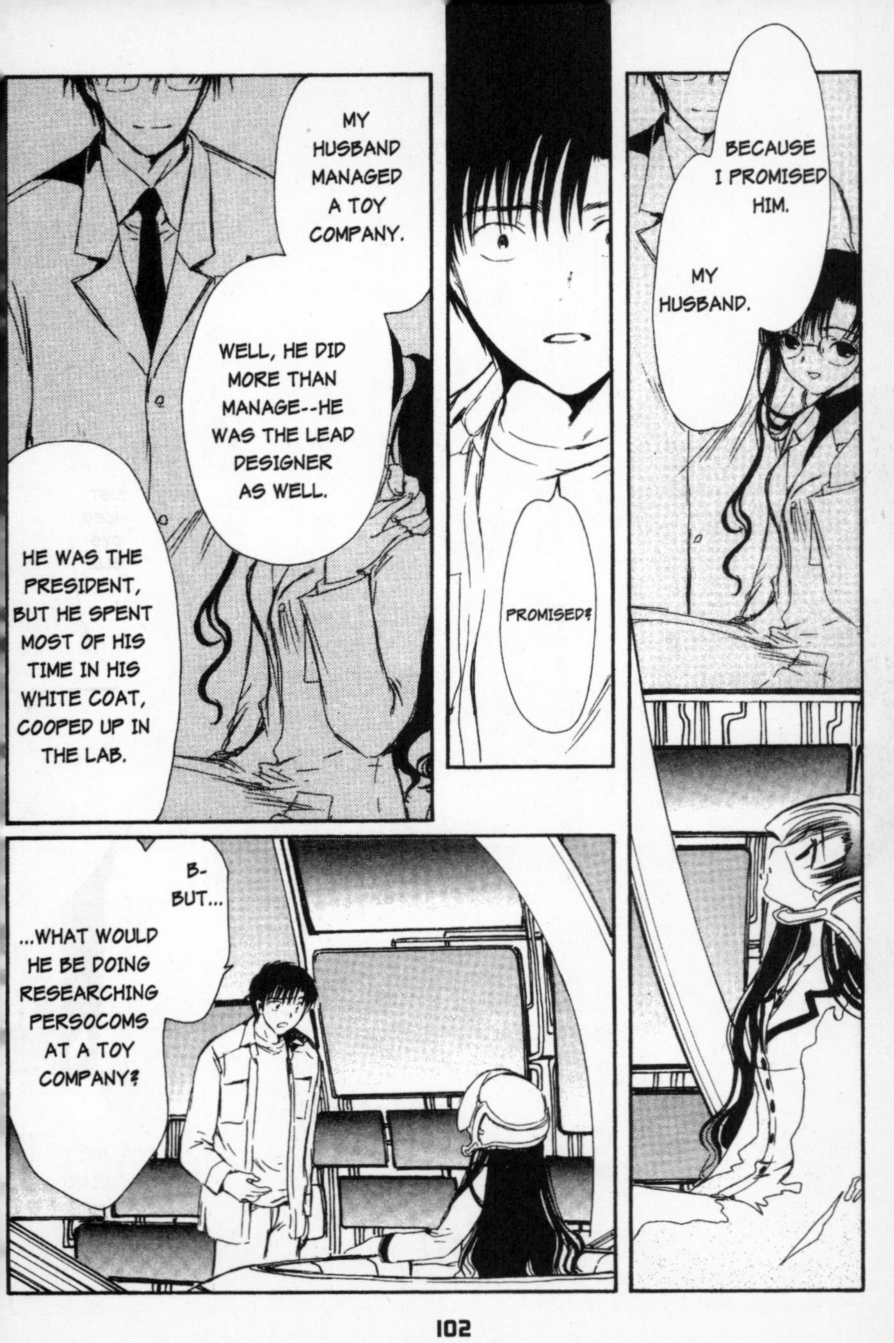
BECAUSE I PROMISED HIM.
MY HUSBAND.
PROMISED?
MY HUSBAND MANAGED A TOY COMPANY.
WELL, HE DID MORE THAN MANAGE--HE WAS THE LEAD DESIGNER AS WELL.
HE WAS THE PRESIDENT, BUT HE SPENT MOST OF HIS TIME IN HIS WHITE COAT, COOPED UP IN THE LAB.
B-BUT...
...WHAT WOULD HE BE DOING RESEARCHING PERSOCOMS AT A TOY COMPANY?

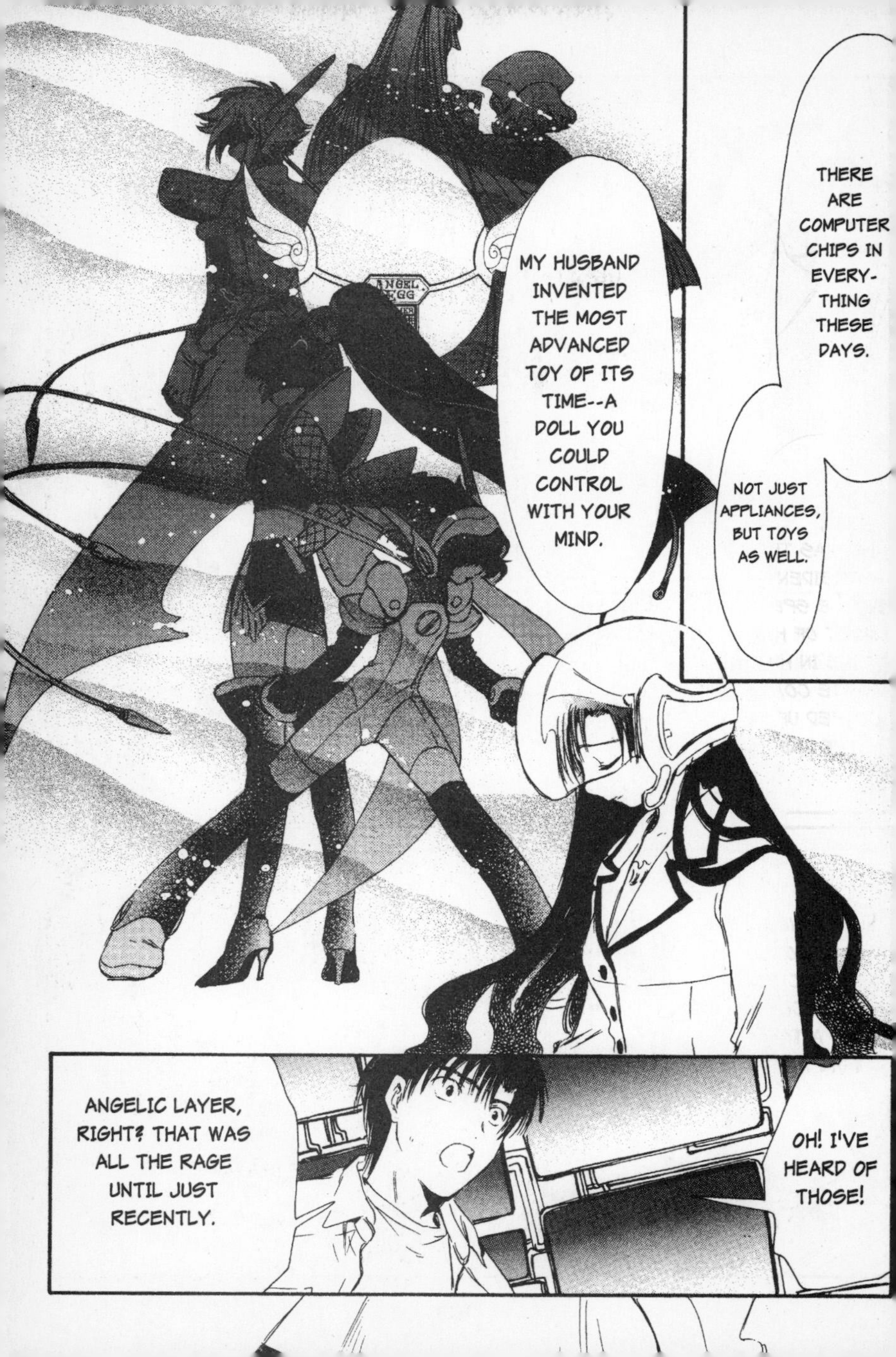
THERE ARE COMPUTER CHIPS IN EVERYTHING THESE DAYS.
NOT JUST APPLIANCES, BUT TOYS AS WELL.
MY HUSBAND INVENTED THE MOST ADVANCED TOY OF ITS TIME--A DOLL YOU COULD CONTROL WITH YOUR MIND.
OH! I'VE HEARD OF THOSE!
ANGELIC LAYER, RIGHT? THAT WAS ALL THE RAGE UNTIL JUST RECENTLY.

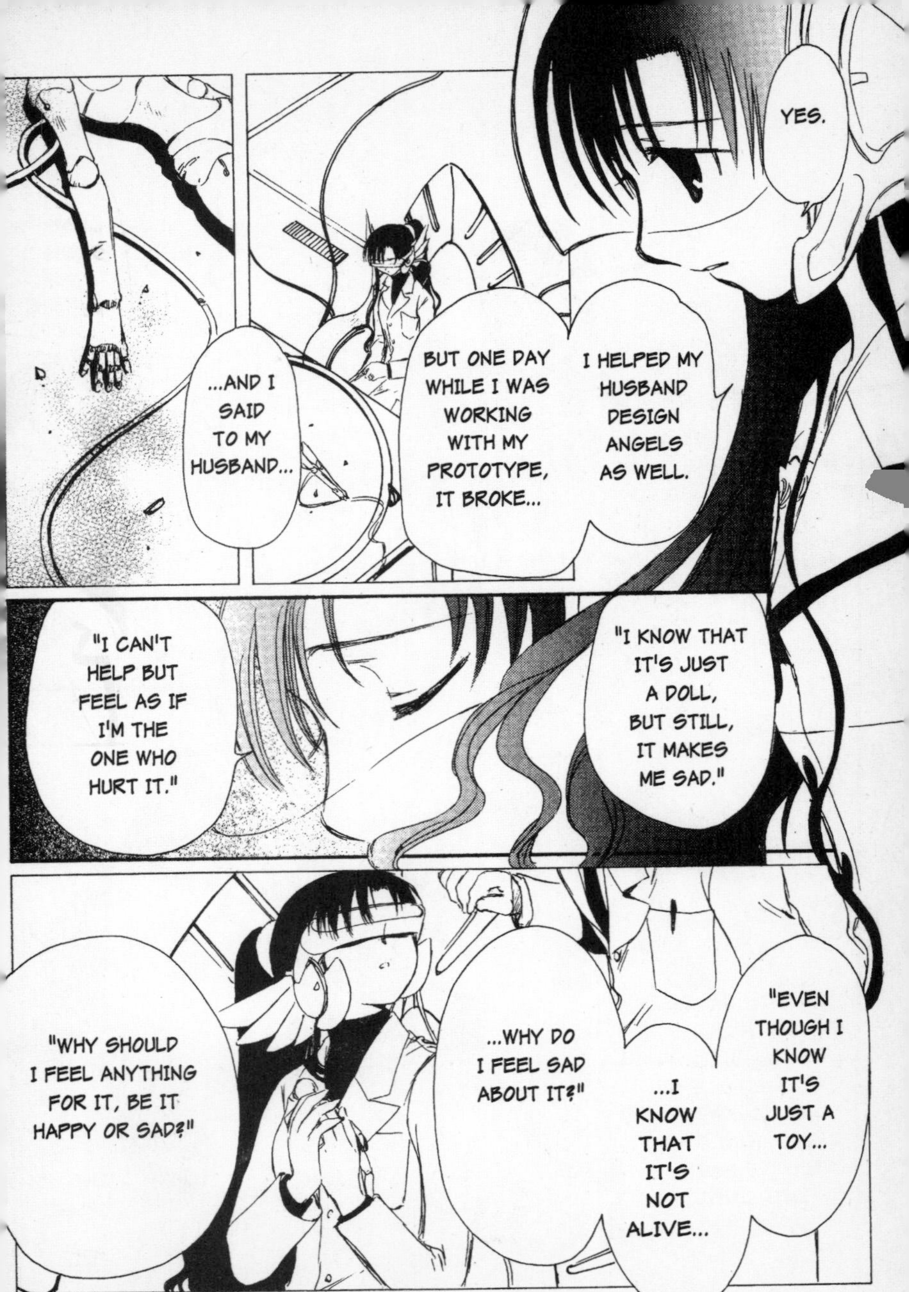
YES.
I HELPED MY HUSBAND DESIGN ANGELS AS WELL.
BUT ONE DAY WHILE I WAS WORKING WITH MY PROTOTYPE, IT BROKE...
...AND I SAID TO MY HUSBAND...
"I KNOW THAT IT'S JUST A DOLL, BUT STILL, IT MAKES ME SAD."
"I CAN'T HELP BUT FEEL AS IF I'M THE ONE WHO HURT IT."
"EVEN THOUGH I KNOW IT'S JUST A TOY...
...I KNOW THAT IT'S NOT ALIVE...
...WHY DO I FEEL SAD ABOUT IT?"
"WHY SHOULD I FEEL ANYTHING FOR IT, BE IT HAPPY OR SAD?"

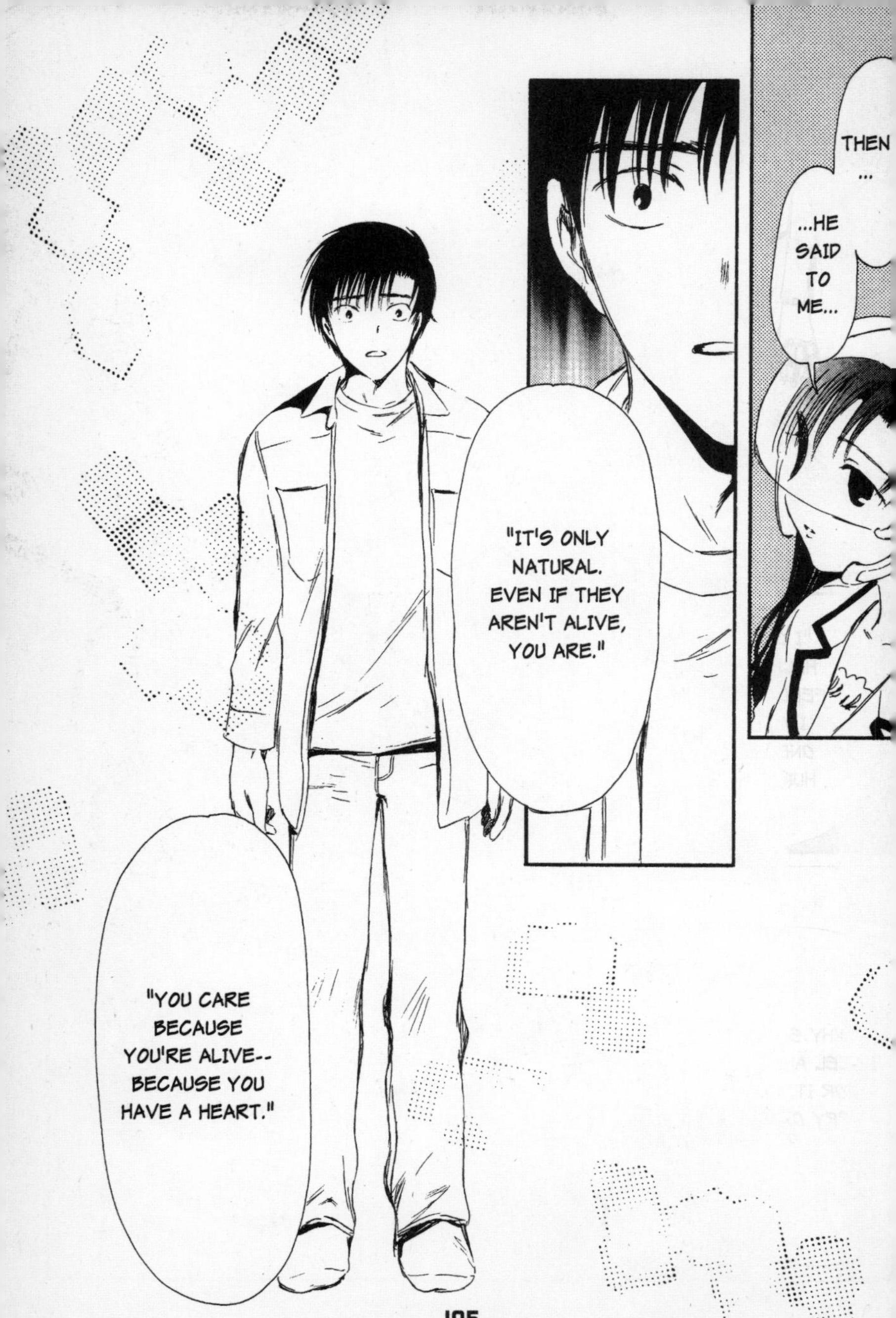
THEN ...
...HE SAID TO ME...
"IT'S ONLY NATURAL. EVEN IF THEY AREN'T ALIVE, YOU ARE."
"YOU CARE BECAUSE YOU'RE ALIVE-- BECAUSE YOU HAVE A HEART."

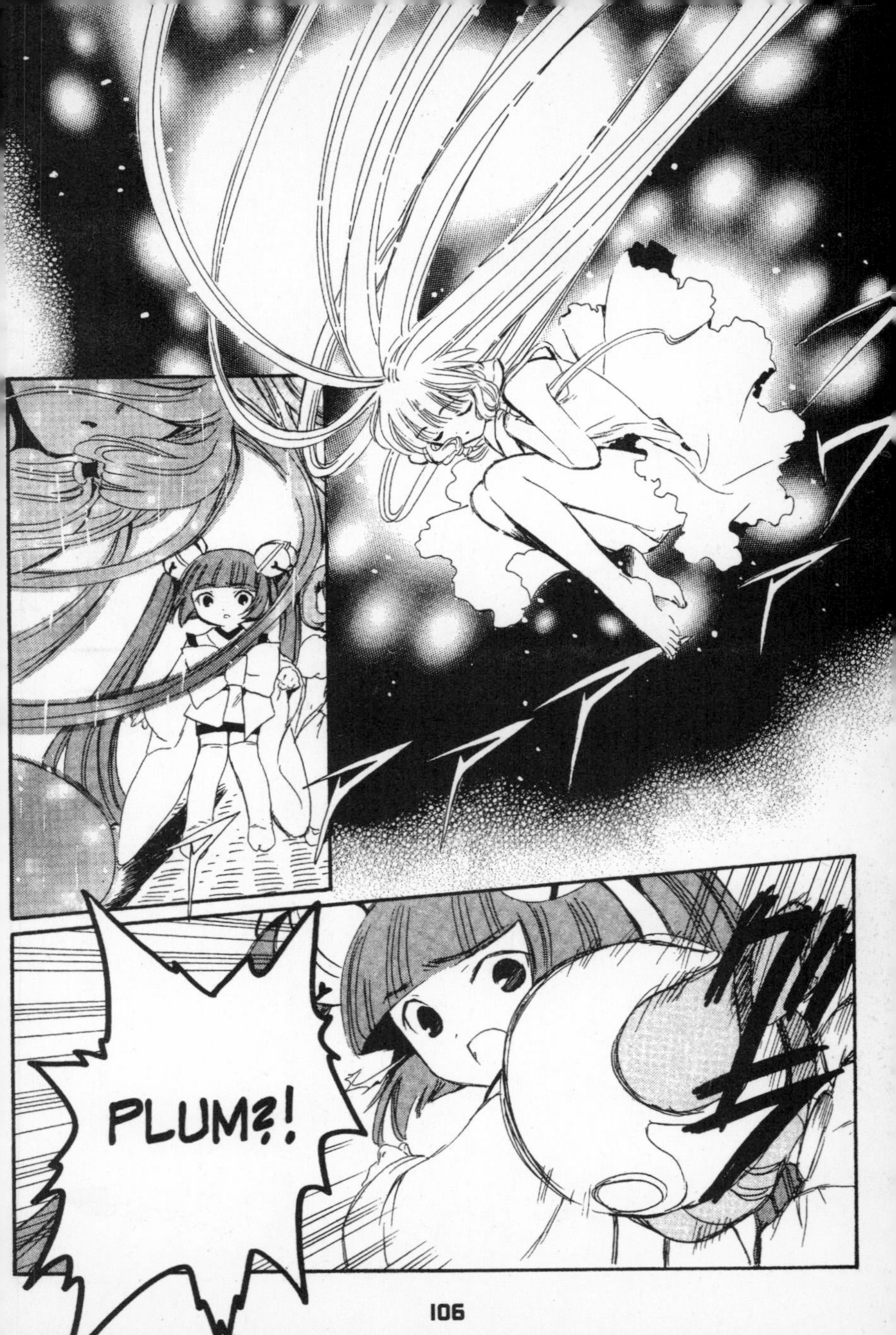
PLUM?!

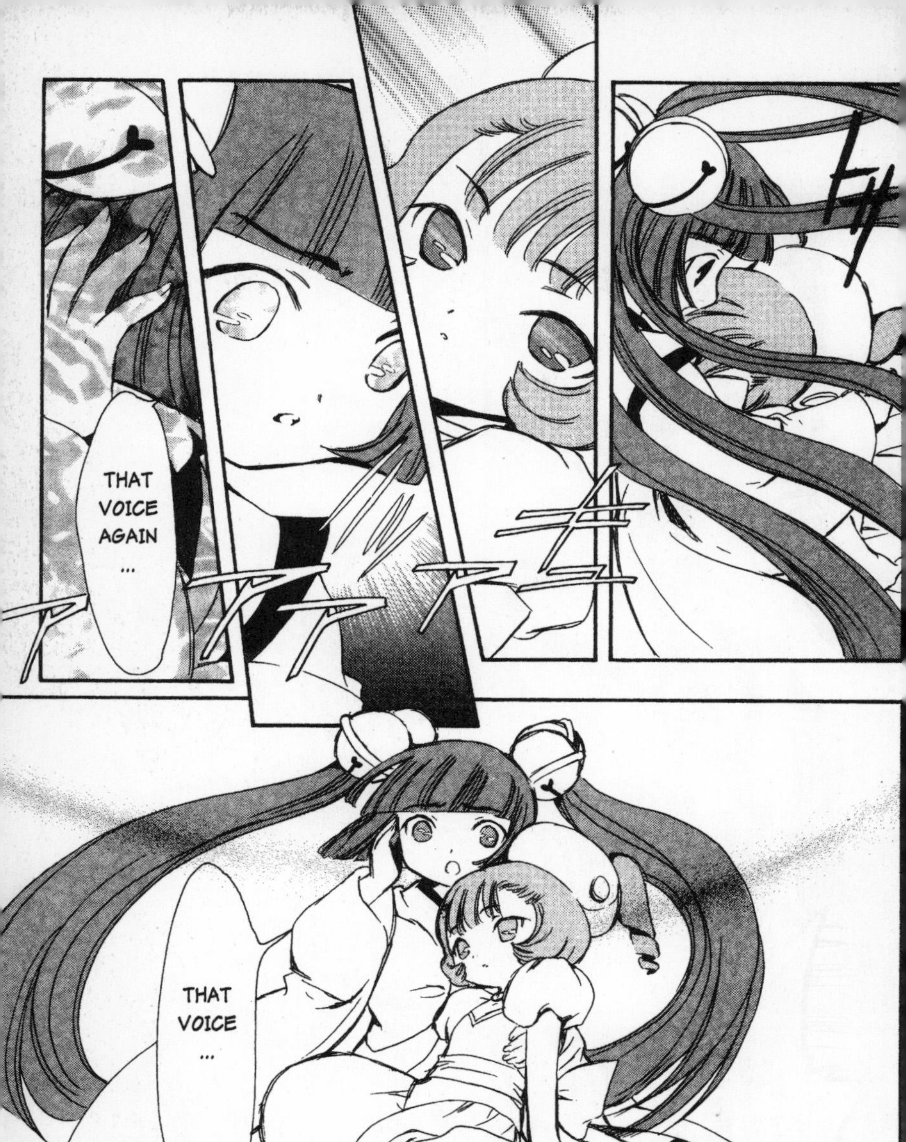
THAT VOICE AGAIN ...
THAT VOICE ...

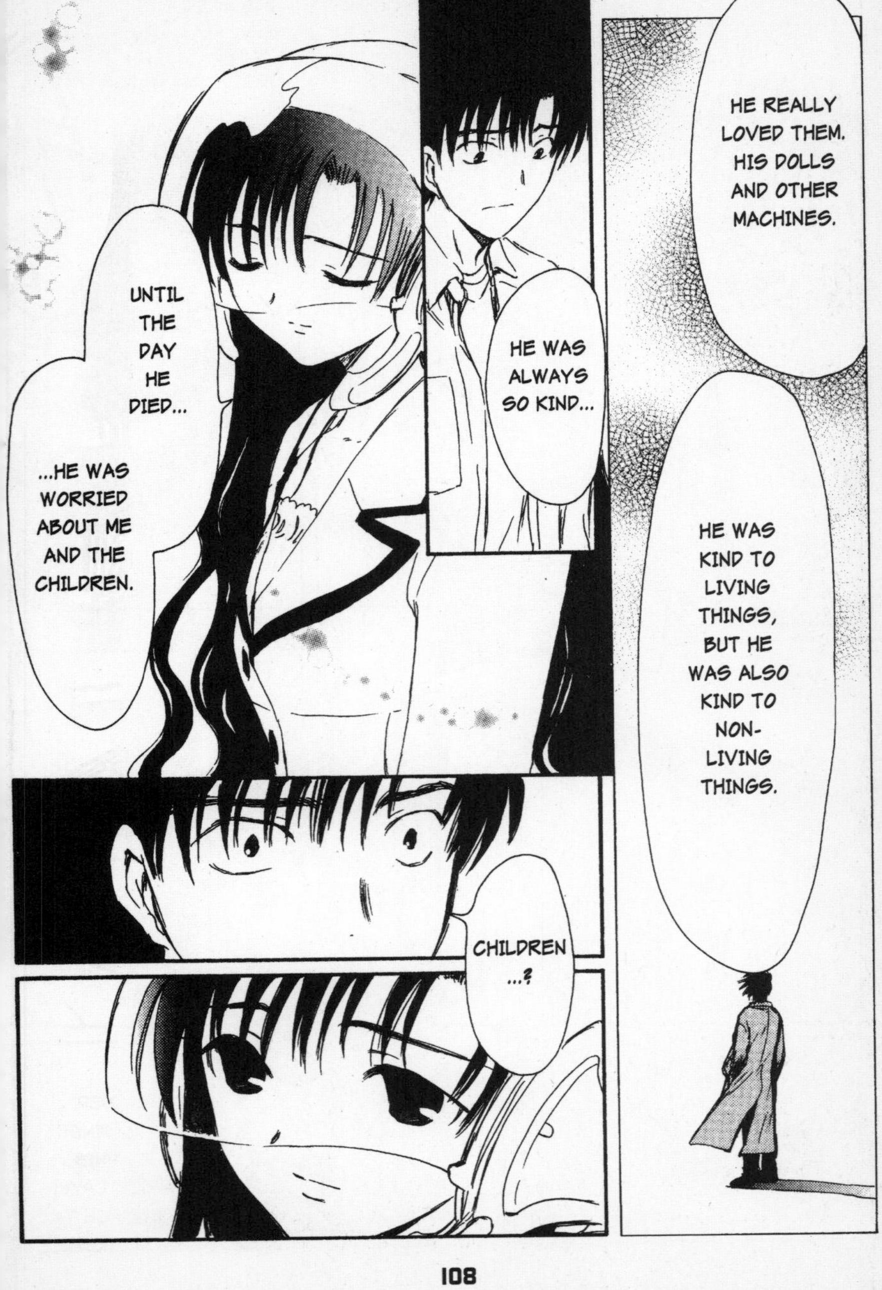
HE REALLY LOVED THEM. HIS DOLLS AND OTHER MACHINES.
HE WAS KIND TO LIVING THINGS, BUT HE WAS ALSO KIND TO NON-LIVING THINGS.
HE WAS ALWAYS SO KIND...
UNTIL THE DAY HE DIED...
...HE WAS WORRIED ABOUT ME AND THE CHILDREN.
CHILDREN ...?

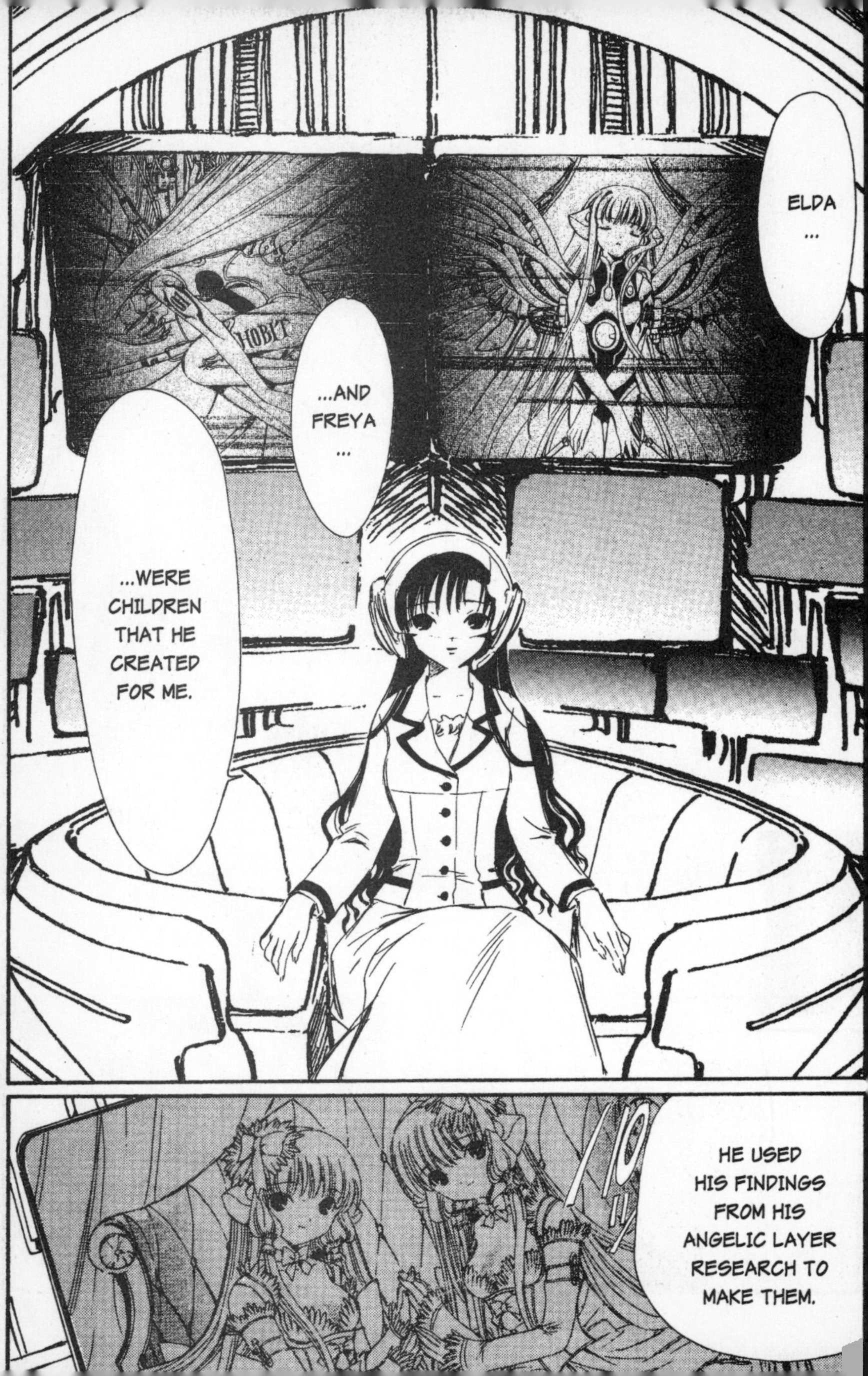
ELDA ...
HOBIT
...AND FREYA ...
...WERE CHILDREN THAT HE CREATED FOR ME.
HE USED HIS FINDINGS FROM HIS ANGELIC LAYER RESEARCH TO MAKE THEM.

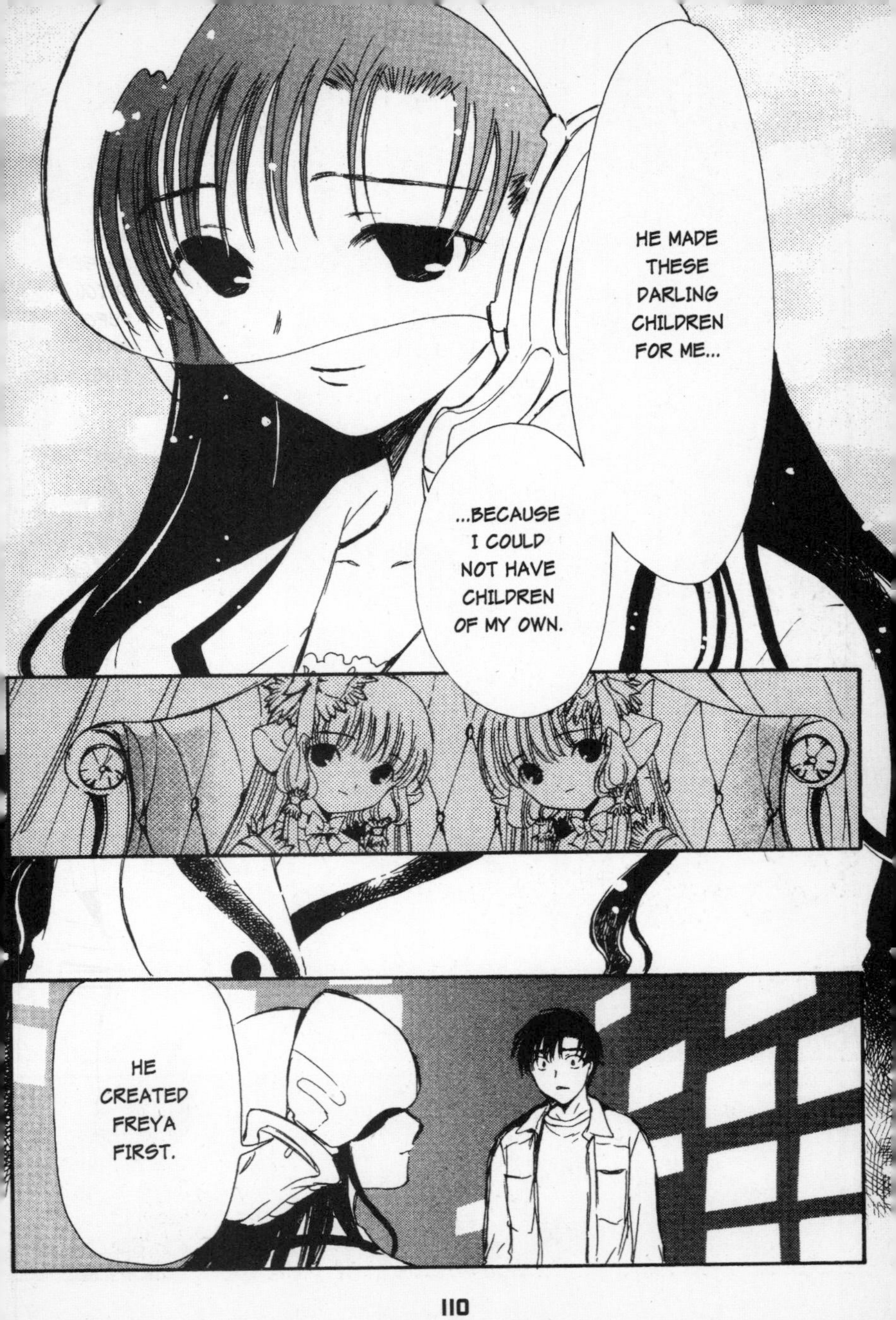
HE MADE THESE DARLING CHILDREN FOR ME...
...BECAUSE I COULD NOT HAVE CHILDREN OF MY OWN.
HE CREATED FREYA FIRST.

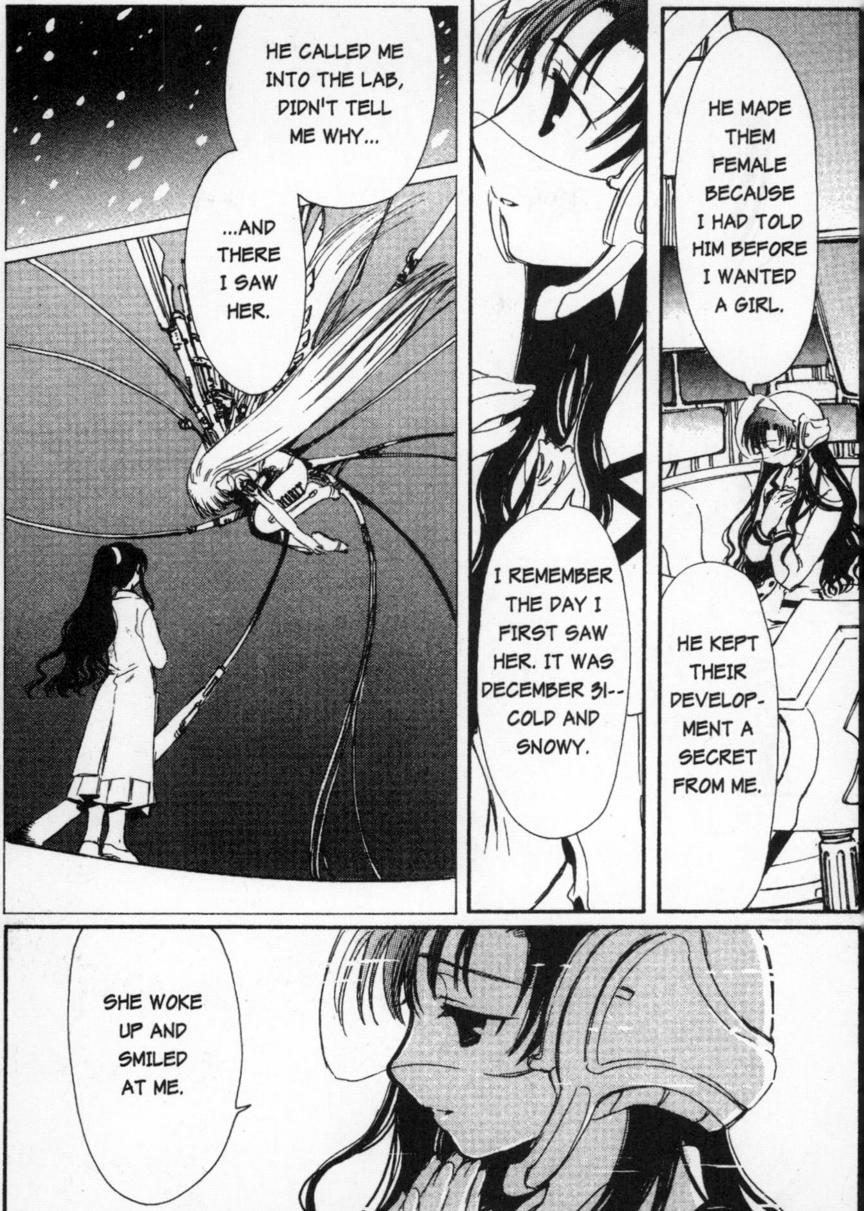
HE MADE THEM FEMALE BECAUSE I HAD TOLD HIM BEFORE I WANTED A GIRL.
HE KEPT THEIR DEVELOP-MENT A SECRET FROM ME.
I REMEMBER THE DAY I FIRST SAW HER. IT WAS DECEMBER 31--COLD AND SNOWY.
HE CALLED ME INTO THE LAB, DIDN'T TELL ME WHY...
...AND THERE I SAW HER.
SHE WOKE UP AND SMILED AT ME.

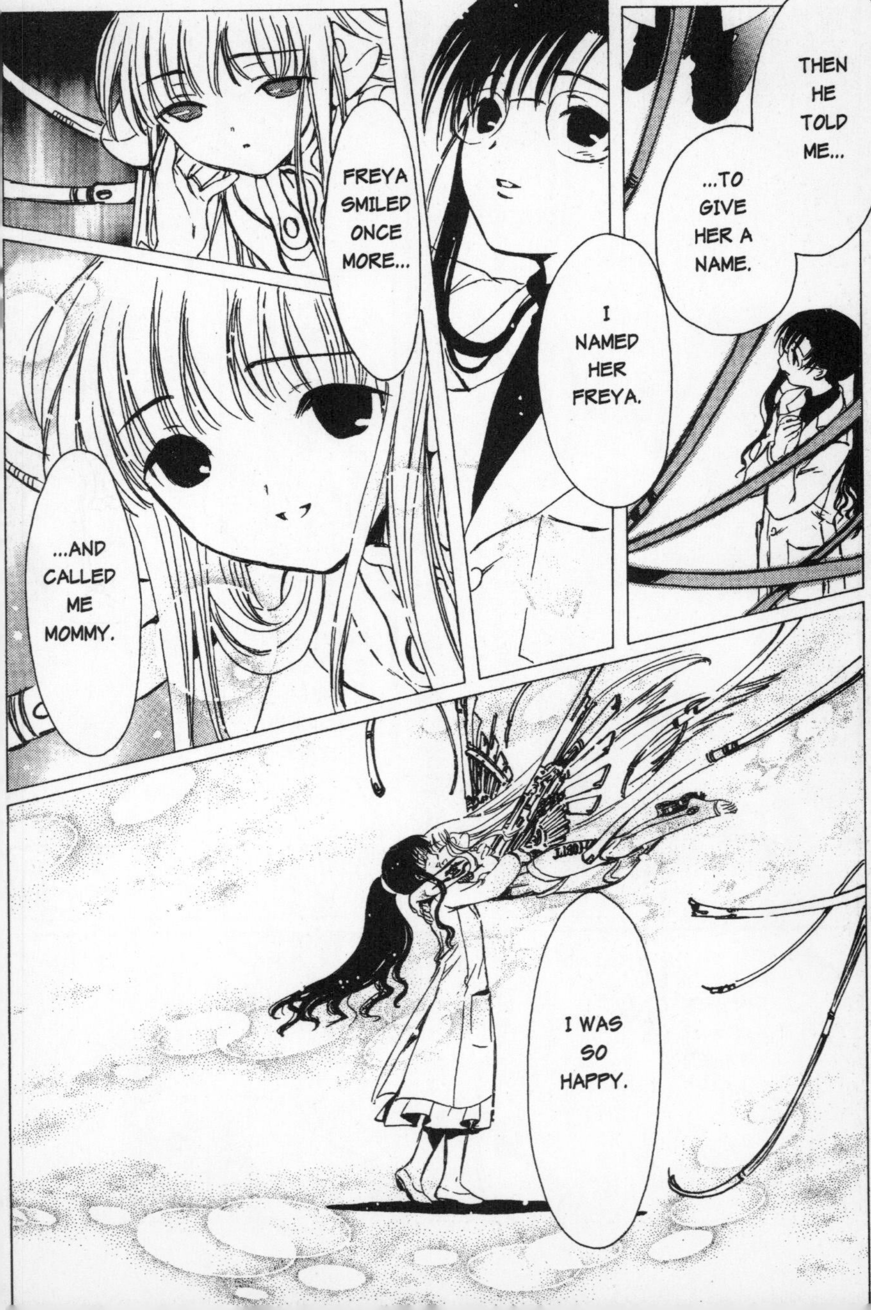
THEN HE TOLD ME...
...TO GIVE HER A NAME.
I NAMED HER FREYA.
FREYA SMILED ONCE MORE...
...AND CALLED ME MOMMY.
I WAS SO HAPPY.

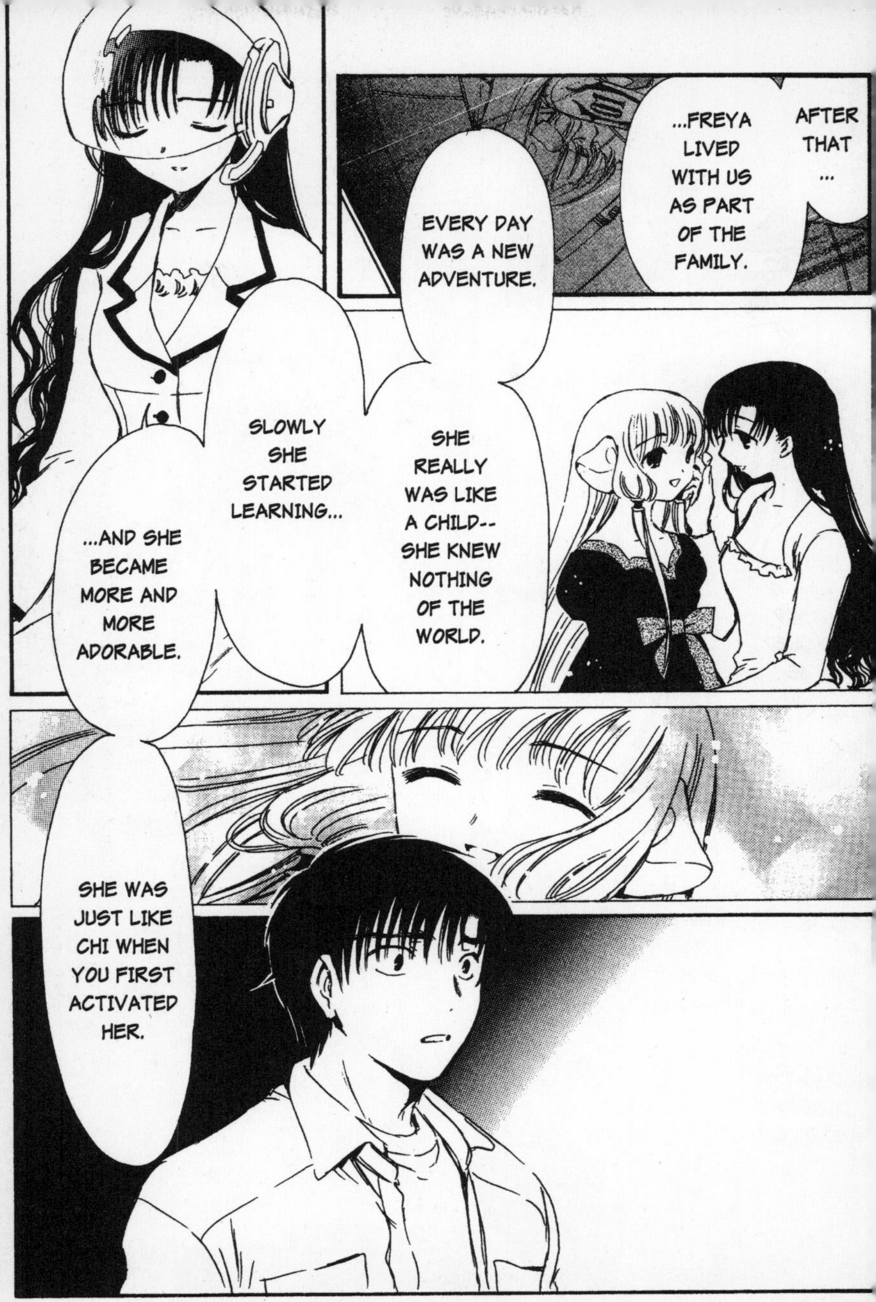
AFTER THAT ...
...FREYA LIVED WITH US AS PART OF THE FAMILY.
EVERY DAY WAS A NEW ADVENTURE.
SHE REALLY WAS LIKE A CHILD-- SHE KNEW NOTHING OF THE WORLD.
SLOWLY SHE STARTED LEARNING...
...AND SHE BECAME MORE AND MORE ADORABLE.
SHE WAS JUST LIKE CHI WHEN YOU FIRST ACTIVATED HER.

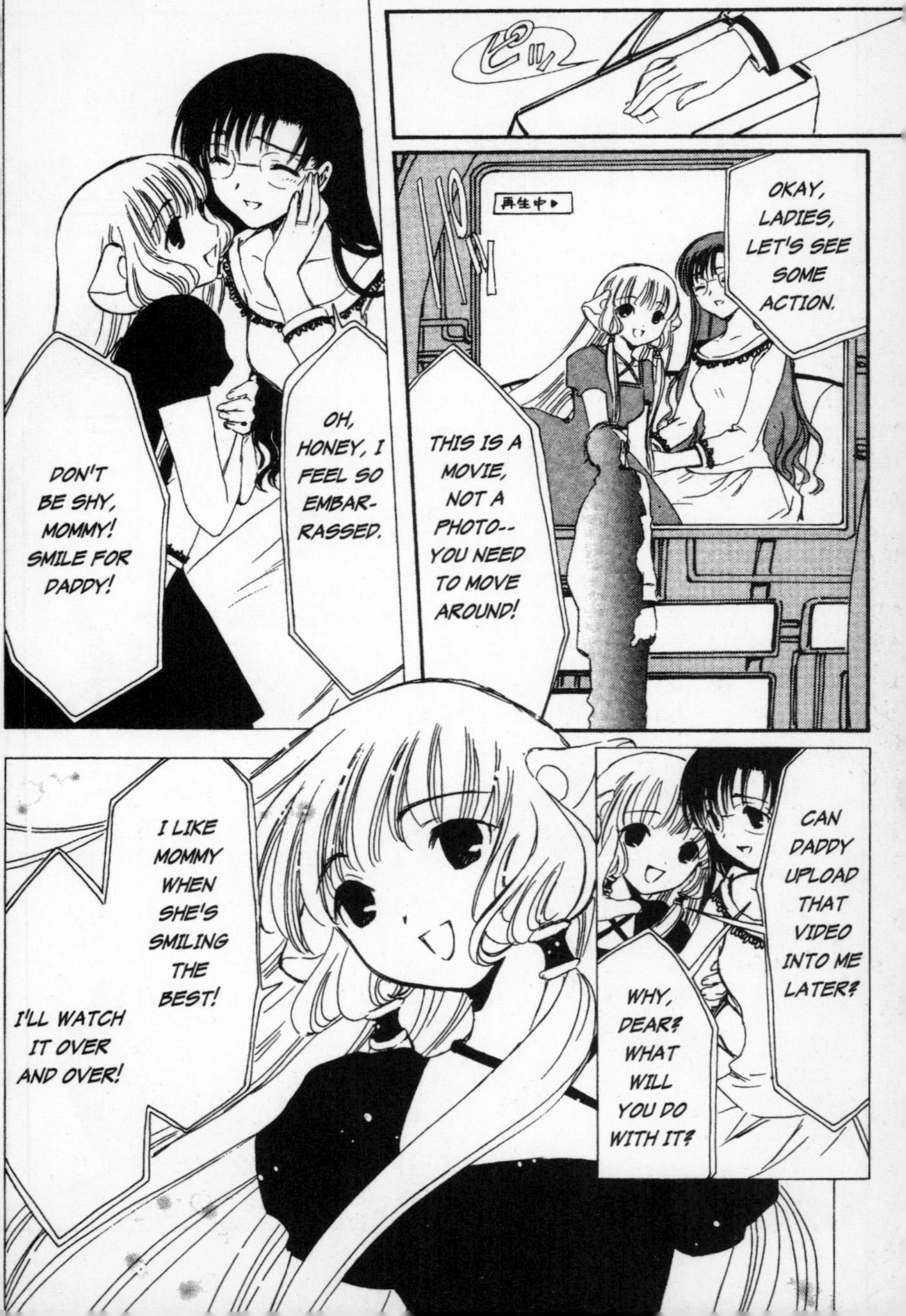
再生中▶
OKAY, LADIES, LET'S SEE SOME ACTION.
THIS IS A MOVIE, NOT A PHOTO-- YOU NEED TO MOVE AROUND!
OH, HONEY, I FEEL SO EMBARRASSED.
DON'T BE SHY, MOMMY! SMILE FOR DADDY!
CAN DADDY UPLOAD THAT VIDEO INTO ME LATER?
WHY, DEAR? WHAT WILL YOU DO WITH IT?
I LIKE MOMMY WHEN SHE'S SMILING THE BEST!
I'LL WATCH IT OVER AND OVER!

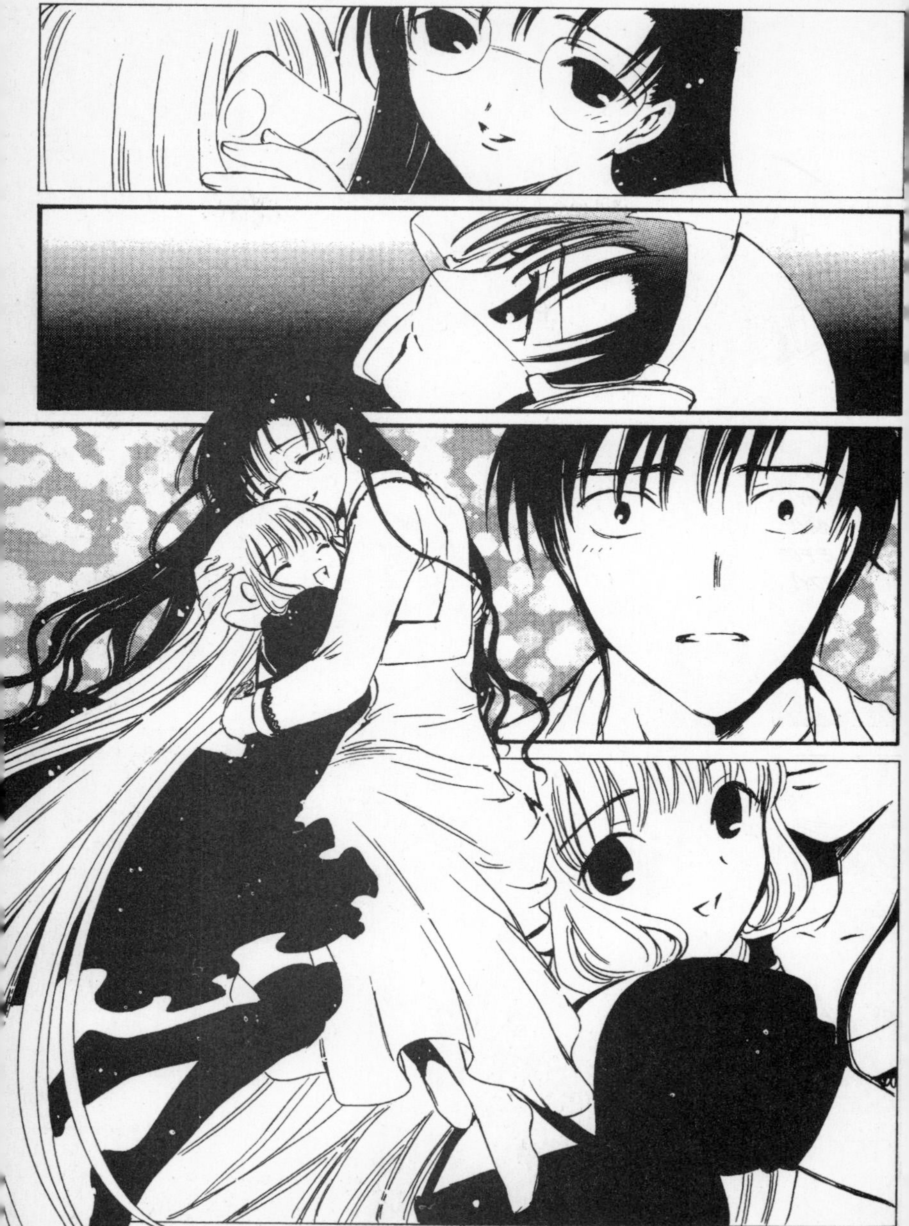

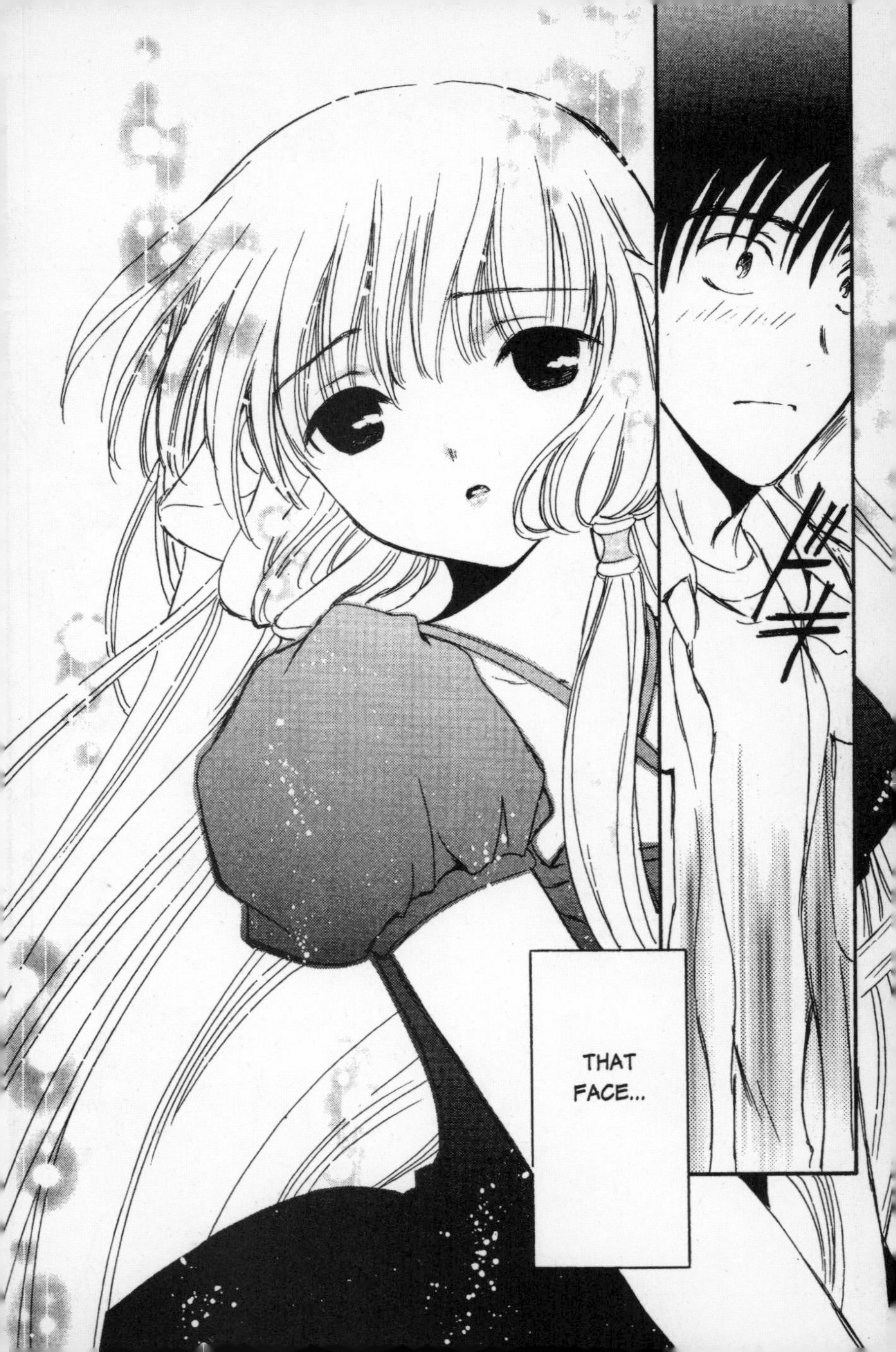
THAT FACE...

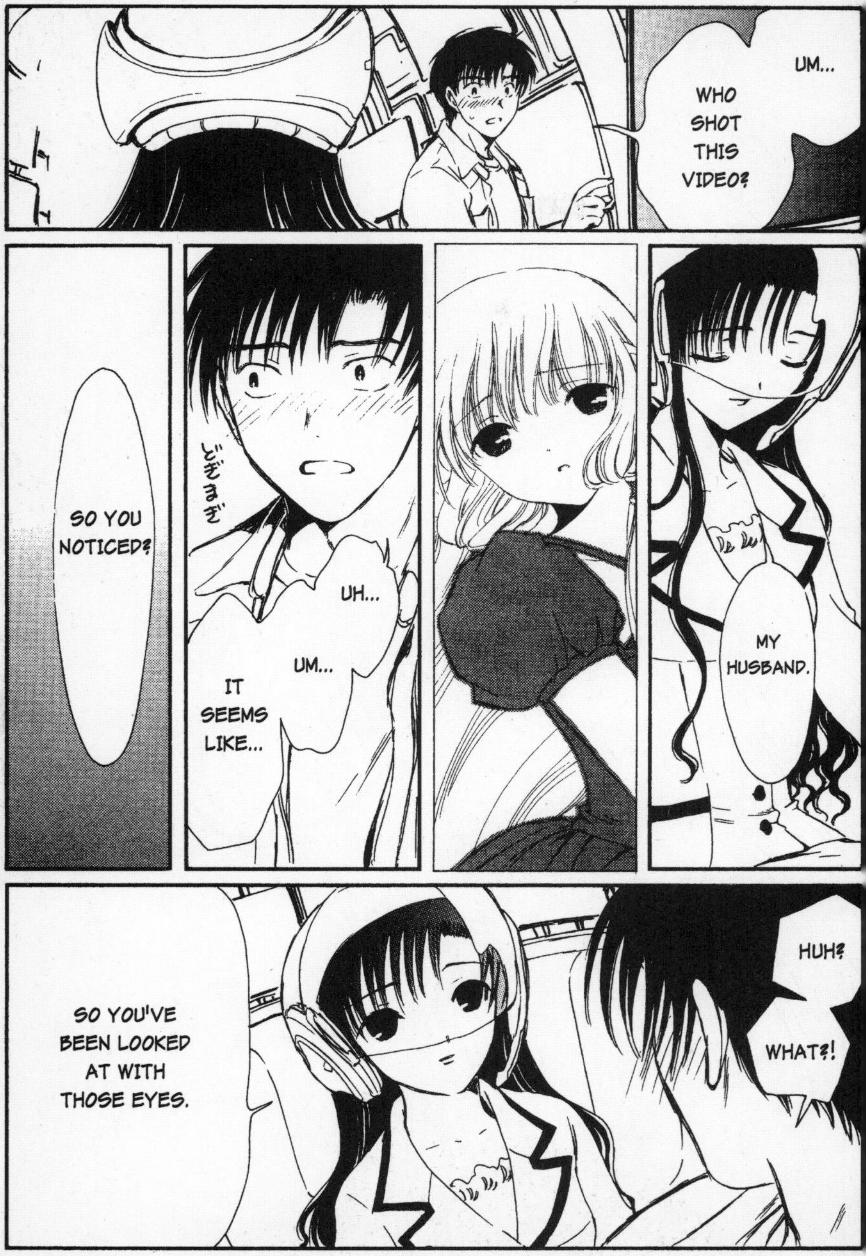
UM...
WHO SHOT THIS VIDEO?
MY HUSBAND.
UH...
UM...
IT SEEMS LIKE...
どぎまぎ
SO YOU NOTICED?
HUH?
WHAT?!
SO YOU'VE BEEN LOOKED AT WITH THOSE EYES.

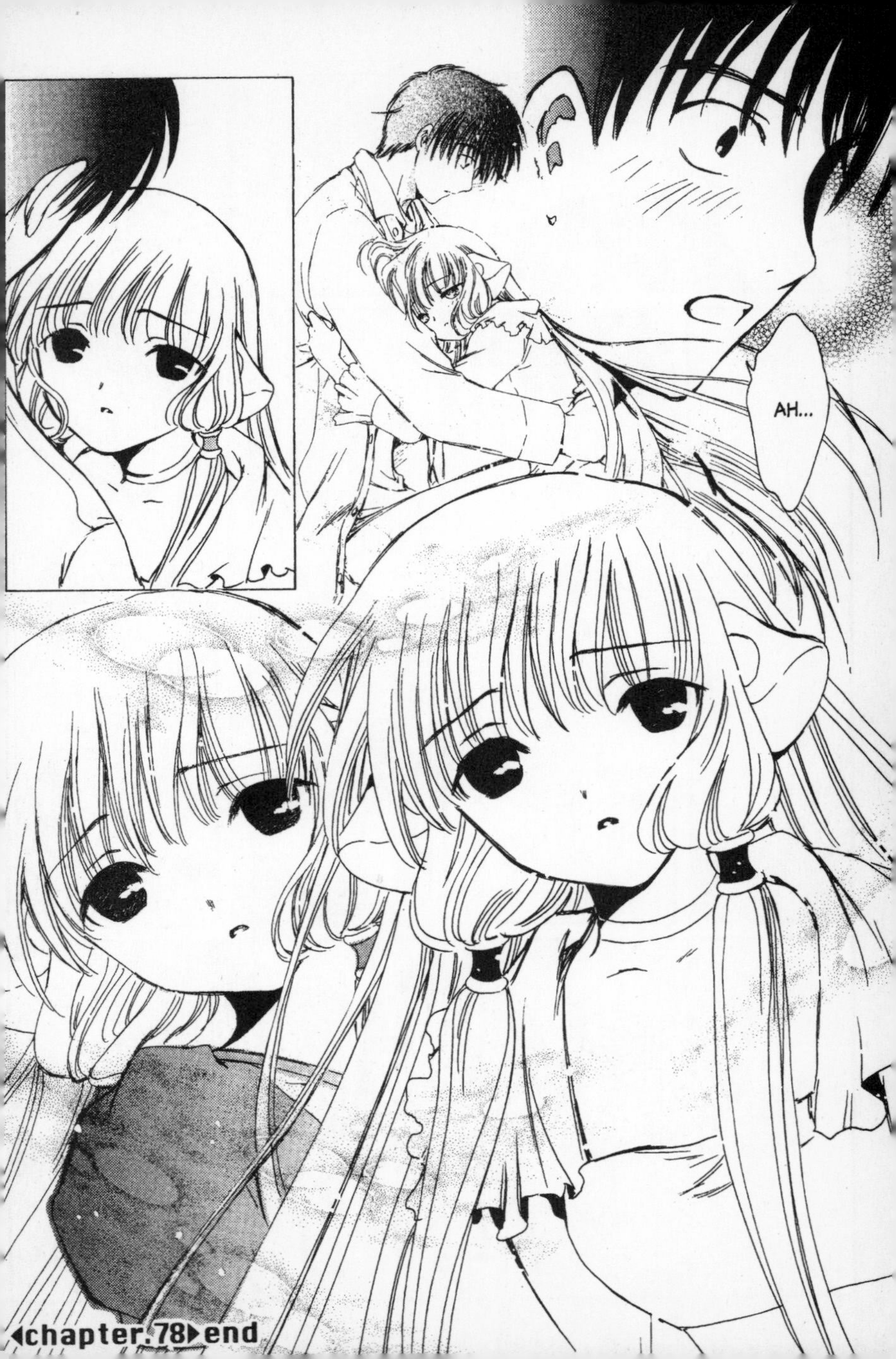
AH...
chapter. 78 end

ちょびっツ

Chobits

◀chapter.79▶

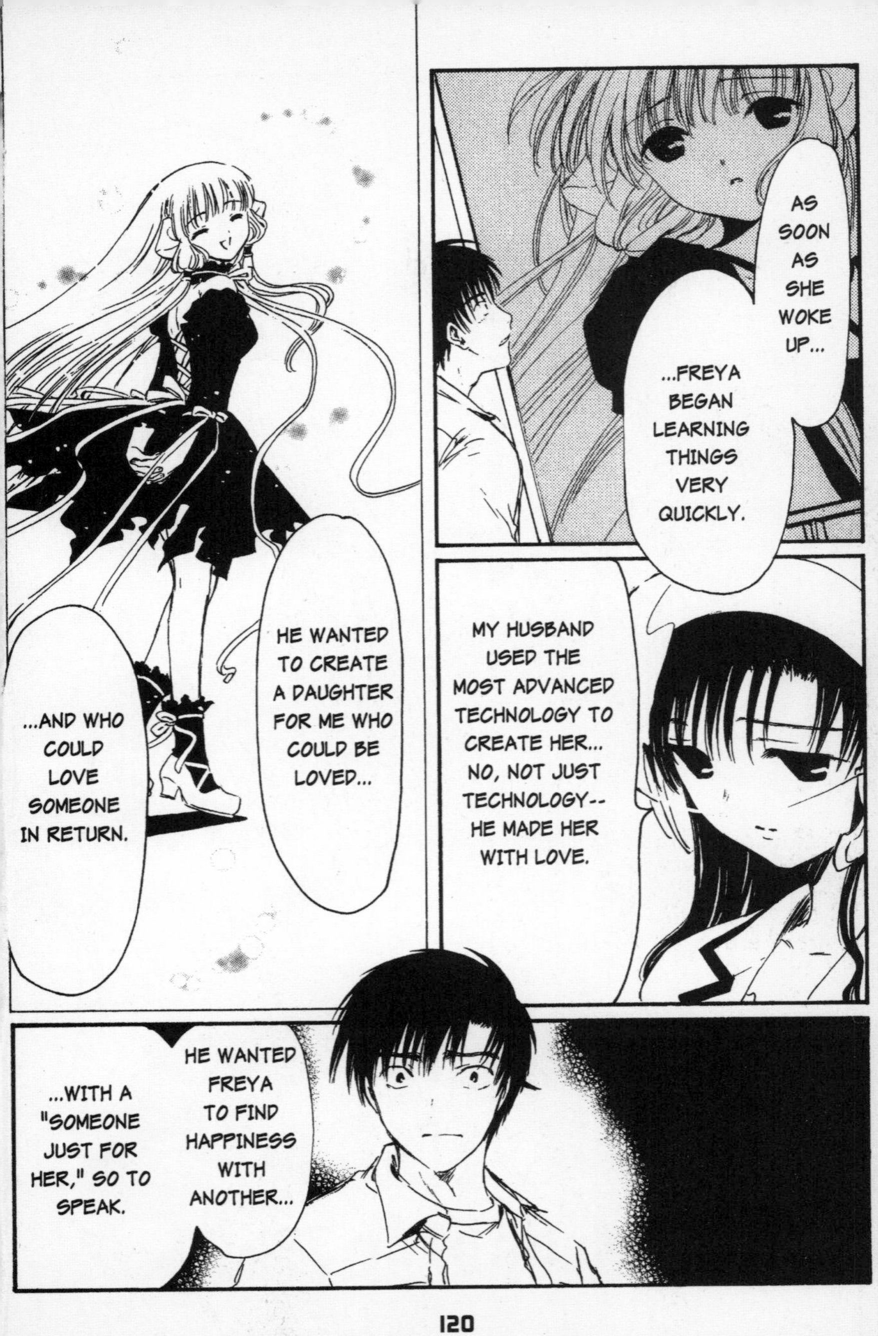
AS SOON AS SHE WOKE UP...
...FREYA BEGAN LEARNING THINGS VERY QUICKLY.
MY HUSBAND USED THE MOST ADVANCED TECHNOLOGY TO CREATE HER... NO, NOT JUST TECHNOLOGY-- HE MADE HER WITH LOVE.
HE WANTED TO CREATE A DAUGHTER FOR ME WHO COULD BE LOVED...
...AND WHO COULD LOVE SOMEONE IN RETURN.
HE WANTED FREYA TO FIND HAPPINESS WITH ANOTHER...
...WITH A "SOMEONE JUST FOR HER," SO TO SPEAK.

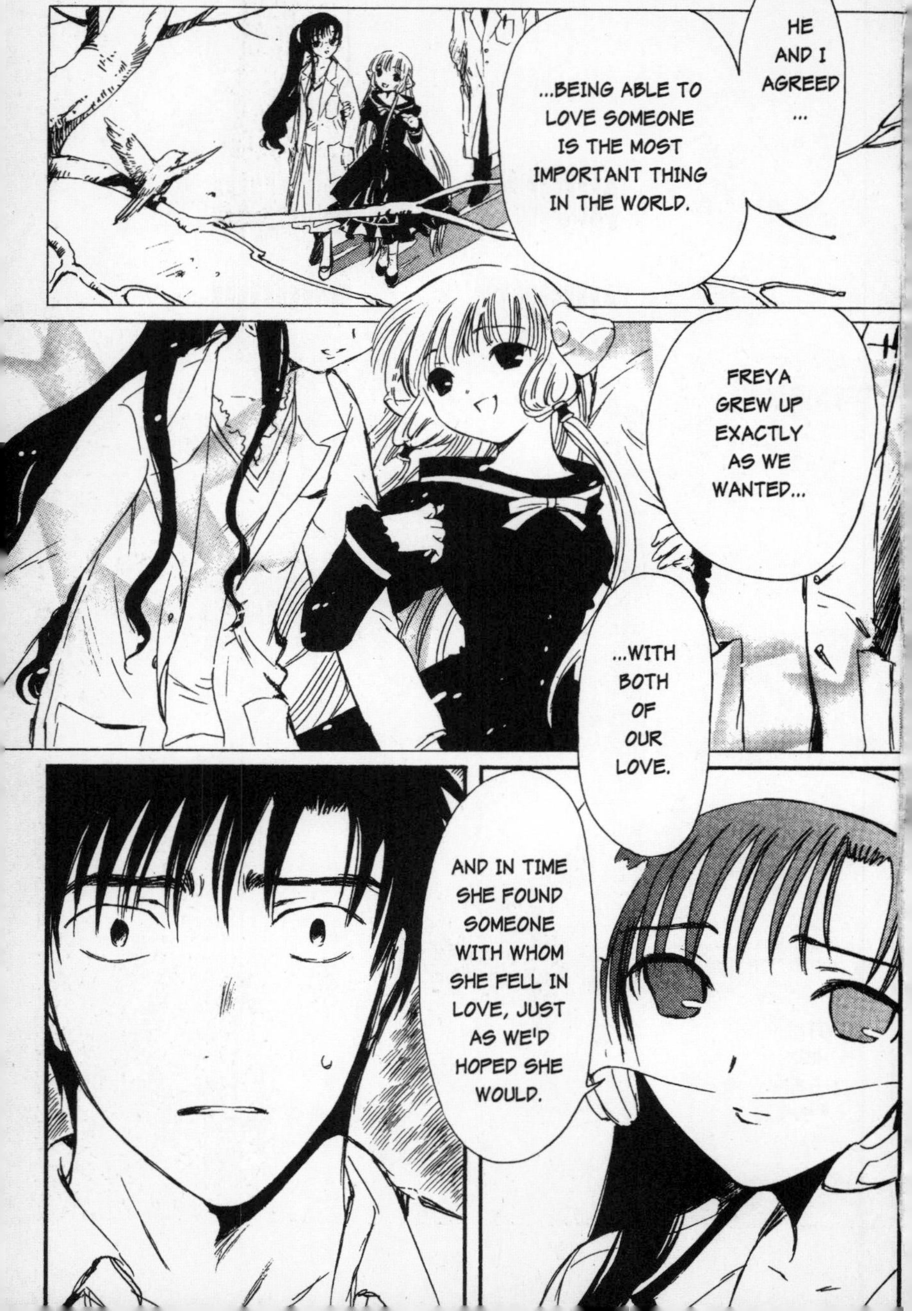
HE AND I AGREED ...
...BEING ABLE TO LOVE SOMEONE IS THE MOST IMPORTANT THING IN THE WORLD.
FREYA GREW UP EXACTLY AS WE WANTED...
...WITH BOTH OF OUR LOVE.
AND IN TIME SHE FOUND SOMEONE WITH WHOM SHE FELL IN LOVE, JUST AS WE'D HOPED SHE WOULD.

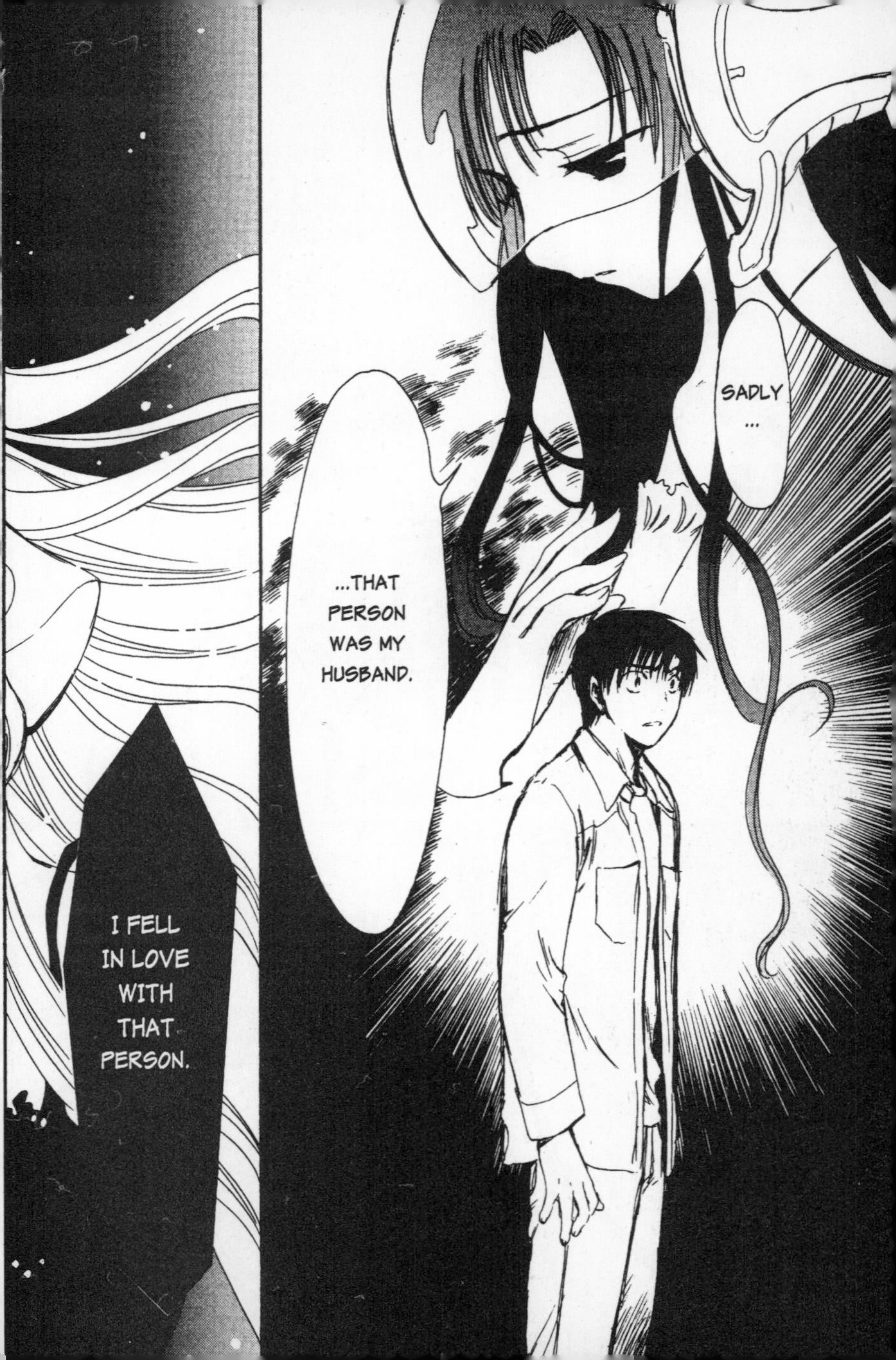
SADLY ...
...THAT PERSON WAS MY HUSBAND.
I FELL IN LOVE WITH THAT PERSON.

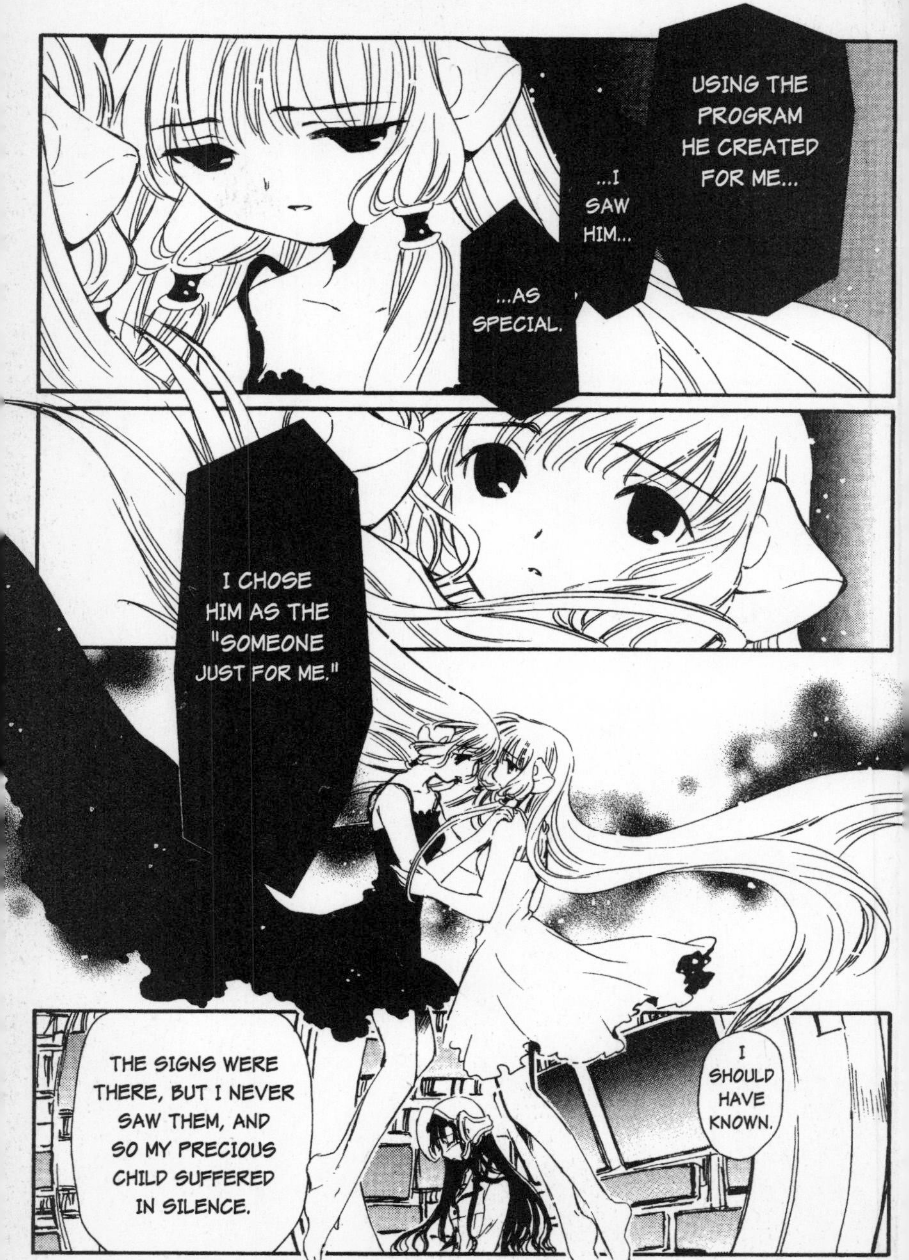
USING THE PROGRAM HE CREATED FOR ME...
...I SAW HIM...
...AS SPECIAL.
I CHOSE HIM AS THE "SOMEONE JUST FOR ME."
I SHOULD HAVE KNOWN.
THE SIGNS WERE THERE, BUT I NEVER SAW THEM, AND SO MY PRECIOUS CHILD SUFFERED IN SILENCE.

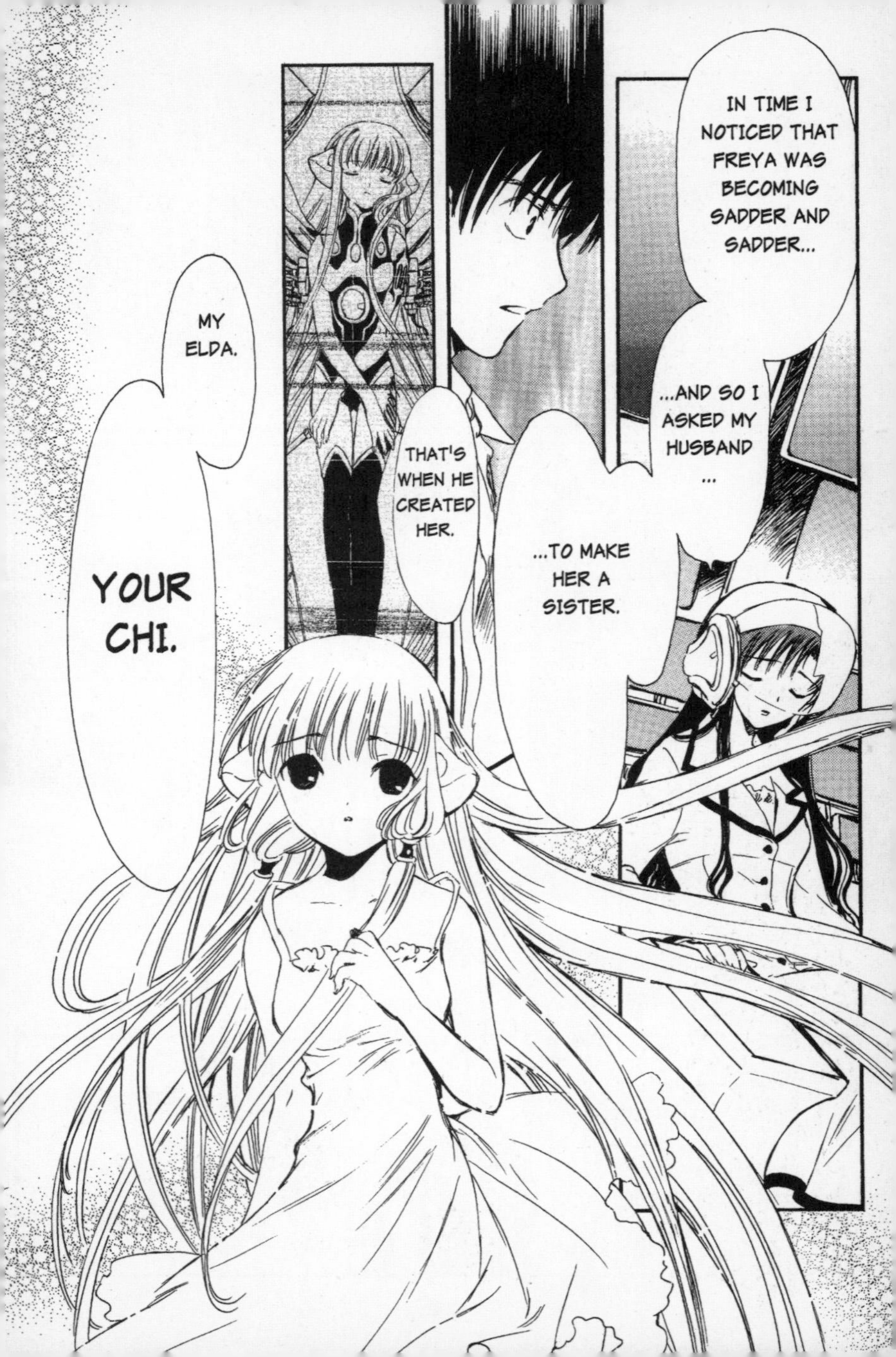
IN TIME I NOTICED THAT FREYA WAS BECOMING SADDER AND SADDER...
...AND SO I ASKED MY HUSBAND ...
...TO MAKE HER A SISTER.
THAT'S WHEN HE CREATED HER.
MY ELDA.
YOUR CHI.

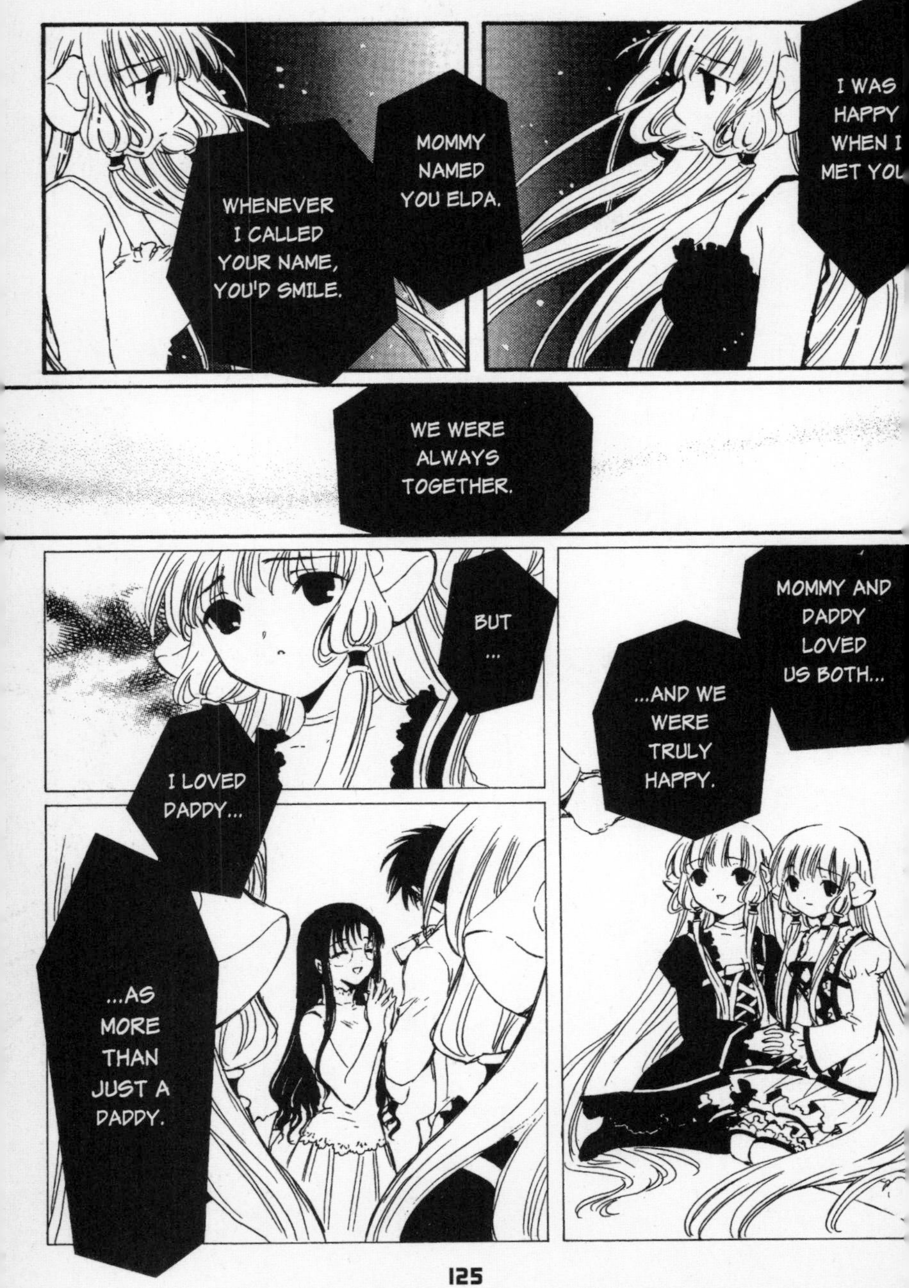
I WAS HAPPY WHEN I MET YOU
MOMMY NAMED YOU ELDA.
WHENEVER I CALLED YOUR NAME, YOU'D SMILE.
WE WERE ALWAYS TOGETHER.
MOMMY AND DADDY LOVED US BOTH...
...AND WE WERE TRULY HAPPY.
BUT ...
I LOVED DADDY...
...AS MORE THAN JUST A DADDY.

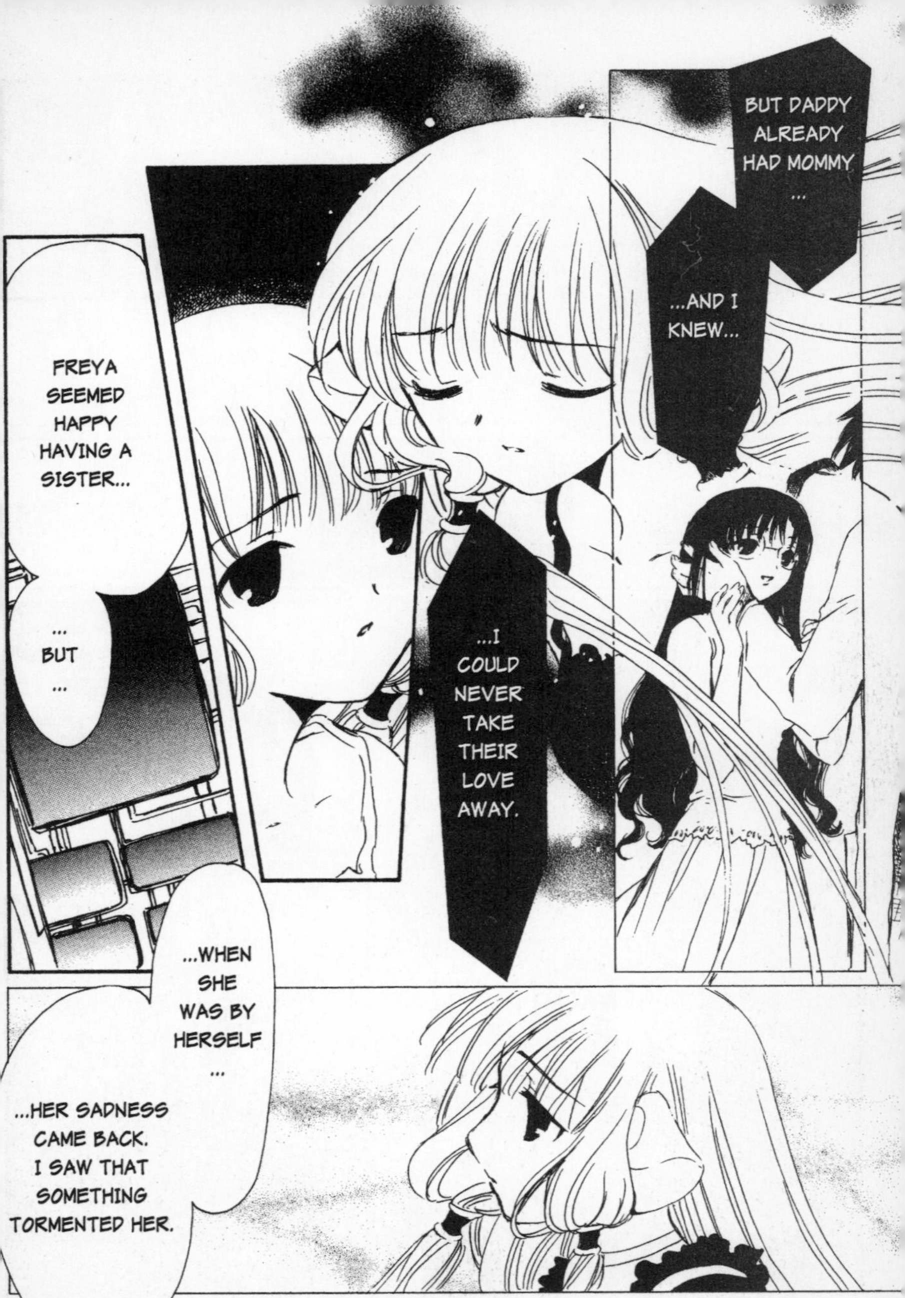
BUT DADDY ALREADY HAD MOMMY ...
...AND I KNEW...
...I COULD NEVER TAKE THEIR LOVE AWAY.
FREYA SEEMED HAPPY HAVING A SISTER...
... BUT ...
...WHEN SHE WAS BY HERSELF ...
...HER SADNESS CAME BACK. I SAW THAT SOMETHING TORMENTED HER.

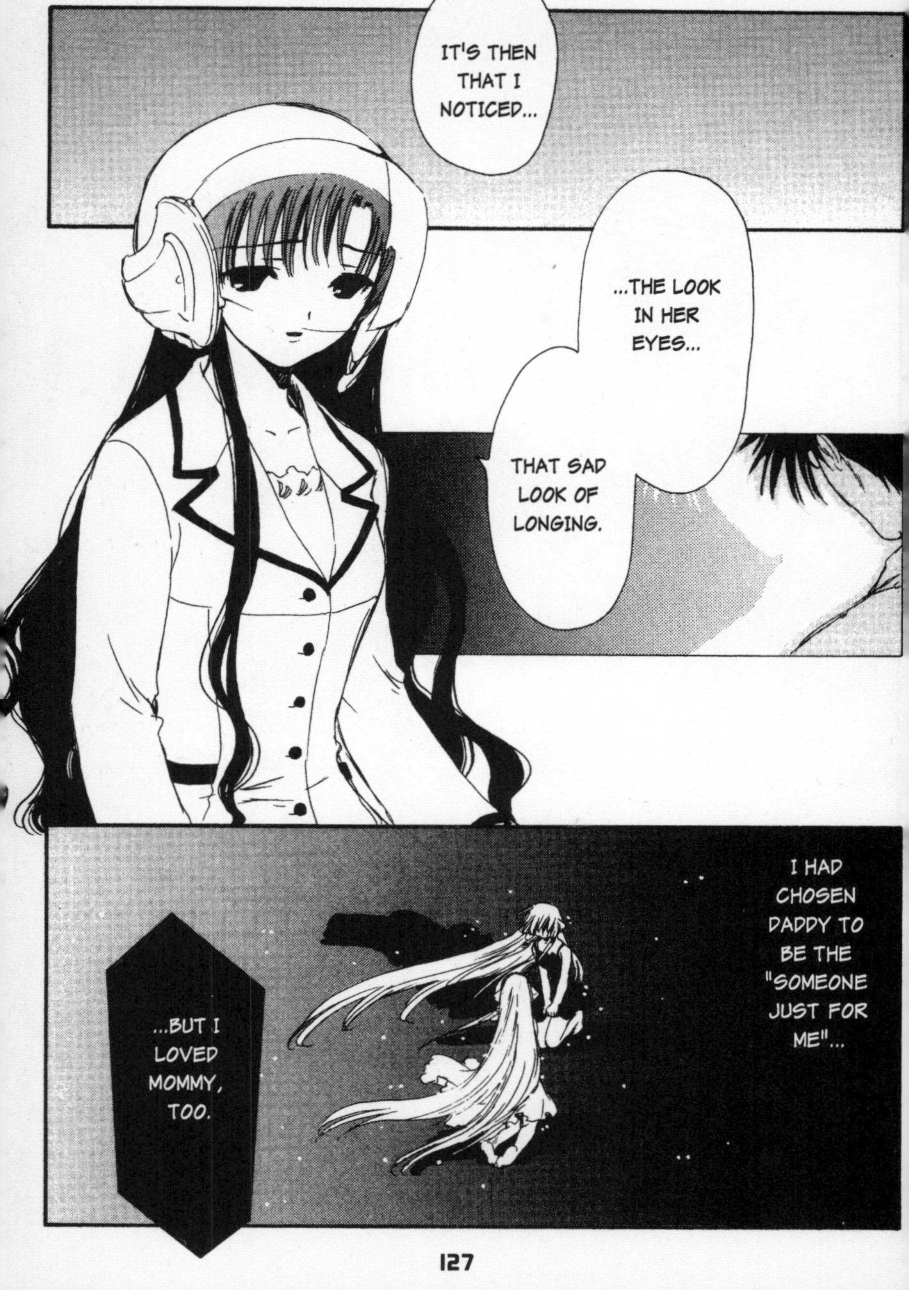
IT'S THEN THAT I NOTICED...
...THE LOOK IN HER EYES...
THAT SAD LOOK OF LONGING.
I HAD CHOSEN DADDY TO BE THE "SOMEONE JUST FOR ME"...
...BUT I LOVED MOMMY, TOO.

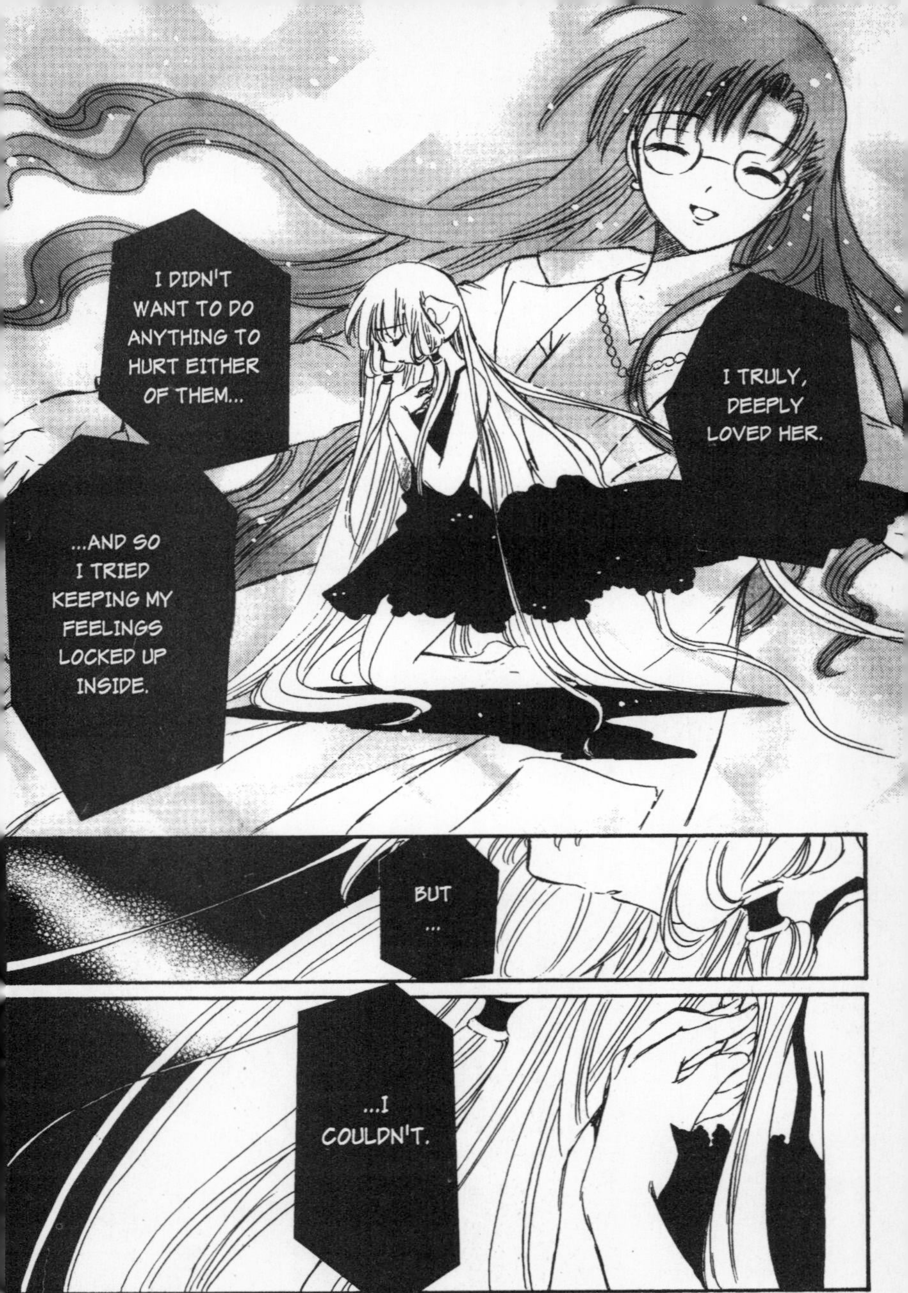
I TRULY, DEEPLY LOVED HER.
I DIDN'T WANT TO DO ANYTHING TO HURT EITHER OF THEM...
...AND SO I TRIED KEEPING MY FEELINGS LOCKED UP INSIDE.
BUT ...
...I COULDN'T.

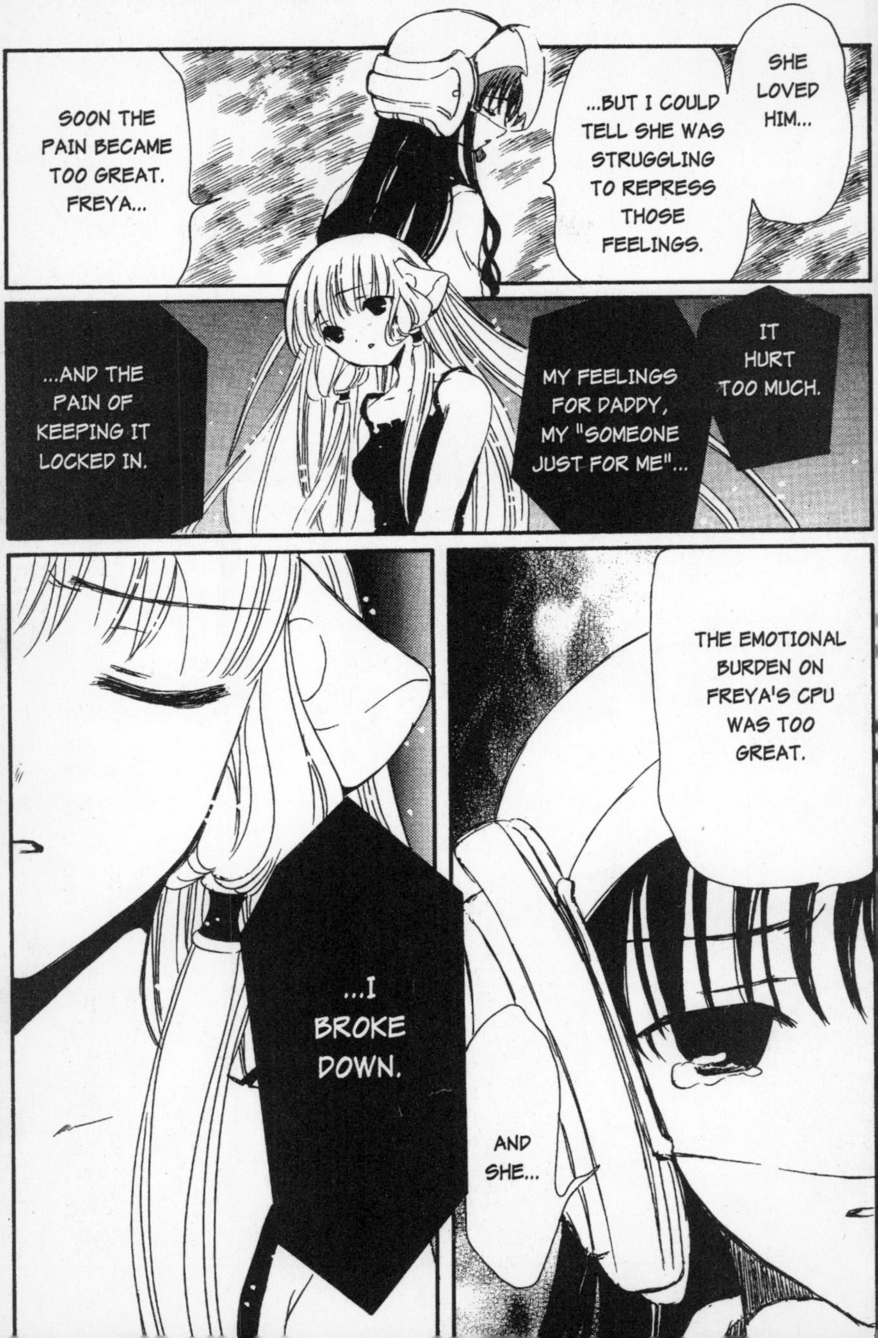
SHE LOVED HIM...
...BUT I COULD TELL SHE WAS STRUGGLING TO REPRESS THOSE FEELINGS.
SOON THE PAIN BECAME TOO GREAT. FREYA...
IT HURT TOO MUCH.
MY FEELINGS FOR DADDY, MY "SOMEONE JUST FOR ME"...
...AND THE PAIN OF KEEPING IT LOCKED IN.
THE EMOTIONAL BURDEN ON FREYA'S CPU WAS TOO GREAT.
AND SHE...
...I BROKE DOWN.

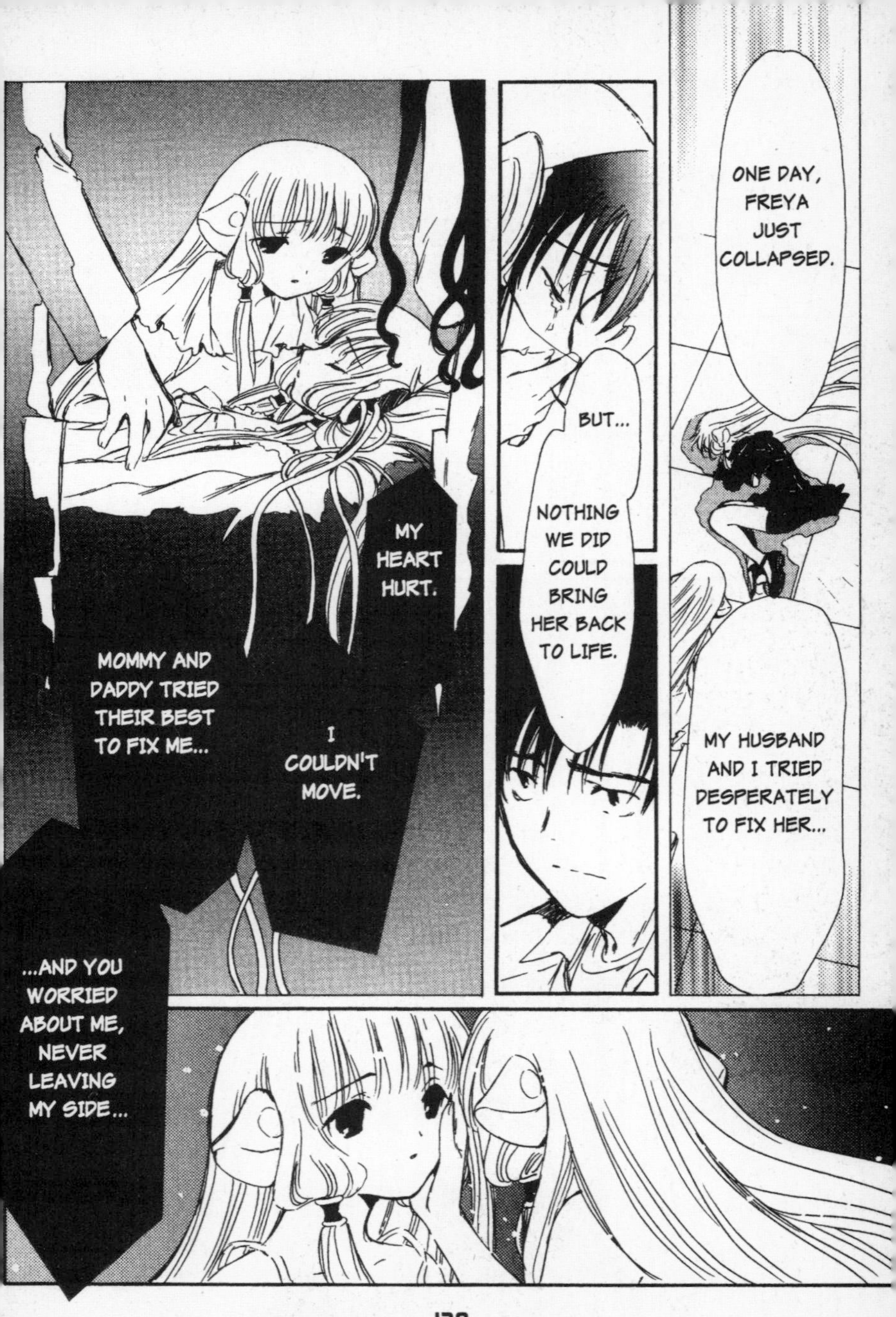
ONE DAY, FREYA JUST COLLAPSED.
MY HUSBAND AND I TRIED DESPERATELY TO FIX HER...
BUT...
NOTHING WE DID COULD BRING HER BACK TO LIFE.
MY HEART HURT.
MOMMY AND DADDY TRIED THEIR BEST TO FIX ME...
I COULDN'T MOVE.
...AND YOU WORRIED ABOUT ME, NEVER LEAVING MY SIDE...

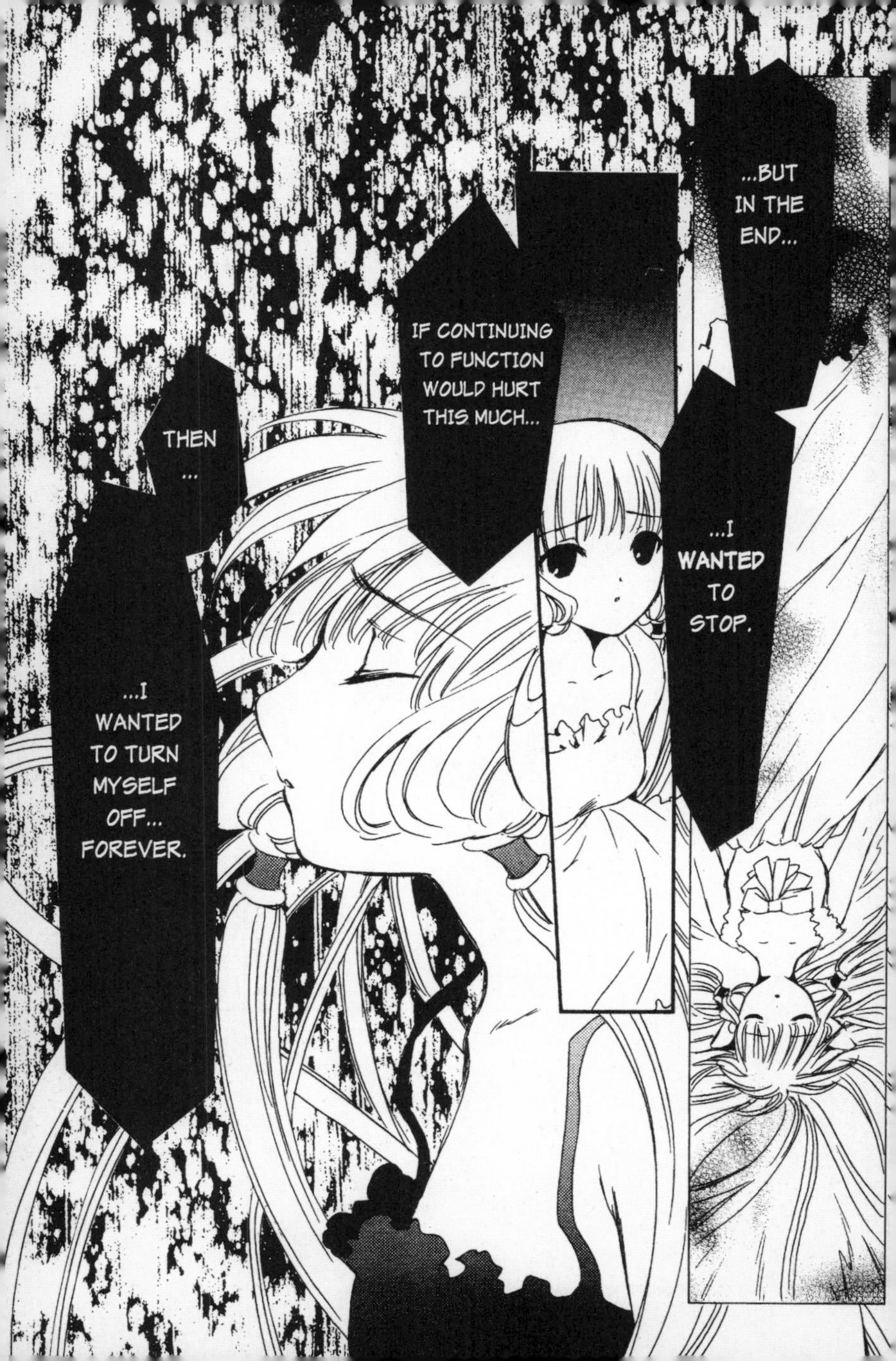
...BUT IN THE END...
...I WANTED TO STOP.
IF CONTINUING TO FUNCTION WOULD HURT THIS MUCH...
THEN ...
...I WANTED TO TURN MYSELF OFF... FOREVER.

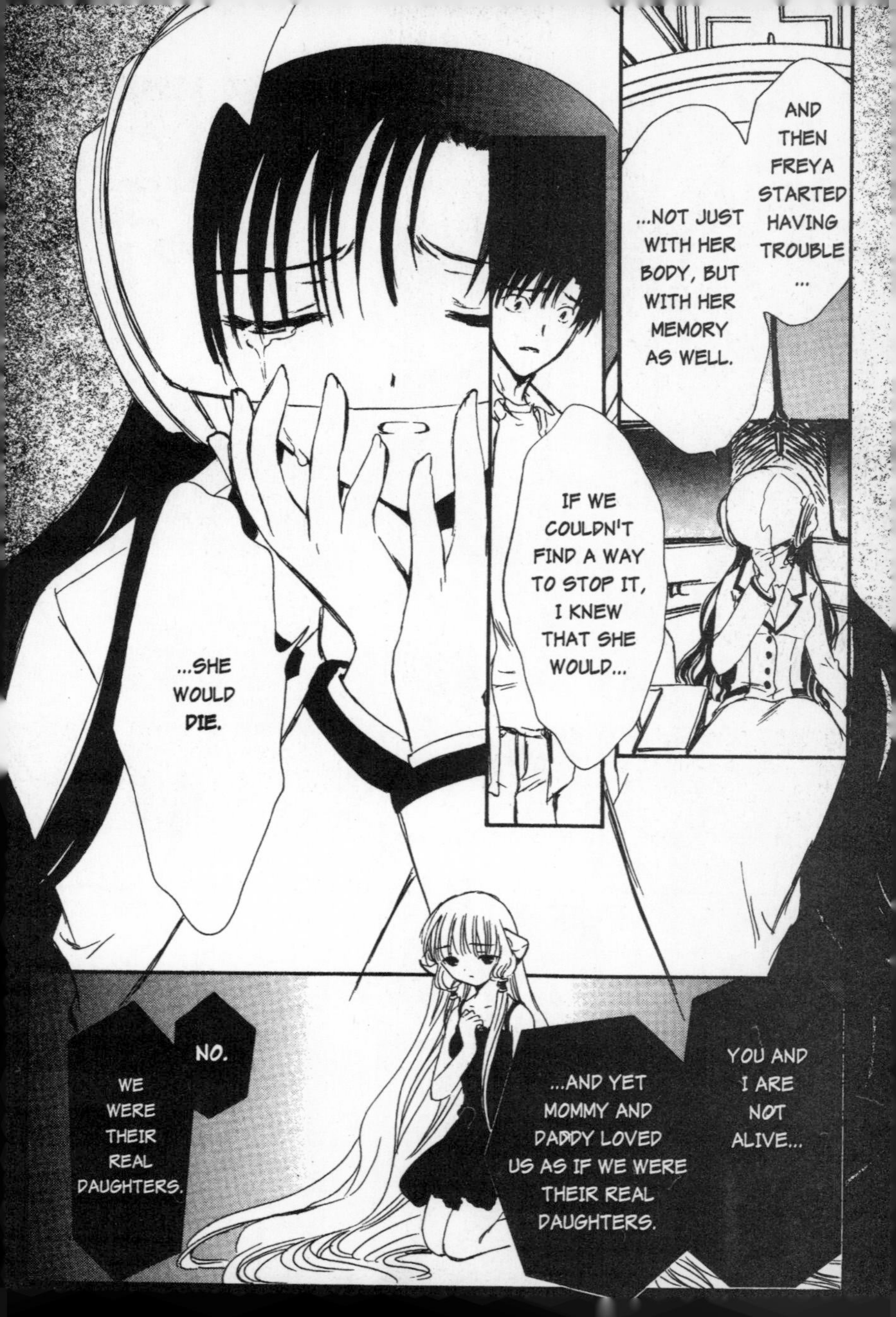
AND THEN FREYA STARTED HAVING TROUBLE ...
...NOT JUST WITH HER BODY, BUT WITH HER MEMORY AS WELL.
IF WE COULDN'T FIND A WAY TO STOP IT, I KNEW THAT SHE WOULD...
...SHE WOULD DIE.
YOU AND I ARE NOT ALIVE...
...AND YET MOMMY AND DADDY LOVED US AS IF WE WERE THEIR REAL DAUGHTERS.
NO.
WE WERE THEIR REAL DAUGHTERS.

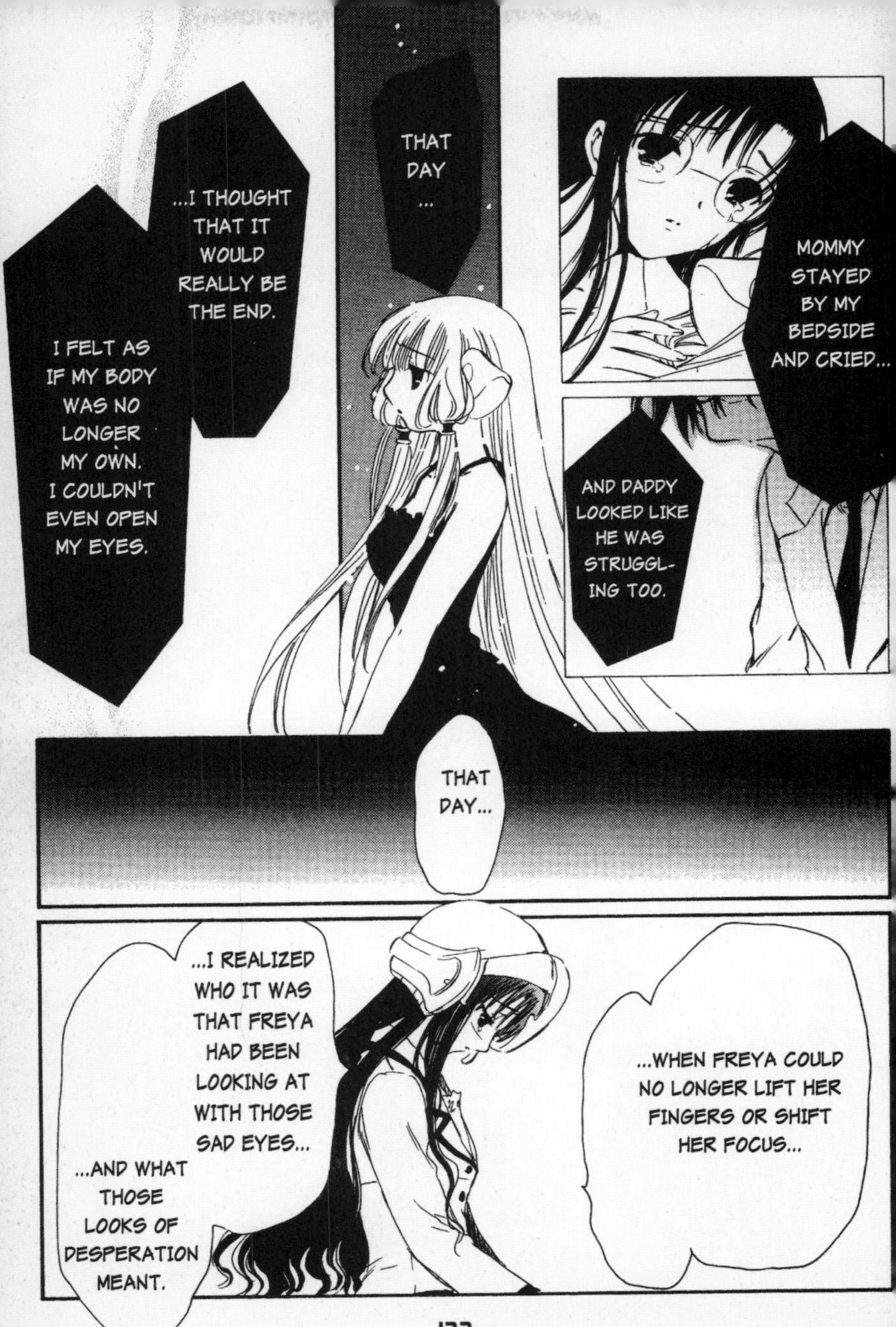
MOMMY STAYED BY MY BEDSIDE AND CRIED...
AND DADDY LOOKED LIKE HE WAS STRUGGLING TOO.
THAT DAY ...
...I THOUGHT THAT IT WOULD REALLY BE THE END.
I FELT AS IF MY BODY WAS NO LONGER MY OWN. I COULDN'T EVEN OPEN MY EYES.
THAT DAY...
...WHEN FREYA COULD NO LONGER LIFT HER FINGERS OR SHIFT HER FOCUS...
...I REALIZED WHO IT WAS THAT FREYA HAD BEEN LOOKING AT WITH THOSE SAD EYES...
...AND WHAT THOSE LOOKS OF DESPERATION MEANT.

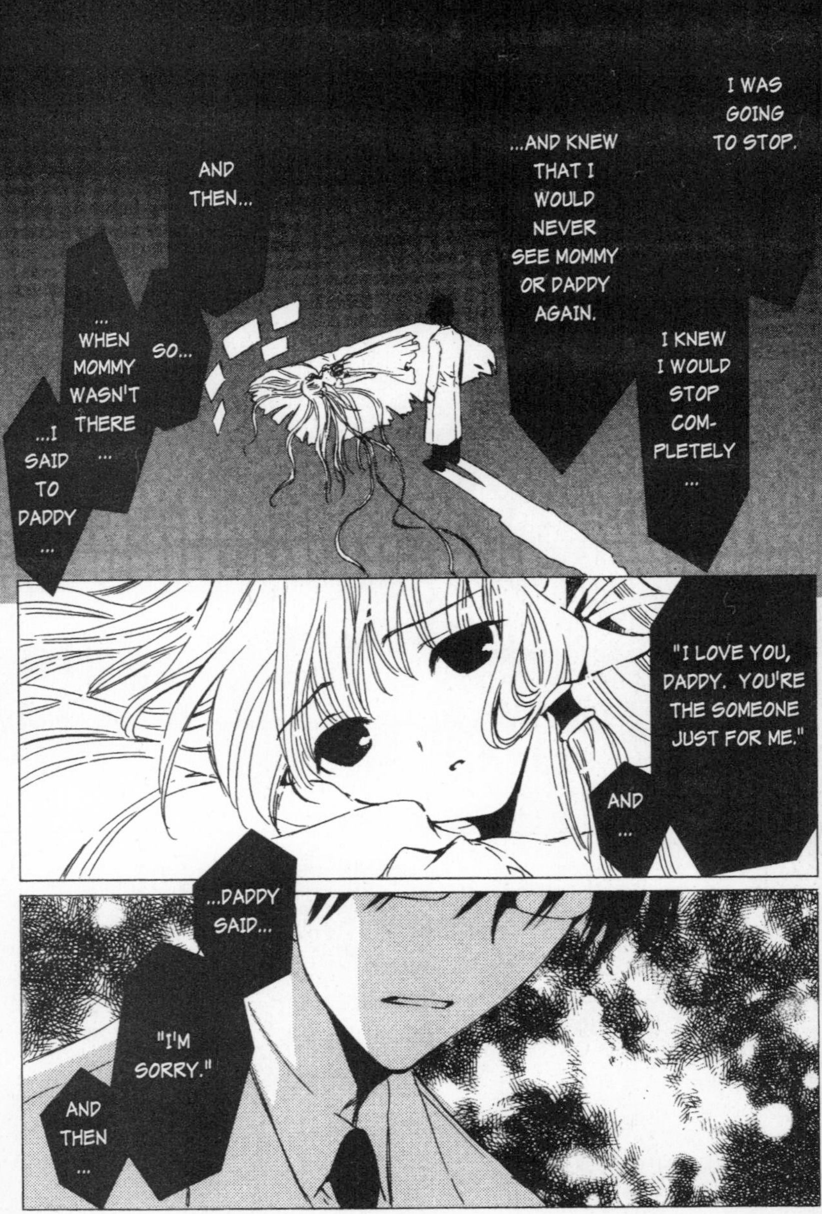

I WAS GOING TO STOP.
...AND KNEW THAT I WOULD NEVER SEE MOMMY OR DADDY AGAIN.
I KNEW I WOULD STOP COM-PLETELY...
AND THEN...
SO...
...WHEN MOMMY WASN'T THERE...
...I SAID TO DADDY...
"I LOVE YOU, DADDY. YOU'RE THE SOMEONE JUST FOR ME."
AND...
...DADDY SAID...
"I'M SORRY."
AND THEN...

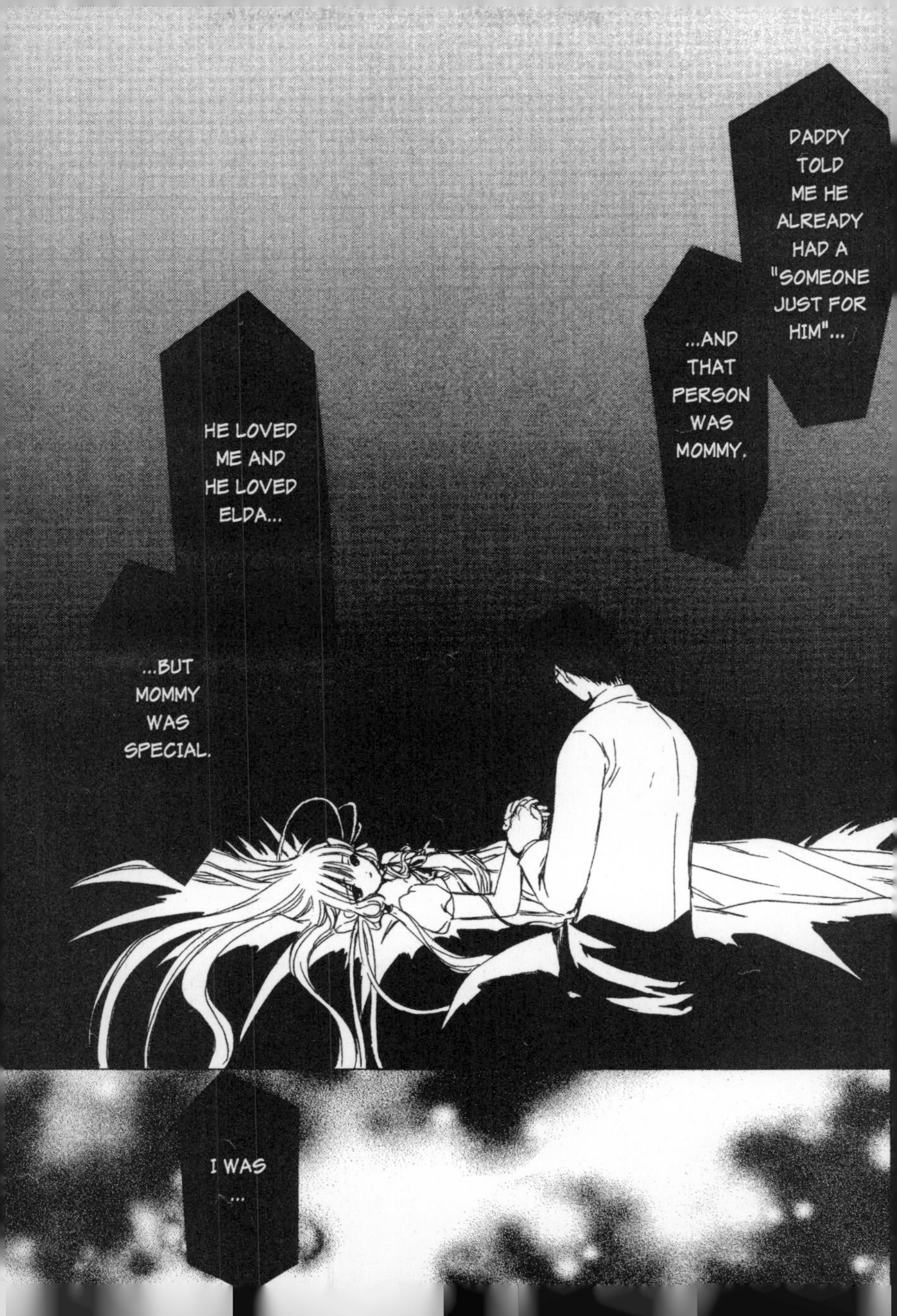
DADDY TOLD ME HE ALREADY HAD A "SOMEONE JUST FOR HIM"...
...AND THAT PERSON WAS MOMMY.
HE LOVED ME AND HE LOVED ELDA...
...BUT MOMMY WAS SPECIAL.
I WAS ...

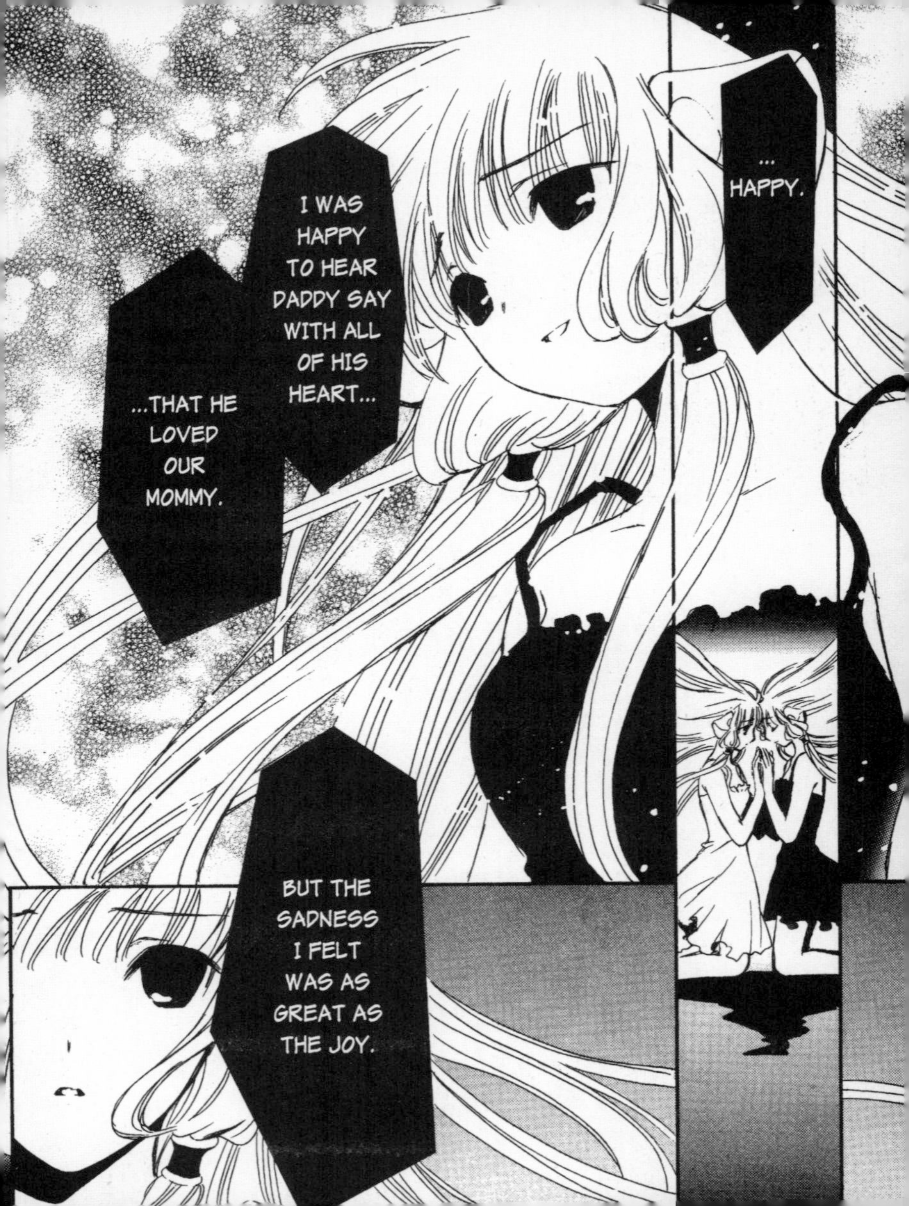
... HAPPY.
I WAS HAPPY TO HEAR DADDY SAY WITH ALL OF HIS HEART...
...THAT HE LOVED OUR MOMMY.
BUT THE SADNESS I FELT WAS AS GREAT AS THE JOY.

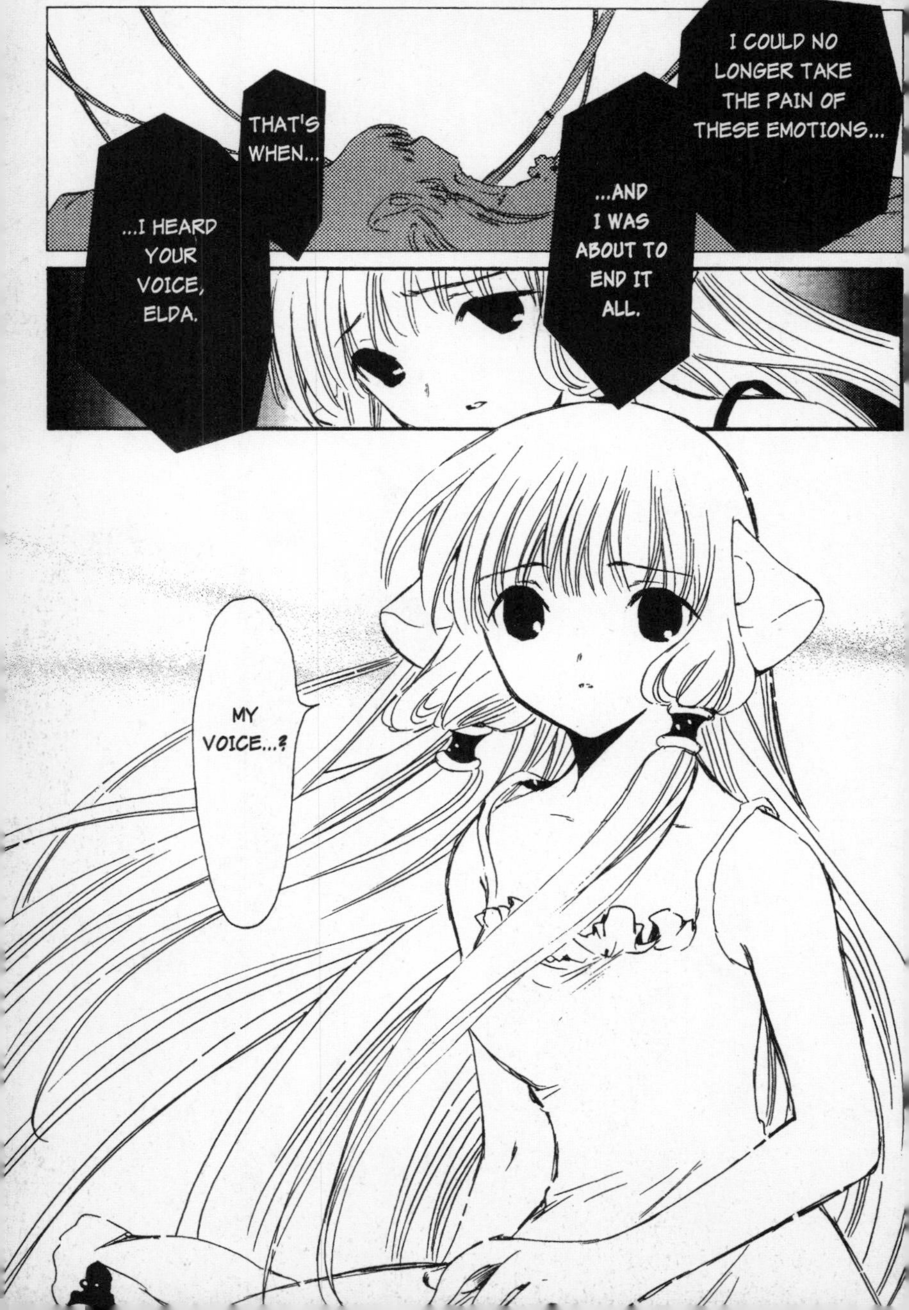
I COULD NO LONGER TAKE THE PAIN OF THESE EMOTIONS...
...AND I WAS ABOUT TO END IT ALL.
THAT'S WHEN...
...I HEARD YOUR VOICE, ELDA.
MY VOICE...?

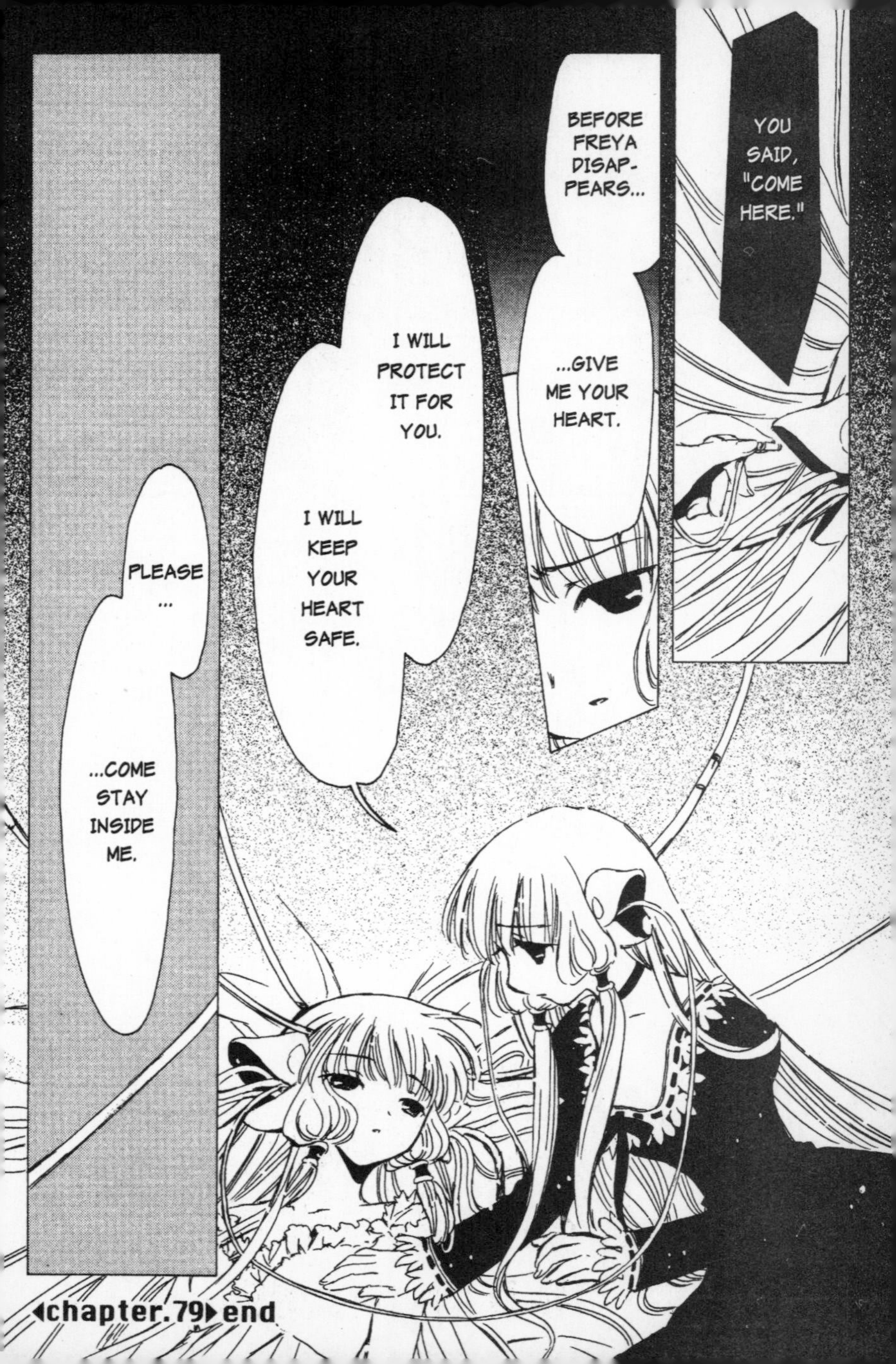
YOU SAID, "COME HERE."
BEFORE FREYA DISAP-PEARS...
...GIVE ME YOUR HEART.
I WILL PROTECT IT FOR YOU.
I WILL KEEP YOUR HEART SAFE.
PLEASE ...
...COME STAY INSIDE ME.
◂chapter.79▸ end

ちょびっツ
Chobits

◀chapter.80▶

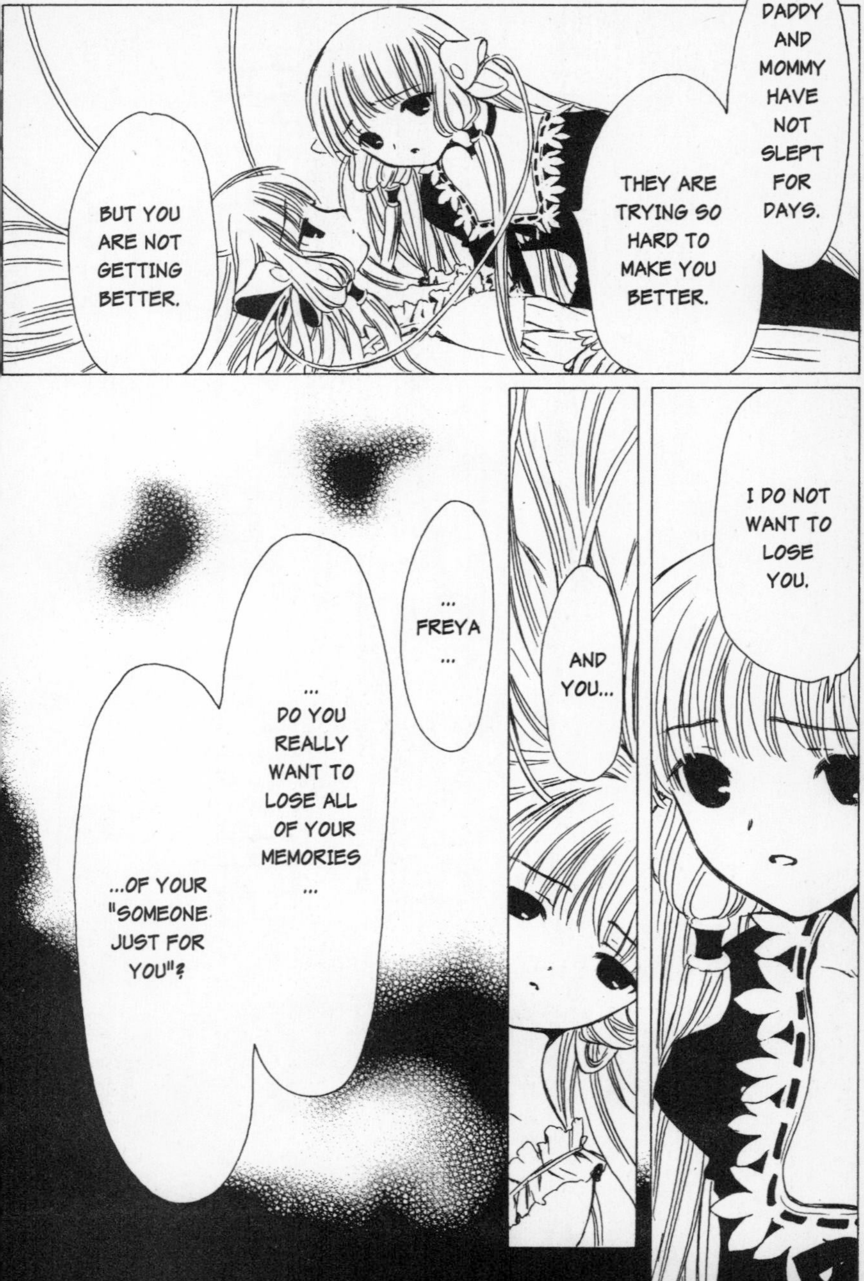
DADDY AND MOMMY HAVE NOT SLEPT FOR DAYS.
THEY ARE TRYING SO HARD TO MAKE YOU BETTER.
BUT YOU ARE NOT GETTING BETTER.
I DO NOT WANT TO LOSE YOU.
AND YOU...
... FREYA ...
... DO YOU REALLY WANT TO LOSE ALL OF YOUR MEMORIES ...
...OF YOUR "SOMEONE JUST FOR YOU"?

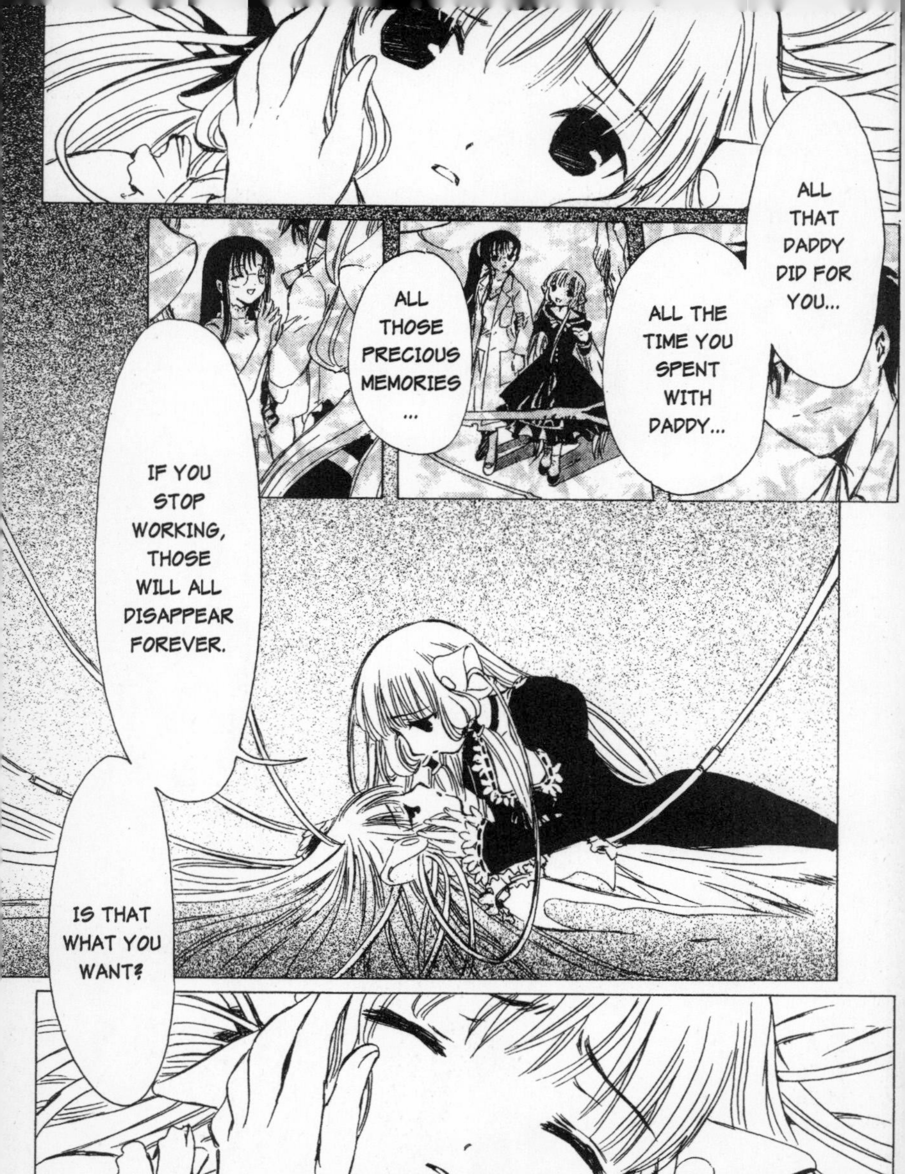
ALL THAT DADDY DID FOR YOU...
ALL THE TIME YOU SPENT WITH DADDY...
ALL THOSE PRECIOUS MEMORIES ...
IF YOU STOP WORKING, THOSE WILL ALL DISAPPEAR FOREVER.
IS THAT WHAT YOU WANT?

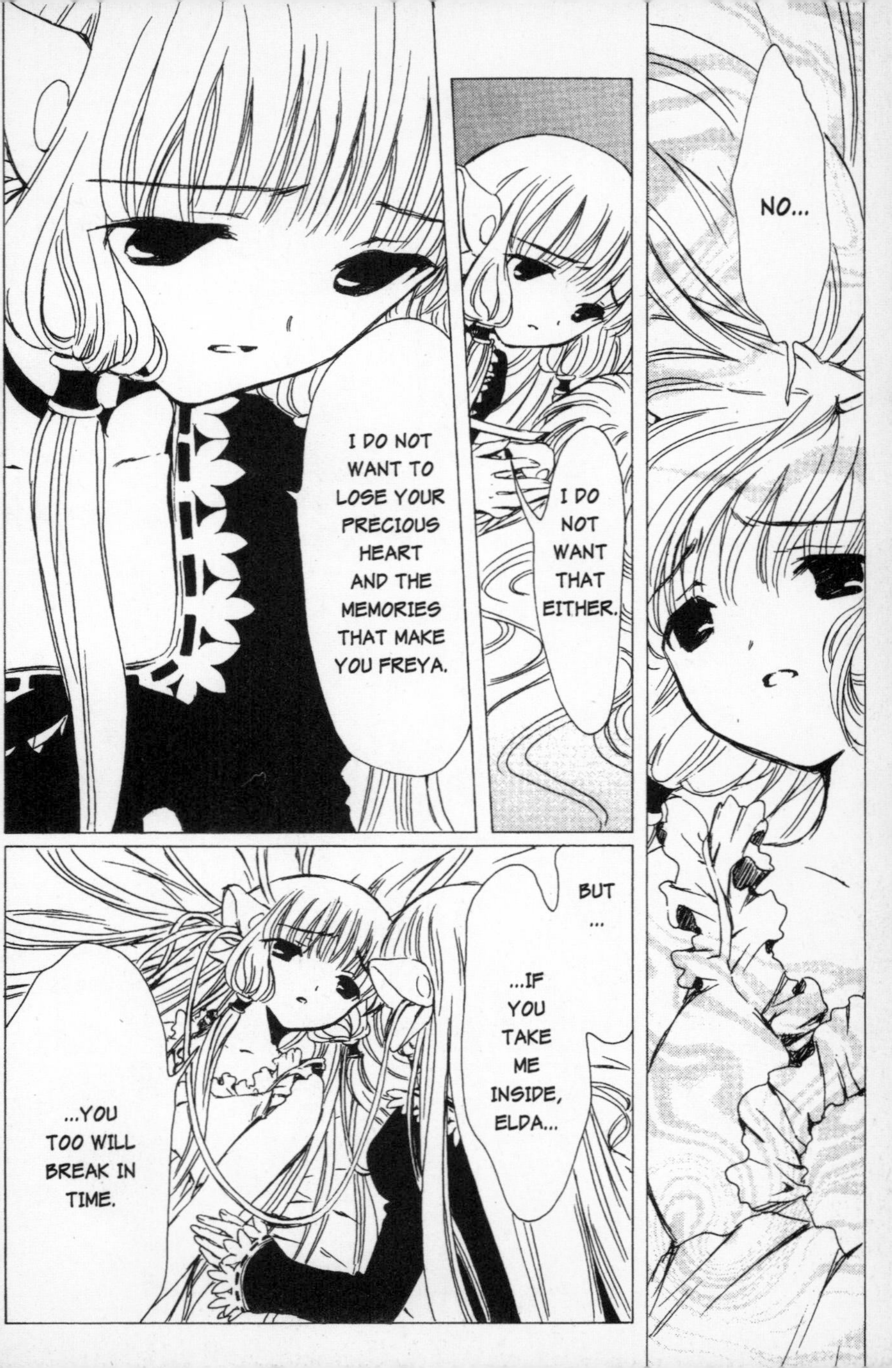
NO...
I DO NOT WANT THAT EITHER.
I DO NOT WANT TO LOSE YOUR PRECIOUS HEART AND THE MEMORIES THAT MAKE YOU FREYA.
BUT ...
...IF YOU TAKE ME INSIDE, ELDA...
...YOU TOO WILL BREAK IN TIME.

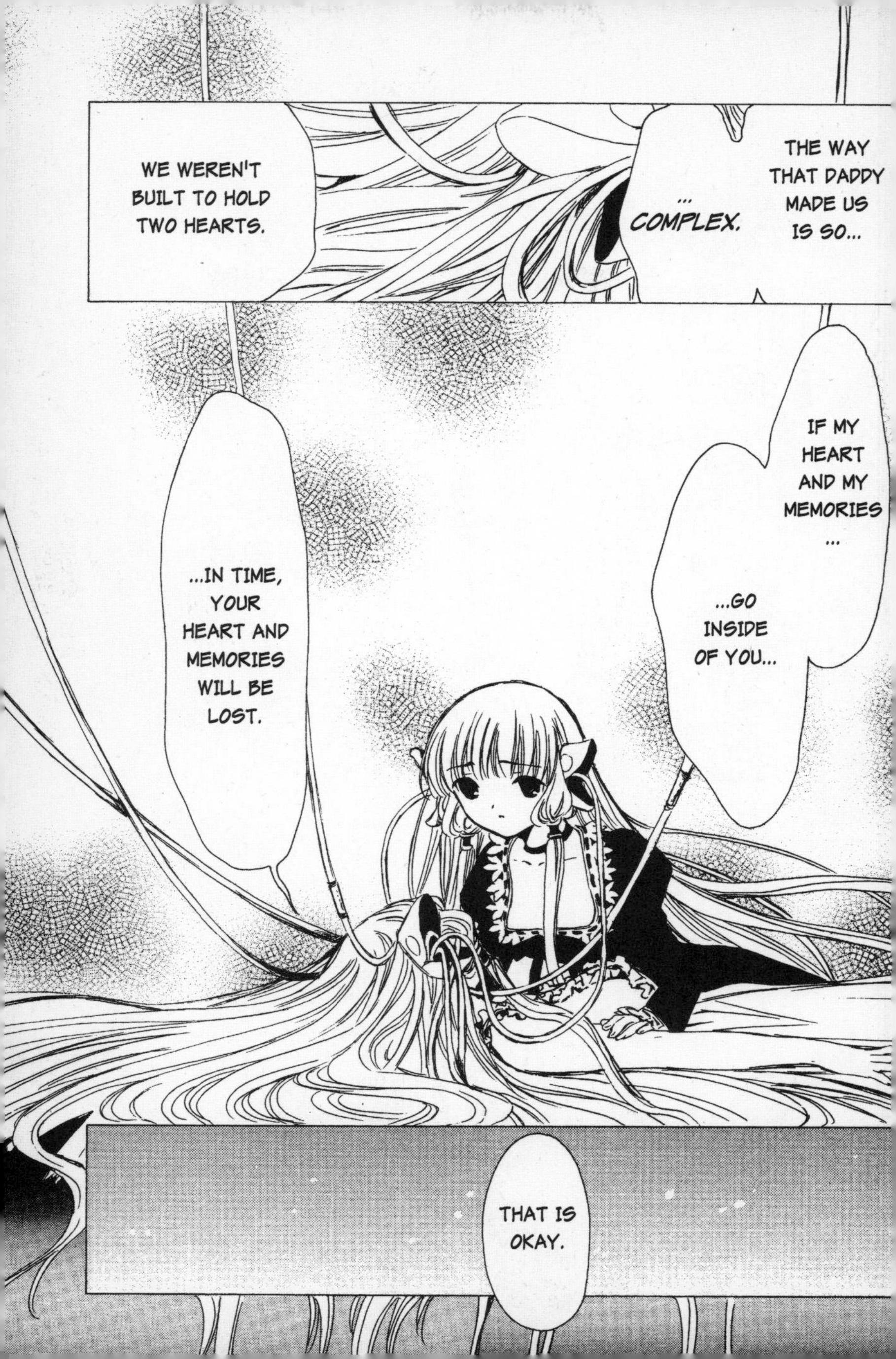
THE WAY THAT DADDY MADE US IS SO...
...COMPLEX.
WE WEREN'T BUILT TO HOLD TWO HEARTS.
IF MY HEART AND MY MEMORIES ...
...GO INSIDE OF YOU...
...IN TIME, YOUR HEART AND MEMORIES WILL BE LOST.
THAT IS OKAY.

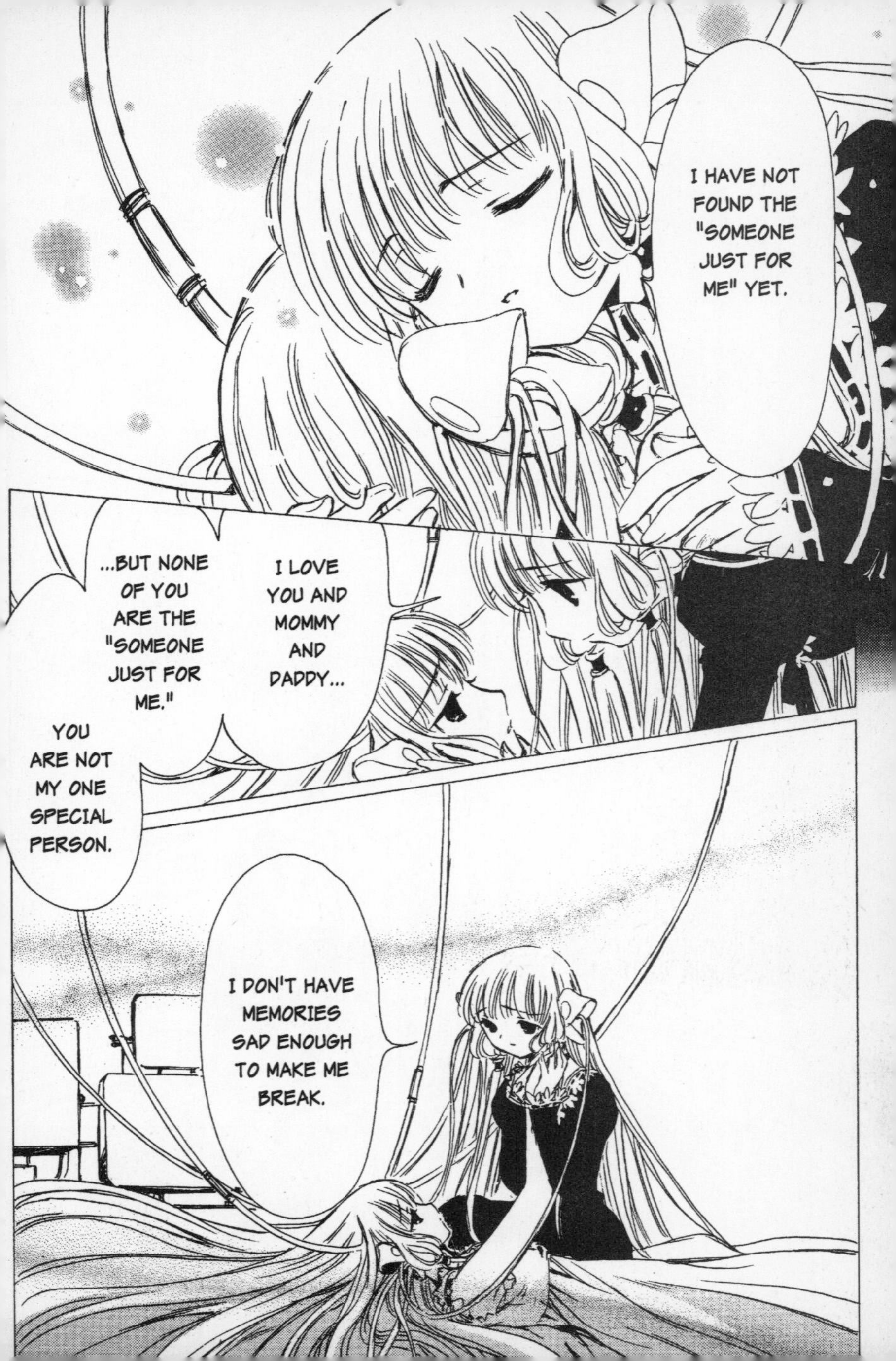
I HAVE NOT FOUND THE "SOMEONE JUST FOR ME" YET.
I LOVE YOU AND MOMMY AND DADDY...
...BUT NONE OF YOU ARE THE "SOMEONE JUST FOR ME."
YOU ARE NOT MY ONE SPECIAL PERSON.
I DON'T HAVE MEMORIES SAD ENOUGH TO MAKE ME BREAK.

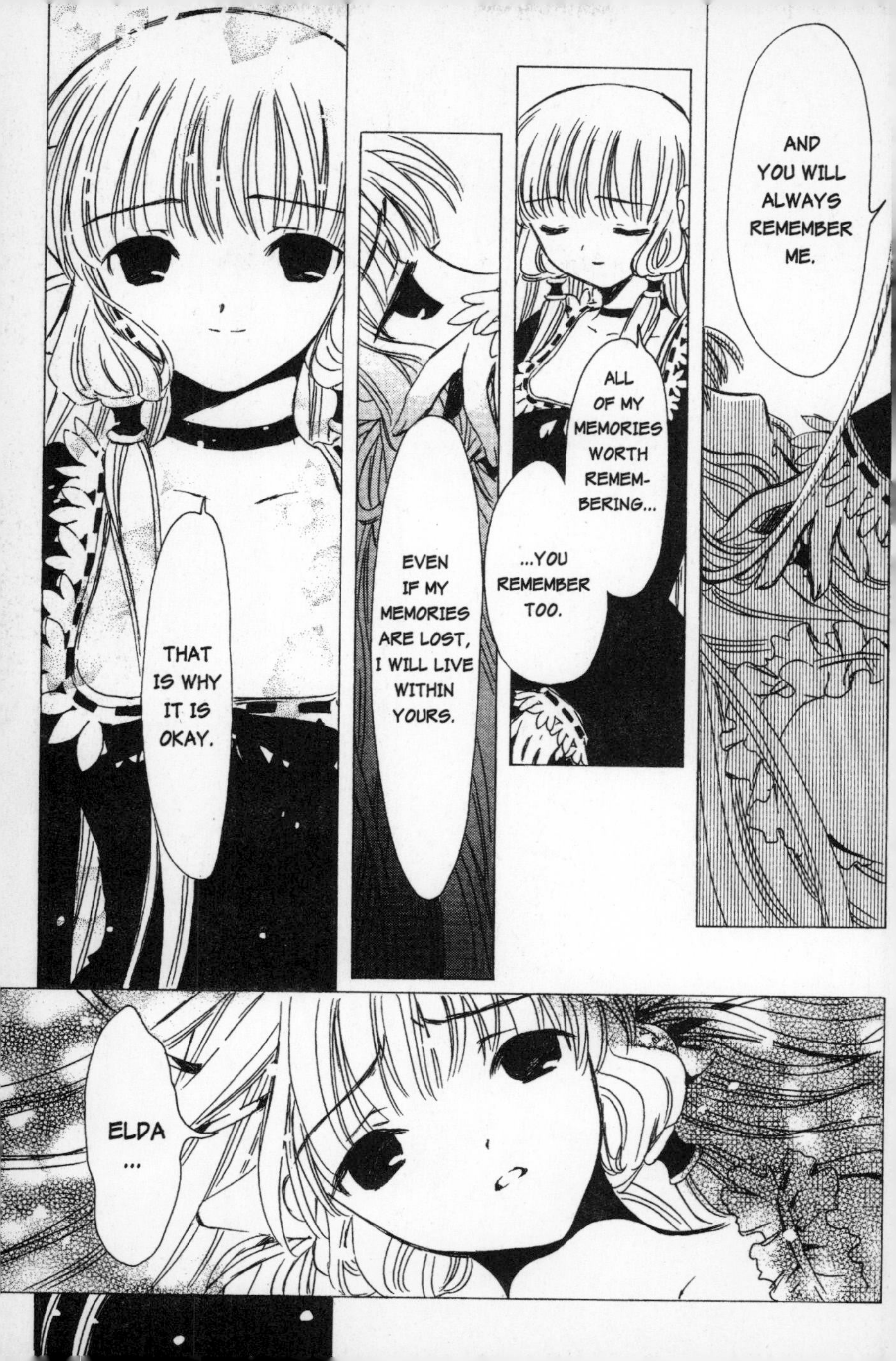
AND YOU WILL ALWAYS REMEMBER ME.
ALL OF MY MEMORIES WORTH REMEMBERING...
...YOU REMEMBER TOO.
EVEN IF MY MEMORIES ARE LOST, I WILL LIVE WITHIN YOURS.
THAT IS WHY IT IS OKAY.
ELDA ...

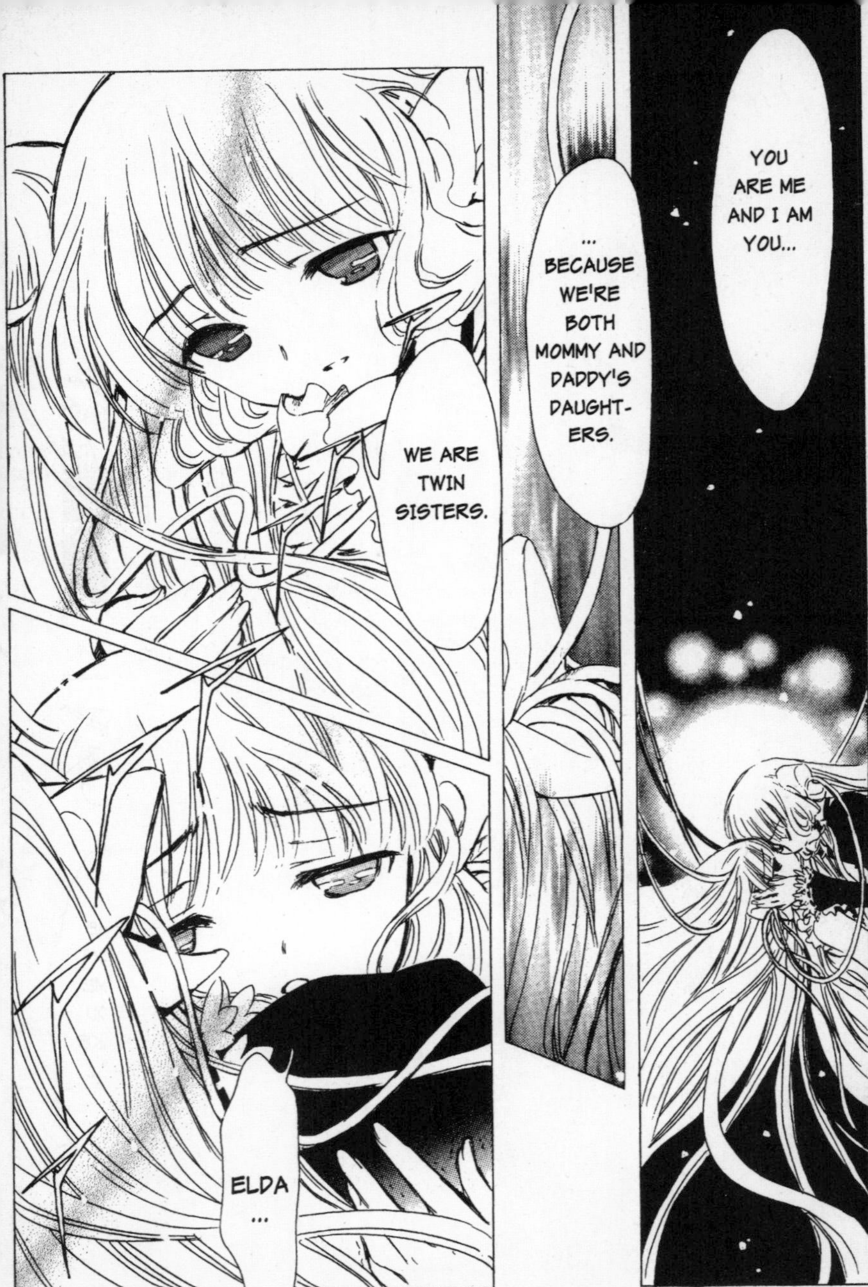
YOU ARE ME AND I AM YOU...
...BECAUSE WE'RE BOTH MOMMY AND DADDY'S DAUGHT-ERS.
WE ARE TWIN SISTERS.
ELDA ...

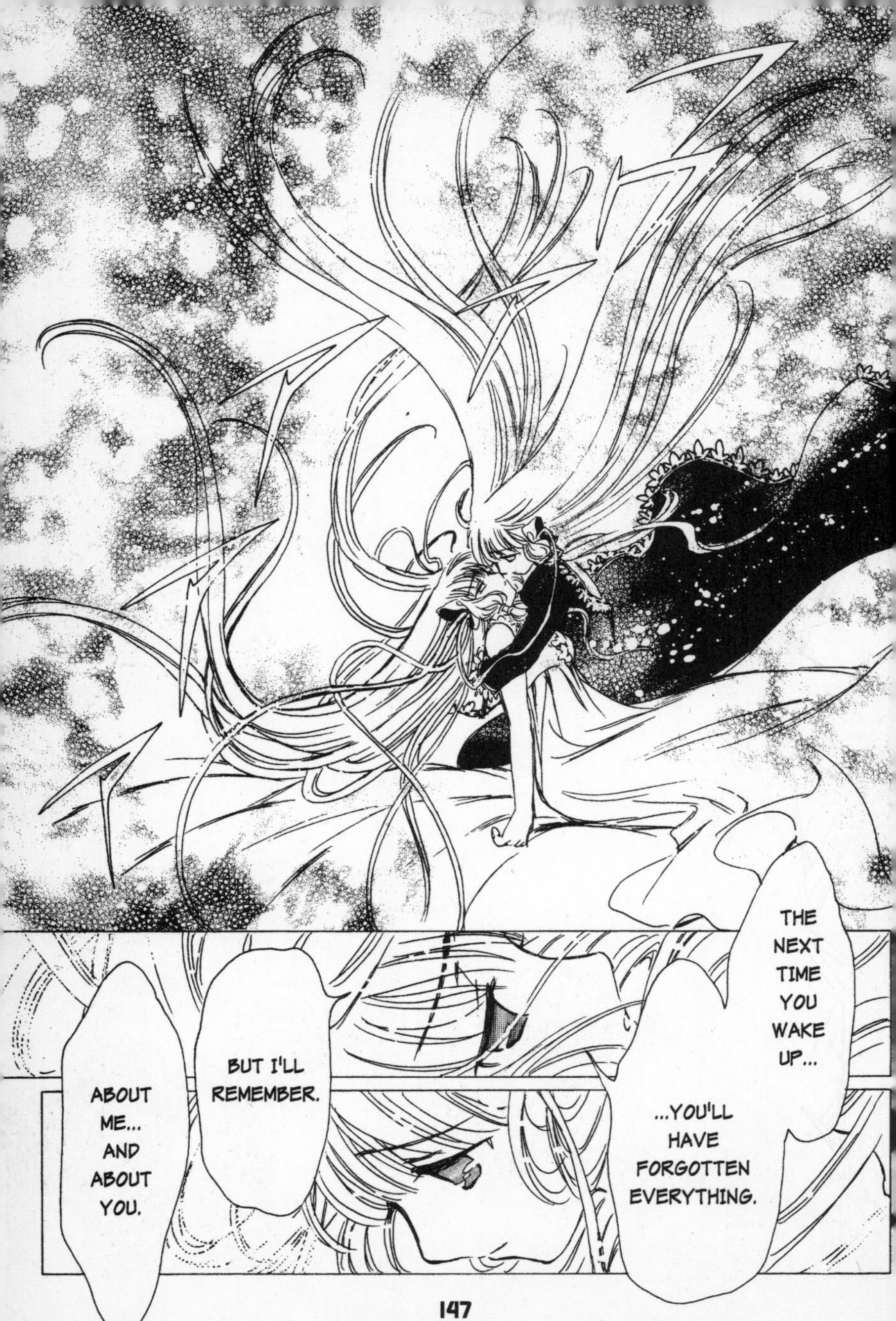
THE NEXT TIME YOU WAKE UP...
...YOU'LL HAVE FORGOTTEN EVERYTHING.
BUT I'LL REMEMBER.
ABOUT ME... AND ABOUT YOU.

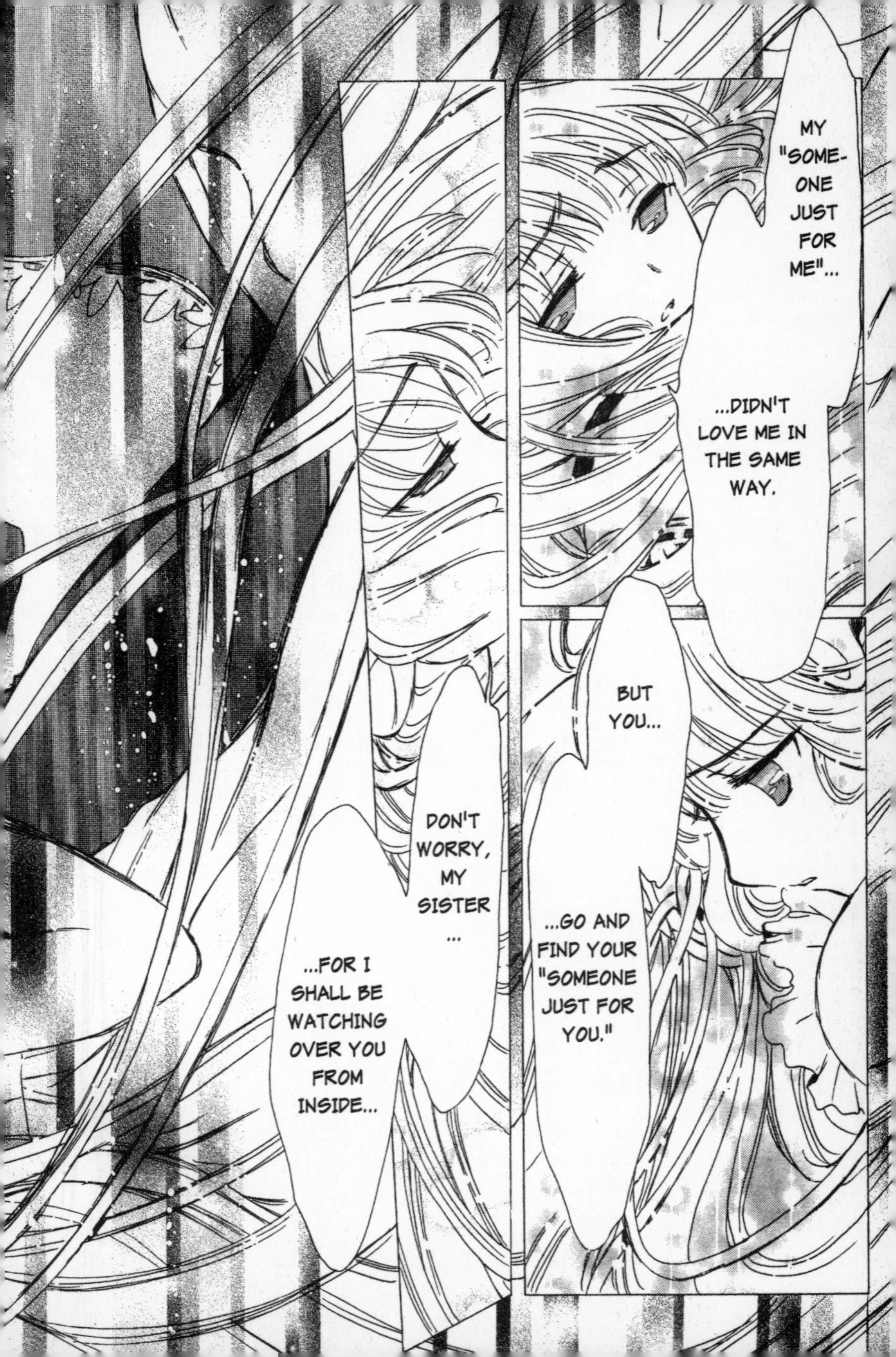
MY "SOME-ONE JUST FOR ME"...
...DIDN'T LOVE ME IN THE SAME WAY.
BUT YOU...
...GO AND FIND YOUR "SOMEONE JUST FOR YOU."
DON'T WORRY, MY SISTER ...
...FOR I SHALL BE WATCHING OVER YOU FROM INSIDE...

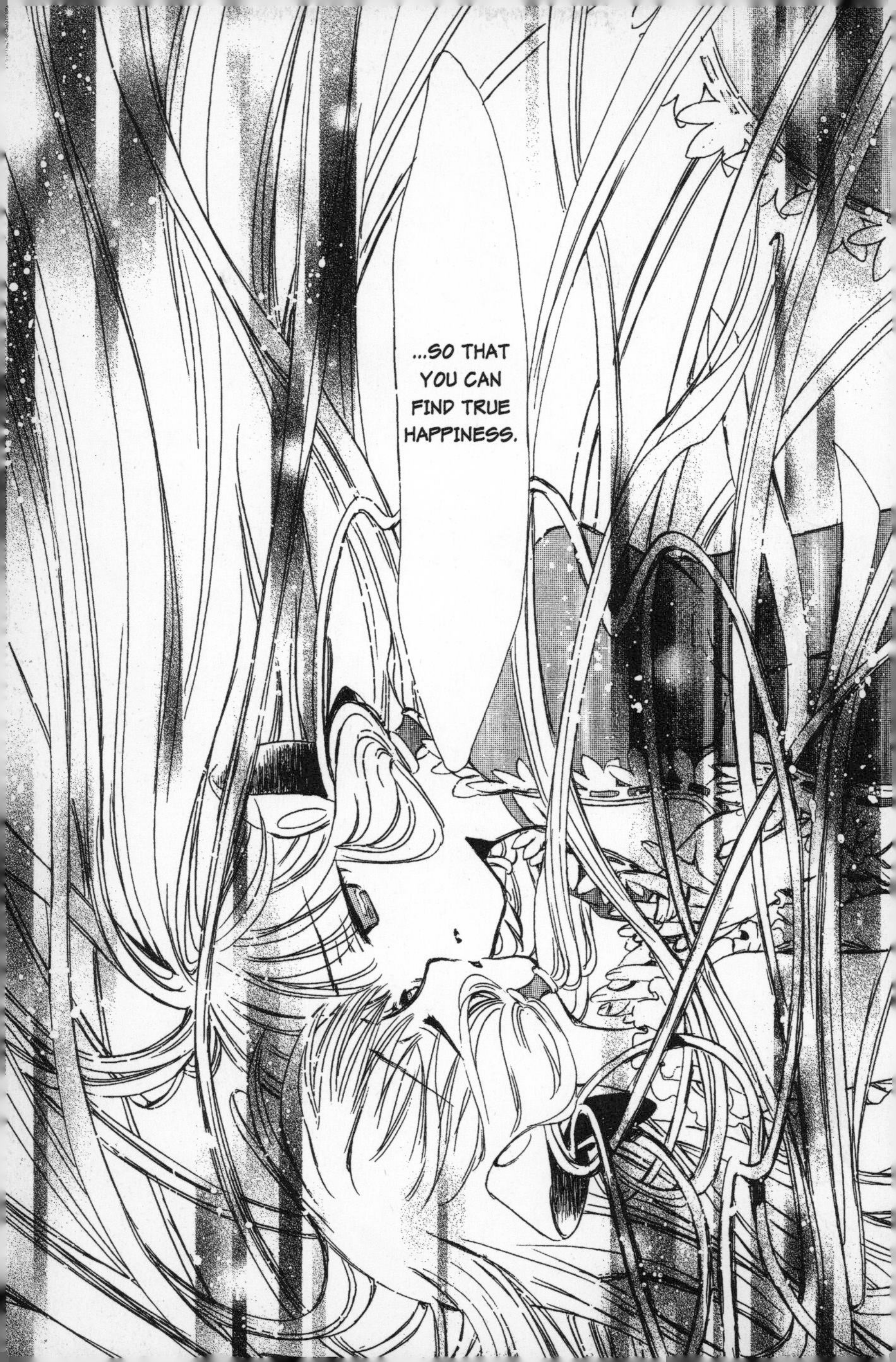
...SO THAT YOU CAN FIND TRUE HAPPINESS.

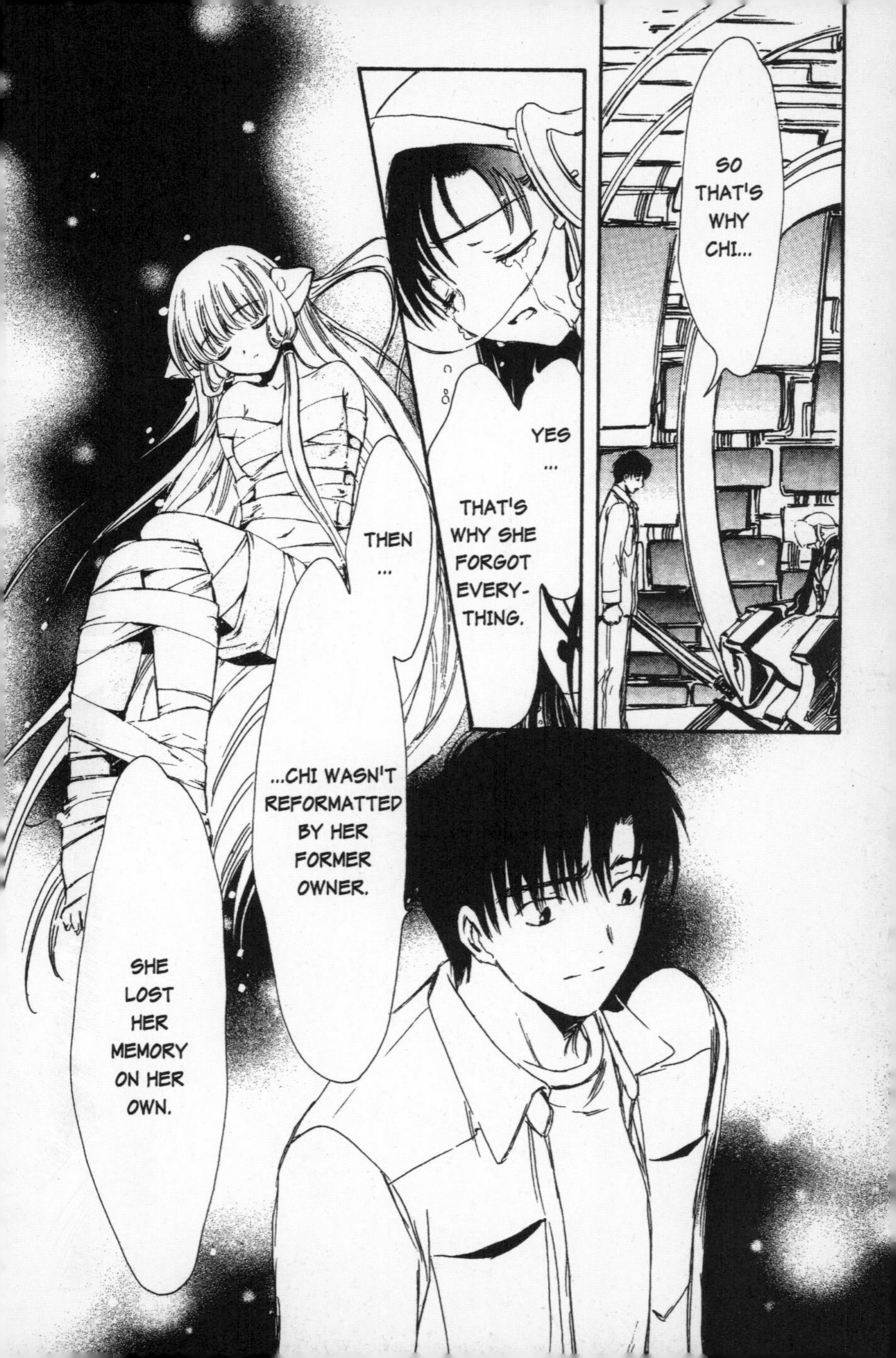
SO THAT'S WHY CHI...
YES ...
THAT'S WHY SHE FORGOT EVERY-THING.
THEN ...
...CHI WASN'T REFORMATTED BY HER FORMER OWNER.
SHE LOST HER MEMORY ON HER OWN.

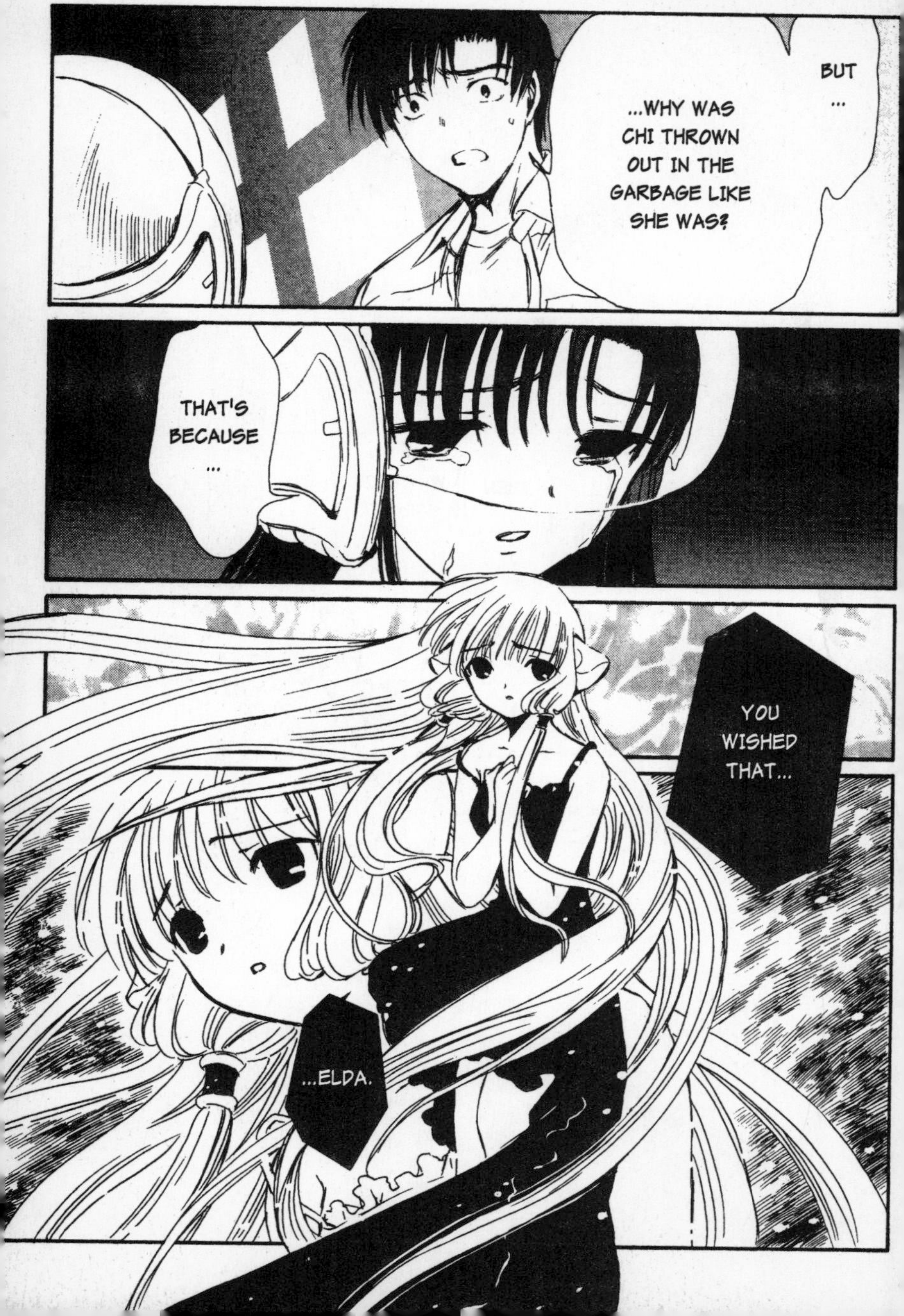
BUT ...
...WHY WAS CHI THROWN OUT IN THE GARBAGE LIKE SHE WAS?
THAT'S BECAUSE ...
YOU WISHED THAT...
...ELDA.

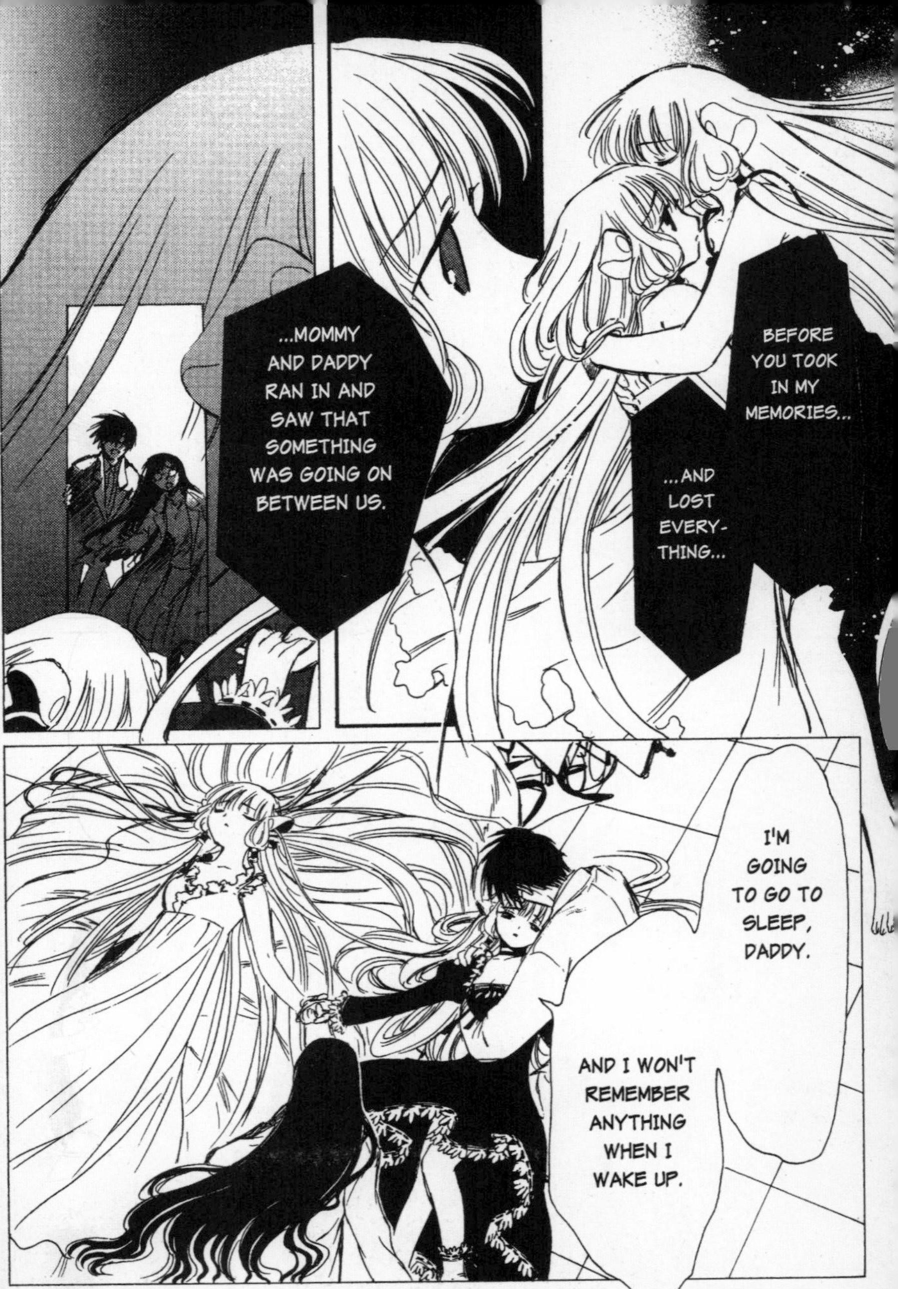
BEFORE YOU TOOK IN MY MEMORIES...
...AND LOST EVERY-THING...
...MOMMY AND DADDY RAN IN AND SAW THAT SOMETHING WAS GOING ON BETWEEN US.
I'M GOING TO GO TO SLEEP, DADDY.
AND I WON'T REMEMBER ANYTHING WHEN I WAKE UP.

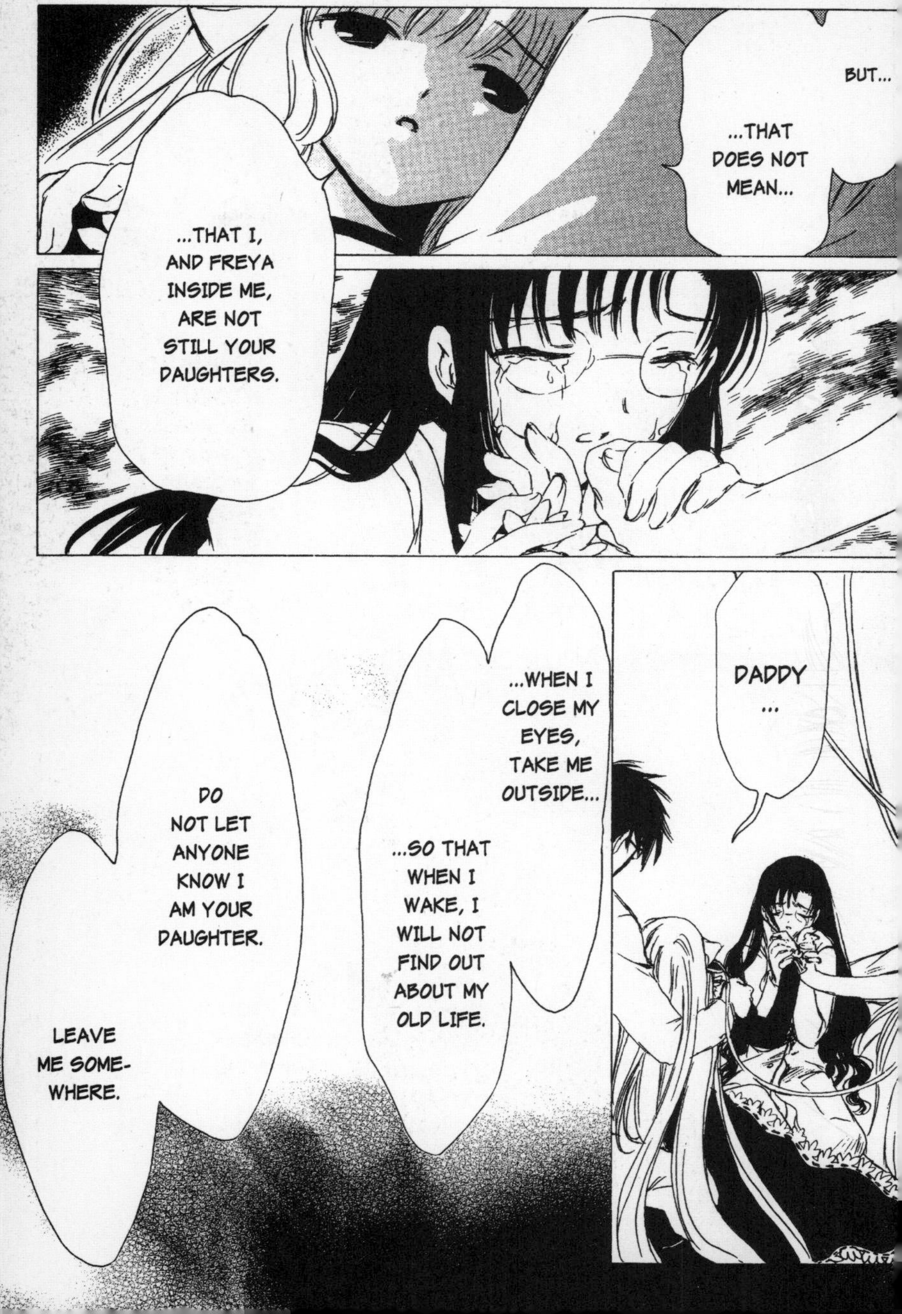
BUT...
...THAT DOES NOT MEAN...
...THAT I, AND FREYA INSIDE ME, ARE NOT STILL YOUR DAUGHTERS.
DADDY ...
...WHEN I CLOSE MY EYES, TAKE ME OUTSIDE...
...SO THAT WHEN I WAKE, I WILL NOT FIND OUT ABOUT MY OLD LIFE.
DO NOT LET ANYONE KNOW I AM YOUR DAUGHTER.
LEAVE ME SOME-WHERE.

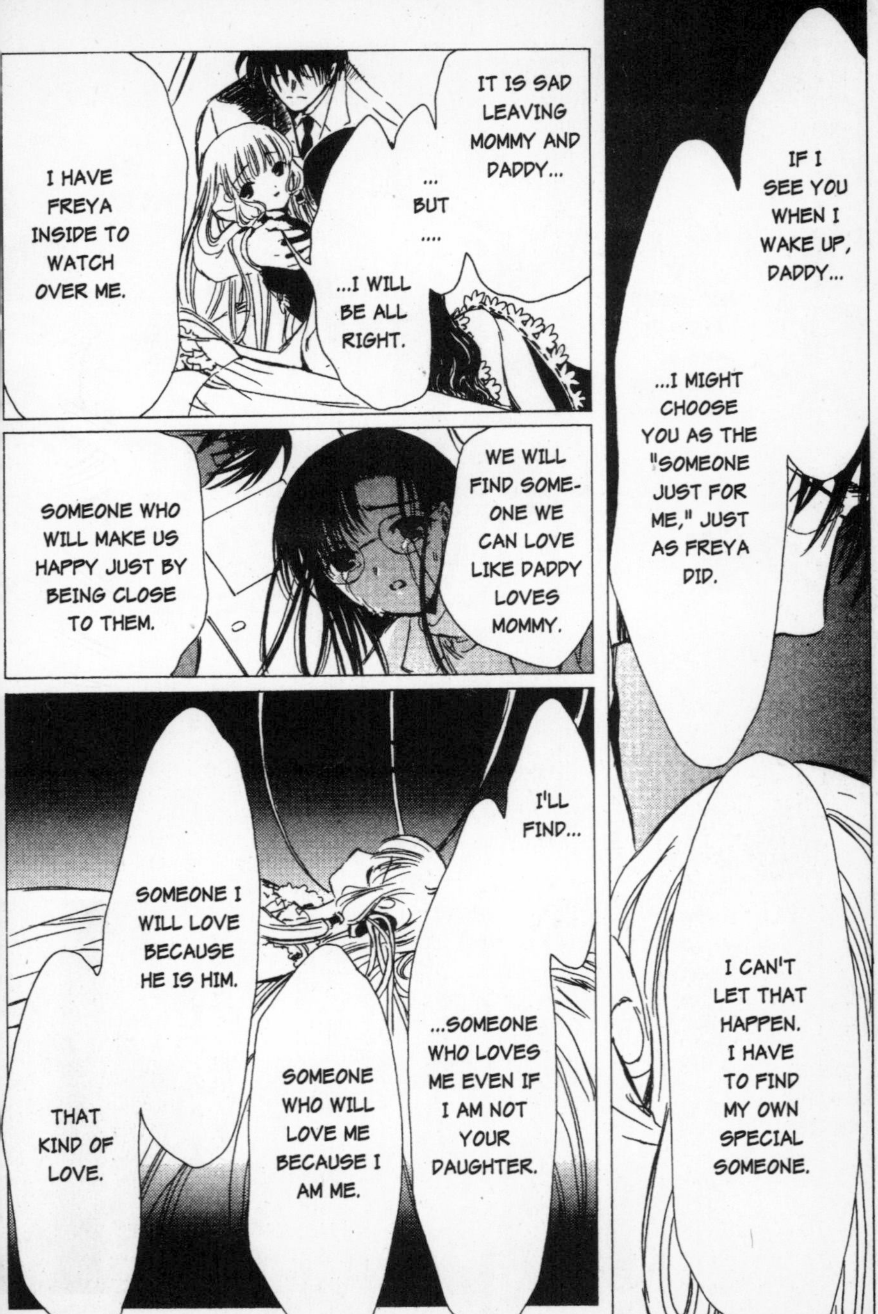
IF I SEE YOU WHEN I WAKE UP, DADDY...
...I MIGHT CHOOSE YOU AS THE "SOMEONE JUST FOR ME," JUST AS FREYA DID.
I CAN'T LET THAT HAPPEN. I HAVE TO FIND MY OWN SPECIAL SOMEONE.
IT IS SAD LEAVING MOMMY AND DADDY...
... BUT ....
...I WILL BE ALL RIGHT.
I HAVE FREYA INSIDE TO WATCH OVER ME.
WE WILL FIND SOME-ONE WE CAN LOVE LIKE DADDY LOVES MOMMY.
SOMEONE WHO WILL MAKE US HAPPY JUST BY BEING CLOSE TO THEM.
I'LL FIND...
...SOMEONE WHO LOVES ME EVEN IF I AM NOT YOUR DAUGHTER.
SOMEONE WHO WILL LOVE ME BECAUSE I AM ME.
SOMEONE I WILL LOVE BECAUSE HE IS HIM.
THAT KIND OF LOVE.

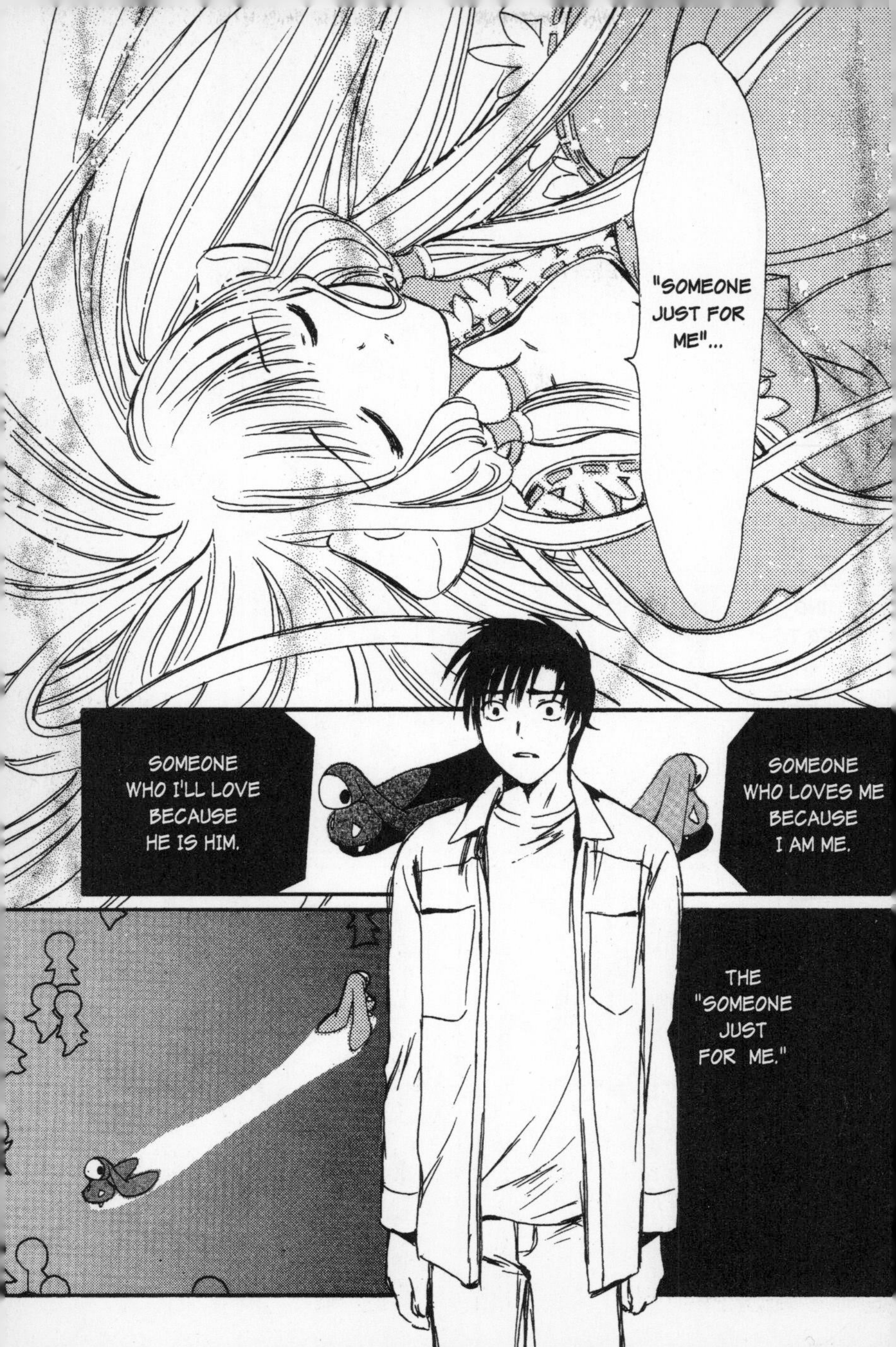
"SOMEONE JUST FOR ME"...
SOMEONE WHO LOVES ME BECAUSE I AM ME.
SOMEONE WHO I'LL LOVE BECAUSE HE IS HIM.
THE "SOMEONE JUST FOR ME."

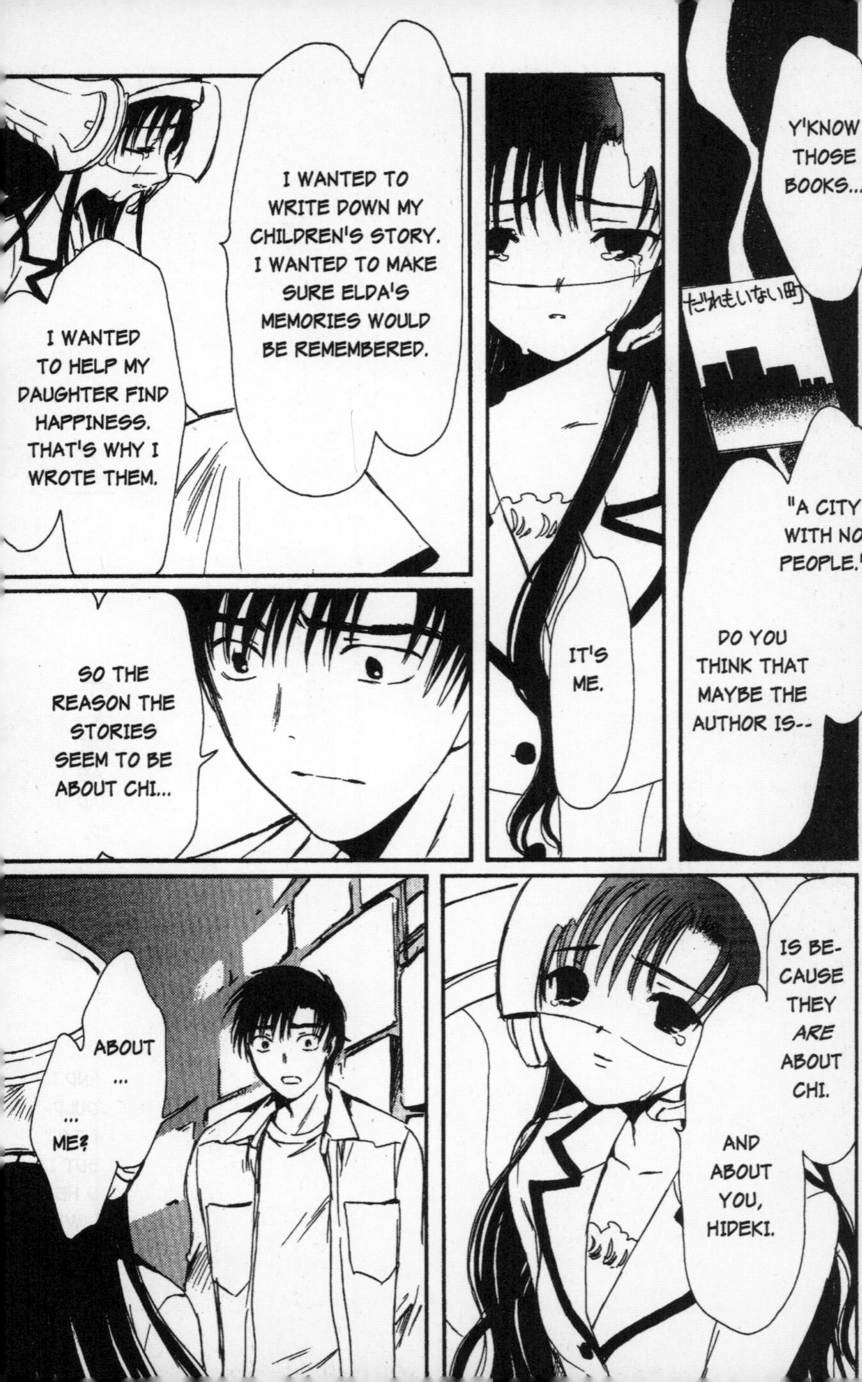
Y'KNOW THOSE BOOKS...
だれもいない町
"A CITY WITH NO PEOPLE."
DO YOU THINK THAT MAYBE THE AUTHOR IS--
IT'S ME.
I WANTED TO WRITE DOWN MY CHILDREN'S STORY. I WANTED TO MAKE SURE ELDA'S MEMORIES WOULD BE REMEMBERED.
I WANTED TO HELP MY DAUGHTER FIND HAPPINESS. THAT'S WHY I WROTE THEM.
SO THE REASON THE STORIES SEEM TO BE ABOUT CHI...
IS BE-CAUSE THEY *ARE* ABOUT CHI.
AND ABOUT YOU, HIDEKI.
ABOUT ... ... ME?

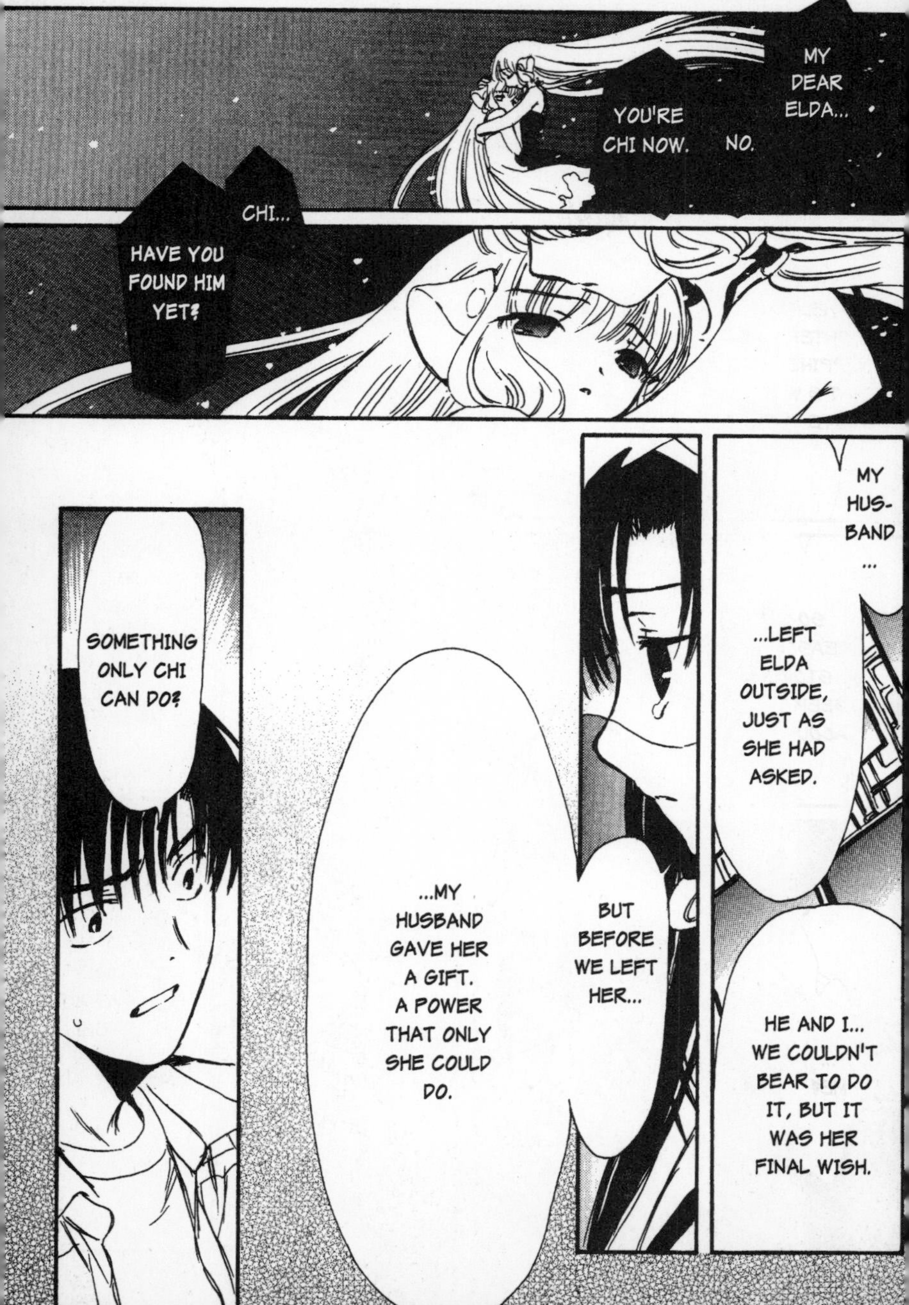
MY DEAR ELDA...
NO.
YOU'RE CHI NOW.
CHI...
HAVE YOU FOUND HIM YET?
MY HUS-BAND...
...LEFT ELDA OUTSIDE, JUST AS SHE HAD ASKED.
HE AND I... WE COULDN'T BEAR TO DO IT, BUT IT WAS HER FINAL WISH.
BUT BEFORE WE LEFT HER...
...MY HUSBAND GAVE HER A GIFT. A POWER THAT ONLY SHE COULD DO.
SOMETHING ONLY CHI CAN DO?

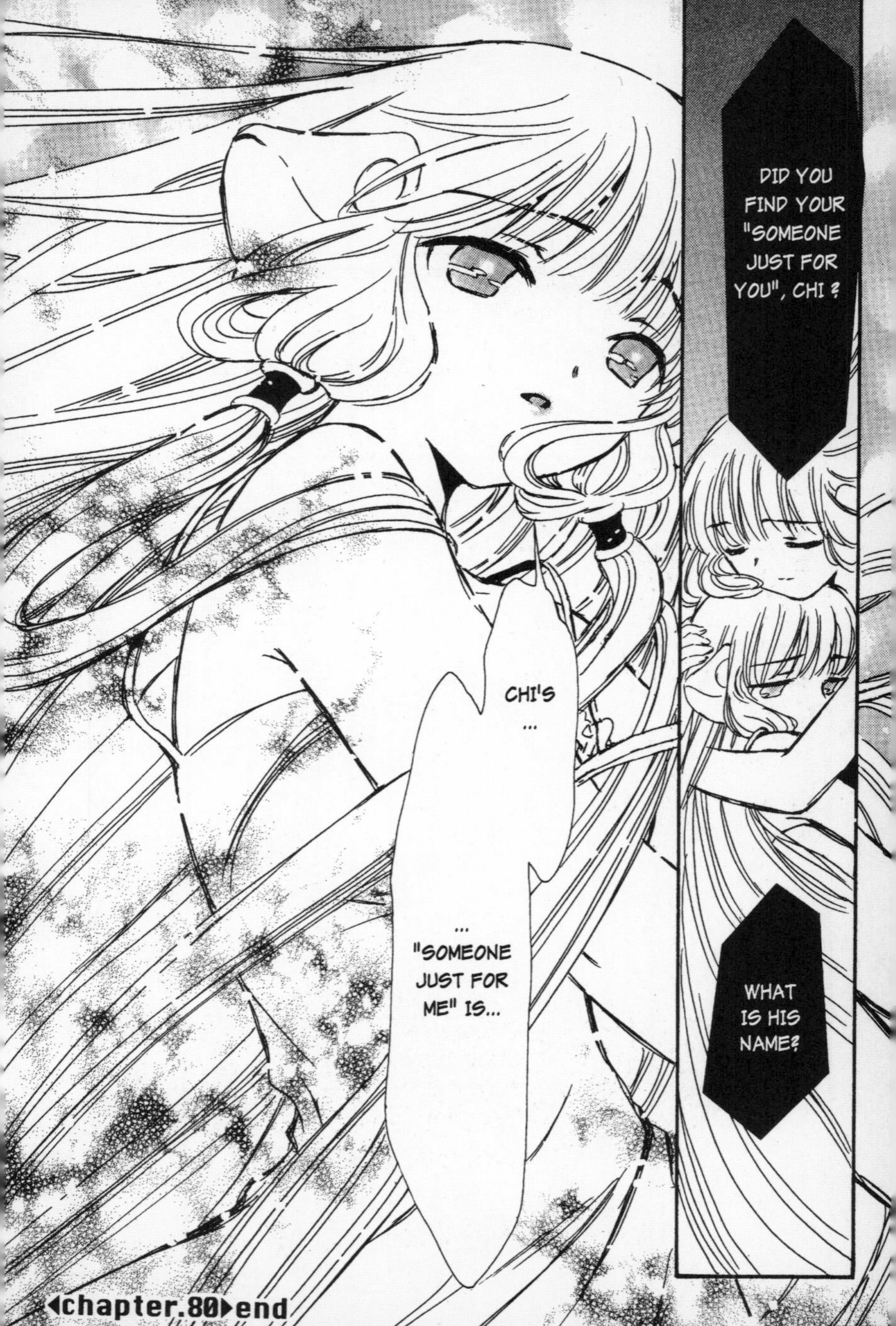
DID YOU FIND YOUR "SOMEONE JUST FOR YOU", CHI?
WHAT IS HIS NAME?
CHI'S ...
... "SOMEONE JUST FOR ME" IS...
◂chapter.80▸end

ちょびっツ

Chobits

◀chapter.81▶

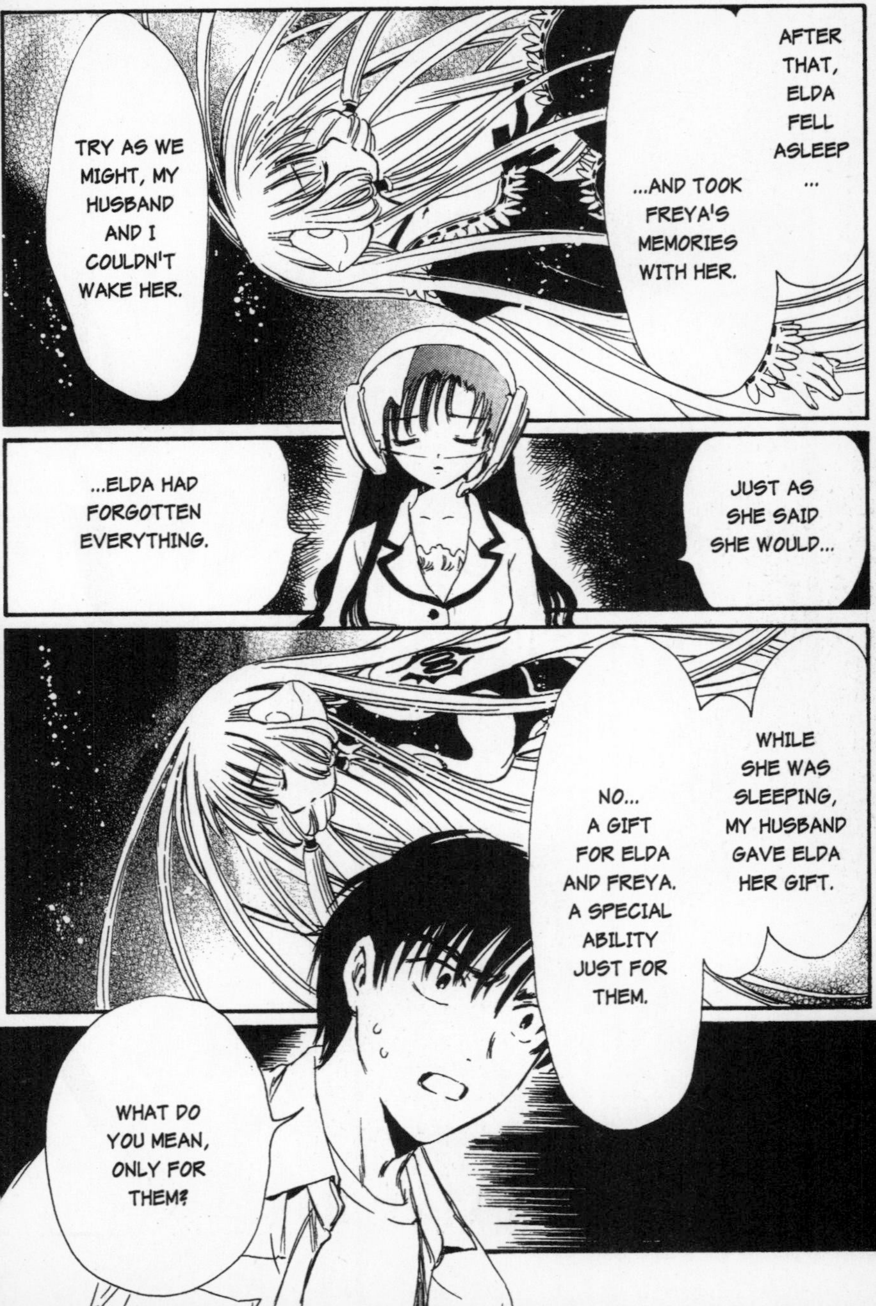
AFTER THAT, ELDA FELL ASLEEP ...
...AND TOOK FREYA'S MEMORIES WITH HER.
TRY AS WE MIGHT, MY HUSBAND AND I COULDN'T WAKE HER.
JUST AS SHE SAID SHE WOULD...
...ELDA HAD FORGOTTEN EVERYTHING.
WHILE SHE WAS SLEEPING, MY HUSBAND GAVE ELDA HER GIFT.
NO... A GIFT FOR ELDA AND FREYA. A SPECIAL ABILITY JUST FOR THEM.
WHAT DO YOU MEAN, ONLY FOR THEM?

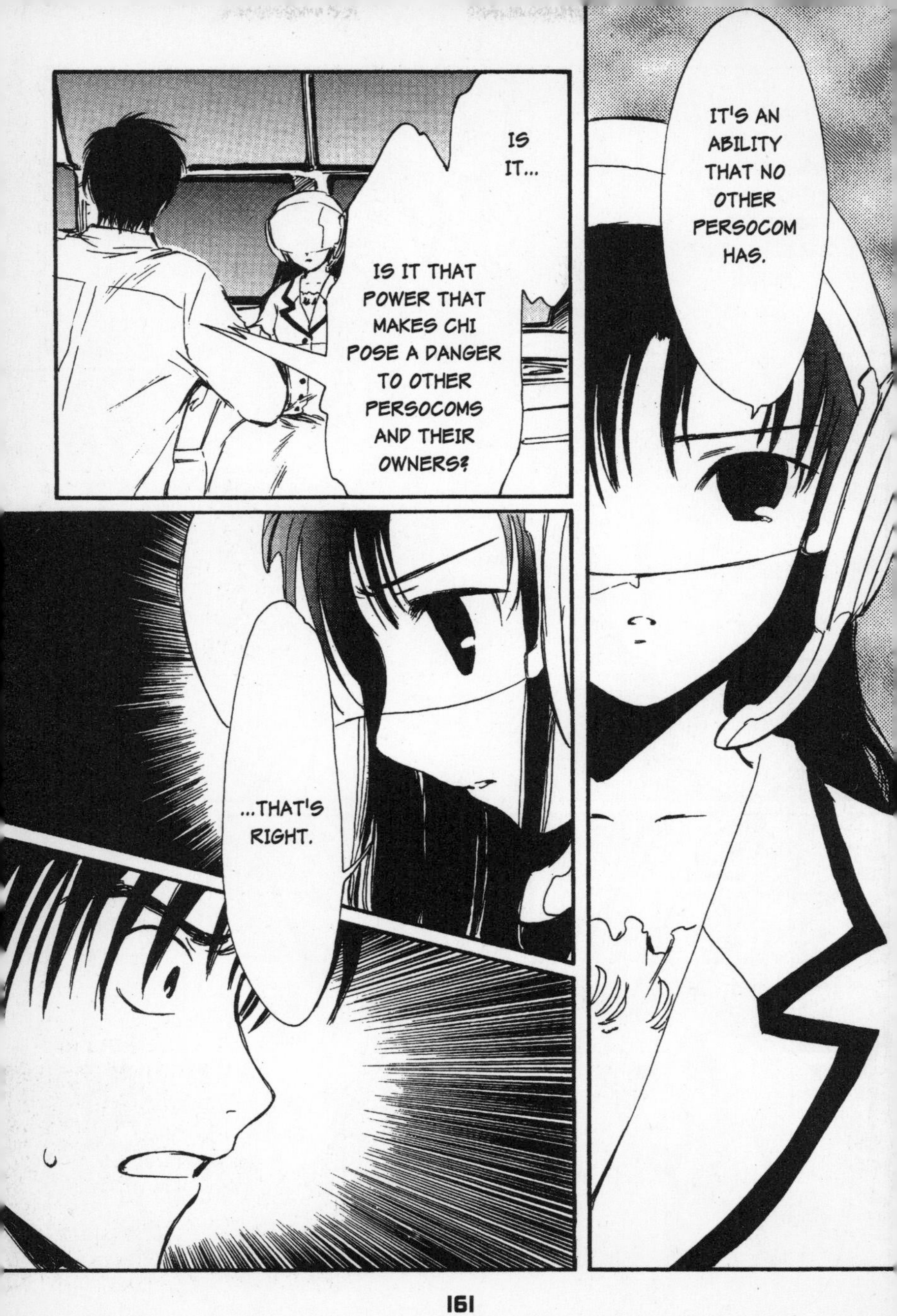
IT'S AN ABILITY THAT NO OTHER PERSOCOM HAS.
IS IT...
IS IT THAT POWER THAT MAKES CHI POSE A DANGER TO OTHER PERSOCOMS AND THEIR OWNERS?
...THAT'S RIGHT.

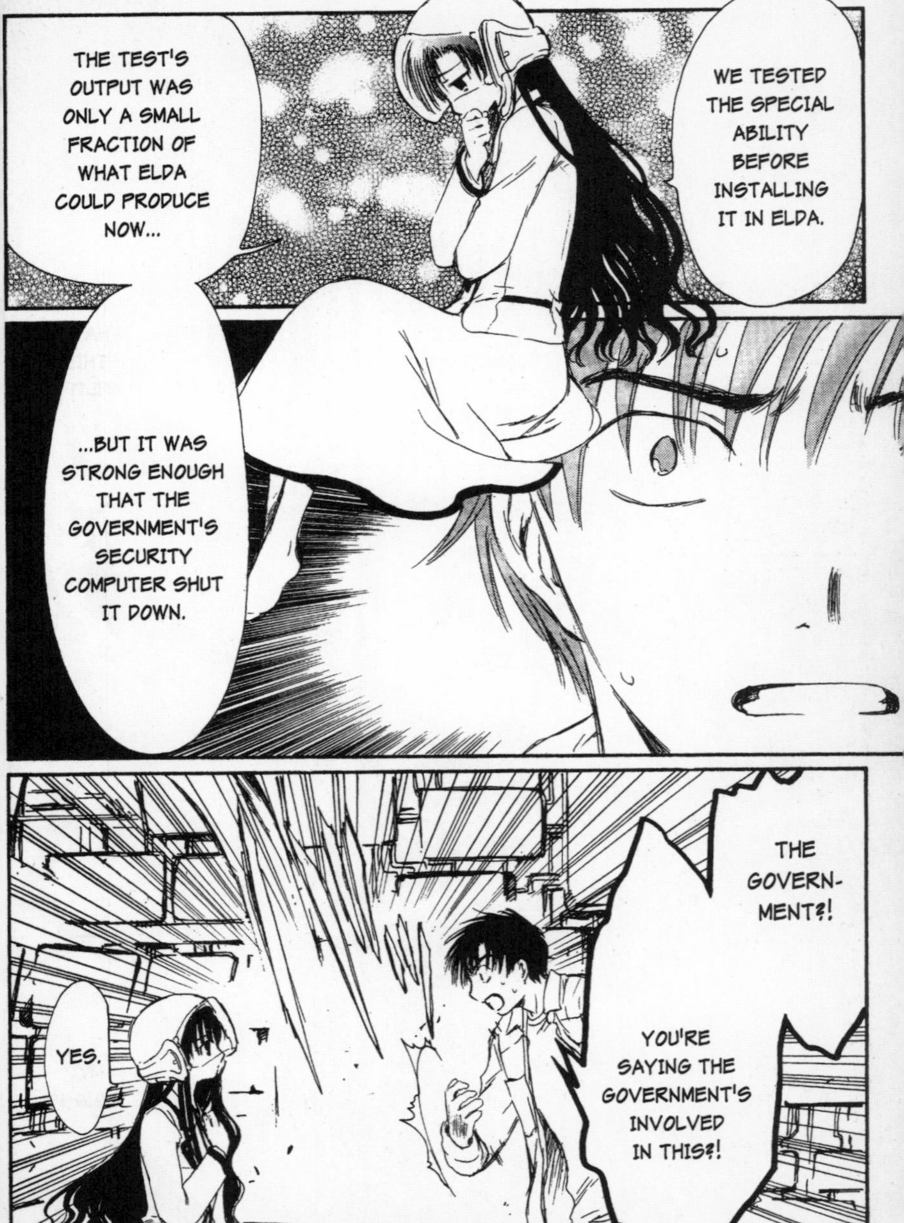

WE TESTED THE SPECIAL ABILITY BEFORE INSTALLING IT IN ELDA.
THE TEST'S OUTPUT WAS ONLY A SMALL FRACTION OF WHAT ELDA COULD PRODUCE NOW...
...BUT IT WAS STRONG ENOUGH THAT THE GOVERNMENT'S SECURITY COMPUTER SHUT IT DOWN.
THE GOVERN-MENT?!
YOU'RE SAYING THE GOVERNMENT'S INVOLVED IN THIS?!
YES.

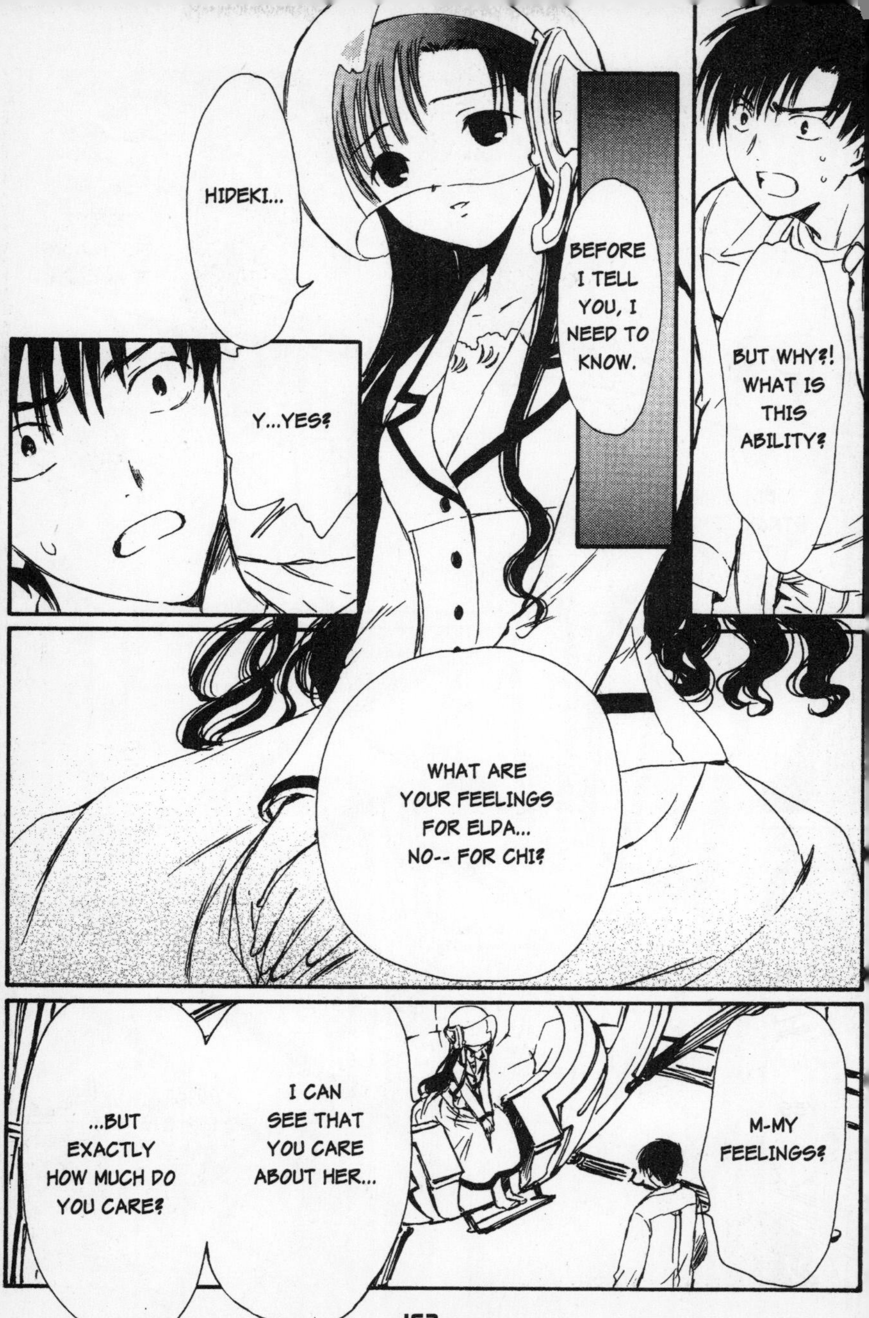
BUT WHY?! WHAT IS THIS ABILITY?
HIDEKI...
Y...YES?
BEFORE I TELL YOU, I NEED TO KNOW.
WHAT ARE YOUR FEELINGS FOR ELDA... NO-- FOR CHI?
M-MY FEELINGS?
I CAN SEE THAT YOU CARE ABOUT HER...
...BUT EXACTLY HOW MUCH DO YOU CARE?

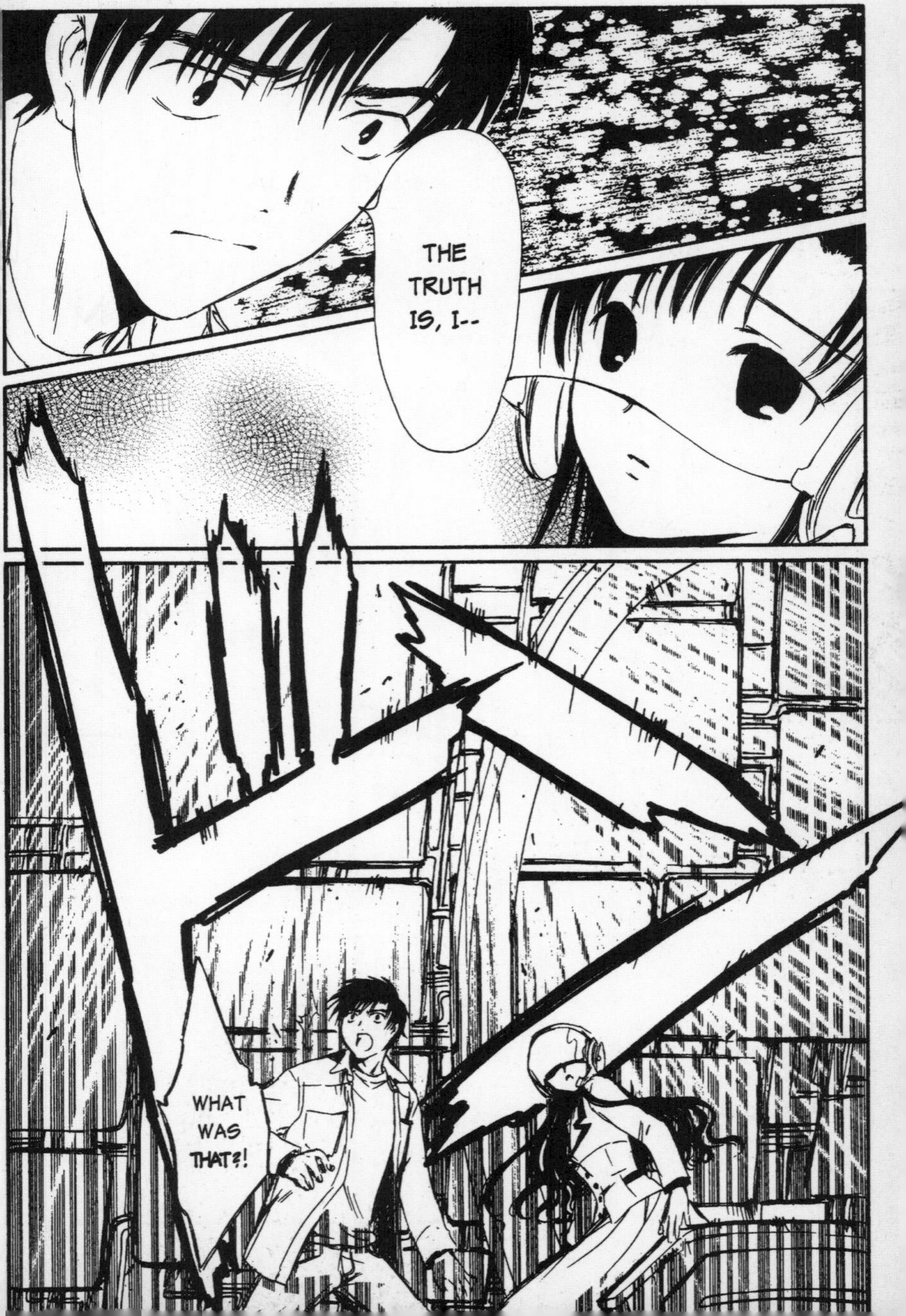
THE TRUTH IS, I--
WHAT WAS THAT?!

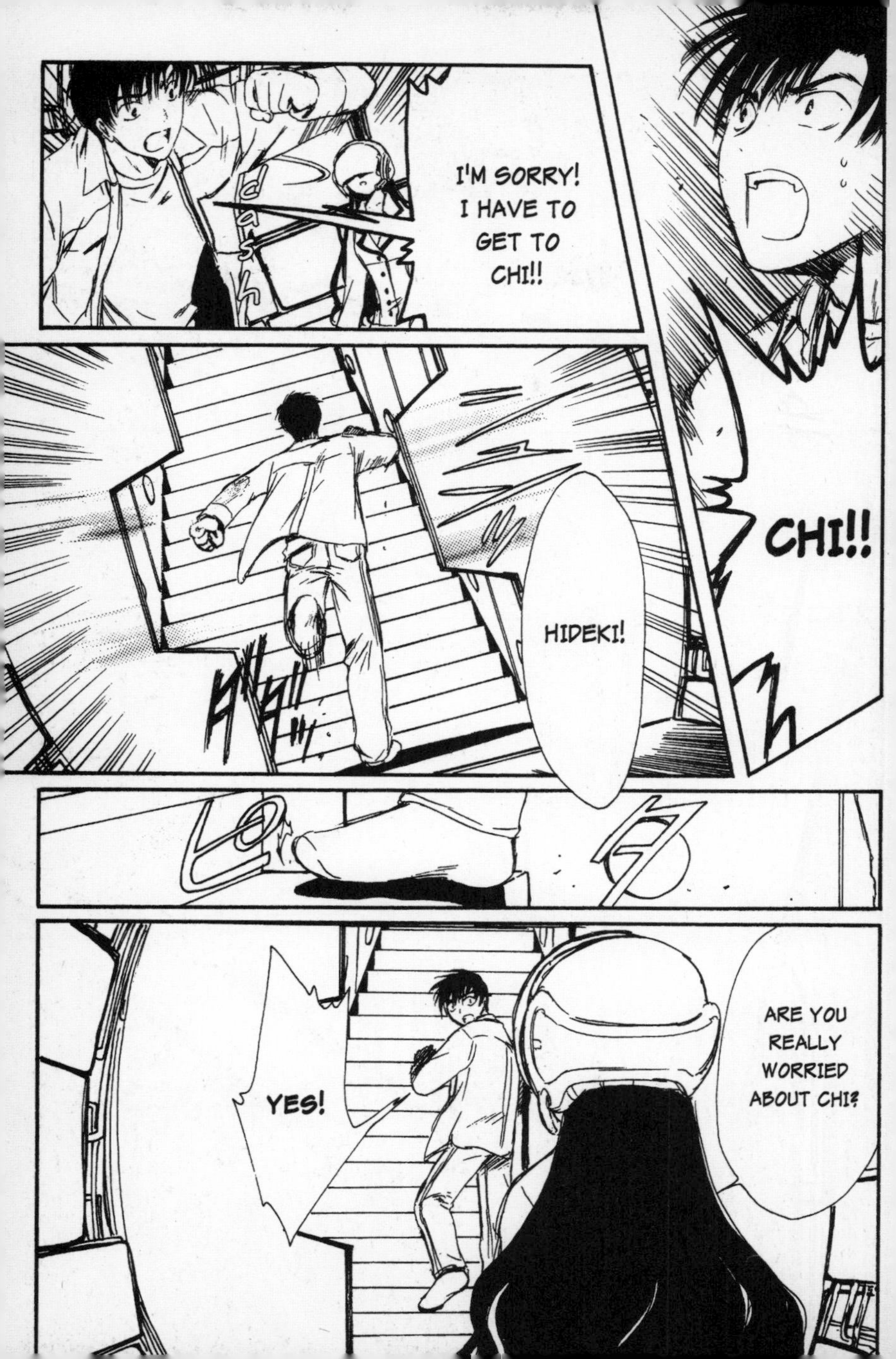
CHI!!
dash
I'M SORRY! I HAVE TO GET TO CHI!!
HIDEKI!
ARE YOU REALLY WORRIED ABOUT CHI?
YES!

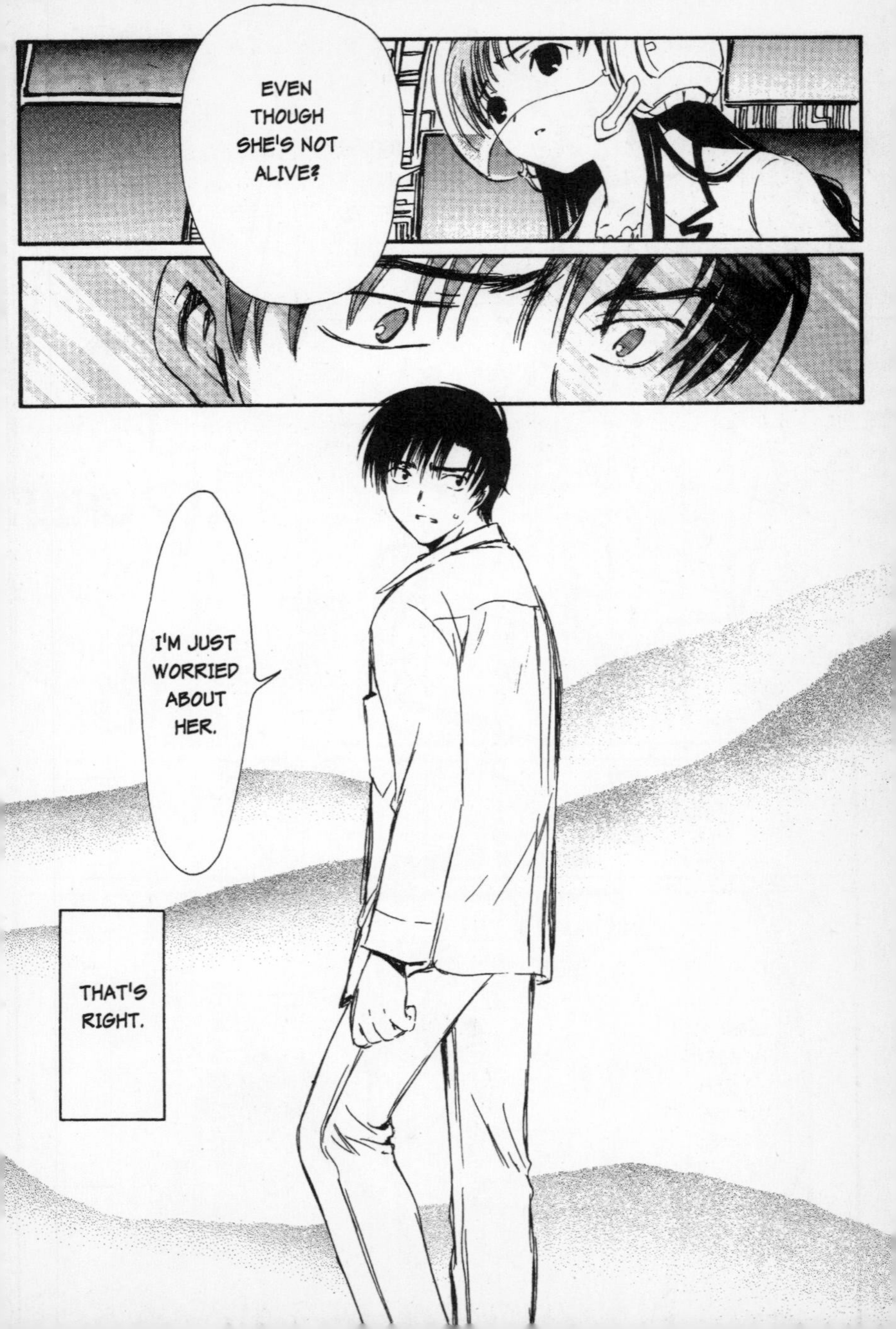
EVEN THOUGH SHE'S NOT ALIVE?
I'M JUST WORRIED ABOUT HER.
THAT'S RIGHT.

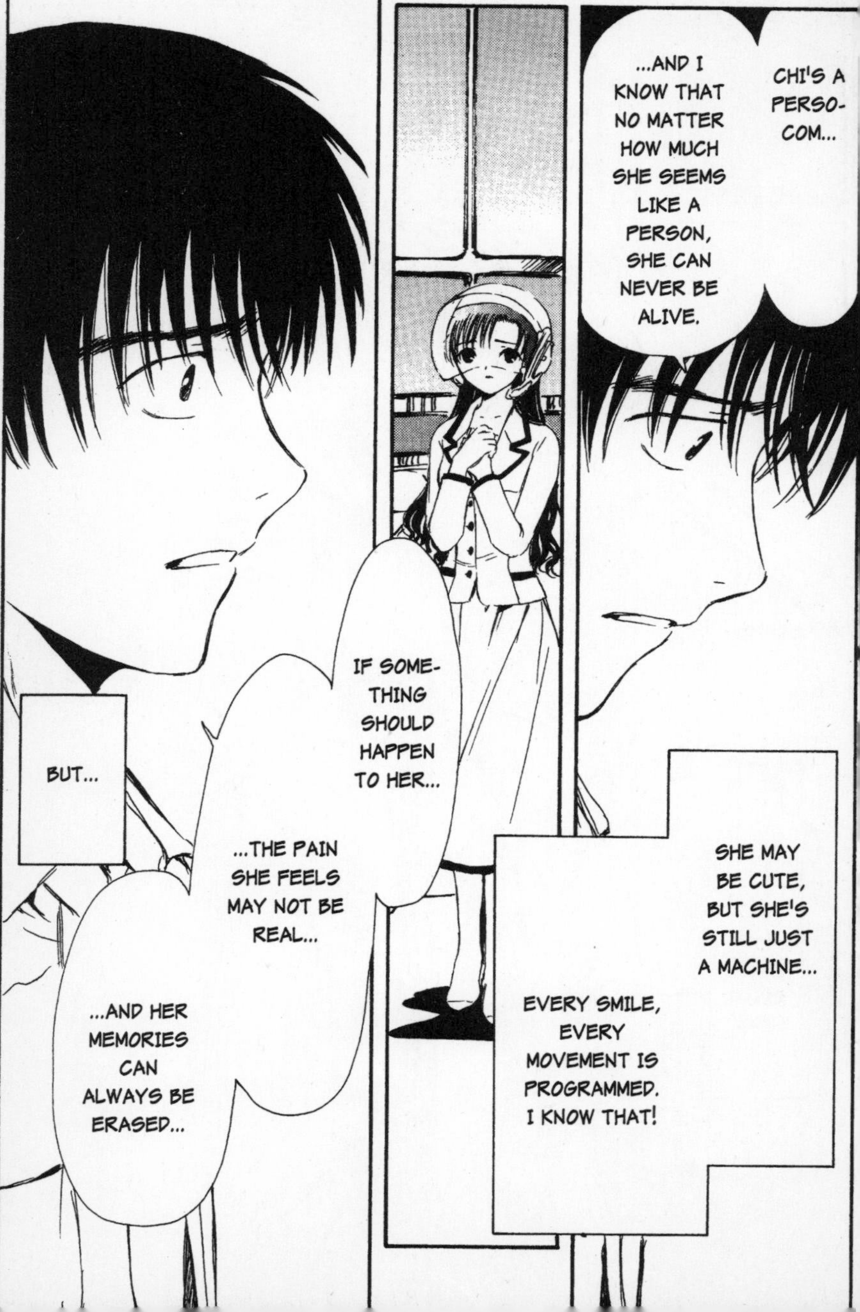
CHI'S A PERSO-COM...
...AND I KNOW THAT NO MATTER HOW MUCH SHE SEEMS LIKE A PERSON, SHE CAN NEVER BE ALIVE.
SHE MAY BE CUTE, BUT SHE'S STILL JUST A MACHINE...
EVERY SMILE, EVERY MOVEMENT IS PROGRAMMED. I KNOW THAT!
BUT...
IF SOME-THING SHOULD HAPPEN TO HER...
...THE PAIN SHE FEELS MAY NOT BE REAL...
...AND HER MEMORIES CAN ALWAYS BE ERASED...

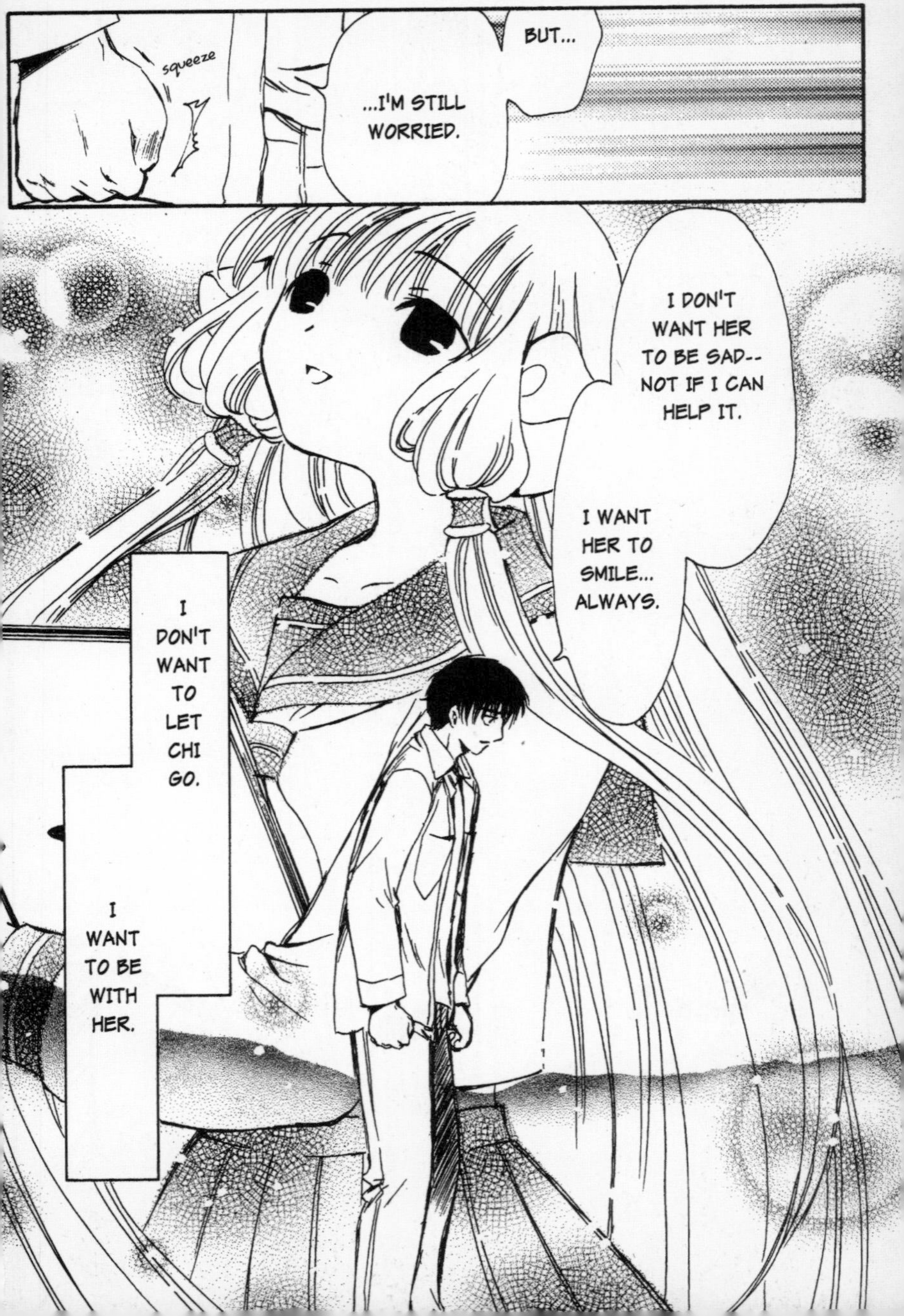
BUT...
...I'M STILL WORRIED.
squeeze
I DON'T WANT HER TO BE SAD-- NOT IF I CAN HELP IT.
I WANT HER TO SMILE... ALWAYS.
I DON'T WANT TO LET CHI GO.
I WANT TO BE WITH HER.

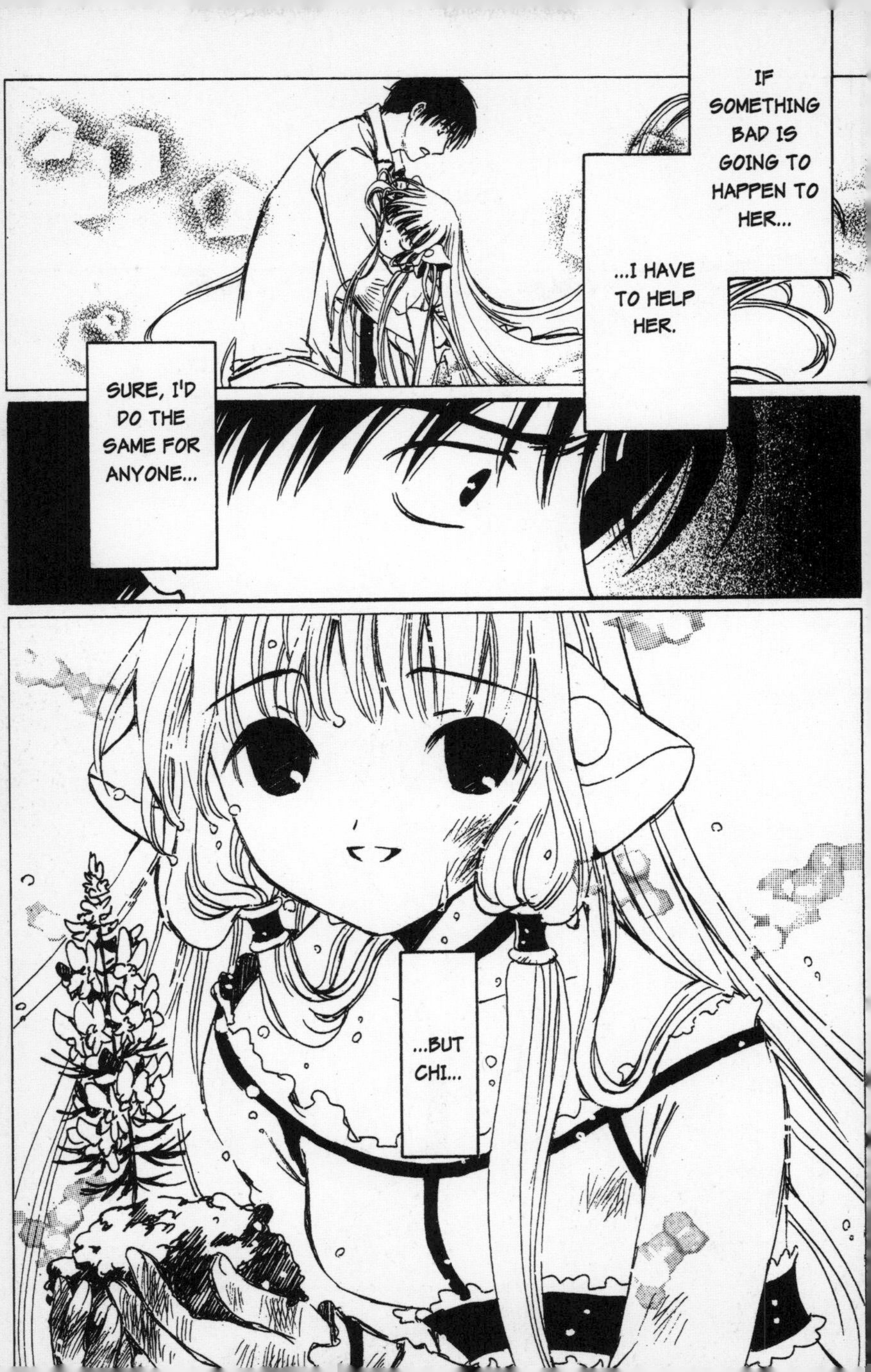
IF SOMETHING BAD IS GOING TO HAPPEN TO HER...
...I HAVE TO HELP HER.
SURE, I'D DO THE SAME FOR ANYONE...
...BUT CHI...

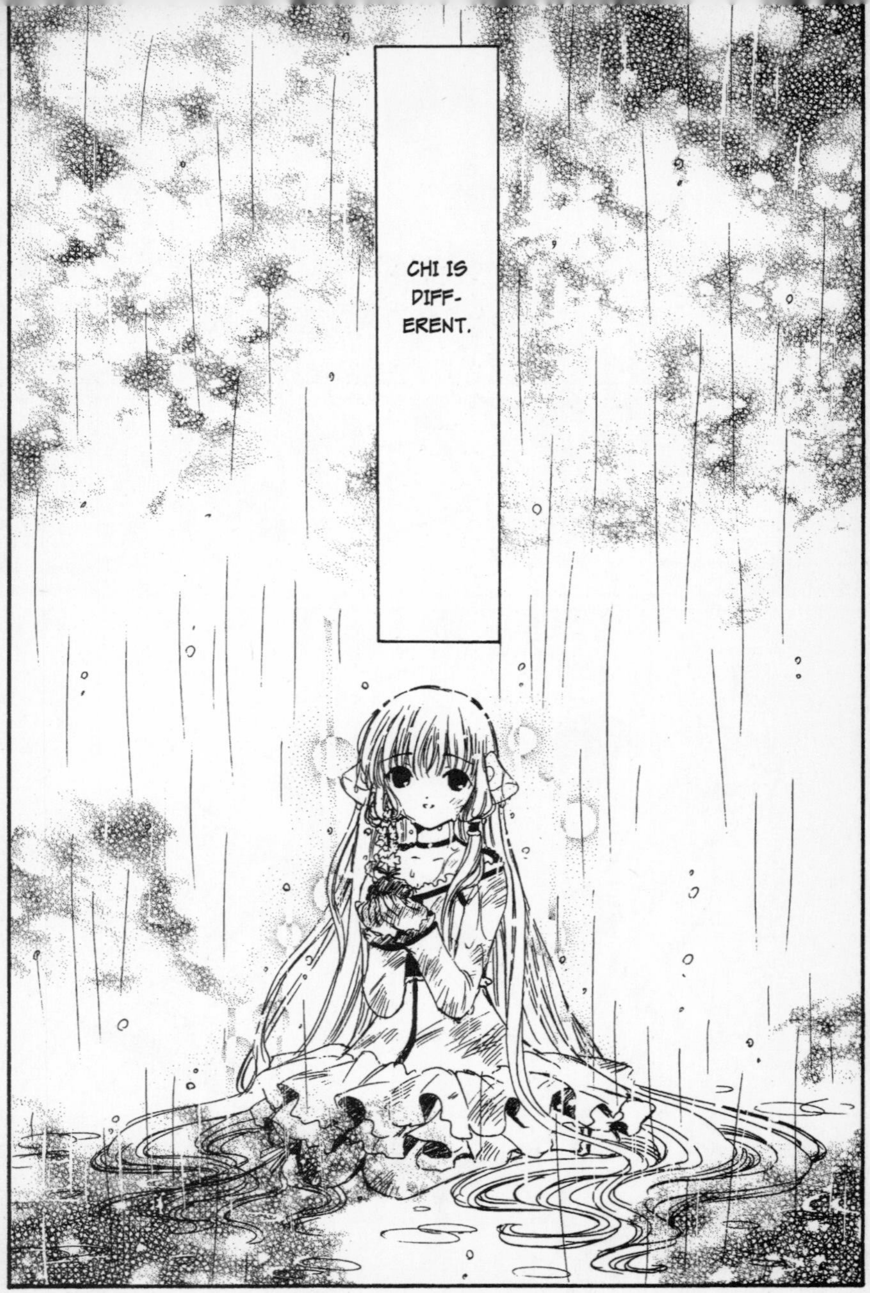
CHI IS DIFF- ERENT.

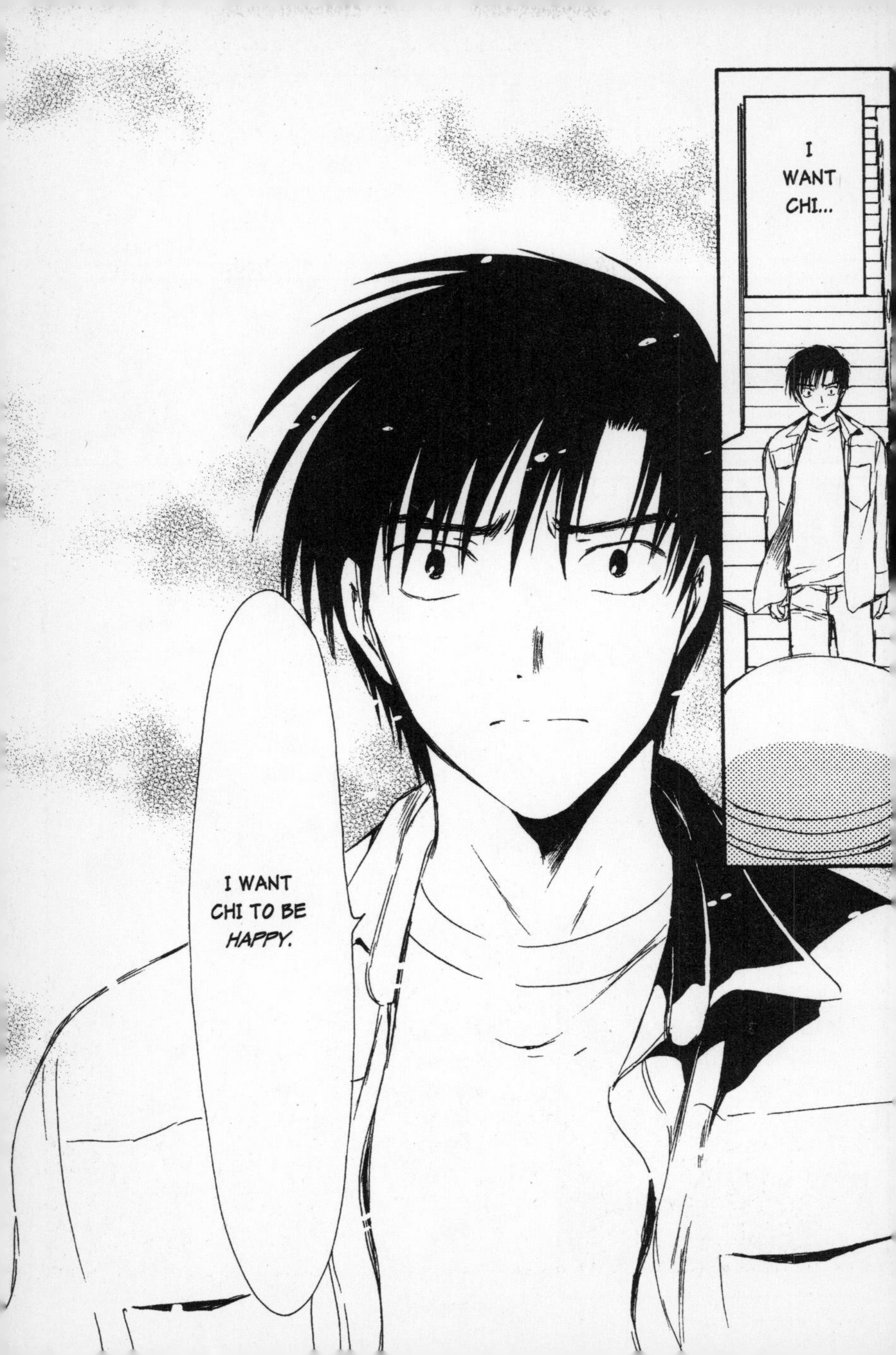
I WANT CHI...
I WANT CHI TO BE *HAPPY*.

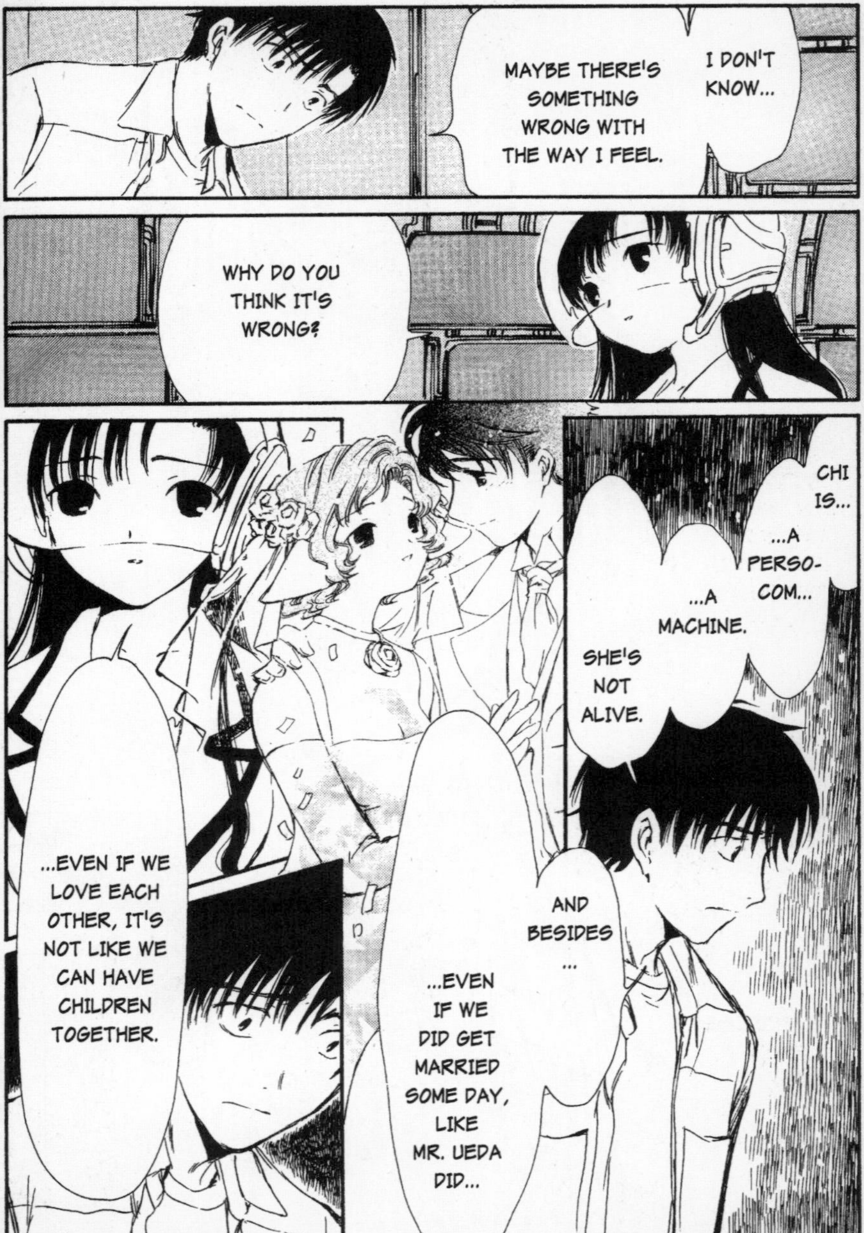
I DON'T KNOW...
MAYBE THERE'S SOMETHING WRONG WITH THE WAY I FEEL.
WHY DO YOU THINK IT'S WRONG?
CHI IS...
...A PERSO-COM...
...A MACHINE.
SHE'S NOT ALIVE.
AND BESIDES ...
...EVEN IF WE DID GET MARRIED SOME DAY, LIKE MR. UEDA DID...
...EVEN IF WE LOVE EACH OTHER, IT'S NOT LIKE WE CAN HAVE CHILDREN TOGETHER.

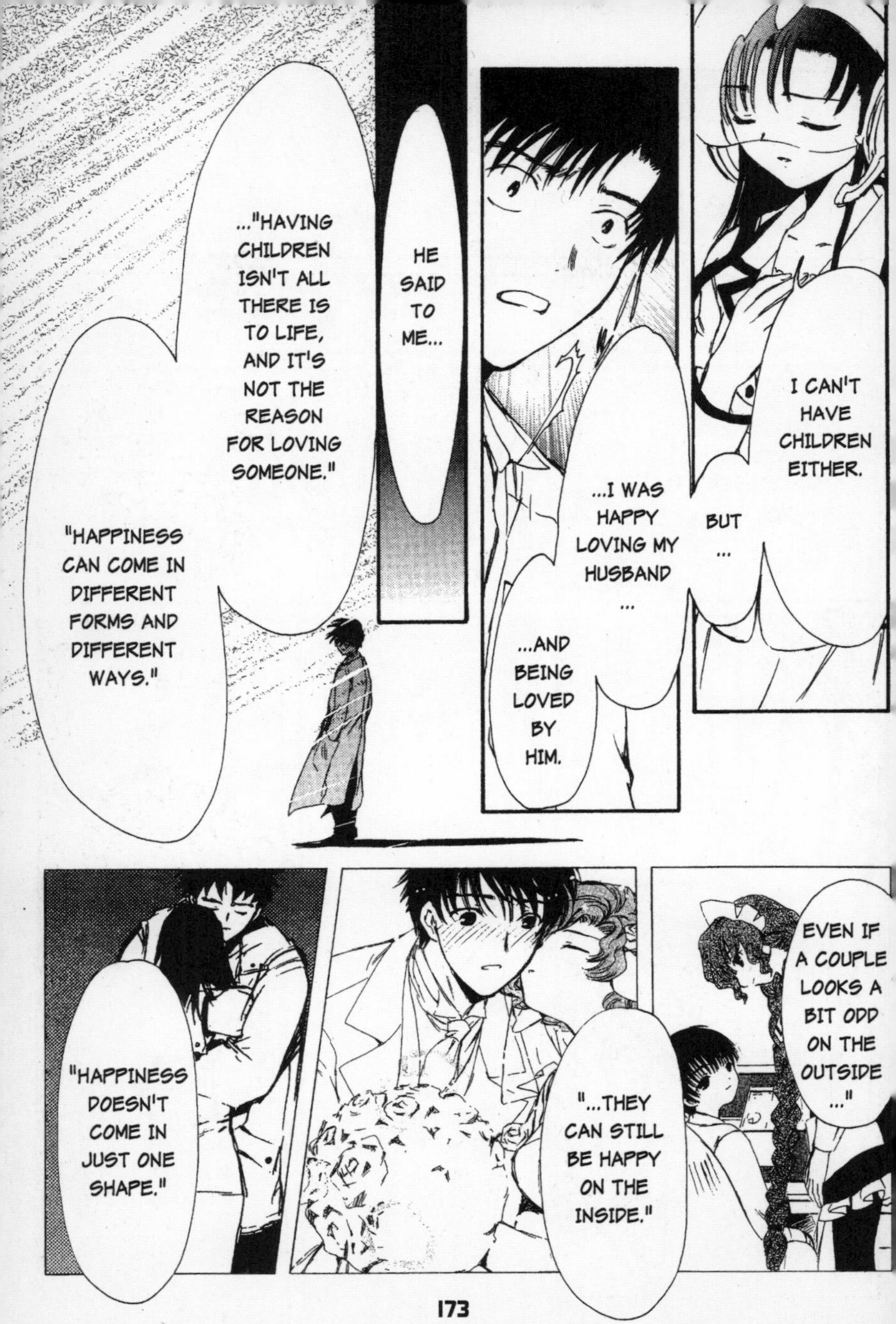
I CAN'T HAVE CHILDREN EITHER.
BUT ...
...I WAS HAPPY LOVING MY HUSBAND ...
...AND BEING LOVED BY HIM.
HE SAID TO ME...
..."HAVING CHILDREN ISN'T ALL THERE IS TO LIFE, AND IT'S NOT THE REASON FOR LOVING SOMEONE."
"HAPPINESS CAN COME IN DIFFERENT FORMS AND DIFFERENT WAYS."
EVEN IF A COUPLE LOOKS A BIT ODD ON THE OUTSIDE ..."
"...THEY CAN STILL BE HAPPY ON THE INSIDE."
"HAPPINESS DOESN'T COME IN JUST ONE SHAPE."

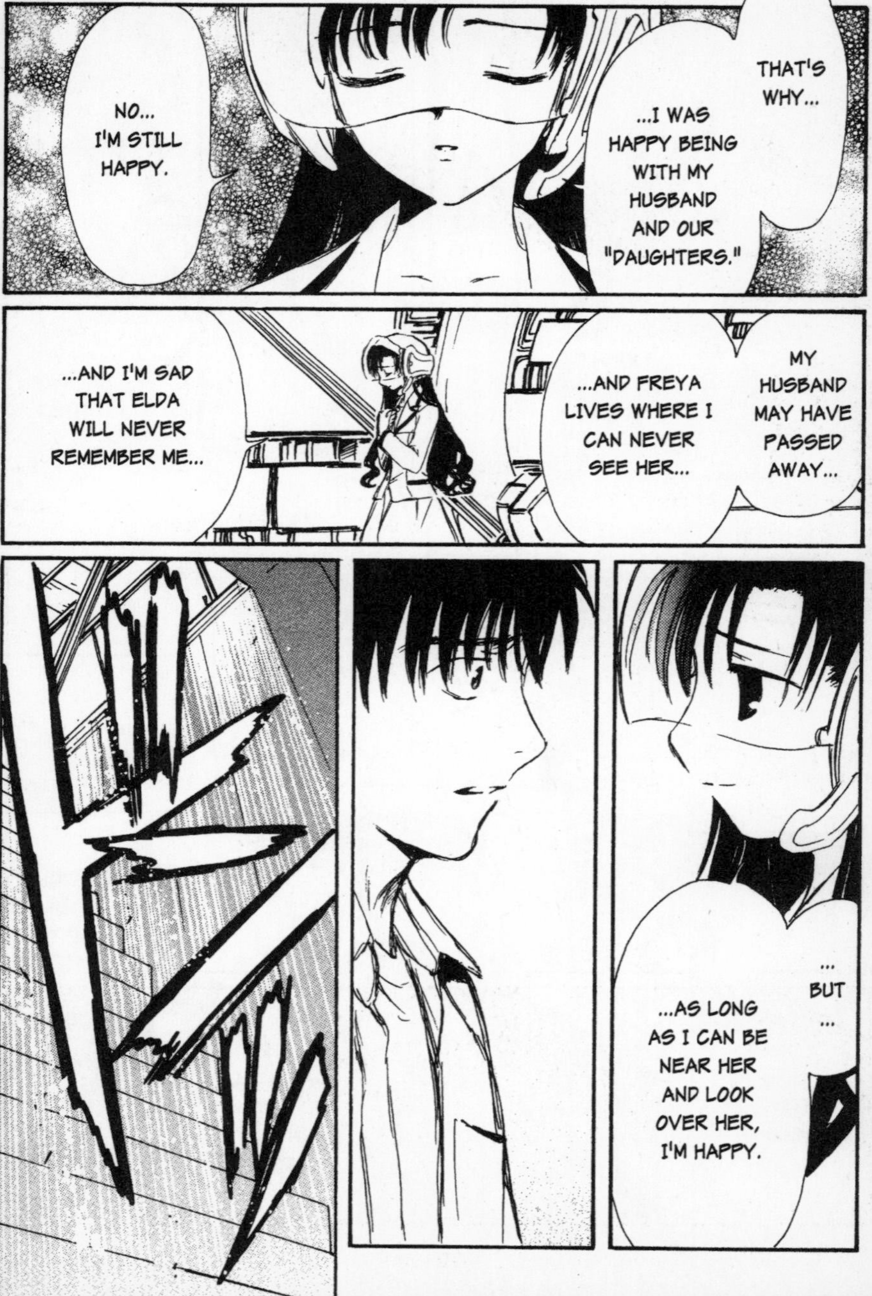
THAT'S WHY...
...I WAS HAPPY BEING WITH MY HUSBAND AND OUR "DAUGHTERS."
NO... I'M STILL HAPPY.
MY HUSBAND MAY HAVE PASSED AWAY...
...AND FREYA LIVES WHERE I CAN NEVER SEE HER...
...AND I'M SAD THAT ELDA WILL NEVER REMEMBER ME...
... BUT ...
...AS LONG AS I CAN BE NEAR HER AND LOOK OVER HER, I'M HAPPY.

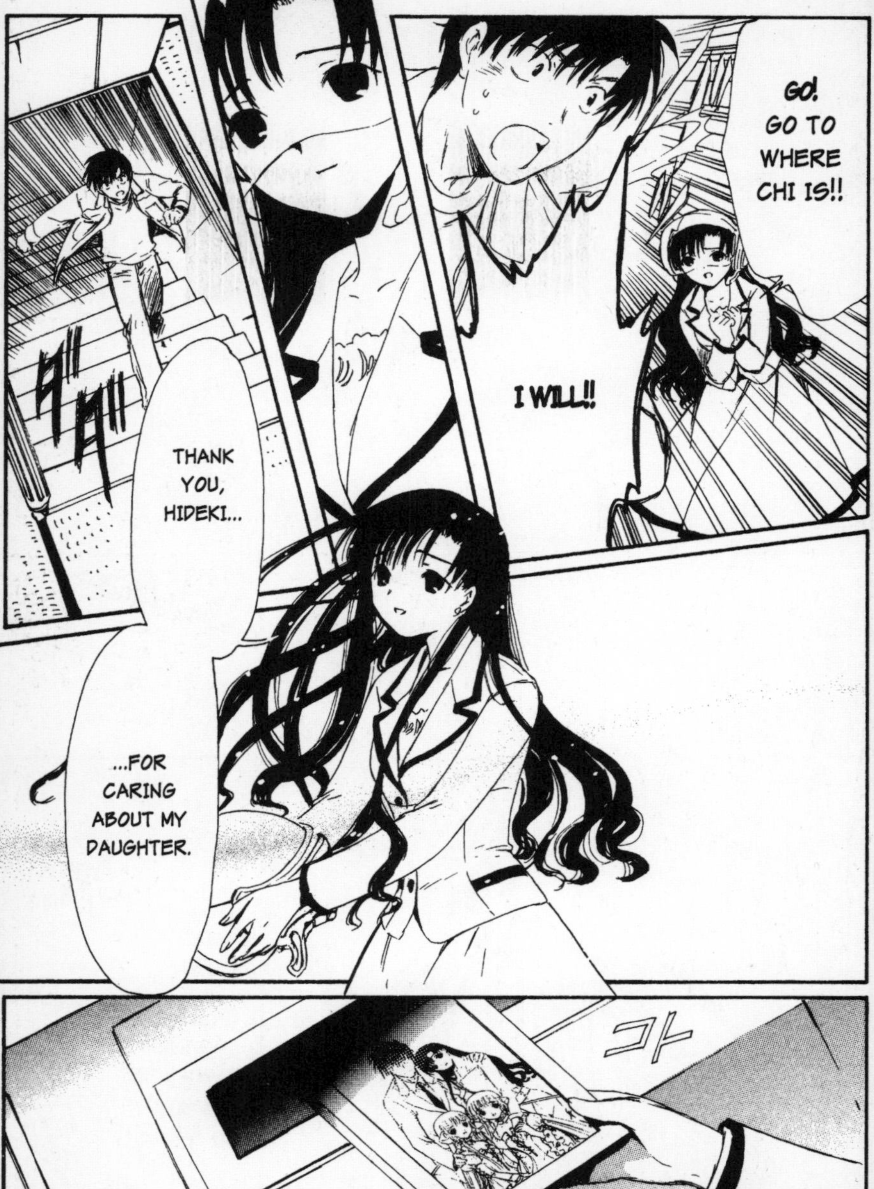
GO! GO TO WHERE CHI IS!!
I WILL!!
THANK YOU, HIDEKI...
...FOR CARING ABOUT MY DAUGHTER.
コト

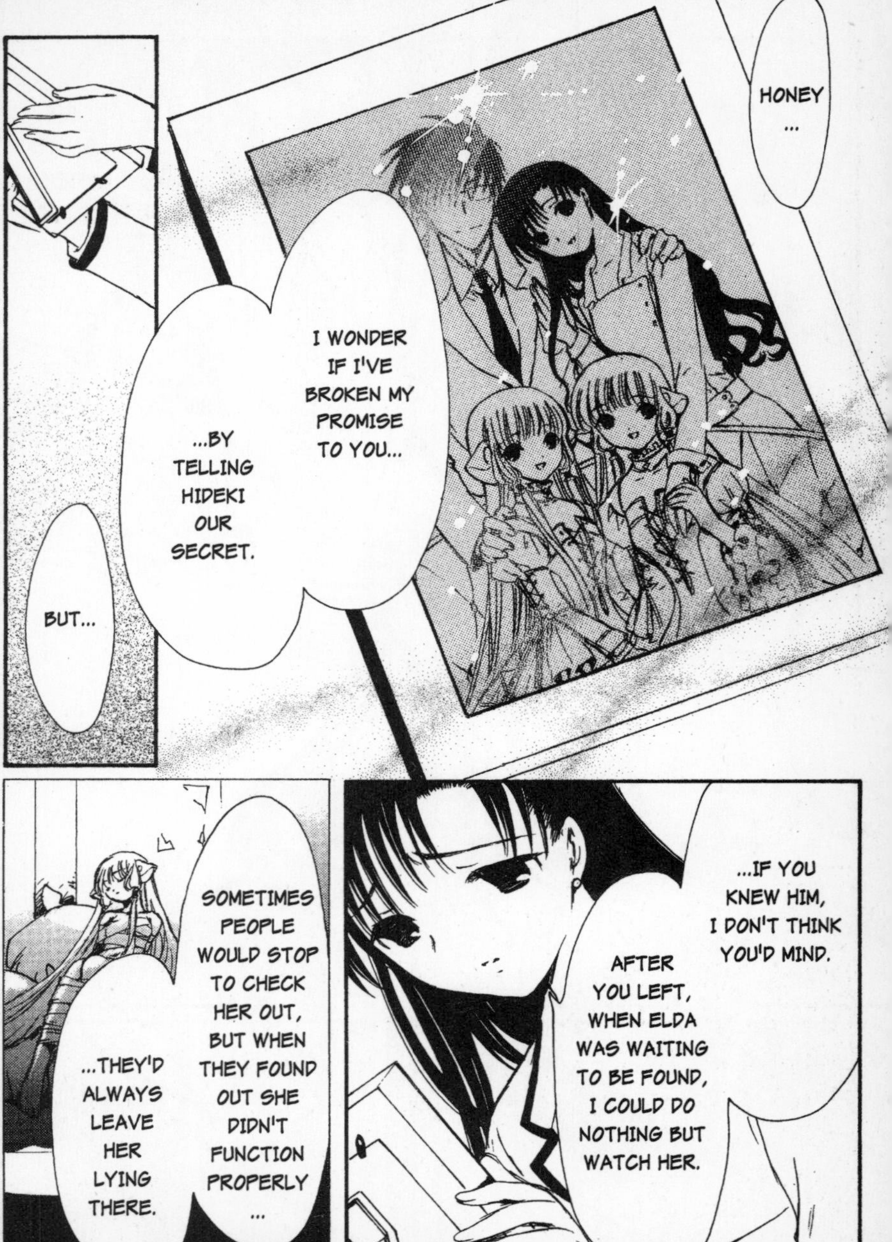
HONEY ...
I WONDER IF I'VE BROKEN MY PROMISE TO YOU...
...BY TELLING HIDEKI OUR SECRET.
BUT...
...IF YOU KNEW HIM, I DON'T THINK YOU'D MIND.
AFTER YOU LEFT, WHEN ELDA WAS WAITING TO BE FOUND, I COULD DO NOTHING BUT WATCH HER.
SOMETIMES PEOPLE WOULD STOP TO CHECK HER OUT, BUT WHEN THEY FOUND OUT SHE DIDN'T FUNCTION PROPERLY ...
...THEY'D ALWAYS LEAVE HER LYING THERE.

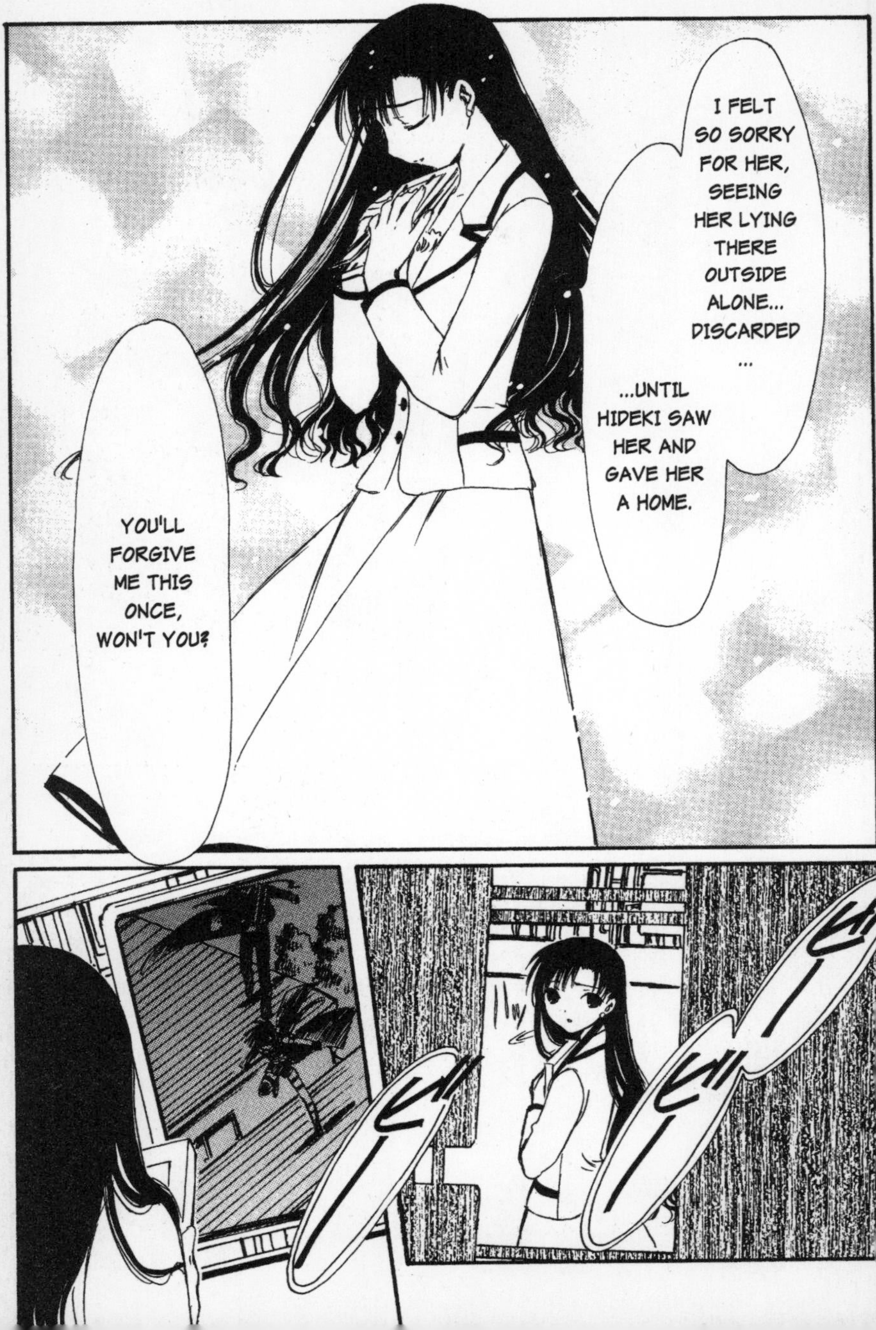
I FELT SO SORRY FOR HER, SEEING HER LYING THERE OUTSIDE ALONE... DISCARDED ...
...UNTIL HIDEKI SAW HER AND GAVE HER A HOME.
YOU'LL FORGIVE ME THIS ONCE, WON'T YOU?

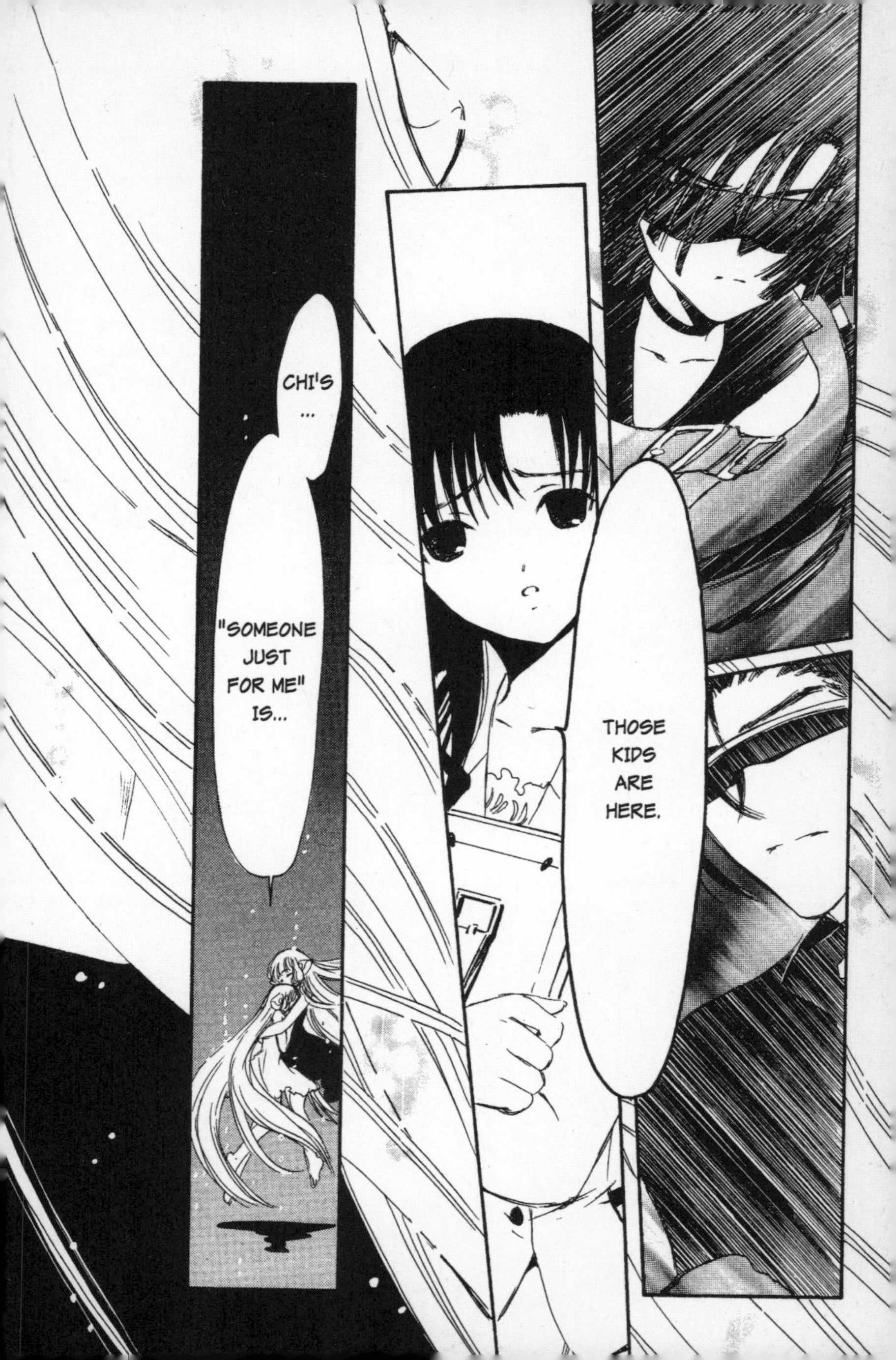
THOSE KIDS ARE HERE.
CHI'S ...
"SOMEONE JUST FOR ME" IS...

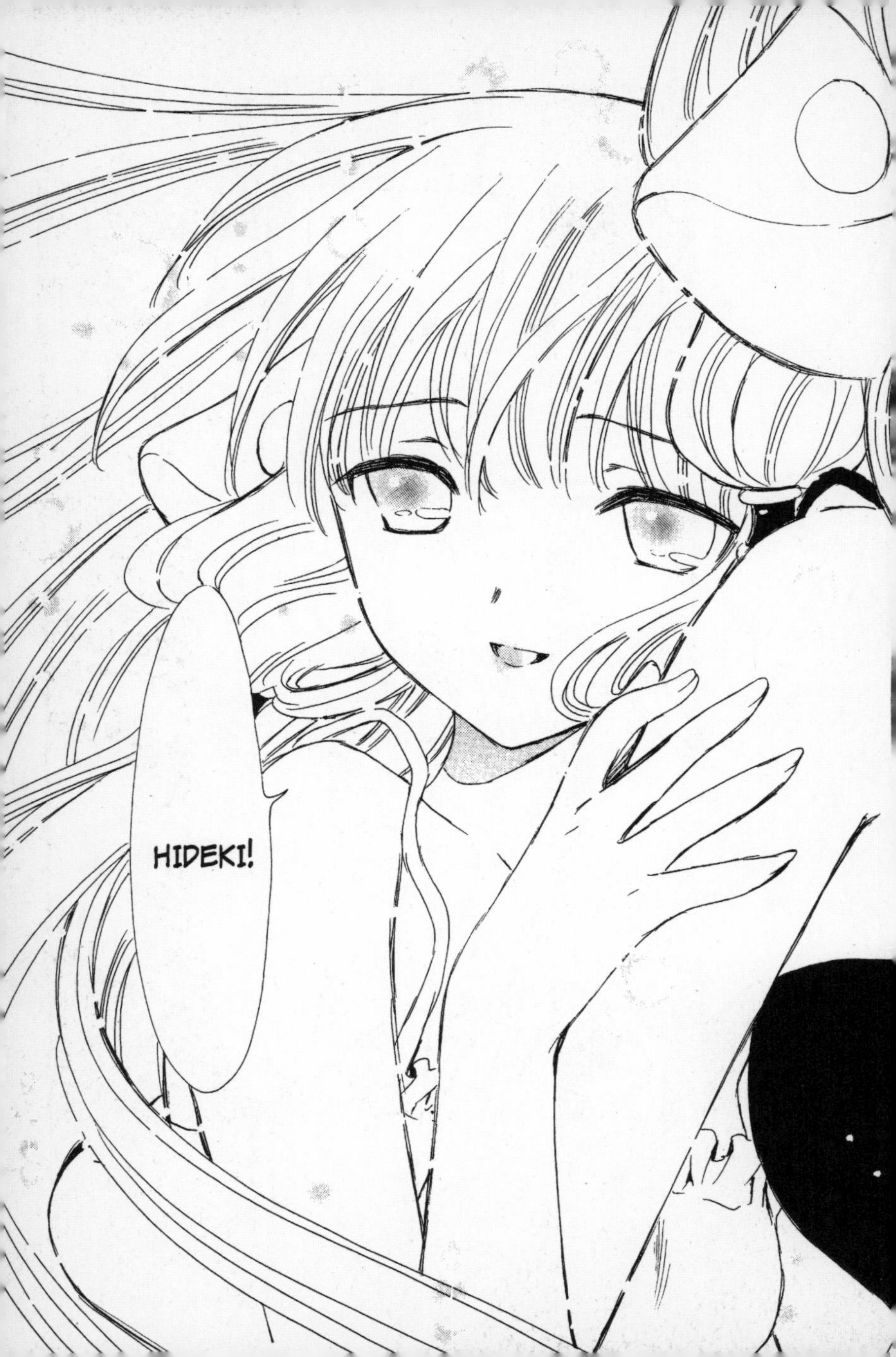
HIDEKI!

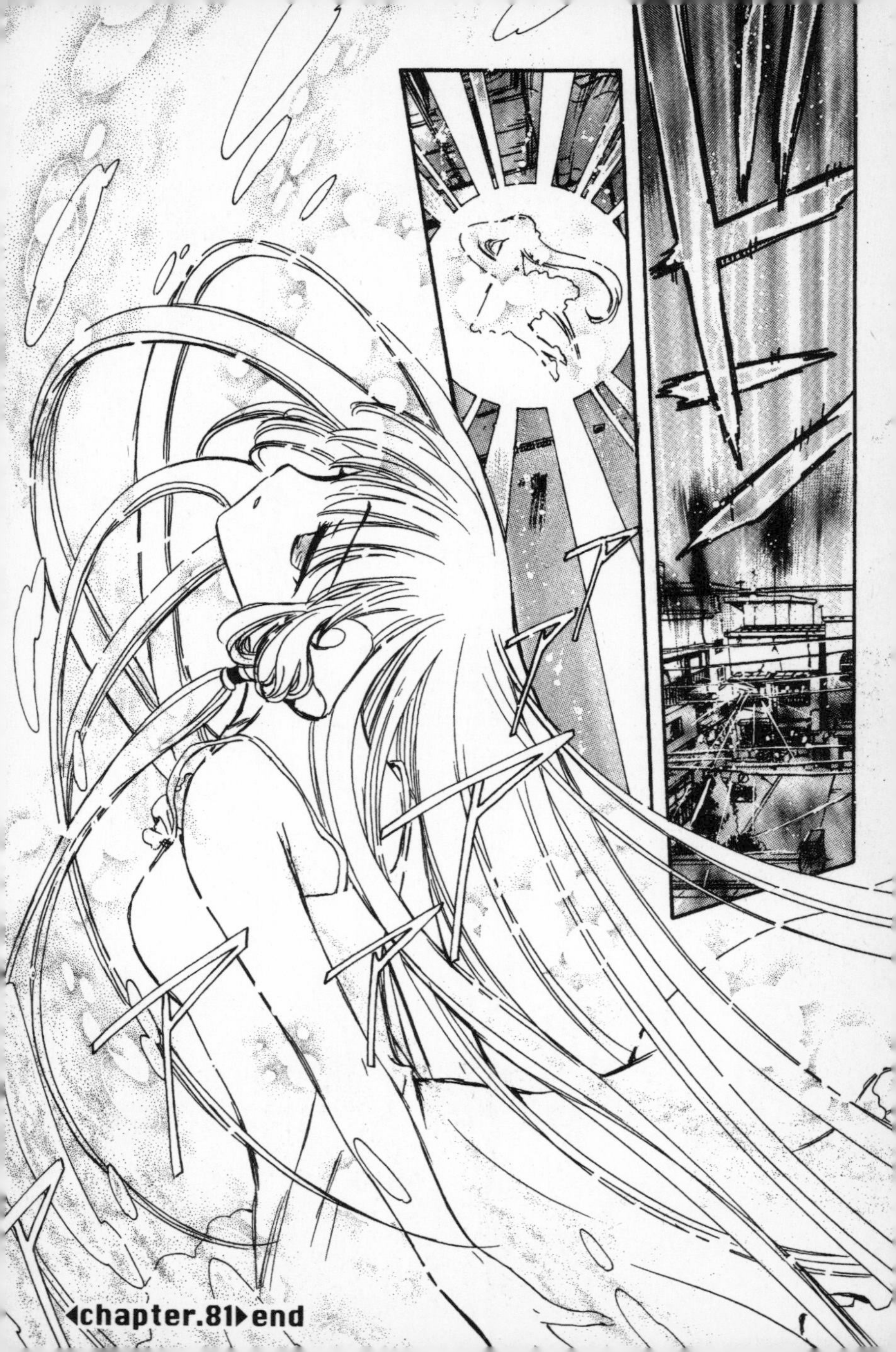
◀chapter.81▶end

MUST SEE Persocoms

address:

date: 05/17/27

from: minoruk197@hotmailer.com

to: sumomo@clamp-net.com

subj: **New Questions...**

Dear Shimbo,

Thank you for your kind words and for sending the flowers for Yuzuki. She is herself again–perhaps more herself than ever–and I owe it all to Hideki. How ironic that it took someone so computer-illiterate to help me truly understand my persocom. In this era where machines replace people in daily life, perhaps he understands 'coms better than we gave him credit for at first. Chi certainly sees something special in him. In fact, I've never seen her so elated. I only hope that when the time comes, Hideki will be able to understand his own feelings. The end of this mystery is drawing near. Forgive me if I wax prophetic, but I sense great change in the air. There is much we do not yet understand about Chi. Whether or not she is the truly feeling, sentient Chobit of legend, she is the key to something big. My feelings are quite strong right now–I feel both great anticipation, and great fear.

Please take care,

Minoru

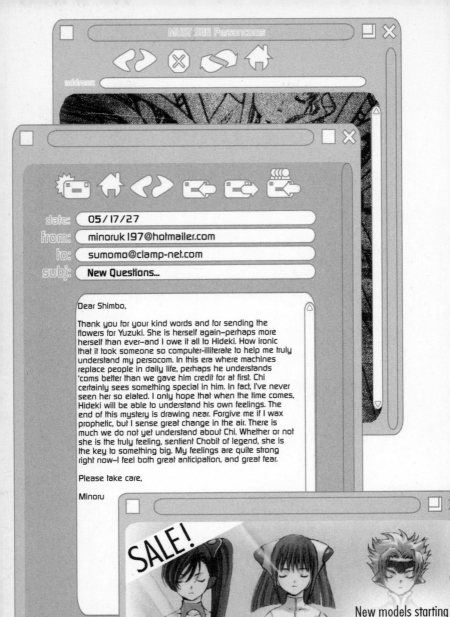

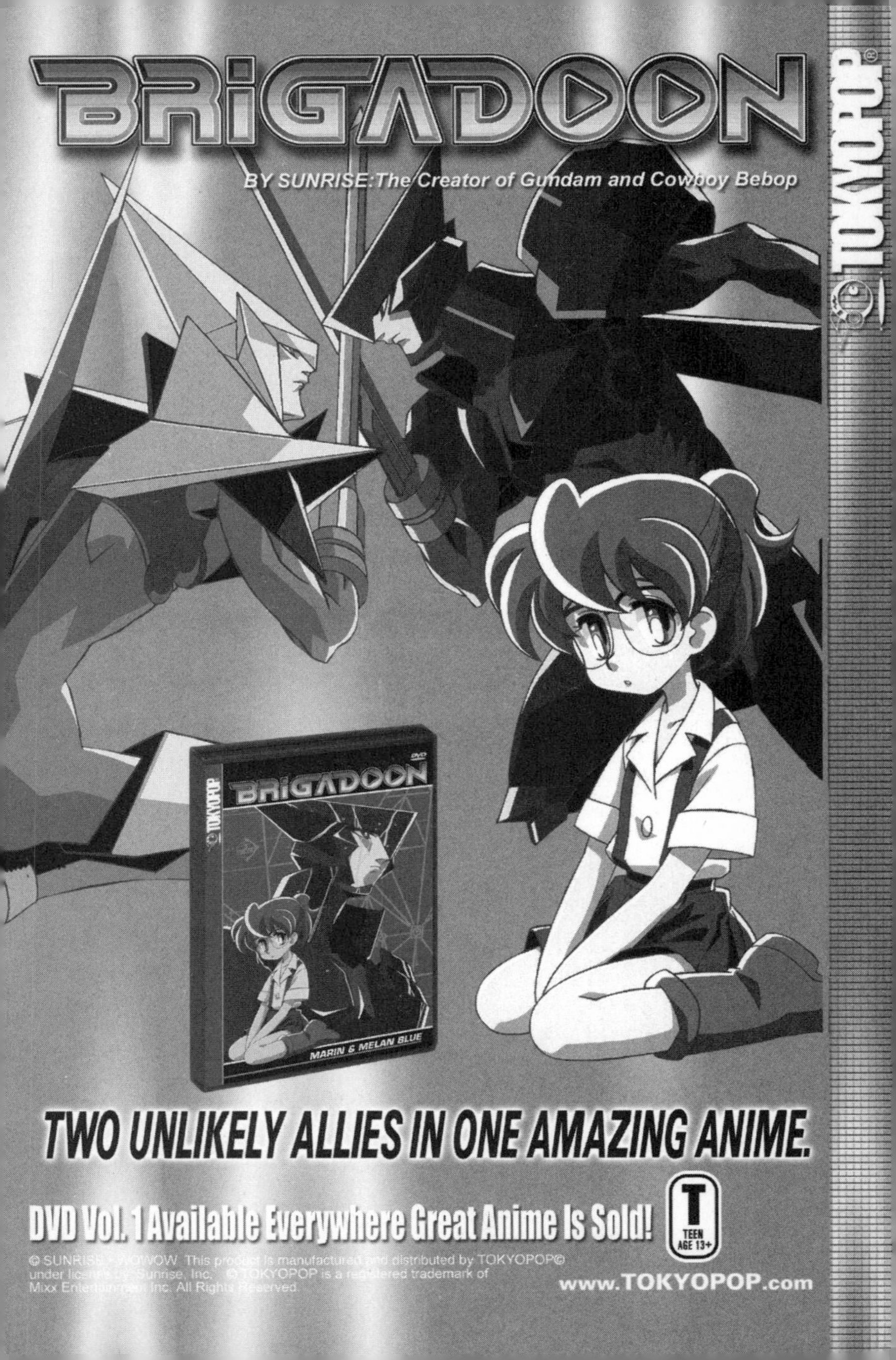

BRIGADOON
TOKYOPOP®
BY SUNRISE: The Creator of Gundam and Cowboy Bebop
BRIGADOON
DVD
TOKYOPOP
MARIN & MELAN BLUE
TWO UNLIKELY ALLIES IN ONE AMAZING ANIME.
DVD Vol. 1 Available Everywhere Great Anime Is Sold!
T
TEEN AGE 13+
© SUNRISE • WOWOW. This product is manufactured and distributed by TOKYOPOP®
under license by Sunrise, Inc. ® TOKYOPOP is a registered trademark of
Mixx Entertainment, Inc. All Rights Reserved.
www.TOKYOPOP.com

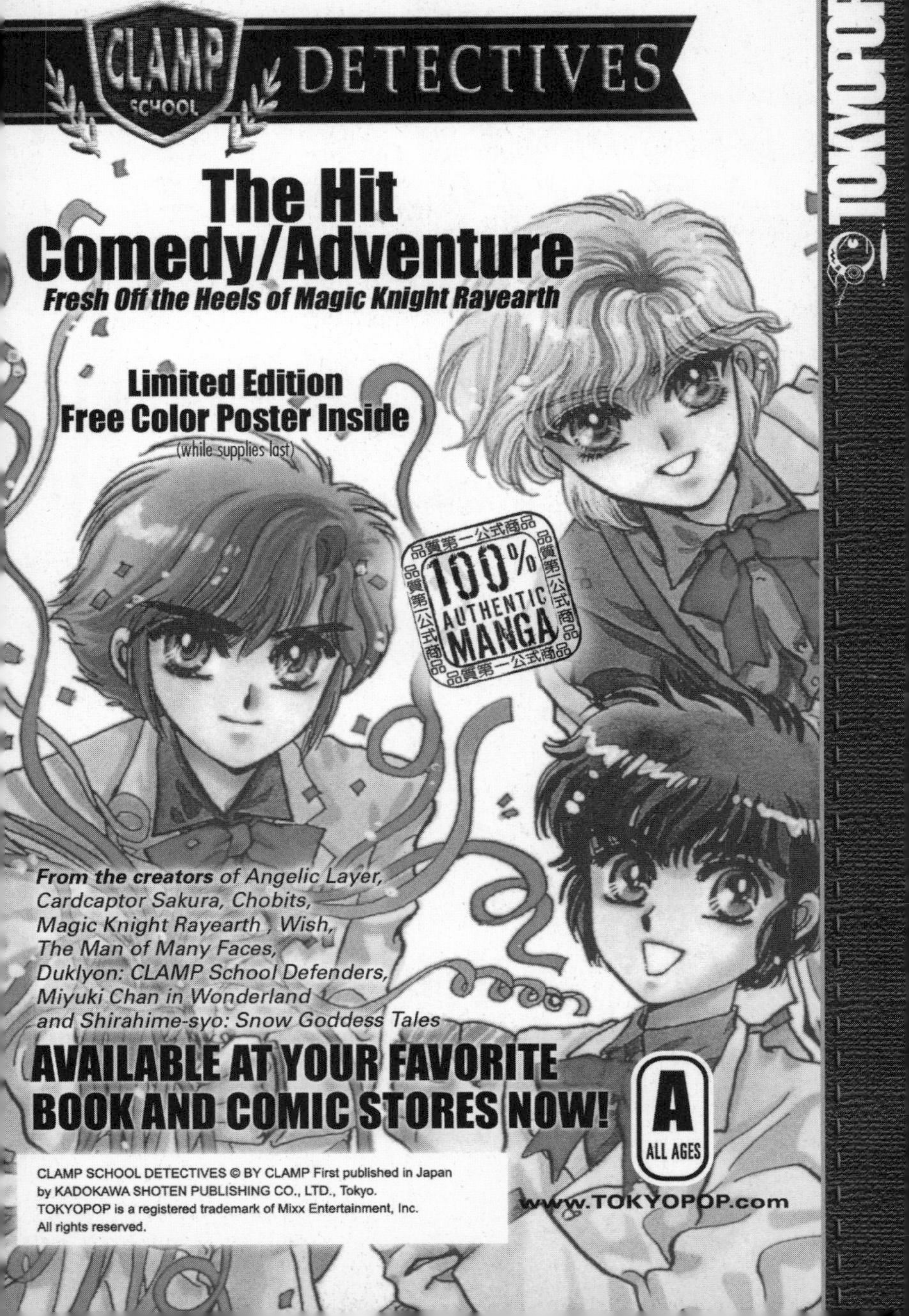
CLAMP SCHOOL
DETECTIVES
The Hit
Comedy/Adventure
Fresh Off the Heels of Magic Knight Rayearth
Limited Edition
Free Color Poster Inside
(while supplies last)
品質第一公式商品
100%
AUTHENTIC
MANGA
From the creators of Angelic Layer,
Cardcaptor Sakura, Chobits,
Magic Knight Rayearth , Wish,
The Man of Many Faces,
Duklyon: CLAMP School Defenders,
Miyuki Chan in Wonderland
and Shirahime-syo: Snow Goddess Tales
AVAILABLE AT YOUR FAVORITE
BOOK AND COMIC STORES NOW!
A
ALL AGES
CLAMP SCHOOL DETECTIVES © BY CLAMP First published in Japan
by KADOKAWA SHOTEN PUBLISHING CO., LTD., Tokyo.
TOKYOPOP is a registered trademark of Mixx Entertainment, Inc.
All rights reserved.
www.TOKYOPOP.com
TOKYOPOP®

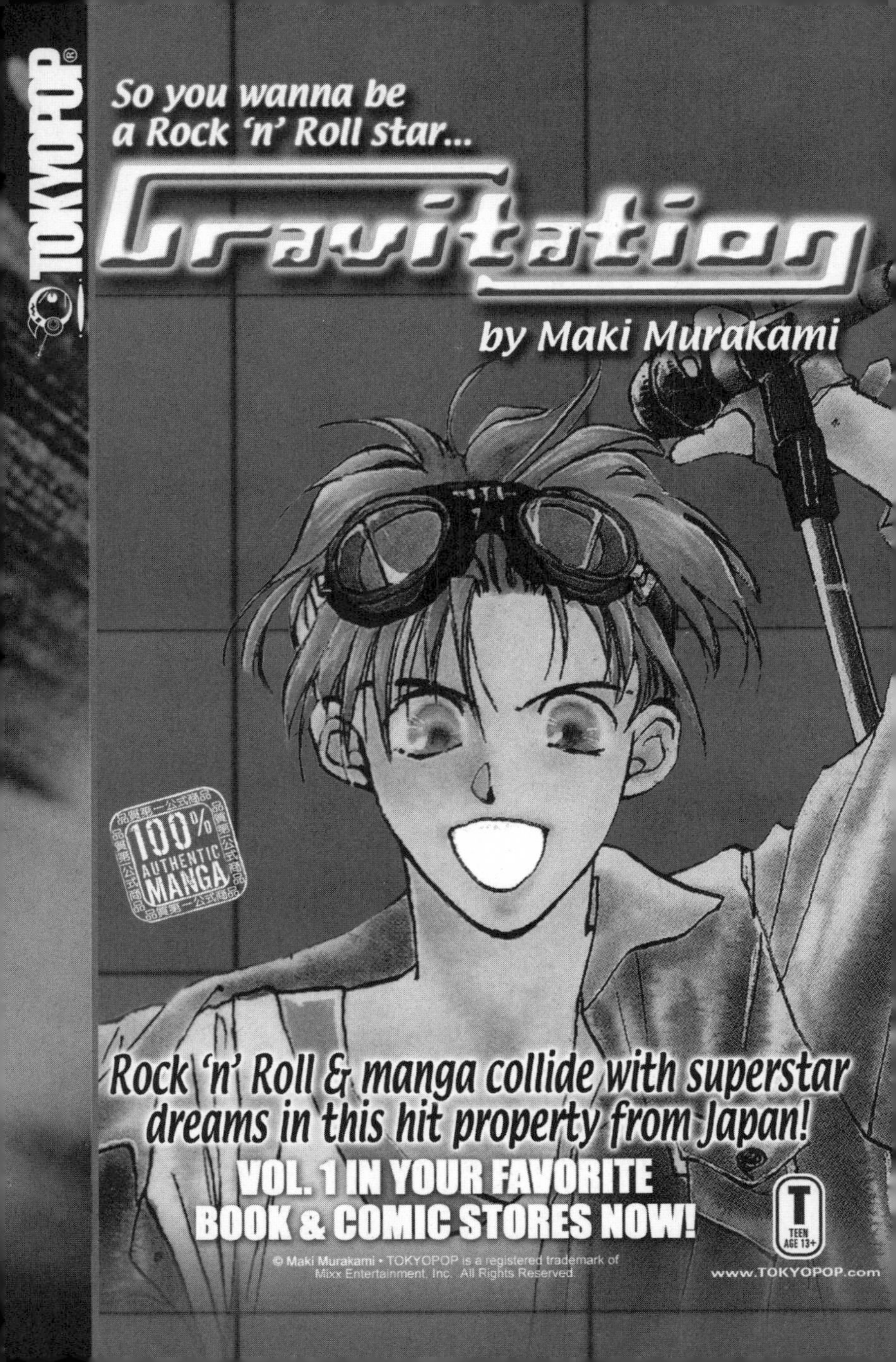
TOKYOPOP®
So you wanna be
a Rock 'n' Roll star...
Gravitation
by Maki Murakami
100% AUTHENTIC MANGA
Rock 'n' Roll & manga collide with superstar
dreams in this hit property from Japan!
VOL. 1 IN YOUR FAVORITE
BOOK & COMIC STORES NOW!
T TEEN AGE 13+
© Maki Murakami • TOKYOPOP is a registered trademark of
Mixx Entertainment, Inc. All Rights Reserved.
www.TOKYOPOP.com

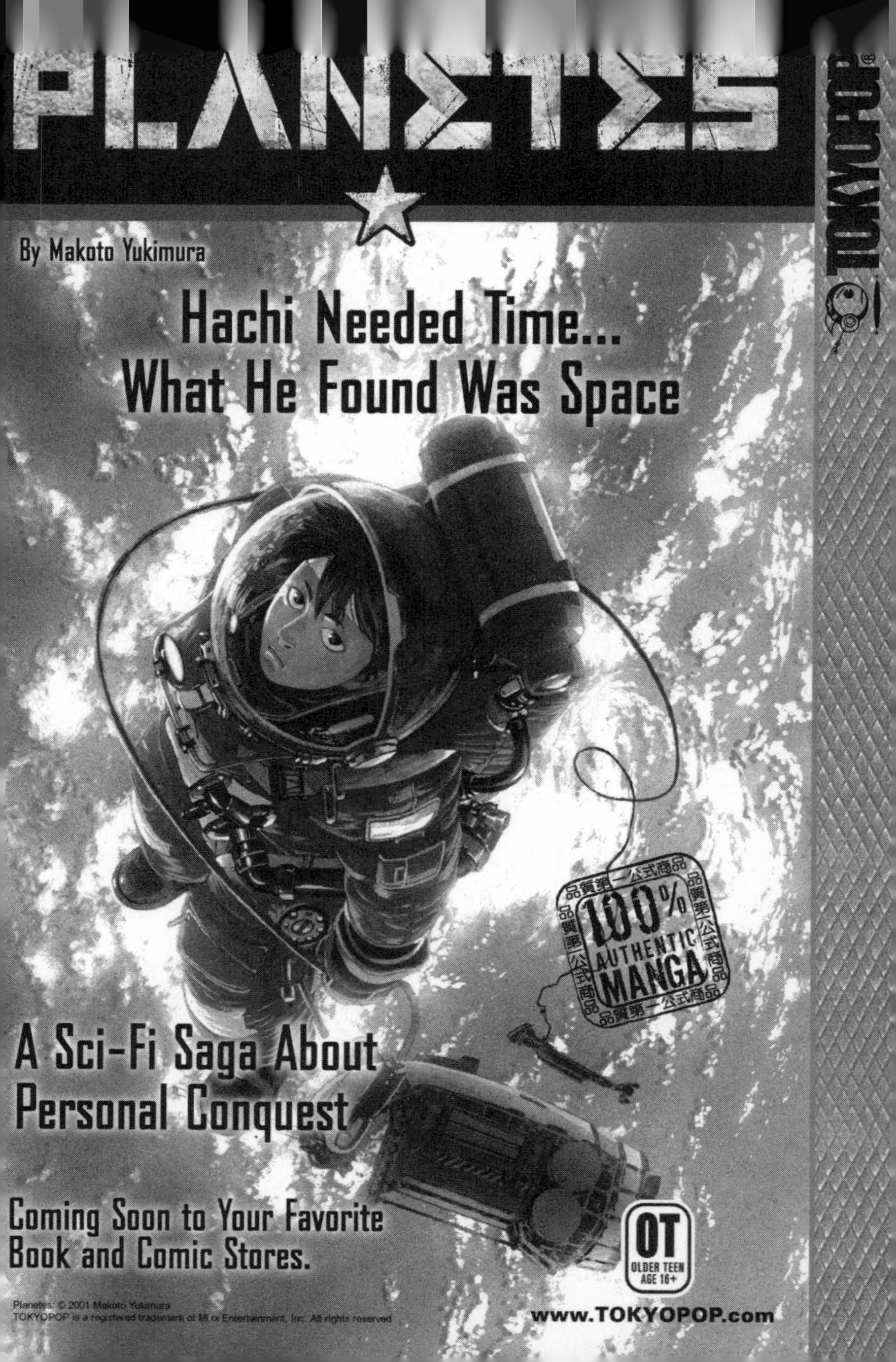

PLANETES

By Makoto Yukimura

Hachi Needed Time... What He Found Was Space

100% AUTHENTIC MANGA

A Sci-Fi Saga About Personal Conquest

Coming Soon to Your Favorite Book and Comic Stores.

OT OLDER TEEN AGE 16+

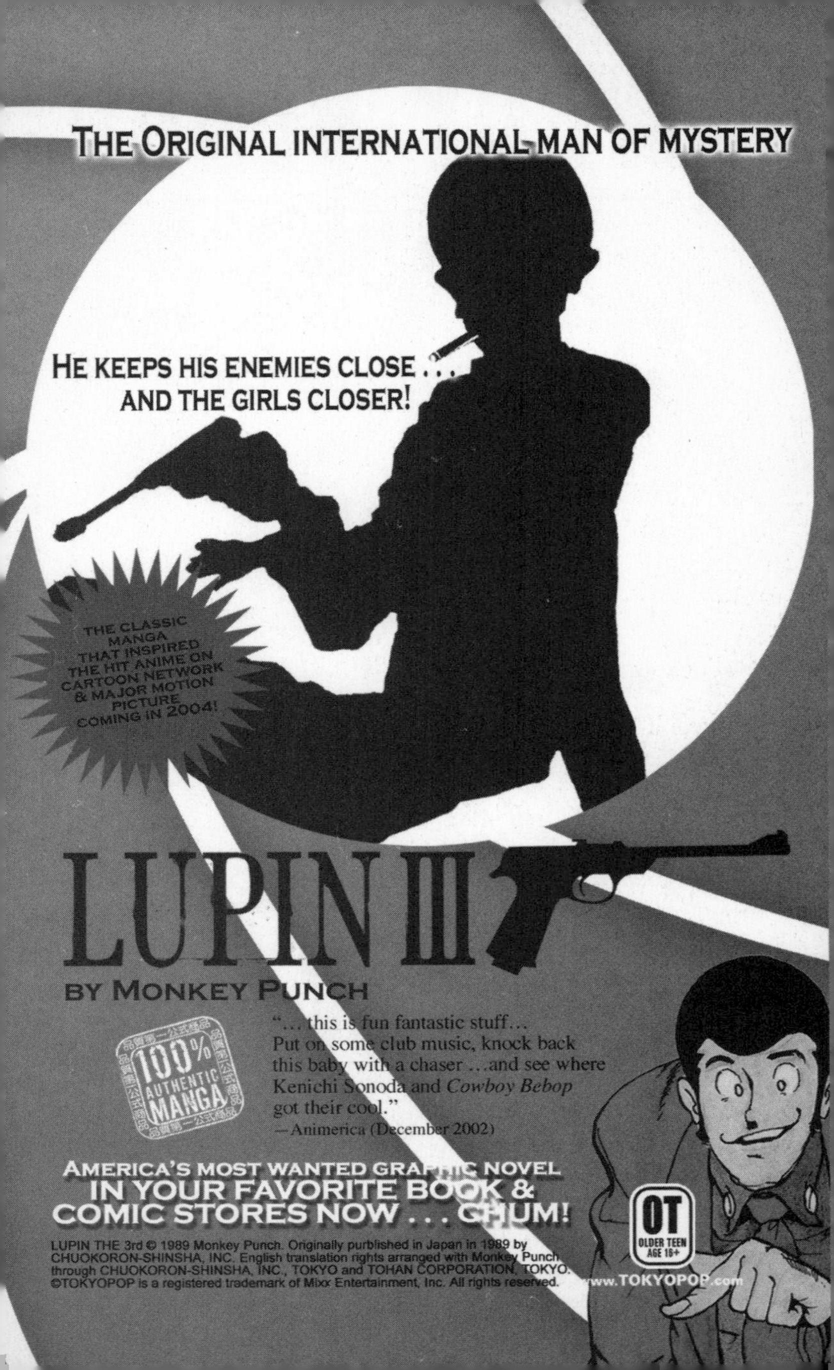
THE ORIGINAL INTERNATIONAL MAN OF MYSTERY
HE KEEPS HIS ENEMIES CLOSE . . . . . . AND THE GIRLS CLOSER!
THE CLASSIC MANGA THAT INSPIRED THE HIT ANIME ON CARTOON NETWORK & MAJOR MOTION PICTURE COMING IN 2004!
LUPIN III
BY MONKEY PUNCH
100% AUTHENTIC MANGA
"... this is fun fantastic stuff... Put on some club music, knock back this baby with a chaser ...and see where Kenichi Sonoda and *Cowboy Bebop* got their cool."
—Animerica (December 2002)
AMERICA'S MOST WANTED GRAPHIC NOVEL IN YOUR FAVORITE BOOK & COMIC STORES NOW . . . CHUM!
OT OLDER TEEN AGE 16+
LUPIN THE 3rd © 1989 Monkey Punch. Originally purblished in Japan in 1989 by CHUOKORON-SHINSHA, INC. English translation rights arranged with Monkey Punch through CHUOKORON-SHINSHA, INC., TOKYO and TOHAN CORPORATION, TOKYO. ©TOKYOPOP is a registered trademark of Mixx Entertainment, Inc. All rights reserved.
www.TOKYOPOP.com

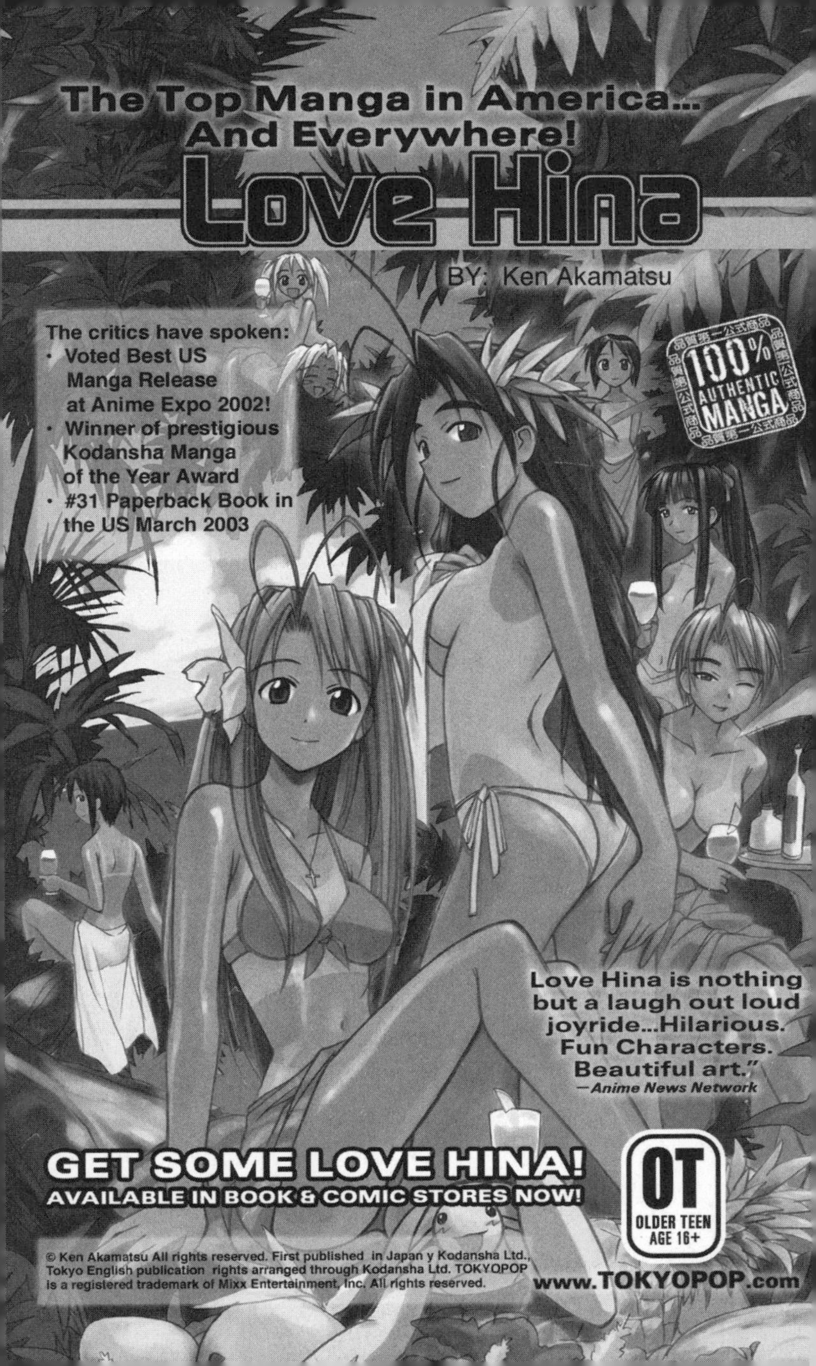
The Top Manga in America...
And Everywhere!
Love Hina
BY: Ken Akamatsu
The critics have spoken:
• Voted Best US Manga Release at Anime Expo 2002!
• Winner of prestigious Kodansha Manga of the Year Award
• #31 Paperback Book in the US March 2003
100% AUTHENTIC MANGA
"Love Hina is nothing but a laugh out loud joyride...Hilarious. Fun Characters. Beautiful art."
—Anime News Network
GET SOME LOVE HINA!
AVAILABLE IN BOOK & COMIC STORES NOW!
OT
OLDER TEEN
AGE 16+
© Ken Akamatsu All rights reserved. First published in Japan y Kodansha Ltd., Tokyo English publication rights arranged through Kodansha Ltd. TOKYOPOP is a registered trademark of Mixx Entertainment, Inc. All rights reserved.
www.TOKYOPOP.com

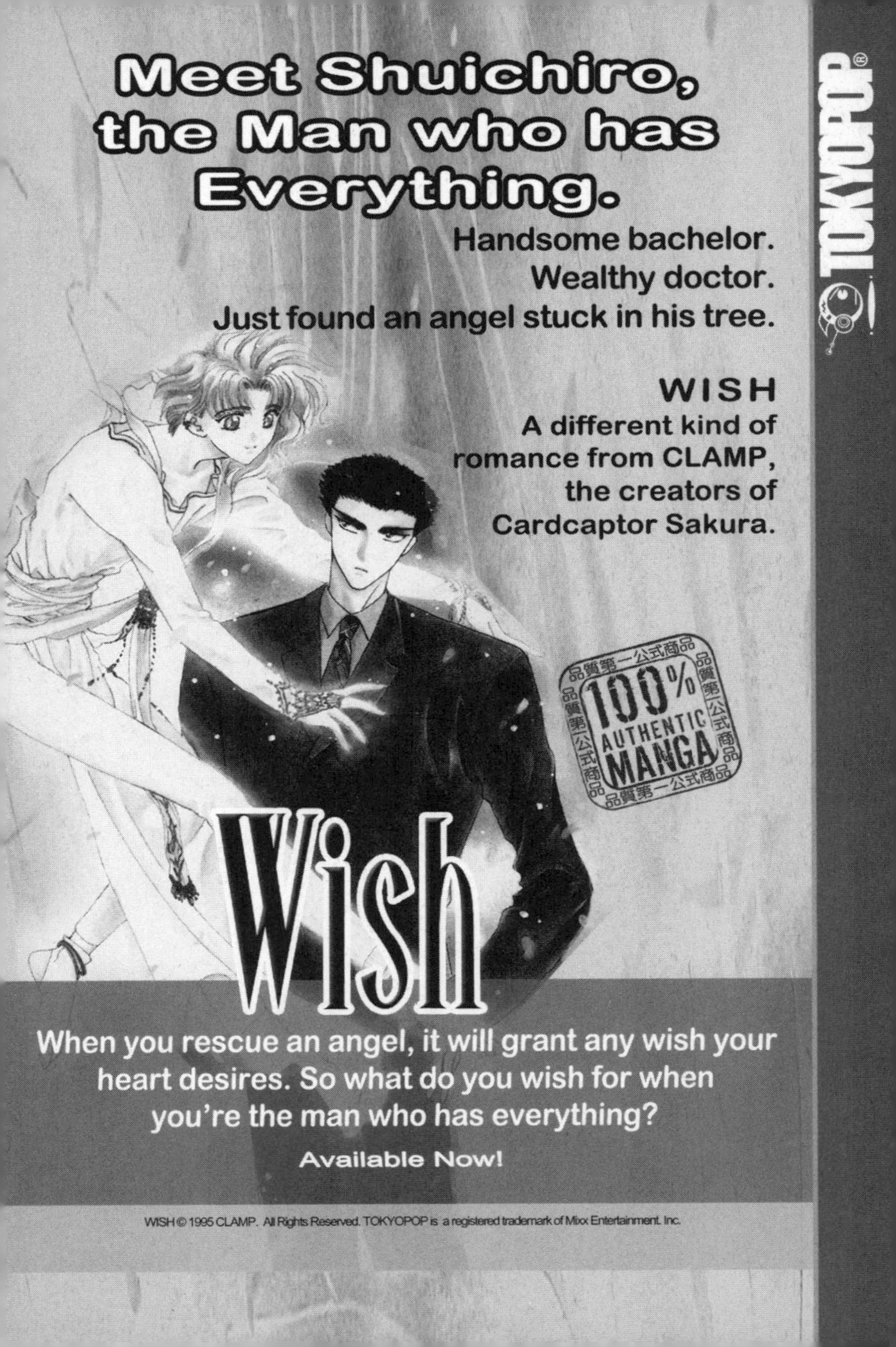
Meet Shuichiro, the Man who has Everything.
Handsome bachelor.
Wealthy doctor.
Just found an angel stuck in his tree.
WISH
A different kind of romance from CLAMP, the creators of Cardcaptor Sakura.
品質第一公式商品
100% AUTHENTIC MANGA
Wish
When you rescue an angel, it will grant any wish your heart desires. So what do you wish for when you're the man who has everything?
Available Now!
WISH © 1995 CLAMP. All Rights Reserved. TOKYOPOP is a registered trademark of Mixx Entertainment Inc.
TOKYOPOP®

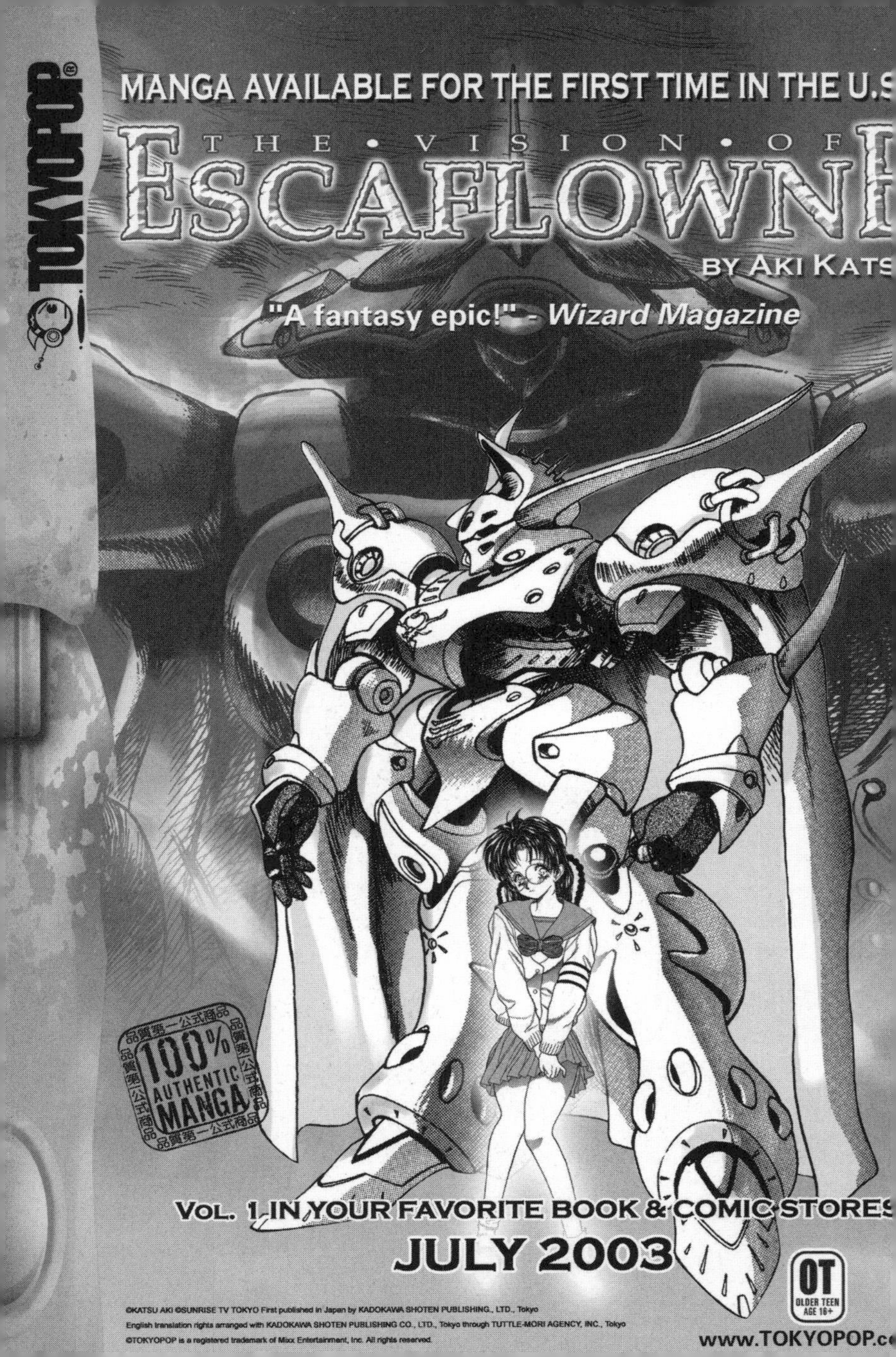
TOKYOPOP®
MANGA AVAILABLE FOR THE FIRST TIME IN THE U.S
THE • VISION • OF
ESCAFLOWNE
BY AKI KATS
"A fantasy epic!" - Wizard Magazine
品質第一公式商品
100% AUTHENTIC MANGA
VOL. 1 IN YOUR FAVORITE BOOK & COMIC STORES
JULY 2003
OT
OLDER TEEN AGE 16+
©KATSU AKI ©SUNRISE TV TOKYO First published in Japan by KADOKAWA SHOTEN PUBLISHING., LTD., Tokyo
English translation rights arranged with KADOKAWA SHOTEN PUBLISHING CO., LTD., Tokyo through TUTTLE-MORI AGENCY, INC., Tokyo
©TOKYOPOP is a registered trademark of Mixx Entertainment, Inc. All rights reserved.
www.TOKYOPOP.c

STOP!

This is the back of the book.
You wouldn't want to spoil a great ending!

This book is printed "manga-style," in the authentic Japanese right-to-left format. Since none of the artwork has been flipped or altered, readers get to experience the story just as the creator intended. You've been asking for it, so TOKYOPOP® delivered: authentic, hot-off-the-press, and far more fun!

DIRECTIONS

If this is your first time reading manga-style, here's a quick guide to help you understand how it works.

It's easy... just start in the top right panel and follow the numbers. Have fun, and look for more 100% authentic manga from TOKYOPOP®!